THE HISTORY OF THE
ROYAL
AGRICULTURAL
COLLEGE
CIRENCESTER

AN INDEPENDENT COLLEGE

ROGER SAYCE

With a Foreword by
HRH The Prince of Wales

ALAN SUTTON

First published in the United Kingdom in 1992 by
Alan Sutton Publishing Limited
Phoenix Mill · Far Thrupp · Stroud · Gloucestershire

First Published in the United States of America in 1992 by
Alan Sutton Publishing Inc · Wolfeboro Falls · NH 03896–0848

British Library Cataloguing in Publication Data

Sayce, R.B.
History of the Royal Agricultural College
I. Title
630.71

ISBN 0–7509–0178–0

Library of Congress Cataloging in Publication Data applied for

Cover picture: Front view of the College *c.* 1860, courtesy of E.J. List,
the Eye Press.

Typeset in 10/12 Bembo.
Typesetting and origination by
Alan Sutton Publishing Limited.
Colour separation by
Yeo Valley Graphics, Wells.
Printed in Great Britain by
The Bath Press, Bath, Avon.

CONTENTS

LIST OF ILLUSTRATIONS

Colour Plates

Between pp. 148 and 149

Between pp. 212 and 213

Many of the illustrations come from College sources. The origins of some cannot be traced. The following are acknowledged with thanks (colour plate numbers are in bold): figure numbers **6, 7** and 15 were provided by the Royal Agricultural Society of England; figure 6 by the Scottish Agricultural College, Edinburgh; figure 13 from a private memoir of Sir Arthur Church; figure 15 by Gwyn Jones of the Agricultural Extension and Development Centre, Reading University; figure **18** by Messrs Knight, Frank and Rutley of Cirencester; figure **29** by E. Cecilia Humphries; figure 35 by the AFRC Institute of Grassland and

Environmental Research, Aberystwyth; figure 59 by the Institute for Agricultural History, Reading University. The photographs taken from College portraits are by Abbey Studios, Cirencester, and the old photographs are by Aerofilms and T.V.A.P. Oxford. The two newspaper cuttings are from *The Graphic*, No. 980, Vol. XXXVIII, Saturday 8 September 1888 (figure 25) and the *Sheffield Independent*, 26 October 1933 (figure 46).

FOREWORD

KENSINGTON PALACE

In 1995 the Royal Agricultural College will celebrate the 150th Anniversary of its foundation. The College has a proud heritage; it was the first institution of its kind in the British Empire. Early in the Victorian era, when new agricultural methods were burgeoning it set out to teach the elements of agricultural science and practice to farmers' sons and of land economy to sons of landowners. The advent of the College generated similar institutions, the first of their kind, in Canada, New Zealand and Australia as well as in the U.S.A. and Japan.

The originators were local; the idea of founding a College in the Cotswolds was first expounded in a speech by one Robert Jeffreys Brown (strangely enough a wine merchant of Cirencester) to a meeting in 1842 of the Fairford and Cirencester Farmers' Club. Yet the thinking became nationwide; the sponsors, mainly leading landowners and farmers, envisaged a series of such colleges throughout the Kingdom. The first shareholder of this independently financed institution was H.R.H. the Prince Consort; since that time successive Monarchs have been Patrons of the College. In my own role as President I enjoy taking a direct interest in the activities of the College.

This book will commemorate the sesquicentennial; it is a history of the personalities who led scientific research, expanded and diffused agricultural knowledge and, above all, educated and trained the future farmers and landowners of the country. In recent years, I am glad to say, the training has broadened in order to reflect a long overdue concern for the protection of the environment and to take a more holistic view of agriculture. The College now teaches young men and women to manage their rural businesses efficiently within the wider context of the living countryside.

The author vividly describes the fortunes of a body which, in pioneering times, suffered the vicissitudes of financial crises, yet has altered with changing farming methods and economic conditions, often by the efforts of the Principals in charge - some autocratic, some progressive, some bringing stability, some with only a short tenure and one an outstanding iconoclast! It is a picture of evolution since the mid-nineteenth century seen through the people at the forefront of agricultural education. Above all it is a story of rugged independence weathering economic storms and of constant development to meet varying circumstances.

PREFACE AND
ACKNOWLEDGEMENTS

Although the Royal Agricultural College will be 150 years old in 1995 there exists no definitive history of it. A thesis and two dissertations have been written in recent years for the purpose of higher degrees and each took a specific aspect related to agricultural education. Articles have been published from time to time but there is no comprehensive work available to the enquirer who might wish to know of its foundation, its aims and objectives throughout its years, its progress towards these, and, above all, of the personalities who fashioned it, guided it, supported it and managed it.

This book is intended to remedy that deficiency, particularly in bringing to life the people who played major parts in the story of the College, the first of its kind in the English-speaking world and a pioneer in agricultural education. It is a fascinating story of vicissitudes and crises, of original research and of periods of relative stability and quietude followed by surges forward in educational stand-ards, and, in the last fifty years, of a quite remarkable expansion of facilities and in the numbers of students passing through.

This variety in its history may be attributed to one single cause: a fierce spirit of independence and a determination to resolve its difficulties in its own way. That, more than any other single factor, has created the 'College spirit', which is the one constant prevailing motive by which successive Governors, Principals, staff and students have acted. It is one reason why the College is, and has been, held in affection by its old students, scattered throughout the world.

When first asked to write this history (the suggestion came from Douglas Fitch, one of the Governors and an old colleague of mine in the Land Service of the Ministry of Agriculture, Fisheries and Food), I demurred. As I told the Chairman of the Governors, the late Charles Coad, and the Principal, Vic Hughes, they could have sought out an experienced historian and trained researcher and commissioned a definitive work.

Just prior to this, Frank Parker, a former Secretary to the Board of Governors had commenced an account of the College based on the minutes of the Governing Body. This would, in itself, be a useful research source. It was suggested to me that what was needed was a descriptive account of the happenings at the College from the outset, based primarily on the personalities who had inhabited the College and guided its fortunes thoroughout the years. Such a history would not necessarily be a standard definitive work but rather a story of the ups and downs of a College which prized its independence and cherished those who had maintained that spirit.

In considering the task I discovered one particular period which was so fascinating that I felt impelled to carry on. This period will be found in Chapter 3: it concerned the principalship of the Revd John Constable, and was one of the most turbulent times in the College's life. Thus it was that this book was started; and, in spite of the difficulties of research where no or few records existed (the College has not, until very recently, possessed any semblance of properly stored and catalogued archives), it was soon discovered that this was not the only period of highly coloured events peopled by men of strong disposition with a determination to build a unique institution and to see it prosper. The reader should not, therefore, expect a learned treatise glittering with detailed facts and erudite expositions of the causes and consequences of the times, but rather a straightforward story of the activities of those whose lives formed part of the College and are of sufficient interest not to require any embellishment.

This book could not have been produced without some very considerable help. My first thanks must go posthumously to Charles Coad (whose sudden death was a great blow to us all) and then to Vic Hughes for their initial encouragement and constant support. Secondly, to the many members of staff, academic, administrative and domestic, my thanks for putting up with my enquiries and helping in the research. Of these I must single out Rachel Rowe, College Librarian, and her staff; with their help I spent many profitable hours delving in the recesses of the main library and in the historical section.

One of my basic sources of information has been the excellent notes prepared by Frank Parker, derived from the records of the Governing Bodies. These are available in the College library for any reader who would wish to clothe my accounts with more detailed facts.

Not unnaturally I sought anecdotal evidence from retired members of the academic staff: Neil Jacobs, former Vice-Principal, Bursar and Registrar; Jim Lockhart, former Head of the Agricultural Department; Dai Barling, former Head of Agricultural Science; John Wibberley, former Head of Agriculture; two former Principals, Professor Gordon Dickson and Sir Emrys Jones; all these read the drafts and offered notes on the periods with which they were concerned. Of the current staff I had help from Martin Keay, who provided some of the illustrations, and from Charles Watkins who read the whole text. The Principal Emeritus, Vic Hughes, read the whole manuscript and so did the present Principal, Professor Arthur Jones.

There was help from outside too: Dr Augustus Voelcker and Sons Ltd;

J.D. Sykes of Wye College, University of London; Professor Peter Wilson, CBE, Professor Emeritus, University of Edinburgh; Ian J. Fleming, of the Scottish Agricultural College, Edinburgh; the Bath and Wells Diocesan Board of Finance; Michael McGarvie, FSA; Professor Bruce J. Ross, Vice-Chancellor, and Brian Robertson, of Lincoln University, New Zealand; the late Earl of Ducie (to whom I am extremely grateful for allowing me the opportunity to scrutinize all the diaries of the 3rd Earl); Professor Colin A. Russell, Department of History of Science and Technology of the Open University; John Creasey of the Institute of Agricultural History and Museum of English Rural Life of Reading University; Mrs Angela Small of the Library of the Royal Agricultural Society of England; and many others who helped and encouraged. To all these I record my grateful thanks.

It has been a demanding, but nevertheless pleasant task mainly because my connection with the College goes back to the days before the Second World War and it allowed me to reminisce. I was fortunate that my father, Roger Sayce, B.Sc., NDA was Vice-Principal in 1937/8 and had worked with Professor Boutflour, Principal from 1931 to 1958, in his early days in Wiltshire in agricultural extension. Otherwise I may not have been a student at the College in the immediate post-war years, nor had the honour to be a Governor. To them both I will always be grateful for my long and cherished association with the Royal Agricultural College.

Roger Sayce
Wantage, Oxon
February 1992

Chapter One

ORIGINS

Agriculture is still without a public institution where it is taught.

R.J. Brown, 1842

The foundation of the Royal Agricultural College took place between 1842 and 1845. The concept was first mooted in 1842, and in 1845 the Royal Charter was granted and the first students were enrolled.

The first positive suggestion for the foundation of an agricultural college in Britain was by Robert Jeffreys Brown, and it was made to the Cirencester and Fairford Farmers' Club at their meeting held in Cirencester on 14 November 1842. Brown took as his subject, 'The Advantages of a Specific Education for Agricultural Pursuits'. Little is known of Brown's background save that he was a local man, a wine merchant, who lived in a house on the Stroud road, known as Further Barton, a property now in the ownership of the College and renamed Trent Lodge. He apparently took a deep interest in agriculture and, aside from being influenced by a Dr Daubeny's address on agricultural education in December 1841 to the Royal Agricultural Society of England, had acquainted himself with what was going on in other countries, as revealed in his speech.

Although this address was to a local farmers' club, which was one of many that were springing up, it received wider attention than just being reported in the local paper, for it was reprinted in full in a national farmers' magazine in the following year.

The speech was a long one, as befitted the times. He started: 'Education, though long neglected in this country, appears not to obtain the attention it deserves; but there are facts which show, that it is still far from being fully appreciated; one is, the common remark, that it may be carried too far. It may be inappropriate, or bad, we allow; but that a man can know too much of what relates to things around him . . . it is not easy to understand.' He considered that education had been neglected by governments, with the funds allocated being inadequate. In his words, '. . . it will be a happy day for England when the cost of schoolmasters exceeds that of her army'. He drew attention to the support given to education in other countries, notably in Austria, Prussia, Saxony, the United States of America (quoting specific sums allocated in the state of New York) and China.

Robert Jeffreys
Brown, the
originator

His concept of education was a wide one, '. . . there are three principles in man never to be lost sight of, or neglected, commonly called the heart, the head and the hands; in other words, the affections, the understanding, and the practice'. In considering how to provide education he noted that it was by class, but that, 'Class education in Great Britain has been almost entirely confined to divinity, physic, and surgery; even the Duke of Wellington was obliged to obtain his military education in France . . . of late the army and navy, engineering, designing, teaching and surgery, have their schools. *Agriculture is still without a public institution where it is taught.*'

He pointed out that agricultural education was needed if improvements and innovations were to be adopted by the 'mass of agriculturalists'. As he said, 'Jethro Tull showed the advantage of drill and horse-hoe culture at the beginning of the last century, whereas in China and Japan it had been practised from the earliest times: and yet it is now only becoming general.' Brown was aware of developments in agriculture for he quoted the work of Bedford, Coke, Spencer, Ducie, Richmond, Sinclair, Morton, Ellman, Davy, Leibig, Young and Marshall. His deduction was that, 'There is still no class of society to whom a good education is so important as the agricultural, not with a view to the wealth and resources of the country alone, but also on account of its position.' He named in detail the elements of agriculture in which education should be given, including the newly emerging sciences applicable to agriculture. He also detailed the institutions abroad now providing such education.

In conclusion he made his main thrust: 'After the enumeration of what has been done elsewhere, it does appear extraordinary that there should be a total absence of any Public School of Agriculture in England. Let us do our part in endeavouring to do away with this deficiency.'

The background to this speech was a period of severe agricultural depression. In fact the country was in some degree of turmoil, following the ending of the Napoleonic wars. Queen Victoria had come to the throne in 1837 to commence a reign with the prospect of at least a decade of crises. Industry in the country, dependent mainly as it was on the textile industry, was starting to face foreign competition. Developing industries, demanding capital injections, led to a decline of handcraft work and consequent unemployment or pittance wages in the urban environment of higher costs.

Agriculture had prospered during the high price regime in the continental wars, but returns had fallen sharply since then. From a peak in 1813 of 109s. 6d. (£5.47) per quarter the price for corn in 1835 had fallen to 39s. 4d. (£1.96) per quarter. It rose slowly only to reach 50s. (£2.50) per quarter in 1845. In spite of this there was agitation over the Corn Laws, introduced in the previous century to protect the home production of corn. These, in effect, provided a floor in the market for corn by providing a single price level, below which imports were stopped. This was the situation in 1815. Pressure from such bodies as the Anti-Corn Law League (founded in 1839) and from urban and industrial interests was opposed by the traditional landowning class and, naturally, the tenant farmers. They feared that repeal of the Corn Laws would result in cheap foreign imports swamping the markets and depressing prices to bankruptcy levels.

But falling prices had diminished their case: imports were starting to rise anyway. Sir Robert Peel, the Prime Minister then heading a Tory administration, had tinkered with the legislation, reintroducing a sliding scale of price levels in 1842. Events moved rapidly and matters came to a head in 1845. A contributory cause of the repeal of the Corn Laws must have been the famine in Ireland as a result of successive potato harvest failures in 1845, 1846 and 1848. It meant that instead of England taking two million quarters of Irish wheat a year, an equivalent amount was needed to be sent to Ireland and that against the disastrous harvest in England in 1845. So the Corn Laws were repealed in 1846.

It was against this background that foundations were laid, not only of the College, but also of two other institutions destined to become enduring symbols of the application of scientific method to agriculture. It demonstrated the faith that the leading protagonists had in the future of farming based on applied research. It was to be the start of what came to be known as 'high farming'.

In 1838, on the initiative of Earl Spencer, the Royal Agricultural Society of England was formed. Its objective was to promote agriculture by 'Practice with Science', its motto down to the present day. It intended to promulgate the results of scientific research and thus to encourage the improvement of crops and livestock. An annual show was inaugurated and the Society organized lectures and commenced the publication of an annual journal in which eminent researchers were invited to report the latest results of their work. Prominent among these were J.T. Way and J.C.A. Voelcker, chemists who were to be among the first professors at the College. Indeed, it was chemistry which was to be the main springboard of the sciences to be applied to agriculture.

Another of the originators of what was to be a leap forward in this transfer of research to the farm, and who was to be deeply involved in the creation of the Royal Agricultural College was Professor Charles Daubeny, a Gloucestershire man who, from 1840, held the Chair of Rural Economy at Oxford University. This Chair, created in 1796, could be said to be at the very start of agricultural education, founded as it was just after the creation of a Chair of Agriculture and Rural Economy in 1790 at Edinburgh University. He was, in addition, Professor of Chemistry and Botany, which two subjects occupied the greater part of his time.

On 9 December 1841 Daubeny gave a lecture to the Royal Agricultural Society of England on 'The Application of Science to Agriculture'. In this he drew attention to the need for 'having some amount of chemical knowledge diffused generally throughout the agricultural community'. 'But how is this important point to be secured?' he asked. His answer: 'It is to the rising generation that we must principally look for improving the practice of husbandry by due attention to its *principles*. . . .'

'It is remarkable', he said, 'that, of all the nations of civilised Europe, England is perhaps the only one which is destitute of any public establishment for the instruction of those designed [*sic*] for agriculture.' [He meant 'destined'.] He referred to the existing institutions at Grignon, near Paris, at Hohenheim, near Stuttgart and to other countries where there were at least the foundations for the teaching of agriculture. In another paper, Daubeny expounded on these institutions for agricultural education already established in other countries. He went on to regret that, 'I . . . have nothing to report of a similar description with reference to our own country.'

He had sowed the first seeds: there started discussions in the meetings of farmers and agriculturalists about the need for agricultural education if scientific advances were to be adopted by farmers.

The second significant move to establish and develop agricultural research was the creation in 1843 of the experimental station at Rothamsted in Hertfordshire. There were 'model farms' set up by some of the progressive aristocratic landowners but these were based on established good farming practices rather than experimental methods. The initiator of Rothamsted was John Bennett

Lawes, joined very soon afterwards by Joseph Henry Gilbert, together destined to be in the van of agricultural scientific research, to stand high among the many progressive researchers that from this time onwards were responsible for the rapid advance of British agriculture and to be knighted in recognition of their pioneering work. In that same year (1843) the Agricultural Chemistry Section of the British Association for the Advancement of Science was formed and one year earlier the Farmers' Club in London had been founded.

So this period, from 1838 to 1843, following the severe agricultural depression, with the prospect of the repeal of the Corn Laws, with an industrial depression post the Napoleonic wars and with famine in Ireland, was to be the fertile ground in which rapid scientific progress in agriculture would grow and flourish in the Victorian era to come. It was from this background that there sprang the first institution in Britain to provide education in agriculture for the coming generation of farmers.

★

It was as a result of Daubeny's assessment of the need for the establishment of agricultural education on a formal basis, to emulate the pioneering examples in other countries and to complement the scientific research now growing into a lusty infant, that Brown had formed his ideas, picking up Daubeny's plea and developing it into support for a national institution for agricultural education.

That speech contained more. Brown was specific and he sketched out the sort of institution that he envisaged. He looked for a farm of between three hundred and five hundred acres on which to establish such a school, '. . . situated on a central part of the Cotswold Hills: the district for its support to be defined, not by any artificial boundary, but by its geological formation. . . .' He saw a wide area of choice and 'scope for an establishment for 200 pupils of 15 to 20 years of age; and it is probable that £20 per annum from each – in addition to the produce of the farm – would defray the expenditure'.

'The estate might be obtained on a long lease. . . .' The teaching and farm buildings were defined: '. . . each pupil to be half the day in class, learning the sciences applied to agriculture . . . and half the day on the farm.'

Brown was concerned that the manual labour would thus assist moral training and that strict discipline was required. As he said, 'This object will be very much forwarded by such a portion of labour as shall still leave sufficient time for mental culture; thus bringing into action two of our principles – the hand and the head – and making both operate (as we hope) on the heart.'

He reckoned that the College could be established by public subscription mainly from the landowners in the district and he ambitiously hoped that every district would have its own college.

★

This long and detailed exposition of Brown's vision of a 'College on the Cotswold Hills' struck a chord with his fellow members of the Cirencester and Fairford Farmers' Club for they unanimously accepted his ideas and at their next meeting on 29 December 1842 a positive resolution was passed:

We, constituting the Cirencester and Fairford Farmers' Club, having fully discussed, and maturely considered the subject brought before us by Mr R. Brown, feel that we cannot too highly estimate the importance of a specific education for those engaged in agricultural pursuits; and the great value to them of a knowledge of those sciences that are in constant operation in the cultivation of the soil, the growth of vegetables, the rearing and feeding of domestic animals; and we think it most essential that the study of these sciences should be united with practical experience.

In order to effect this we propose, (with the united means of landlord, tenant, and others) to establish a college for 200 pupils on a central part of the Cotswold Hills, with about 500 acres of land attached; that the pupils should employ one portion of their time in the schools; and another portion in assisting in the cultivation of the farm. The funds necessary for such an establishment cannot be exactly determined, until the plans and estimates we are now engaged in obtaining are complete. When the amount is ascertained, we think the capital may be raised in shares of £25 each, and we expect that an annual payment of £25 or £30 by each pupil will be sufficient to defray the expenses of the college.

The advantages of an institution of this kind to the landowner, as well as to the occupier, are too obvious to require any comment; and we confidently rely on their cordial co-operation and support.

Our fellow countrymen who are not so directly interested, are become aware that the welfare and prosperity of our country; as, also, the happiness and comfort of our whole population, is much dependent on the increased product of the soil, which our population is eminently calculated to promote; we, therefore, entertain the most sanguine hopes, that our plan will meet with general approval and receive attention from all classes.

We have thought it right thus to present our ideas to the public; and, after allowing time for the consideration of the subject, some of our members will take the liberty of waiting personally on the landowners, occupiers, and the public generally, of the Cotswold district; and when we have procured a subscription of the means for carrying out our views, we shall then call a public meeting of the shareholders, to meet at this place, when details of the plan will be laid before them.

EDWARD BOWLY, Chairman.

Cirencester, 29 December 1842.

★

This resolution adopted Brown's ideas almost in their entirety; the exception being the fees to be paid for each pupil. Brown thought that £20 per annum per pupil would be sufficient; the Club considered £25 to £30 per annum a more realistic figure. In the event both were wrong; the estimates were much too low. It is the first indication that the promoters were venturing into unknown territory and they were to find this so in many other ways besides the financial hazards involved.

A small team of the promoters carried out the promise made in the last paragraph of the resolution that 'some of our members will . . . wait . . . personally on the landowners, occupiers, and the public generally. . . .' Messrs Robert Brown, Edward Bowly and James Kearsey, a tenant farmer of Tarlton, travelled around the district to explain the proposal and to solicit financial support by inviting the promise of the purchase of shares at £25 each.

Edward Bowly, the chairman of that meeting, a supporter from the very first of the idea and eventually a Governor of the new College, was a leading local landowner, noted as an improver of cattle and sheep, a promoter of agricultural improvements and of technical education. He was a breeder and judge of shorthorns and a member of the Council of the Royal Agricultural Society of England. Fond of fox hunting, he was a tall, thin man, erect and distinguished in character, very courteous, friendly and jocular in manner – altogether the right person to lead those seeking support for this unique venture.

★

As a result of putting forward the ideas at these meetings and of the visits of Bowly, Brown and the others, another meeting was convened on 22 April 1844, with Earl Bathurst, the principal landowner of the area, in the chair, to translate the idea into concrete proposals for the intended college. Brown read a long report from the Committee of the Cirencester and Fairford Farmers' Club. In all probability it was written by Brown for it recapitulated much of what had been contained in his seminal speech of 1842 and carried the matter much further forward:

> On the necessity of an establishment of a school of agriculture upon some plan or other, all were agreed. . . .
> The Club eventually came to the resolution that the establishment of agricultural colleges, with example farms attached, in which young men . . . should be instructed in those branches of knowledge which would best qualify them for the pursuit of agriculture, would be the most desirable course; and they determined that an effort should be made to found a college in their own district.

It is worth noting that the Club took a broad view and though proposing a college in its own district thought that it might become one of many.

★

A prospectus had been prepared, and circulated, with a view to obtaining patronage and for an eventual public meeting to gain such support. There was long and lively discussion after which, with one dissentient, resolutions were passed, the principal one stating: 'That it is expedient to provide an Institution in which the rising generation of farmers may receive instruction, at a moderate expense, in those sciences, a knowledge of which is essential to successful cultivation; and that a farm form part of such Institution.'

A committee was then formed to carry forward this proposition: it was of eminent local landowners and others and included, Earl Bathurst, the Earl of Ducie, Edward Holland, Dr Daubeny, Charles Lawrence, Edward Bowly, Raymond Cripps, and, of course, Robert Jeffreys Brown, all of whom were destined to play leading parts in the creation of the Royal Agricultural College. Earl Bathurst was elected President and Brown became the Secretary.

The lone voice of dissent came from a Mr John Nicholls of Harnhill. He was caustic about the proposers: '. . . by whom was this agricultural college proposed? By Messrs Brown and Bowly; and who are they? Very respectable men in their situations, no doubt; but what do they know about farming? I never heard tell of Mr Brown being anything of an agriculturalist, but it is true that Mr Bowly has lately become a considerable agriculturalist and exhibitor of stock; yet it was not for him . . . to come forward and tell us we know nothing of our business.' His comment on the benefits to the boys who would attend was, '. . . I can assure Mr Brown that he would do farmers more good, by impressing upon them the habits of frugality, industry, and temperance, instead of offering them liquors and the college.'

Brown's response was moderate: 'He fully concurred with Mr Nicholls that no education, unless it was practical, would be of any good to the farmers, but he believed that the proposed plan was the only means to provide this, and unless it did so, he would have nothing to do with it.'

Nicholls received short shrift from the Chairman, Earl Bathurst, who said that his friend Mr Nicholls had the happy knack of misunderstanding sometimes, to which Nicholls facetiously retorted that he had also the 'happy knack of wishing to be set right by your Lordship'!

And so, with this seemingly gentlemanly exchange the only grit in the smooth proceedings, the plan was adopted.

★

The newly formed committee convened a 'General Meeting of Subscribers and Friends of the Proposed Agricultural College' at Cirencester on 1 July 1844. At this meeting the first of the definitive steps towards the setting up of the college was announced. Earl Bathurst had offered a site for the college and its farm. This was for a lease of forty-eight years of a farm of 430 acres near to Cirencester, on his estate, known as Port Farm, also previously known as Starveall Farm. The site for the college buildings was to be let on a longer lease of ninety-nine years. It lay one mile from the town and between the Stroud and Tetbury roads. In addition, his Lordship offered a loan not exceeding £2,000 at a moderate rate of interest, intending it to be one half of the expense of the necessary buildings.

Earl Bathurst's generosity had been preceded by other support he had been giving to the project. In May 1844 the obtaining of a Charter was already being mooted and Earl Bathurst had spoken to Sir Robert Peel and to Lord Dalhousie, the Vice-President of the Board of Trade, and the prospect seemed favourable. Mr Gladstone was also approached.

At this meeting a Committee of Management was formed with the intention that it should be responsible for applying for a Charter for the college, arranging the lease with Earl Bathurst, calling in subscriptions and generally acting on behalf of the shareholders.

In addition a meeting was proposed to be held at the showground of the Royal Agricultural Society of England at Southampton on 24 July, subject to the agreement of that Society. A deputation consisting of the Earl of Ducie, Edward Holland, Dr Daubeny, Edward Bowly, Robert Brown and others was appointed to obtain the sanction of the Council of the Society to hold the public meeting under its patronage. But the sanction was refused so the deputation decided to hold its own public independent meeting at the Freemasons' Hall, Southampton.

The 2nd Earl of Ducie, third Chairman of the Council

Philip Pusey, MP presided at this meeting. He was a leading member of the Society and he was backed by the Duke of Richmond who proposed the resolution, seconded by Dr Lyon Playfair, the Consulting Chemist to the Society, 'That schools of agriculture are much wanted in this country; in which a knowledge of the sciences now admitted to be essential to the successful pursuit of agriculture may be learned, in connection with the practical working of a farm on the most approved principles.'

A second resolution proposed by a Mr Escott was, 'That the plan for the establishment of an agricultural college near Cirencester, explained by the deputies attending that meeting, is calculated to achieve that object.'

The meeting was poorly attended, mainly because many of the agricultural visitors were at the implement yard which was being visited by the Duke of Cambridge. But those attending were very influential landowners and scientists; the press report of the time said, 'What, however, the meeting lacked in point of numbers was made up by the great respectability of the parties present.' In addition to those proposing and seconding the resolutions there were Earl Spencer, Professor Buckland and Dr Daubeny.

It seems fitting that the Society, founded in 1838, should have had in its numbers several who supported the concept of an agricultural college, but the support was never more than lukewarm and thereafter the Society was not particularly active in its promotion. A possible reason for this may have been that the College turned out to be utilized more by the sons of well-to-do landowners rather than by the sons of tenant farmers, though that was not the original intention. Writing in the journal of the Society at a later date (1865), Charles Lawrence, one of the founders, said of the Society, 'The Council has, neverthe-less, been recently reminded that it has hitherto neglected one important duty of those enumerated in our Charter, namely, "to take measures for the improve-ment of the *education* of those who depend on the cultivation of the soil for their support".' So perhaps this reflected a general disinterestedness on the part of the Society rather than any specific attitude towards the college at Cirencester.

★

These happenings were beginning to catch attention nationally and attracted the contributors to *Punch*. The sophisticated attitude of the day towards farming and countryside affairs was steeped in ridicule of the bucolic inhabitants. The magazine had a field day:

We are happy to find that there is to be a College of Agriculture, and that the worthy clodhopper will henceforth have his Alma Mater, like the Cantab, and the honest highlow of industry will tread the sacred groves of Academus as well as the aristocratic Oxonian. We see no difficulty in organising the College of Agriculture, and we can suggest a few of the probable professorships. Of course there will be a chair of new laid eggs, which the professor of poultry would be well qualified to occupy. Degrees will be conferred in guano; and a series of lectures on the philosophy of making hay when the sun shines would, no doubt, be exceedingly popular. We should also propose that, previous to matriculation, every student should be required to undergo an examination on moral philosophy in connection with chaff, and the efficacy of thrashing by hand when the ears are unusually lengthy. Corresponding with the university Master of Arts, there could be Bachelors of Barley, and the undergraduates might be brought direct to the Agricultural College from the Plough, as they are now brought to Universities immediately from Harrow. The examination papers would be at first difficult to frame, but the following may be some guide for preparing them:

Find the square root of a stick of horse-radish. Describe the Milky Way, distinguishing the whey from the milk, and chalking out the way by which the milk gets there.

We merely throw out these hints, but the Professors themselves will be better able to frame the necessary questions for the use of students. Clover will offer a wide field, and hay, though rather dry, will be the sort of food that the students may take advantage of.

This ponderous and strained humour managed to bring some levity into the equally ponderous but intensely serious debates that had transpired to date, but which were to achieve their objective.

★

On 27 March 1845 the Charter of Incorporation was granted by the sovereign in response to the petition made by Henry George, Earl Bathurst, Edward Bowly, Raymond Cripps and Robert Jeffreys Brown and this conferred on the proposed institution the title of 'The Agricultural College', 'in which College the science of Agriculture, and the various sciences connected therewith, and the practical application thereof in the cultivation of the soil, and the rearing and management of stock, are intended to be taught to pupils who have attained the age of fourteen years or upward'. Although this was the title granted by the Charter, from the outset the College was referred to as 'The Royal Agricultural College' and was so called in the first prospectus issued in 1846. Later in the century this use was called into question and on application, Queen Victoria in Council conferred the prefix 'Royal' upon the College, although there were further or Supplementary Charters granted in 1849 and 1870. The fact that there was royal patronage from the beginning was the reason for the assumption of the title.

At last, therefore, the efforts of the originators had borne fruit and this was the culmination of their campaign to generate support for the formation of their brainchild, the 'College in the Cotswolds'.

The Charter constituted the association of Governors, or Proprietors and Donors as a corporate body according to a Deed of Settlement which had been granted slightly earlier on 27 February 1845, and vested the management in a Council consisting of the President, Vice-President and Secretary together with the Governors and Proprietors. It gave powers to raise monies and to hold and manage lands and properties in accordance with the Deed of Settlement. The Council could make all necessary by-laws. By the Charter Earl Bathurst was appointed the first President and the Earl of Ducie the first Vice-President.

A Governor was defined as being the holder of five or more shares, a Proprietor a holder of less than five shares and a Donor as a contributor of £30 towards the institution. The Donors were not eligible for election to the Council but were permitted to attend the General Meeting of the associated members. The capital of the association was to be £12,000, in shares of £30 each with no one person holding more than ten shares, with power to increase the amount to £24,000, and to declare a dividend of not more than 4 per cent. The Deed gave full powers to the Council regarding the management of staff and of the farm.

One significant feature of the Deed was that preference was to be given, in the admission of students, to the nominees of Proprietors and Donors. Each Proprietor could nominate one student for every share held and each Donor one student for every £30 contributed. The significance which became apparent later on was that if sufficient of the Proprietors and Donors exercised their rights then this would in practice determine to some extent the type of entrant, particularly if their sons or the sons of their tenants were to be nominated. This is in fact what happened.

By the time the Charter was granted the quest for shareholders was nearly completed, having started after the meetings in the previous year and the initial £12,000 was easily subscribed. The list of shareholders was impressive, particularly in numbers of nobility as well as other landowners and tenant farmers. At the top was His Royal Highness, Prince Albert, the Prince Consort, the possessor of five shares, who also became Patron. Among the peers there were the Dukes of Cambridge, Bedford, Buccleuch, Cleveland and Grafton; the Marquises of Downshire, Exeter, Lansdowne and Northampton; Earls Fitzhardinge, St Germans, and Granville; Lords John Russell, Villiers and Sudeley. The leading agriculturalists who purchased shares were such as the Earl of Leicester of Holkham Hall, Norfolk; Richard Tull of Crookham, Newbury, Berkshire and the Earl of Radnor of Coleshill. These were, of course, in addition to the original promoters and supporters of the project. One interesting shareholder was Isambard Kingdom Brunel, the engineer, who purchased five shares numbered 572 to 576 in the later issue in 1847.

The result of the taking up of shares and the formation of the Company in accordance with the Deed of Settlement was that there were sixty-four Governors. The Council comprised twenty-six members and the Chairman appointed was Mr Edward Holland; from this Council a committee was appointed to draw up the by-laws and regulations for the College.

★

With the finances and the land thus assured the Council set about creating the College on the land leased from Earl Bathurst. They appointed as architects Messrs Daukes and Hamilton of Gloucester and Cheltenham, following a competition for the design of the College buildings. They were the winners from forty entries. The design utilized the existing farmhouse of Port Farm and the seventeenth-century tithe barn, but did not retain any of the other buildings of the farm.

A contemporary description of the proposed building was reported, in 1845, in a newspaper of that year:

The situation is well chosen, it being on Lord Bathurst's grounds, known as Port Farm, near the railway station, at the junction of the Stroud and Tetbury roads. Thus, the edifice will present a perspective of two bold fronts; the principal front, 190 feet long, will have a southern aspect, commanding an extensive view over North Wiltshire. The ground slopes in every direction, and a more beautiful and healthy site could scarcely be pointed out; in one direction having the view above described – on the other the park and woods of Lord Bathurst. The farm itself will be attached to the main building; it will be altered to meet the domestic requirements of the institution, and decorated sufficiently to be in character with the new structure, which, with this addition, will form an entire frontage of nearly 250 feet.

The design is in the Tudor style, of three stories high; the upper storey being lit by picturesque, old fashioned dormer windows, of the style so prevalent among the collegiate buildings of Oxford. The centre is occupied by a bold tower, 80 feet high; with a turreted newel of 100 feet, intended as an observatory, for meteorological and other scientific purposes. The materials are limestone from the quarries adjacent; the quoins, window-dressings, &c., being of freestone; and half the elevation is already completed.

The Building will include a large Dining Hall, Classrooms, Laboratory, Museum, besides ranges of Sleeping Apartments on two floors. The Head Master and Pupils will reside in the College.

The School will be under the management of the different Professors, who will be constantly on the spot; the instruction will be conveyed not merely by lecture, but also by individual study and *practical* working. Mr Way has been chosen as the Chemical and Geological Professor. Professors will be engaged to instruct in Botany, Natural History, Mathematics, and Physics, Drawing, Mechanics, Geometry, Dynamics, Levelling, Mapping, Surveying, Building, Hydrostatics, &c., more particularly as they have a reference to Agriculture. The structure and treatment of the Diseases of Cattle will be taught.

ROYAL AGRICULTURAL COLLEGE, CIRENCESTER.

Architect's impression of the proposed College in 1845

The reference to the farm buildings could not have been quite accurate, for apart from the retention of the old farmhouse and the tithe barn, the new farmstead was to be built off a separate entrance from the Tetbury road, some way away from the College proper. This description was taken from the architect's drawings, for the artist's sketch accompanying the report shows some different details from the finished buildings. The reference to Oxford college design was relevant, for the structures enclose a quadrangle and the entrance hall is typical of such colleges. The description of the style as Tudor has some merit but a better reference would have been Gothic.

Tenders were sought on a competitive basis and the successful one chosen was from Mr Thomas Bridges, a Cirencester builder, for the sum of £3,674. This did not include the chapel, which was to be built two years later, nor the tower, also added later. The work started in April 1845 and was completed, in accordance with the terms of the contract, exactly one year later in April 1846. By today's standards this was a remarkable feat.

★

However, the Council did not want to wait for completion of the College before accepting students. In the previous year (1844) they decided to advertise for a

Principal (actually it was for a Headmaster, but the title was changed after the first appointment): It was in September 1844, when the Committee of Management was set up, that the search for a Principal was started. By November 1844 the salary was fixed at £200 per annum plus £1 per head for every student admitted over fifty.

The Council considered seven names for the post: Young, Townsend, Hall, Buckland, Wade, Scales and Law. Later on they interviewed two more: Pears and Phelps. The successful applicant was John Scales, a Norfolk farmer, who was appointed on 24 December 1844. His wife was appointed matron. A bailiff was also appointed.

★

The desire to make a start now that the finance had been secured and the Royal Charter granted caused the Committee to hire accommodation and accept a first intake of students. Two houses in Thomas Street, Cirencester, were leased and on 15 September 1845 twenty-five students were admitted. By then, in addition to Scales, some staff had been recruited. J.T. Way was appointed as Professor of Chemistry as from 25 March, S.P. Woodward as Professor of Geology, Natural History and Botany, J. Robinson as Professor of Veterinary Surgery and M. Bravender for Civil Engineering and Surveying.

The by-laws and regulations had been formed and provided procedure for the admission of students:
1. Based on the Deed of Settlement students were admitted only on the nomination in writing of a Proprietor, or of a Donor of £30.
2. The minimum age was fourteen, and the maximum eighteen, students not being allowed to continue in residence beyond the end of the half-year after their twentieth birthday.
3. No student was to be accepted who did not at least possess a competent knowledge of reading, writing, grammar and arithmetic. All students had to produce a certificate of moral character.
4. The fees were £30 per annum for students between the ages of fourteen and sixteen, though no more than one third of the total number would be admitted at that sum; £40 for students between the ages of sixteen and eighteen; £50 per annum for students from eighteen upwards. There was also a charge for the maintenance of the library, museum and laboratory which would be fixed by the Council.
5. The College sessions commenced on 6 October and 6 April each year and there were two vacations – one of four weeks, commencing on such day in June after the 24th, and the other of six weeks, commencing on such day of December after the 15th, as the Principal with the approval of the Council would decide.
6. Three months' notice was required for the removal of a student.
7. Regular attendance at daily morning and evening prayers and Divine Service

on Sundays (Church of England) was required, though as it said in the first prospectus, 'the sons of dissenters may respectively attend such places of worship as their parents shall, by letter to the Principal, request'.

8. Non-resident students, of any age, were admitted on the recommendation of a shareholder or Donor on payment of £30 in advance.

These regulations smacked more of a school rather than a College, but then the lowest age of admittance was fourteen and so boys would be coming straight from school. With only ten weeks for vacations, forty-two weeks of tuition in College seems a long time and an exercise in endurance for the staff. However, the day was divided into mornings for lectures and studies and afternoons for work on the farms.

The syllabus arranged comprised Chemistry, Geology, Natural History, Botany, Veterinary Art and Farm Accounts as basic subjects, with a choice from Mathematics, Natural Philosophy and Practical Engineering. During the half day on the farm the students were required to keep a Farm Diary. The course was of two years and led to the College Diploma (Member of the Royal Agricultural College – MRAC), and the final examinations were to be held immediately preceding the summer vacation. These examinations were to be conducted by external examiners appointed by the Council.

The Principal and the professors were to be appointed by the Council. This is of note for it was later that powers were devolved to the Principal to engage and to dismiss all staff, and such powers were to be the cause of a troubled period in the history of the College in the coming years. The Principal was given overall responsibility for the well-being of the College and for the superintendence of all its departments. It was his job to fix the order of the day (to be announced at breakfast each day), to regulate the frequency and duration of lectures and examinations, to conduct morning and evening prayers and to enforce discipline. The professors were given board and lodging in the College, unless given special permission to live out by the Council; this was to be another source of friction eventually. They were entirely responsible for the control of students in their respective lecture rooms and for the content of their instruction.

The Royal Agricultural College commenced agricultural education to students on 15 September 1845 when the twenty-five students housed in Thomas Street received their first instruction. Mr John Scales, the new Principal, was directly responsible for their welfare. They awaited the completion of the College buildings due in the April of 1846.

★

The first phase had ended. Three years after Robert Jeffreys Brown had sown the seed of agricultural education the harvest had commenced with the first students sitting at the feet of the teachers of 'Practice with Science'. His speech to the local farmers' club had not only reflected the members' need to express their feelings about agricultural education but had touched a wider audience and had received the backing of academics who looked for the transfer of developing scientific principles into practical application on the farm.

What was equally, or perhaps more, important was that it had been recognized by the aristocratic landowners who had the power and influence to make it happen. They, with some of the wealthier tenant farmers, had the financial resources to invest in the project.

It was a speculative venture: there was a considerable degree of risk, for the promoters were moving into unknown territory. They could only guess at the market; they started out by envisaging a College for the sons of tenant farmers, but really had little knowledge of what the demand might be. In order to encourage investment by potential shareholders they devised the system of priority for places to be reserved, in effect, for the sons or nominees of the Proprietors and Donors, thereby restricting entry to one class of person. Yet, it is possible that without this they would not have achieved the immediate success in raising the capital from those best able to pay – the nobility, the landed classes and the larger farmers. In addition, a contributory factor was the enthusiastic support of the burgeoning scientific world and influential national figures, from the Prince Consort, and by implication the monarch, downwards. Had this taken place in modern times it would have been regarded as a highly successful publicity campaign using the media available and tapping the right market for sponsors.

The concept was in keeping with the times; it was ambitious; it was based on the use of the corporate body, the shareholding company with the facility to raise capital; it had the noble imprimatur of a Royal Charter; it reflected the Victorian thought of expansion and of grand designs; it deserved to be successful. All was set with the establishment of the first agricultural college in the kingdom for it to forge ahead.

★

ARVORUM CULTUS PECORUMQUE

The shield and crest of the College has below it the motto: *Arvorum Cultus Pecorumque*. There is, unfortunately, no record of exactly when the motto was devised and by whom. It may have come from one of the original founders or from someone associated with the foundation of the College. It has a classical derivation.

Writing in the *College Journal* of 1980/1, Ross Leckie wrote of his close investigation of this feature. He said: '. . . what does it mean? . . . Which of those forty founding members of the founding committee proposed [this] as the College's motto, we do not know. Yet we do know that the College's founders were all men of education; the majority of them had studied at Oxford or Cambridge, where Latin was a part of the curricula.'

The College sh...
and crest. *Top*
1895, *right*: 190...
bottom left: 1922...
right: 1954

Leckie reported that his enquiries of 'those current in all walks of the College's life' revealed an understanding that it meant: 'The Cultivation of the Fields and of Beasts'. He threw some doubt on the translation of *cultus*: he went to the likely source of the phrase – Virgil's *Georgics*, Book 4, line 559:

'*Hactenus, super arvorum cultu pecorumque canebam.*'
The *Georgics*, written between 36 and 29 B.C. . . . is a didactic poem in 4 books, ostensibly concerned with agriculture in all its forms . . . it is a moralising poem, Virgil shows how the simple virtues make the farmer free from ambition, avarice, corruption; how the life of toil can result in serenity and contentment. . . .

Quite apart from this particular context, the word itself bears considerable resonance; its usual meaning is 'honouring', reverence, veneration. . . . What *cultus* does not mean is simple, straightforward cultivation or tillage.

Thus the College motto means 'tending the fields and the beasts', or possibly even 'caring for the fields and the beasts'. I believe that the College's founders realised that they were using a loaded term. . . .

This thought that the founders were, in their selection of the motto for the College, presenting a double message, was also expounded by E. John Wibberley. He also concludes that the motto is taken from Virgil's *Georgics* – '*Haec super arvorum cultu pecorumque et super arboribus*' – and quotes the translation by Lonsdale and Lee (1898) as: 'So I have been singing of the tillage of fields, and the tending of herds and of trees.'

He also makes clear that *cultus* refers to 'caring' and that the College motto may be translated as 'care for your fields and your livestock'. But he interprets another meaning; he tells that *cultus* has also the meaning of 'worship', that is, as Leckie has it, 'reverence, veneration'. 'Thus,' says Wibberley, 'one might suppose the founders had the intention of advocating, "God honouring stewardship of the land, its crops and its animals".'

This may be stretching the intentions of the founders' interpretation of the motto, but two facts support it. The first is the emphasis placed on daily prayer in the curriculum and the provision of a handsome College chapel, and the second is the College Prayer:

Oh, Lord, our Heavenly Father, who hast gathered together Thy servants in this College to study the laws and working of this earth, for the better care and use of the same, Grant that in the pursuit of knowledge and in the labours of our hands we may be directed by Thy guidance and may in all thing become obedient to Thy Heavenly Law and Will. Grant this, O Father, for the love of Him who has taught us the beauty of this earth and the dignity of labour, Thine only Son Jesus Christ.

Both Leckie and Wibberley wrote their interpretations of the College motto against a background of the modern agricultural philosophy of the application of science to the increase of profit and of the desire to optimize efficiency. At the time of the creation of the College and its motto, the first striving to these eventual goals can be seen, but it is a return to the caring role of agriculture that is now stirring – so the founders may now be seen to be justified in the ideals with which they started out.

Chapter Two

A TROUBLED START, 1845–59

Unless the requisite funds are immediately found you cannot receive back the pupils before Christmas. . . .

Edward Holland, 1847

It is difficult to know what the thinking was behind the appointment of John Scales, for there is no record save that the post of Headmaster (as it was first called, and almost immediately renamed Principal) was advertised in the national and agricultural press, and interviews were held. Apart from their names we do not know anything of the other applicants nor of the criteria that the Committee set for this decision. What we do know is that there was no guidance based on previous experience available to them, for there were no institutions for agricultural education to which appointments had been made. The main consideration must have been the same as it would be today – is the post to be occupied by an agriculturalist or by a teacher or, if available, by someone with both qualifications? There was, in addition to the education of the students, a farm to be run, on at least semi-commercial lines, i.e. it should show no loss and preferably a profit. There were other matters to be thought of: the need for moral supervision and religious training, and the possibility of research. Not the least, in addition, was the need to control the financial state of the College.

There was a farm to manage. Earl Bathurst had offered the lease of 430 acres of land, at a rent of £648.18s.0d (£648.90). It was virtually unequipped with buildings since those at Port Farm were to be absorbed into the new College buildings.

The necessity to manage this farm must have ranked high in the judgement of the Council, particularly as it was at the end of 1844, with the autumn cultivations to be dealt with and the need to clean up the farm, when the search for the first Principal began. It was completed by 24 December 1844 with the appointment of John Scales.

★

John Scales was a farmer from Norfolk, though at the time he took up the post he was managing an estate in Sussex. Born at Cottingham near Kingston-upon-Hull

A photograph
thought to be of
John Scales, the first
Principal

on 21 March 1794, he had the misfortune to be taken prisoner by the French when travelling by boat from Hull to London. He was ransomed by his father, who, after a spell in London, bought a farm at Halvergate in Norfolk when John Scales was fourteen years of age. Four years later this property was sold and a large farm purchased at Beachamwell in West Norfolk, comprising 3,500 acres. Although Scales had intended to take up medicine, his father fell into ill health and could no longer manage the farm so he had to take over with little or no knowledge of agriculture. He had been a very keen naturalist and continued with this abiding interest, travelling extensively. He seems to have been more than just a gifted and enthusiastic amateur and certainly built up an extensive naturalist collection and wrote copious notes. On the death of his father he moved from Beachamwell and took the tenancy of a farm at Helhoughton under Lord Charles Townshend of Raynham. This tenancy ended in 1842 (we do not know the reasons why) and he left Norfolk to become manager of the Battle Abbey Estate in Sussex, the property of Lady Webster. It was from here that he came to the College and took up his post in March 1845 when the Royal Charter was granted.

He arrived at the College with experience of farming in Norfolk, which county was held in high regard for progressive farming, and with some reputation as an entomologist, ornithologist and botanist, though not with any academic qualifications in those subjects. It must be wondered whether any of the other applicants for the post were better qualified: it would be surprising if there was no one with academic qualifications. It must be concluded, therefore, that the Committee put practical farming experience at the top of their list of the desirable features of a Principal.

Scales has left behind a memorandum in the form of a letter to the shareholders setting out to justify his management of the farm. It was written in 1847 after his dismissal the previous year on the grounds of mismanagement of the farm and of inability to teach. When he took over he was faced with immediate problems. For a start, the previous tenant, Stevens, was allowed a holdover and it was not until April 1845 that his disposal sale took place. Although the College had obtained pre-entry from 1 February, the cultivations that were necessary for the spring cereal and root crops were put back and the purchase of horses and material was held up until after the sale. It was a cold and wet spring and he said that he was unable to start preparing one hundred acres of land for turnips until the middle of May, which land was 'a mass of couch grass'. He had many other complaints: '. . . our neighbours were getting forward with their sowing, from having the advantage of winter tillage, and shortly afterwards the season set in remarkably wet, cold and unpropitious, and, as soon as the weather took up, the turnips were attacked to an extraordinary degree by wire-worms, grubs and earwigs; the same wet weather spoiled all the sainfoin hay in the neighbourhood which happened to be cut'.

The tale of troubles had not ended: 'We had not, at that time, received our new one-horse harvest carts; I was, therefore, obliged to be entirely dependent upon the kindness of Earl Bathurst for the accommodation of waggons, so obligingly furnished to me by Mr Anderson, his Lordship's Steward. . . . I unfortunately had no straw provided to thatch any part of the corn-stacks, except through the kind accommodation of Earl Bathurst. . . .' He summed up all his woes:

> The farm was engaged under peculiar circumstances and disadvantages, – the outgoing tenant remaining, and occupying the premises a month longer that was expected with live and dead stock. The premises were then immediately pulled down, to make room for the College: consequently there were no stables for horses, until two sheds were temporarily enclosed for them at the small field-barn; no buildings or convenience for new or other implements, which caused me to purchase as few as possible; no place to use as granary or store-house, for mixing and keeping artificial manure, or even to lock up necessary implements. In addition to this, there was no residence for myself upon the farm, which compelled me to have one in the town, at a distance of $1\frac{1}{2}$ to 2 miles from the respective parts of the farm.

He had difficulty in some of his dealings with merchants, agents and others. There was a long-running saga from May 1845 to March 1846 about the purchase of two working horses – Cleveland Bay mares. He retained an agent in Durham to purchase them and insisted on a tight specification in spite of the lack of horses for sale at that busy time. In the end they were found unsound by the College veterinary surgeon, disputed by the vendor and the matter was eventually settled by the College paying the agent, Mr Wetherell, his reduced bill of £110. But it wasted a great deal of time which could not have pleased the Council, dragged into it as they were.

This response to the charges of incompetence that were made against him in 1846 was certainly lively and must be judged as a catalogue of the difficulties he faced at the outset, not, perhaps of his success or otherwise in dealing with them. He was bound to put as good a face on his own actions as he could as the charges that were made later on were of extreme incompetence and negligence.

★

At the start, part of the two leased houses was reserved for Scales and his wife. The first twenty-five students were housed there, of whom the first five were:
1. John Coleman of Wandsworth
2. John George Stubbs of Cannock
3. Antony Bliss Kittermaster of Meriden
4. John George Rodney Ward of Over Stowey, Somerset
5. Henry Tanner.
So Scales was not only responsible for managing the academic resources of the

College and of the farm, but he also had to look after the students in the same house.

The Council laid out the arrangements in detail:

> . . . Mr and Mrs Scales shall have for their private use the drawing room, parlour and two bedrooms and chief staircase and entrance. The pupils shall have the use of the dining room for meals; small room and common room on the ground floor, and the passage from the dining room through the Hall to the garden, together with free use of the garden, also four large dormitories, two washing closets and back staircase, a room on the first floor being reserved for a sick room, and one for a linen room.

The establishment to be conducted by Mr and Mrs Scales with the assistance of a cook, housemaid, kitchen maid and manservant. Mr and Mrs Scales will dine with the pupils, and preside at the breakfast table.

The board provided by the College will consist of:

Sunday	Boiled beef and pudding.
Monday	Mutton roast or boiled and bread and cheese.
Tuesday	Pork or bacon and pudding.
Wednesday	Roast beef and Yorkshire pudding.
Thursday	Irish stew and bread and cheese.
Friday	Mutton roast or boiled and pudding.
Saturday	Miscellaneous and bread and cheese.
Beverage	Table beer or water.
Breakfast	Coffee and tea with bread, butter and cold bacon.
Tea	Tea and bread and butter or bread and cheese.

The Master and prefects will carve and the servants wait at table.

Order of the Establishment. Bell call at 5.30 summer; 6.30 winter. *Prayers* to commence at 6.0 summer; 7.0 winter. *Roll* called over. *Breakfast* to commence 7.30 summer; 8.0 winter. *Dinner* at one. *Tea* at six. *Prayers* at 9.0. Tray bread and cheese. *Bed* immediately after. The prayers and scriptures will be read by the Principal, and the pupils are expected to observe the greatest decorum in dress and behaviour.

The Principal will give out after breakfast or overnight the duties of the outdoor class for the day. The course of study in the different schools will be put in writing for the guidance for the Pupils, at the commencement of the term or session. Directly after breakfast the classes will pass on to the farm or schools. The Principal and Professors will be assisted in the duties of the College by a Prefect and sub-prefect for every 12 students; chosen from the highest class, their duty being to preserve order and enforce bye-laws and to report any breach of discipline to the Principal. The pupils will pass, without stopping, by the direct route to the Farm, and no pupil, except prefects, will be allowed to go into the town without leave and never without a companion unless sent by the Master or Professors, and it will be arranged that the

Principal or some Professor shall always be with the students. The most gentlemanly behaviour will be required at all times, and the students will be expected to salute the Principals and Professors on meeting them. No smoking or taking of snuff will be sanctioned, nor will any pupil be allowed to buy wine or spirits for private use, or to contract any debt except by allowance of Professors for school articles.

On the farm the pupils will keep a diary of all operations and other incidents, they will take part in every description of labour and occupation.

This tight and strictly ordered regime probably derived from taking school rather than college discipline as an example and was possibly necessitated by the type of student who was first entered. Mainly between fourteen and sixteen they were later to be described as, '. . . rough, wild, half-educated lads, who were in many cases sent there because there was nothing else could be done with them'. It added to the load imposed on Scales for it had not at first been intended that he should have to take charge of the boarders. The first appointed Professor of Mathematics, Agricultural Engineering and Natural Philosophy was George Townsend and he was to take up residence with the students in the Cirencester house and be in charge. Unfortunately, he died shortly after his appointment, and so Scales took over the role.

This arrangement lasted until the students moved in to the College buildings on 30 April 1846, though some of them had to sleep in the classrooms! In May of that year numbers were up to thirty-five and by the end of the summer vacation ninety were enrolled.

Before then the deficiencies in the choice of Principal were becoming apparent. At the very time that the regulations for the Thomas Street houses were being promulgated the Council recorded: 'The Council making allowance for the difficulties Mr Scales has to contend with, still feel it proper to express their dissatisfaction with regard to the general management of the farm, and call upon him to state in writing on Friday the general system he intends to pursue in the occupation.' At their next meeting they did not find Scales's explanations satisfactory.

To add to the problem of the competence of this first Principal it was becoming apparent that he was not capable of teaching; by November 1845 the Committee had decided that the attempt to combine in the post of Principal the responsibility for the management of the farm and the administration of the College had failed and that the two aspects should be split. So, in January 1846, Scales was made Farm Superintendent and Professor of Agriculture, and a new Principal was to be appointed. This did not last very long for in July 1846 Scales resigned. Indeed, he was asked to resign because the Committee had reached the conclusion that he was incompetent to carry out either of the posts.

Perhaps the opprobrium which descended on Scales should be tempered by a recognition of the conditions he had to contend with at the outset. Nevertheless in subsequent histories of the College some hard words were said. He was described 'by an Old Professor' in the report of the jubilee celebrations of 25/6 July 1895 as: '. . . the first Principal, one Scales, who, if the report did not belie him, was a broken-down Norfolk farmer, with a tongue that was perpetually wagging'.

In later correspondence, in October 1847, Robert Brown, writing to a Mr Edwards, a shareholder who had complained of the state of the College farm, said:

> We were extremely injured by a wrong choice of our farmer in the first instance, and are still suffering from his mistakes and negligence. That gentlemen was recommended by leading agriculturalists of the eastern counties, and, after the mess he got us into, I think they will be extremely cautious of recommending an agriculturalist from their district again to us. . . . The management of the farm by our late superintendent was the derision not of our good farmers only, but of the bad ones, and with reason. Whenever they had abundant crops of swedes and turnips, with half the means that we had, we were obliged to send our flock out to tack. . . . A most beautiful crop of seed hay was so secured, as to be little better than straw; some say it was not as good. A great deal of corn was put up so badly that it stunk in the ricks, and afterwards so neglected that one wheat-rick was a perfect burrow for rats all the winter.

Scales departed; in spite of the criticisms of his farming there were other comments that he had raised the standard of the cultivations that were carried out and he was thought to have made the introductory speech at the opening of the College. The original handwritten draft of this speech still exists and a typewritten copy of it states that the speech was probably made in March 1846. At this date, immediately prior to the occupation of the College buildings, Scales had been replaced as Principal and was Farm Superintendent and Professor of Agriculture, so it is unlikely that he would have made the speech then. In the speech there is a statement that, 'I have the honor to be appointed to carry out these expectations the whole establishment being (at present) under my control and management with the assistance of Professors.' This does establish that it was made by the Principal, but which one? It goes on, 'The department of theoretical and practical Agriculture will be taught by myself. . . .' This may mean that the post of Principal combined with that of Professor of Agriculture, in which case it points to Scales as the writer and to the speech having been made earlier than January 1846, when the next Principal was appointed. In fact it would have to have been made before November 1845 when the posts of Principal and Professor were divided. Thus it will have been made at or about the time when the first students arrived to start in Thomas Street.

The speech has an academic background, referring as it does to the early history of agriculture and the first attempts at agricultural education. It starts by saying of the College, 'as it is the only one of its kind in the Kingdom the difficulties are the greater not only as to its construction but also as to the general organisation of it, a knowledge of which can only be acquired progressively: for having no precedent (at least in England) to guide us, an institution of such magnitude can only be got into a system of general good management and which can only develop itself in course of time by practical working'. It brought the sciences of chemistry and botany to the forefront of the proposed syllabus. It expounded a philosophy towards farming that set the tone for the College and its farm for many years to come:

> The farmer's object is to raise the greatest possible amount of produce from the soil by such means as will afford him the largest profit and there can be no doubt that the more scientifically he proceeds the more effectually will both objects be gained.
>
> It is not sufficient that he already gets what he considers a fair return for his capital and industry if by other modes he could obtain more: if he neglects them, he injures himself, his family and the public.

The parting words appear to have been a homily to the young men who were to pass through the College, ' "Time is an Estate" – a truth strictly applicable to those who spend, in a useful and improving manner that leisure which the vicious and ignorant spend in idleness.'

★

The person appointed on 7 January 1846 to replace Scales as Principal was the Revd George Christopher Hodgkinson MA of Trinity College, Cambridge, aged thirty. At the time he was Second Master of the Royal School (probably the King Edward VI Grammar School) at Bury St Edmunds, Suffolk. Before that he had been Principal of Hull College, Hull, a large public school. He came with many glowing references to his abilities as a schoolmaster.

This was a quite extraordinary change of course for the Council. From the first appointment of a Principal with knowledge of agriculture but none of teaching they moved to a Principal who was a teacher pure and simple with no knowledge of agriculture. Hodgkinson was neither an agriculturalist nor a scientist, disciplines one would have thought essential in the head of an agricultural college.

The choice of Hodgkinson was not unanimous; there were three candidates before the Committee: Hodgkinson, Alexander and Haygarth. The first voting was 11, 6 and 4 respectively with two abstentions. On a second division Hodgkinson won by 12 votes to 10 for Alexander, with Haygarth eliminated, a narrow majority, with one abstention. In both divisions Edward Bowly, who was certainly one of the most influential on the Committee, did not vote. Haygarth was to appear again and become Principal in 1851.

However, on his arrival on Lady Day 1846, Hodgkinson found that, in addition to Scales as Farm Superintendent and Professor of Agriculture he had on his staff some capable men. J.T. Way, Professor of Chemistry, was among the first to be appointed in 1845. He had studied chemistry under Daubeny at Oxford who was instrumental in putting him into the College. He was to be the first of a long line of agricultural chemists who occupied this chair and who, after doing research at the College, went on to achieve eminence in their field. He was also Consulting Chemist to the Royal Agricultural Society of England for a short time while at Cirencester and continued in this post when he left the College.

The responsibility for running the farm after Scales left was taken over by Thomas Arkell, also a shareholder of the Company. He farmed at Pen Hill. He was also a member of the Council and was expected to pull the farm round and put it under sound management. He also occupied the Chair of Agriculture but had no experience of lecturing and found it difficult. Although he was successful in bringing the farm up to an acceptable standard the Committee decided that the post of Professor of Agriculture should be separate from that of Farm Superintendent.

Arkell was replaced as Professor of Agriculture by John Wilson, aged thirty-four, who came to the College after training in Paris where he had studied medicine and chemistry under Payen, Bousingault and Gay Lussac. He was a fine sportsman and an excellent horseman. Wilson was also appointed Vice-Principal and was to become a strong leader of the scientific staff.

The Professor of Geology, Natural History and Botany was S.P. Woodward, later to become Professor of Natural History at the British Museum. The Professor of Veterinary Surgery (then known as 'The Veterinary Art') was J. Robinson and the Professor of Surveying and Practical Engineering was M. Bravender, a shareholder and College Secretary.

The syllabus in January 1847 was for a course of two years, commencing in mid-summer, made up of two sessions each year and with vacations being of a month commencing in June and six weeks commencing just before Christmas. The *theroetical* instruction comprised:

 1. Oral instruction in practical agriculture
 2. Elementary geometry applied to surveying, levelling, cubage of solids, etc.
 3. Mechanics applied to agricultural implements, to the erection of sheds and construction of roofs, etc.
 4. Hydraulics applied to drainage and irrigating
 5. Designing and drawing of plans for implements and buildings
 6. Chemistry and General Physics
 7. Geology and Mineralogy
 8. Botany, Vegetable Physiology and Natural History
 9. Principles of the Veterinary Art
10. Methods of Farm Accounts.

The *practical* instruction comprised half of each day spent on the farm and taking part in all the manual operations of husbandry.

It soon became apparent that Hodgkinson intended to run the College on much the same lines as he would expect in a Grammar School. Having an academic background and training he inclined to a more theoretical approach and to less practical application of the teaching on the farm. At the same time, during 1847, it was becoming evident that, because of Arkell's inability to lecture, and with the advent of a professor who was more experienced in the teaching of agriculture and with the knowledge of its practical application, that there should be a change. So Arkell resigned in August 1847 in order that Wilson could take over. Wilson was proving a forceful character and readily accepted the dual role. Once again the management of the farm and the teaching of agriculture was in the same hands as it had been when Scales accomplished both.

Nonetheless, the problems for the College were not dissipating. For Hodgkinson to carry out his object of increasing the theoretical content of the syllabus the staff had correspondingly increased. He had started with some highly competent staff and his policies did not meet with their concurrence. There was friction leading later to the resignation of at least one of the senior staff.

★

Throughout 1846 admissions were steady but the target figure of one hundred was proving elusive. It was not until towards the end of the year that the total admissions since commencement reached that figure, with a rather smaller number actually in residence. The expansion plans were still being put forward by the Council. In March it was proposed to erect a new wing capable of extending accommodation to two hundred as well as providing a new lecture theatre. It was intended to fund this by the issue of a hundred more shares and to keep the cost below £2,500. This got as far as the acceptance of a tender of £2,493 but by May it was realized that money was not forthcoming from the College's usual source, the landed interest, and so it would be necessary to have a public issue of shares.

Plans had been prepared for a new set of farm buildings to consist of a barn, fodder rooms, feeding house and lean-to, stable, cart and implement sheds, harness room and pigsty, workshops, and cattle and sheep sheds. At the same time it was decided to construct an approach avenue to the College direct from the Tetbury road. To save costs the College would supply materials and put the labour to tender. This was obtained at £2,748.

To finance these developments it was decided to increase the authorized capital to £24,000 and to issue four hundred more shares. An Extraordinary General Meeting of the Court authorized the Council to borrow at a rate of interest not exceeding 5 per cent.

Further capital expenditure was necessary to provide a chapel for the College. This was not in the original plans although it had been envisaged. It was, however, funded by subscriptions from the Proprietors and Friends of the College.

It was designed by Mr Daukes, of Daukes and Hamilton, the architect of the College, and built by Bridges in 1847. It is an excellent example of Victorian decorated gothic, in the same style as the main College and was built to form an extension of one side of the quadrangle. It is 73 feet by 24 feet.

★

By the middle of 1847 the financial situation was acute. There had been a deficit in the income and expenditure accounts of £1,423 15s. 6d. (£1,423.77) at 31 March 1846 and by the end of May 1847 this was £6,719 4s. 3d. (£6,719.21) with future requirements estimated at £6,500.

At another Extraordinary General Meeting of the Court the fees were raised to £50 per annum. It must have been seen at the time that this would not solve the situation but the original fallacy had been to set the initial fees much too low and at this time a doubling of the fees, which is what was probably necessary to hope to cover the liabilities, would have forfeited future admissions.

At the next meeting of the Council Hodgkinson presented his scheme of education. His way out of the financial chasm was to alter the tenor of the teaching to one of a wholly theoretical basis. It would have changed the College into more of a high school rather than adhering to its original intention of teaching 'Practice with Science', the principle it had borrowed from the Royal Agricultural Society of England. It is surprising that the Council, which still comprised the founders, should have contemplated such a radical alteration in its objectives. No doubt, as is generally the case, they were driven by the realities of rapidly increasing deficits in the accounts.

An immediate consequence of this scheme prepared by the Principal was that one of the professors opposed it vehemently. Professor J.T. Way regarded the scheme as having 'duties such as he could not perform'. He added to the Council, 'Your Principal has made an unjust, unfair and unconditional proposal that I cannot fall in with them nor can I perform them nor were they the conditions under which I was engaged.'

It was not the first time that there had been friction between the Principal and his senior staff. The Council promptly gave notice to Way saying that they 'would seek someone who would carry out the duties he would not perform'. So Way, already displaying the qualities of the eminent chemist he was to be, was lost to the College, and he would not be the first so to go as a result of quarrelling with his Principal. Way left to become full-time consulting chemist to the Royal Agricultural Society of England. He had set up the College chemical laboratory in the tithe barn on the Giessen System. This was based on the laboratory that Leibig (Baron Justus von Leibig) operated in at Giessen University in Germany for teaching students. Leibig had developed the study of artificial manures, including the mineral elements, and based on application in the insoluble form. Way showed the logical development in the soluble form. He had been responsible for the work on the analysis of the ashes of plants which was the first research commission that the College had received (it was from the Royal Agricultural Society of England) and he had published a book on the *Absorptive Powers of Soils*. He was succeeded by Edward Frankland who did not stay long and was, in turn, replaced by Dr John Buddle Blyth. He came with an excellent reputation. He had been trained at Giessen under Leibig and produced glowing references from his German professors. He, too, did not last long, leaving in June 1849. He eventually became Professor of Chemistry at Queen's College, Cork.

By April 1847 the Chairman of the Council, now Edward Holland, who had taken over from Raymond Cripps, was reporting the College's liabilities as £8,000 and asking for a general meeting of the shareholders to be called, for the works at the farm buildings to be stopped and for shareholders in arrears to be pressed for payment. He presented the report of the Council to a meeting of shareholders at their Annual General Court on 2 June 1847. It set out in detail the financial difficulties that were being faced by the College and outlined the causes of this lamentable situation.

He made the initial, and obvious, point that the difficulties were inherent to any large and novel undertaking and, '. . . most peculiarly so to one having for its object the teaching of the science of agriculture. . . . These difficulties have been increased from time to time', the report continued, 'partly from the apathy, and in many instances from the distrust displayed by those who it might be imagined would be most benefitted by the successful establishment of the Institution.'

The first causes had been the additions to the buildings found necessary, the expensive farm buildings and dwellings for farm servants. There was a lack of capital. When the authorized capital had been increased to £24,000 by the issue of four hundred shares only two hundred had been subscribed. A balance sheet of income and expenditure from the start to 22 May was presented. It showed a deficit of £6,719. Of this, £4,192 was owed to the banks and the major liabiities were for the College buildings.

The Council had suspended operations on the farm buildings and postponed other works. They sought to excuse the difficulties:

> The Council . . . beg to draw attention to the fact that no radical error has been committed. On the contrary, it may be considered a matter of surprise, that in an undertaking of such magnitude, and of so novel a nature, where there were no precedents for guidance, no machinery ready at hand with well assayed experience for conducting the operations, and above all, where the funds have been throughout inadequate to the undertaking, there should be such few errors to receive, and those few should be of so retrievable a nature.

Their recommendations included reducing the number of staff in order to save costs, opening an office in London in order to show the College as a national rather than a local institution, and finally ensuring proper educational standards of students on entry.

At a meeting held on 10 June 1847, the General Court accepted the resolution passed at the meeting of the shareholders, '. . . that, in order to pay off existing liabilities, to complete the Buildings requisite for the reception of 130 students, and to stock and carry on the Farm in a satisfactory manner, a sum of £14,000 will be required'. They recommended increasing the authorized capital of the Company by £12,000, to be raised by four hundred additional shares of £30 each. The resolution regarding staff cuts was accepted, thus reducing the staff to the Principal and three professors, the whole of whose salaries was not to exceed £1,100 per year.

The report with its recommendations was accepted by the shareholders. This radical rescue plan resulted in the dismissal of Principal Hodgkinson for it meant the end of his 'scheme'. His successor was at hand – the Professor of Agriculture, John Wilson, FRSE, FGS.

A Committee of Management was formed primarily to effect the reduction in staff. It was made up of five members of the Council: J.H. Langston, J.J. Mechi, Edward Holland, R.J. Brown and J. Kearsey. This small body was likely to prove more effective in the management of the College instead of the rather unwieldy Council of twenty-six members.

★

Hodgkinson had proved to be a Principal who wanted to run the College on a tight rein. The College had turned from a farmer as Principal to a teacher, one whose ideas were theoretical and who sought to constrain the staff and students within his own ideas of running an institution that he saw, basically, as a school. His relations with the staff do not seem to have been very harmonious – he had a dispute with the matron, resulting in her dismissal, and he imposed strict discipline on the students. The Council had difficulties with him after he had been given notice for he was noticeably tardy in giving up occupation of the Principal's residence and continued afterwards to seek compensation. He was the first of the products of Trinity College, Cambridge to be made Principal (the others to come were Haygarth, Constable and McClellan). All were basically scholars trained more in teaching and not scientists or agriculturalists.

In spite of this harsh regime of Hodgkinson, it seems that at least Wilson flourished. He had taken over the management of the farm and continued as Professor of Agriculture successfully. Since he came to the College as an experienced agriculturalist as well as with scientific qualifications he had showed the right combination of qualities to be desired in the Principal of an agricultural college.

★

Impression of John
Wilson, Principal
1847–51, when
Professor of
Agriculture and
Rural Economy at
the University of
Edinburgh 1854–85

In spite of the optimism regarding the rescue plan, only about half of the new four hundred shares authorized were taken up, thus leaving the College in a precarious position and the abandonment of the whole undertaking seemed imminent. There seemed to be no other way out but insolvency and liquidation.

It was at this nadir of the fortunes of the College that rescue appeared in the form of the Chairman of the Council, Edward Holland. He had been constant in his support of the College and of its originator, Robert Brown. Writing to Brown on 28 April 1847, he had said:

> You must not croak, my old friend – and you shall have your niche *still* in the College Entrance Hall.
> Thank you for the list of subscribers to the guarantee fund – it will be useful to me . . . the annual meeting of the shareholders takes place (by charter) on Wednesday 2nd June and I therefore make choice of that day for laying our financial position before our shareholders . . . (you) are *not* I hope going to take any notice of a letter in print by 'John Scales' which has today reached me. Yours very truly and by no means disheartened but the reverse.
>
> Ed. Holland

Unfortunately, though the promise by Holland was thoroughly deserved there is no 'niche' in the entrance hall of the College which might have contained the bust of Robert Brown. The reference to the letter in print by Scales may well be to that which he wrote after his departure with all his woes and complaints, and cited earlier. The meeting of 2 June was, of course, the one at which the radical plan to raise £14,000 and to cut the staff was agreed. But when Holland came to report the College accounts to the Council on 28 July 1847 the deficit was up to £10,800 and the College was in dire straits and facing extinction.

On 5 August the Council received the following letter from him:

> Dumbleton, Evesham
> July 29th 1847
>
> Gentlemen
> Unless the requisite funds are immediately found, you cannot receive back the pupils before Christmas, and the probability is, that if you remain closed until then you will lose those who are now ready to come to the College.
> Under the circumstances, I beg to state that I am willing to advance from time to time, between this and Christmas, such sums as may be necessary for the payment of pressing demands, upon the following conditions:–
> 1. That I have absolute control over both the College and the Farm.
> 2. That all receipts, whether arising from shares, donations, assets, Farm Sales or from any other source, shall from this date be passed to my credit, at one or other of the Cirencester Banks, as I may direct.
> 3. That whenever such College and Farm Payments passed to my credit are

sufficient in amount to balance my account, and that I am repaid all that I have advanced, together with all interest I may owe to the Bankers, then, in such case the surplus, if any, is to be placed by me (to the credit of the College) in the hands of the Treasurers.

I remain, Gentlemen,
Faithfully Yours
Edward Holland.

This munificent offer was accepted without reservation by the Council: there was no other way out of the financial abyss.

On 21 September 1847, Robert Brown wrote, as Honorary Secretary to the Council, a letter to shareholders telling them that the liabilities of the College had been met, '. . . through the liberality of an individual member of the Council, who has shown his confidence in the ultimate success of the Institution by advancing a large sum to meet immediate liabilities; the difficulties in the way of re-opening the College have been removed, and the students returned on 30th August. Forty-nine are in residence and others enter at the beginning of the quarter'.

This letter was an appeal to existing shareholders to purchase more shares or to induce others to subscribe in order to meet the target of £12,000 by the sale of four hundred shares at £30 each.

★

Arkell had resigned from management of the farm; he had improved matters considerably. A new Farm Bailiff was appointed.

Holland reported to the Council on 22 September 1847. He said that Wilson had 'well fitted into the arduous task he has undertaken'. By now the Revd E. Sendall had been appointed Master and Chaplain and he occupied the house in Thomas Street, Cirencester. The College had reopened in the autumn of 1847, thanks to the regeneration of funds by Holland, with thirty-two in-students and two out-students. This number was increased to forty-nine in-students and five out-students before the end of the session, and by Christmas to fifty-six in-students and thirteen out-students. In view of the increasing number of out-students, especially those under the age of twenty-one, it was felt necessary for accommodation to be provided for them, and they were lodged and boarded with the Revd Sendall.

'Order and harmony, good feelings and good discipline prevail. . . .', reported Holland. The implication is that it had not been so under Hodgkinson. The work on the construction of the farm buildings was resumed and the new Bailiff was proving satisfactory. Work, too, on the chapel was progressing well, but this, of course, was being separately financed by donations.

When the first contract had been placed for the construction of the College buildings the tower was deferred. Now, thanks to the generosity of Earl Bathurst, this was provided and the Hon. W.L. Bathurst donated the clock.

An innovation by Holland (proposed in the June report of Council) was to have an office in London opened for publicity purposes and to make it easier to offer shares and attract donations. It was created and put under the management of Philip Bowers, the new Secretary, at 26 King William Street.

Holland made regular reports to the Council; in December he reported that things were going better under Wilson and by that time he had advanced the College £3,560.

In May 1848 the Principal reported that the chapel would be ready at the end of the vacation, though further subscriptions were needed to finish it. The farm buildings also were nearly ready, as well as the dairy and two cottages. But he had a different tale to tell about the farm. The accounts had been badly kept, the livestock were in poor condition and the sheep flock was suffering from a lung disease so serious that it would have to be got rid of!

Another effect of the control being handed over to Holland was that the fees were increased to £80 per annum for in-students and £40 per annum for out-students. The reasons were given in the report of the Council to the Annual General Court on 6 June 1848: 'When the Council two years ago reported to the General Council of Shareholders that the charge of £30 per annum did not produce sufficient sum for carrying on the Institution, the Meeting passed a resolution that the charge should be increased from £30 to £50 a year. . . . The Council have however to report that in spite of the exercise of due economy the present annual charge of £50 . . . is not sufficient to cover the current expenses of the year.'

The report went on to outline the improvements in teaching and in accommodation that were being carried out and which would justify an increase in fees:

Since the Annual fee was raised from £30 to £50 . . . the students who have entered into residence are of a different class to those who joined in the first instance.

The parents of these students demand additional comfort for their sons. They require that Professors and Teachers shall be of the highest grade and that the education afforded to their sons shall be superior (in the particular branch which we profess to teach) to what can be attained elsewhere. They not only demand but are willing to pay for these advantages. It would be the height of folly not to meet their wishes, especially since the very existence of the Institution depends on our doing so.

The Council then recommended the increase to £80 per annum, a 60 per cent increase, which brought the fees at last to somewhere near an economic level. What had been also discovered over these first two years was that the idea that by working on the farm students would pay for their board and keep was not practical. What this increase did mean was that there could no longer be any place for the sons of the smaller tenant farmers, and the type of student attracted would be mainly from the middle classes and the landowners. Judging from the Council's report this was clearly understood.

The College accounts presented on 31 May 1848 showed a deficiency of £12,590 6s. 6d (£12,590.32). The capital assets were £22,235 8s. 5d (£22,235.45). The liabilities were about £5,000 each to the banks, Edward Holland and general creditors. The share issue had only produced £6,750, against the expectation of £14,000.

One year after Edward Holland had taken over control of the College he addressed a letter to the Council:

> Dumbleton
> Evesham
> August 10 1848

Gentlemen,

A year has now elapsed since you entrusted me with the entire management of your institution. During that period I have advanced a large sum towards its support, under the hope through Mr Wilson's able management it would speedily become an effective engine for advancing Agriculture as a science, and that funds still requisite for the firm establishment of so noble an Institution would have been raised during the course of my term of management.

As regards the advance which the Institution would make under Mr Wilson's superintendance I have not been deceived. The system he adopted is working admirably, whilst the gradual increase of pupils denotes the return of public favor. The scheme however for raising the requisite funds has been unsuccessful, and the pecuniary difficulties of the College as shown by your last report to the shareholders still exist.

I cannot any longer continue to uphold the Institution as I am now doing, and request you therefore under these circumstances to meet in Council that you may decide upon the course to be pursued.

> I remain, Gentlemen
> Faithfully yours
> [signed] Edward Holland

★

On receipt of this letter the Council decided to try to raise £13,000 and to pay back Holland £2,340 by increasing the borrowing from the banks. A meeting of shareholders was called and they were persuaded that application should be made to the Queen for a Supplementary Charter to enable the Association to increase its capital by £20,000. In the middle of March there was due to the banks some £4,323 and to Holland £6,328. In the meantime a mortgage was to be arranged, while efforts would be made to raise funds by the issue of additional shares.

The College in

The Supplementary Charter was granted on 7 July giving the necessary authorization, but the share issue was unsuccessful. Following the agreement of Earl Bathurst to the assignment of the leases of the College and the farm as security for a loan, and the personal guarantees of Earl Bathurst, the Earl of Ducie, Mr Thomas Henry Sutton Sotheron-Escourt MP, Mr James Haughton Langston MP and Mr Edward Holland, a loan of £15,000 for a term of ten years at 5 per cent interest was negotiated with Messrs G.I. Pennington, E. Penhryn and the Hon. G.F.S. Elliott. The five guarantors were appointed as a Committee of Management of the College and farm. The Earl of Ducie and Mr Holland also offered to become guarantors for the Gloucestershire Banking Company and the County of Gloucester Bank respectively for the sum of £2,500, to be advanced by each to cover an estimated deficiency on the College farm buildings and interest for the year to midsummer 1850. These arrangements were confirmed by the Council on 7 September 1849.

So although direct control by Holland came to an end with this scheme for financing the debts of the College, as a member of the Committee of Management he remained in joint control and was clearly *de facto* in charge as he was also Chairman of the Council.

Edward Holland, although a man strong and resolute in his actions, was quiet and gentle in manner with a great kindness of heart and a strong vein of humour. He was a martyr to ill health and suffered in later years from gout. He was very much an experimental farmer particularly on the strong clays that he farmed. His ability to hold on to his beliefs was apparent during the great debates on the repeal of the Corn Laws. He was prepared to take a different line from that of most agriculturalists of the day. Knowing the effect that the repeal would have he came to an agreement with his tenants that their future rents should vary with the price of wheat. His enthusiasm for agricultural education did not stop with the constant support he gave to the fledgling College: as a leading member of the Royal Agricultural Society of England he persuaded it to offer scholarships to boys intending to make agriculture their career. In fact, he was an equally strong participant in that Society's affairs as he was in those of the College and he rose to be President.

★

The change of Principal did not, it seems, wholly remove difficulties with the staff. The Revd Sendall, College Chaplain, had left in 1848 and been replaced by the Revd G.M. Tandy, who after a short period in the office was himself replaced by the Revd Daniel Mitford Cust in December 1848. On 25 April 1849 he was dismissed by the Chairman of Council, Edward Holland, the reasons being stated as, '. . . on more than one occasion you have acted independently of (the Principal) in matters connected with the Pupils, and with your position as Chaplain . . . in particular, that you lately, without previous communication with him, took certain of the students to a confirmation at Cricklade'.

Holland's letter continued, 'When I had the pleasure of an interview with you on the 14th March last, I distinctly explained that you were not in any way allowed by the Council to act independently of the Principal. I can therefore only regard this act as a breach of discipline which cannot be overlooked; and I therefore (with regret) feel it my duty to give you notice that your services as Chaplain and first Master of the Royal Agricultural College will not be required after the expiration of the present term.'

This was, as often the case in such disputes, just the culmination of disputes between the Principal, Wilson, and the Chaplain over matters of delegation of duties. Cust protested against his summary dismissal and the Council set up a Committee of Inquiry headed by T.H.S. Sotheron-Escourt. In July 1848 the

Committee took as evidence the correspondence that had passed between the Principal and Cust, heard their accounts, and came down in favour of the Principal. Cust maintained that he did have independence in all control of matters relating to the moral and religious discipline of the pupils; in this, the Committee decided, he was mistaken – the by-laws and prospectus were explicit in giving the Principal overall responsibility for the pupils, and the terms of the correspondence prior to his appointment did not warrant the opinion he held. His immediate dismissal following the confirmation incident was upheld.

There was, however, an equally serious consequence of the affair. Dr Blyth, Professor of Chemistry, had written a letter protesting against the manner of Cust's dismissal, and asking that each Professor 'should know exactly the position in which he stands, and how far he is to have the control in his own department without being subject to constant interference. . . .' It was very strongly worded and extended the matter by asking that a searching inquiry be made, 'not only into the present system of education, both theoretical and practical, but also into the management of every department of this Institution . . . and at the same time [to] prevent the introduction into its management of principles of government which would not be tolerated in a private seminary'. Strong words! Buckman, Professor of Botany and Geology, supported Blyth. When questioned by the Committee, Blyth refused to confirm that he would not make the letter public. The Committee reported, 'After this publication, we cannot hope from Dr Blyth for a cordial co-operation with the Council or Principal, and we recommend that it should be intimated to him, that after the present date, his connexion with the College is closed.'

Blyth departed; like Way he was starting on a notable research career. While at the College he had edited Leibig's *Natural Laws of Husbandry*. He was replaced by Dr J.C.A. Voelcker, destined to become the leading agricultural chemist of his time and to bring honour and status to the College until he, too, was to leave as the result of a quarrel with his Principal.

★

As reported by Holland the farm was not making headway under Wilson in spite of the fact that he probably had more experience than his predecessor. It was not paying. Wilson was an excellent lecturer and a personality more fitted to being in charge of the students and the staff than previous Principals. But he still faced great difficulties in running the College on the restricted staff. When the salary bill had been reduced along with the issue of further shares in the middle of 1847 at the first attempt to save the situation, Woodward, the first Professor of Natural History, had been given notice. The same had happened to Bravender who had been responsible for Surveying as well as being the College Secretary.

The situation after Holland had taken over and, after the Supplementary Charter and the mortgage had been obtained, was still serious enough for it to be

Plan of the Co
buildings and
in 1852

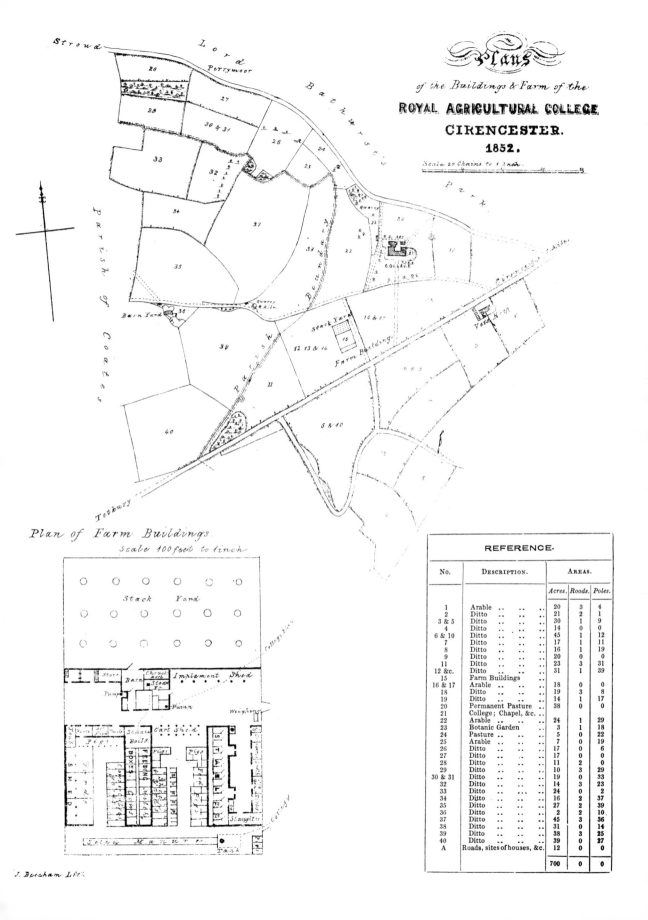

Plans of the Buildings & Farm of the
ROYAL AGRICULTURAL COLLEGE
CIRENCESTER.
1852.

Scale 20 Chains to 1 inch.

Plan of Farm Buildings.
Scale 100 feet to 1 inch.

J. Beecham Lith.

No.	Description	Areas		
		Acres.	Roods.	Poles.
1	Arable	20	3	4
2	Ditto	21	2	1
3 & 5	Ditto	30	1	9
4	Ditto	14	0	0
6 & 10	Ditto	45	1	12
7	Ditto	17	1	11
8	Ditto	16	1	19
9	Ditto	20	0	0
11	Ditto	23	3	31
12 &c.	Ditto	31	1	39
15	Farm Buildings			
16 & 17	Arable	18	0	0
18	Ditto	19	3	8
19	Ditto	14	1	17
20	Permanent Pasture	38	0	0
21	College; Chapel, &c.			
22	Arable	24	1	29
23	Botanic Garden	3	1	18
24	Pasture	5	0	22
25	Arable	7	0	19
26	Ditto	17	0	6
27	Ditto	17	0	0
28	Ditto	11	2	0
29	Ditto	10	3	29
30 & 31	Ditto	19	0	33
32	Ditto	14	3	23
33	Ditto	24	0	2
34	Ditto	16	2	37
35	Ditto	27	2	39
36	Ditto	2	2	10
37	Ditto	45	3	36
38	Ditto	31	0	14
39	Ditto	38	3	25
40	Ditto	39	0	27
A	Roads, sites of houses, &c.	12	0	0
		700	0	0

contemplated that the College would have to revert to becoming a school. This was because it was thought that the principal drain on the College resources was the science schools. It was this proposed abandonment of the collegiate principle together with the limited resources that caused Wilson to resign in 1851. This happened to be at the very time that he was assisting by acting as deputy juror at the Great Exhibition, where he worked along with Prince Albert. In 1853 he was sent as a Royal Commissioner to the United States, and in the same year he was created a Knight of the French Legion of Honour, in recognition of his distinguished services to agricultural science. In the following year he was made Professor of Agriculture and Rural Economy at Edinburgh University. This he filled with distinction for thirty-three years. In 1860 he published an important work on, *Our Farm Crops, being a popular Scientific Description of the Cultivation, Chemistry, Diseases, Remedies, etc., of the various Crops cultivated in Great Britain and Ireland,* for many years a standard work on the subject. His obituary, published in the *North British Agriculturalist* said of him: 'His work as a teacher has been often criticised with undue acerbity. He did undoubtedly maintain a cold and distant manner towards the majority of his students, and his method of teaching was not perhaps the best suited for the slower members of his class, but his success as a teacher may be seen from the fact that nearly all the important Chairs of Agriculture in this country, and many of those abroad, are held by gentlemen who studied under him.'

Wilson can be regarded as the first successful Principal; he did appear to fill more of the requirements of a Principal of an agricultural college than those who went before him. It is understandable that he would not want to stay at a college that was about to revert to being a school; he was more fitted to be at a great university and so it proved.

★

One of the leading characters in the foundation of the College and at the heart of affairs during the various crises that had been undergone was Charles Lawrence, a member of the Council. He wrote an article on the history of the College in the *Journal of the Royal Agricultural Society of England* in 1865 (2nd series, Vol. I, pp. 1–9). In it he said about agricultural education, at that date, that, '. . . we are not aware of the existence of any institution in England especially devoted to the instruction of those who require that knowledge and experience which improved agriculture calls for, with one exception . . . the only institution of its kind in England . . . the Agricultural College of Cirencester'. He also said of the early setbacks that the College suffered:

> The expression of opinion in favour of an institution of this kind was so strong and general as to render the early administrators of its funds somewhat over-sanguine as to success. This lead to a premature extension of the College

by the immediate erection of some buildings, which it had been originally intended to leave till time should show what amount of accommodation was necessary. The day of reckoning, when it arrived, presented a result in conformity with experience in such cases – the buildings, with all the incidents essential to the actual occupation, had involved an outlay considerably beyond the estimates.

At that date, 1865, near to the events themselves, Lawrence recognized the causes of the stuttering start – fees too low to meet other than the bare cost of keeping the students – as he said, '. . . the demands caused by the keen appetites of youngsters spending the greater part of the day in the invigorating air of the Cotswolds'.

Lawrence was always interested in the application of science to agriculture and carried out experiments in farm machinery on his farm which was next to the College farm. He was concerned to build up fertility in the soil and he was visited by Leibig. He wrote many articles for the journal of the RASE. He was a staunch supporter of the College from the very start and was held in high regard for his benevolence at Cirencester. He made a practice of keeping his farm open for the students, the first of the numerous farmers who, throughout the history of the College to the present day have helped by willingly allowing the use of their farms to assist the tuition of the students.

★

In place of Wilson the Council appointed someone well known to them, the Revd J.S. Haygarth. He was, according to the anonymous author of the 1859 history of the College, '. . . a gentleman who had long been known, and esteemed, by the farmers of the district, as well as by many members of the Council; and who, moreover, had practically acquired a considerable knowledge of agriculture'. We have heard of him before, for he had been a candidate for the post when Hodgkinson was selected. He was another product of Trinity College, Cambridge, but this time one with some agricultural knowledge. Not a great deal is known about Haygarth or about the events of his period in office up to his death in 1859; there are few records for there are no minutes of the meetings of the Court, Council or Committee of Management in existence.

What can be gleaned shows that the College entered into a more placid time and it can only be because Haygarth managed capably and efficiently. When he arrived he carried out a careful examination of the current affairs of the College, particularly to look at the assumption that the excessive expenditure was attributable to the science departments. He found that this was not so; these schools did produce a large income and he re-established them at a high level of efficiency. Those professors who had received notice to leave, so it seems (they are not named), were re-engaged and the intake of students resumed, once the

The Revd John S.
Haygarth, Principal
1851–9

belief that the College would close at the Christmas Term 1849 had been scotched. He soon had the accommodation available filled up.

Haygarth had difficulties in finding a suitable farm manager. The first occupant, Robert Vallentine, was there from February 1851 to August 1853, to be followed for a year by a Mr Austen. Then Haygarth made an excellent choice: he appointed John Coleman, MRAC, as Professor of Agriculture and Farm Manager.

John Coleman was the very first student to be registered at the College. He was aged sixteen when he arrived and was the nephew of Robert Jeffreys Brown. When he left with his Diploma, he went as estate agent to Albury Park near Guildford, Surrey. He came to the College in 1856 and during the six years of his control the farm made a profit of about 5 per cent per annum, based on the annual valuation of all the farming assets. Like some others who left at the same time in 1862, such as James Buckman and Sir George Brown, because of friction with the Principal, John Constable, he flourished in an eminent career in agriculture. For twenty-two years he was agent for the Yorkshire estates of Lord Wenlock on the Escrick property and in 1865 he became agricultural editor of *The Field*, which post he held for twenty-three years. He was very active in the Royal Agricultural

Society of England, often judging and writing at shows. In his later years he was an honorary professor of the College. A prolific writer, he produced a large illustrated volume on *The Cattle of Great Britain* and followed this with a similar book on sheep and pigs, eventually amalgamated into one volume entitled, *The Cattle, Sheep and Pigs of Great Britain*. A large, robust man with a powerful physique he played cricket for 'The Gentleman of Yorkshire'. The College can be proud of its very first student.

★

From the time that Haygarth took over until his demise in 1860 the College prospered and the early vicissitudes were left behind. Haygarth provided a stable platform for this development and he was ably assisted by the strongest and most talented staff that the College had had to that date.

In 1852 the staff was:

Chemistry and Chemical Manipulation – J.C.A. Voelcker, Ph.D., FCS.
Geology, Zoology and Botany – James Buckman, FGS, FLS, &c.
Veterinary Medicine and Surgery – G.T. Brown, MRCVS.
Surveying, Civil Engineering and Mathematics – William Sowerby, AICE.
Manager of Farm – R. Vallentine.

The prospectus for 1852 was headed by His Royal Highness Prince Albert as Patron, Earl Bathurst as President and the Earl of Ducie as Vice-President, and the objects were set out:

> The object of this Institution is to afford such a course of education as will be most useful to those whose destined profession is to connect them with Agriculture, at home or in the Colonies; whether as Owner or Occupiers of Land, Surveyors, Land Agents, or Stewards. In the case of the younger Students, considering that the choice of a profession is not often made at the early age at which they will be received, it is intended, without losing sight of Agriculture, or the sciences connected with it, to offer such an education as will qualify them for any calling or profession, at as moderate a cost as is compatible with the advantages offered, and with the liberal scale on which the comforts of the Students will uniformly be arranged.

This is very wide ranging and the introduction of a course for the younger student was a novel innovation of Haygarth's. What was said about this was:

> The course of Instruction pursued with regard to the younger students, and those whose future profession may not be determined, will embrace all the branches of a good education. Instruction will be afforded in Arithmetic, Algebra, Mathematics and Natural Philosophy, Surveying and Mensuration, History and Geography, also in Modern Languages and Classics. It will

depend on the wishes of Parents and their views for the future profession of their Sons, whether they are instructed in the whole course, or whether portions of it be omitted.

It seems that Haygarth was aiming at teaching schoolboys what they should otherwise have learnt at school, either to prepare them for the College Diploma course or just to offer a school course for those who then would go on to a profession, not necessarily that of agriculture or surveying and land agency. If it were the former it may have been because there were insufficient students offering themselves with the basic education essential for the Diploma course or it may have been simply another means of utilizing the College resources to earn fees. The latter reason would be a reflection on the basic education of the farmers' sons that the College was seeking to teach. Whatever the reason this Junior School, which it was, was dropped not long after its introduction.

The main course was offered as a two-year course but this could be telescoped into one year if desired by students, 'where time is of consequence'.

The prospectus makes clear the authority of the Principal so that there was not likely to be a recurrence of an episode such as arose with the Revd Cust. 'The management of the whole establishment of the College is committed to the Principal, who is responsible to the Council for everything, except the Cultivation of the Farm, which is committed to an Agriculturalist of practical experience . . . the Principal will – with this reservation – superintend and control every department of the College.' To make doubly sure that the College Chaplain could in no way misunderstand the limits of his responsibility, it went on: 'He [the Principal] will carefully attend to the Religious instruction and moral discipline of every In-Student, and will exercise such supervision over the conduct and pursuits of the Younger Out-Students as the nature of their relations with the College will permit.' Now there really could be no doubt.

★

The College had by 1859 come a long way from the early days of repeated financial crises. It had changed, too, in its objectives. The history as written in 1856 stated:

> . . . there is one subject that has caused disappointment to the originators of the undertaking, viz., – that the primary object of giving an education adapted to the wants of their calling, to farmers' sons at a small charge has not been fully carried out; this has arisen from several unavoidable causes: – In the first place, £30 was found to be totally inadequate to board and lodge, not boys, but men; with the comforts that were expected, and at the same time defray the expenses of so complete an Institution, where the Professors were so highly qualified. . . .

However, it was thought that the courses that had been developed under the notable professors, such as Voelcker, Buckman and Brown, were now appreciated and that 'the flow to . . . the College is constantly increasing: it is a mistake that the cost is too great; judging by what it teaches theoretically and practically, it is the cheapest Institution in Europe. . . .'

Even allowing for the hyperbole of a document written to extol the virtues of the College, the comments are justified by the facts, for no longer was the College living from hand to mouth and there seemed to be a steady population of about one hundred students, though this was still only half the original plan for two hundred.

★

There was one part of the College which had, from the start, progressed steadily and which had begun to build up a reputation which enhanced the College's prospects. This was the Chair of Chemistry. Way, Blyth and Voelcker were all proponents of the pioneering work of Leibig. He had published his famous book, *Chemistry and its Application to Agriculture and Physiology*, in 1840. Rothamsted had been started in 1842 by John Lawes, later Sir John Lawes. Leibig was the discoverer of artificial manures; these had not been in existence before. His work burst on the agricultural research scene as a revelation; what was then needed was the applied research to make practical his theoretical work.

J.T. Way, having studied at the Giessen laboratories of Leibig, set up the College chemistry laboratory in the old tithe barn on the Leibig principles. He was an excellent research chemist and it was from his publications on the *Absorptive Power of Soils* that he gave Leibig's theories a practical application. Blyth and Voelcker carried on the work, particularly Voelcker, whose name will forever be associated with potash and unexhausted manurial values.

Buckman, too, was one of the first to do pioneer work. Professor of Natural History at the College, he awoke a real agricultural interest in plant breeding, particularly with oats and parsnips.

Lastly, in this spell with Haygarth as Principal, the foundations of the Veterinary Art (as it was then often referred to) were being laid by George T. Brown, later to become Sir George Brown.

★

Little is known of Haygarth's character and personality, save that in 1862, at the fourth dinner of the newly formed Old Students' Club, the Hon. C. Carnegie spoke warmly of him:

Perhaps it is necessary for me to say here, for the benefit of those who were not at the College at the time Mr Haygarth was Principal, that he was a man possessed of very gentleman-like feelings and many brilliant accomplishments which, however, he did not bring so prominently forward as the strong commonsense which he possessed, and we may say that from very small beginnings he brought the College to the state of efficiency of which we are still reaping the fruits.

Haygarth was successful in that he correctly diagnosed the science departments as those to be encouraged as the stable base on which the College could prosper; he established a core staff of highly talented men; the College farm, which increased from 430 to 700 acres for a time, was no longer a source of worry; the buildings were now complete and there was no lack of students.

He died suddenly in 1860; had this not happened the likelihood is that he would have retired with honour and thus would have been the first Principal not to have been dismissed.

Chapter Three

THE CONSTABLE REGIME, 1860–79

If there had been more of a conciliatory spirit shown by the Principal, much ill-will would have been spared.

Edward Holland, 1862

In 1860 there commenced one of the most turbulent and dramatic periods of the College, even though there had been vicissitudes from its inception in 1845, which had been caused by material factors, mainly financial.

With the appointment of the Revd John Constable, another product of Trinity College, Cambridge and no agriculturalist, to succeed the Revd J.S. Haygarth, authority for hiring and firing professors, and indeed all staff, was delegated by the Council to the Principal. This was to a Principal who chose stern discipline as the way to produce efficiency; with an evidently autocratic manner there are the makings of turbulence, especially if those for whom he is responsible are of equally strong intellect. Since its inception the College had attracted men active in scientific research and they needed a liberal atmosphere in which to flourish. During Constable's time as Principal there were on the senior staff as professors such men as Voelcker, Church, Fream, Tanner, Buckman, Brown, Jarman and Coleman, all of whom eventually achieved high distinction in their particular fields.

An understanding of the events which culminated with the resignation of so many of these men needs the background of their individual characters and of their scientific attainments. A significant number, on leaving the College, went on to make their name resound in the field of agricultural research.

But first let us look at the leading character in the dramas which unfolded in the years following his appointment in 1860. The Revd John Constable, MA (Oxon.), born in 1824, was thirty-six years old on taking up the post. He came out of the same academic stable as Hodgkinson, Principal from 1846 to 1847, and Haygarth, Principal from 1851 to 1860. From the very start of Constable's tenure there was a degree of resentment among the staff since he came as a very long and close friend of Haygarth, the former Principal. It is possible that a contributory

The Revd John
Constable, Principal
1860–79

cause for this resentment may have been an amendment which had been made to
the College by-laws and regulations which gave the Principal authority to
appoint and dismiss professors. We shall see that this 'hire and fire' clause would
lead later to a flare-up as a result of which most of the professors resigned in 1862
and it spilled over into the public arena doing the reputation of the College
immense harm. Nonetheless, credit must be given to Constable for the enhanced
academic standing that he achieved for the College and for the improvements
carried out in his time. The chapel was completed, the museum enlarged, the
Botanic Gardens 'nearly entirely made', and, perhaps the most important, the
debt got under control. Though student numbers decreased Constable's plans
received the approval of the Council, and by his ability and energy, combined
with the assistance of staff chosen by himself, the College regained its former
number of students and enhanced its reputation as a teaching establishment.
Constable must certainly have been a man of enormous energy for at one time
he undertook 'all the Mathematical work, Mensuration, Mechanics and
Bookkeeping', for which his university education can hardly have prepared him.
This may have been by *force majeure* since his energy, discharged into stern
discipline and an unremitting adherence to procedures, had lost him the very staff
who might have undertaken these tasks! In modern parlance his staff manage-

ment was plainly deficient, and staff relations frosty and lacking in effective communication.

Constable took over with the intention of establishing a policy more attuned to education through scientific discipline and the practical application of scientific principles: in other words 'Practice with Science', the theme of the Royal Agricultural Society of England. This was the title of a series of papers that he published in 1867.

His aim was to have the College regarded as of the same rank as the university colleges. In so doing it became necessary to raise the standard of entry and he looked for a standard of qualification equivalent to that granted by the Oxford and Cambridge Local Examinations Board in 1858. The consequence of this objective would materially change the original concept of a college for the sons of tenant farmers, for they were unlikely to have been able to give their sons that public school education which would allow them to attain the standard of university entry. So the change to accepting the sons of landowners, which was initially caused by the need to rationalize the financial structure through increases in fees to a realistic level, was now to be accentuated by this change in the academic performance required for entry.

Not only this, but Constable sought to impose a stricter internal discipline by regular examinations. He established weekly and termly examinations, and a student could not progress without passing the sessional examinations.

Diploma group in the late nineteenth century

The College Diploma, the passing of which would lead to the qualification of MRAC, was to be raised to honours degree status. Students were also prepared for the Diplomas of the Royal Agricultural Society of England and the Highland Agricultural Society of Scotland. To lift the College to this higher level of academic attainment it followed that staff commensurate with these standards would need to be employed. Indeed, it was a natural consequence of the new policy that scientists rather than schoolteachers were attracted not only because here was the prime, and only, agricultural educational establishment, but there would appear to be open opportunities for research in what was a well-equipped establishment. So Constable was responsible for the development of research at a national and international level and, albeit it was not his primary intention, for several of the staff so attracted to go on to national eminence.

Another effect of this lifting of the standards was to cause interest in the work of the College outside the kingdom. Other countries, particularly the United States of America and Japan, took note of the teaching and performance being achieved.

The period 1860 to 1879 was undoubtedly a productive time for the evangelistic nature of the College's teaching, for in spite of vicissitudes the influence of the College was being felt on the other side of the world. In New Zealand the impetus for agricultural education resulted in the province of Canterbury acquiring land for the purpose of endowing a school of agriculture. The University College in Christchurch was, in the 1870s, contemplating a school of agriculture. It is interesting that the way was being forged through the establishment of agricultural chemistry as the primary science to be researched and taught. A class in this subject had been started in 1876 and endowments established for the funding of a school of agriculture. The first connection with the RAC was with one of the members of the committee formed to report on the administration of the funds; this was Edward Cephas Stevens (1837–1915), educated at Marlborough and the Royal Agricultural College. He was a Christchurch land agent and financier. In 1878, with the buildings available for the foundation of the school, applications were invited for the post of Principal. Of two applicants interviewed one was William Edward Ivey, MRAC, FIC, FCS. Ivey was forty years of age when he was appointed on 29 March 1878. He was Australian born, educated in England, including the diploma course at the College and had farmed in England. He became a chemist and had jobs superintending experimental farms in Victoria. His appointment carried the salary of £600 per annum with residence. Both he and Stevens based their recommendations for the curriculum on their experiences at the RAC. Stevens advocated liberal courses and an intake of mature students who already had a good basic education which would enable them to undertake further technical education. Ivey was given full rein to organize all teaching, technical and practical, and the support functions, including catering and finance.

Ivey based his teaching on a three-year course leading to a certificate following the RAC pattern. This remained the qualification attainable at Canterbury until Ivey's death in 1892. Shortly afterwards the university authorities in New Zealand gave first consideration to the establishment of a degree at the school and it became the Canterbury College of Agriculture. Stevens continued the link with the RAC for he became Chairman of the Board of the College in 1899, a post which he continued to occupy for sixteen years. It is of interest *vis-à-vis* the College fees that Ivey started by providing board for students at £50 per annum. He provided this himself and actually lost money when the Board requested a reduction to £45. Eventually, as in the case of the RAC, it had to be increased to cover the running costs. Incidentally, no charge was made for tuition! In the first decade of operation Lincoln College apparently lived from hand to mouth during a period of countrywide depression.

In 1978 Sir Emrys Jones, B.Sc., Hon. LLD (Wales), Hon. LLD (Bath), then Principal of the Royal Agricultural College, was invited to give the oration at the centennial assembly of Lincoln College. He quoted I.D. Blair, in his book commemorating the 75th anniversary of Lincoln College, as saying, 'If the age of institutions of this kind can be measured from the date they opened their door for student enrolment, then Lincoln stands junior certainly to Cirencester and apparently to the Ontario Agricultural College, Guelph.' He also said: 'Ivey was a distinguished ex-student of the Royal Agricultural College. . . . He obtained his Diploma (with Honours) in the year 1860 and his name is proudly enshrined on the wall of the dining hall at the College as one of the outstanding students to have graduated in 1860. . . . the first lectures must have made a deep impression on Ivey's young and attentive mind.' Ivey certainly adopted the Cirencester policy of teaching scientific agriculture with the practical training to come afterwards. Yet in spite of his professed adherence to the teaching of technical matters first, he differed in one respect from the Cirencester methods in that he advocated compulsory farm work for students, a criticism he made of the Cirencester courses. But it had no effect on the College which has not required 'compulsory farm work' from students from that day to this!

Following a visit to the College, Mr Ezra Cornell was so impressed by its work that he offered the New York Government over £100,000 to go towards the funding of a single institution. The result was Cornell University in New York, one department of which was planned and modelled on the College. The interest taken by Japan in the work of the College came to light in 1989, when Professor Tajima, Head of the International Agricultural Development Department at Tokyo University, visited the College. He brought with him documents describing the role played by the College in the establishment of Tokyo Agricultural University and the development of modern methods of rice production. Professor Tajima's documents indicated that the links first developed with the visit of a Tajori Tamita in 1870 for discussions with Constable, who later arranged for five members of his staff to go to Japan where they lived and taught for the next five years. College professors who obtained posts in Japan after leaving the College were Edward Kinch, who was Professor of Chemistry from 1876 to 1881, and John Adam McBride, who was Professor of Veterinary Surgery and Anatomy from 1866 to 1876. As a result of McBride's tour of five years a school of veterinary science was established at Yeddo (Tokyo), modelled on Cirencester and opened by the Emperor of Japan.

Some idea of Constable's philosophy towards agricultural education may be gleaned from extracts from his lectures. In 1863 he wrote, 'The continued prosperity of a nation depends mainly on the condition of its agriculture (quoting from Leibig's *Natural Laws of Husbandry*) . . . intellect and money may be advantageously and successfully employed in the cultivation of the soil . . . our first object is the education of our students, so that their future career may be successful and that the intelligence and capital of the country may be attracted to the cultivation of the soil.' He referred to the RAC as, 'not merely a place where scientific truths and theories are urged . . . but . . . where we hope to develop the mental, moral and religious capabilities of youth'. He believed, 'the more severely trained by the study of abstract science a mind may be, the more rapid is the advancement made by such a mind when its powers are concentrated on progressive studies'.

Constable's attitude towards monitoring the progress of his students was expressed by him, 'Against the possibility of those who profess themselves students not profiting by instruction imparted in lectures, we seek to guard ourselves by catechetical lectures and weekly examinations. . . .' A far cry from modern, liberal ideas of education!

As we note, his regime was a tough one especially for the student, seemingly under constant scrutiny. But Constable did see education as a development of the capability of the student's power of self learning. 'We hope, by our system, to lay a good foundation on which each student may build effectively for himself. The principles of farming may be taught – how to put these principles into practice each man must learn for himself. . . .'

★

We will return to the achievements of Constable but for the moment let us have a look at the professorial staff that he had on his strength.

John Christopher Augustus Voelcker was appointed Professor of Chemistry in 1849 at the age of twenty-seven. He succeeded J.T. Way who had left to become the first appointed chemist of the Royal Agricultural Society of England. He was a German and was educated at the University of Gottingen where he studied under Professor Wöhler, probably the greatest teacher of chemistry in any country, and obtained his Ph.D. in 1846. He had also attended Justus von Leibig's lectures on agricultural chemistry at Giessen. From there he became assistant to Professor Gerrit Jan Mulder at Utrecht and in 1847 was assistant with James Finlay Weir Johnson at the Agricultural Chemistry Association of Scotland in

John Voelcker,
Professor of
Chemistry 1849–62

Edinburgh. He married in 1852 and during his time at the College he was Consulting Chemist to the Bath and West of England Agricultural Society, and in 1855 was appointed Consulting Chemist to the Royal Agricultural Society of England, working with John Lawes at the experimental farm at Woburn. In his research he carried out experiments and laid down trials into the use of farmyard manure and artificial fertilizers, identifying potassium as a plant nutrient. He worked on the various aspects of feeding farm animals. 'There can be no doubt that, both in the matter of purchased manures and purchased feeding-stuffs, his analyses, papers and reports have done much to raise the standards of such articles and leave no one to blame but the purchaser himself if he does not get value for his money.'

Voelcker, with his own laboratory at the College and with technical assistants, quickly established a pre-eminent role for the analytical agricultural chemist, following in the footsteps of his predecessor, J. T. Way. He collected and analysed samples for farmers from all over the country. This was to stand him in good stead when he later extended this work to found a consultancy. Furthermore, his time at Cirencester enabled him to develop by strict application his skills in lecturing and writing, since he had arrived still basically as a German speaker.

He left the College in 1862 and was appointed an honorary professor with the requirement to lecture once a year. Voelcker became eminent in his field: he was elected a fellow of the Royal Society in 1870 and was one of the founders and one of the first Vice-Presidents of the Institute of Chemistry of Great Britain and Ireland, established in 1877; his advice was constantly sought in technical and legal inquiries (in which he was 'absolutely fearless in his dealings with manufacturers and merchants, and was no respecter of persons', and he, 'did a great deal to raise the standard of integrity in the fertilisers and feeding stuffs trade'). He was a prolific contributor to the *Journal of the Royal Agricultural Society of England*. He died in 1884 of paralysis and heart failure. His work was carried on by his son, John Augustus (1854–1937), who succeeded him both as Consulting Chemist to the Royal Agricultural Society of England and as Director of the Society's farm at Woburn. To this day the consultancy which bears his name carries on the analytical work.

He was followed in the Chair of Chemistry by Arthur Herbert Church, MA (Oxon.), D.Sc., (Oxon.), FIC, FRS, FSA, who was eventually created KCVO in 1909. In 1879 he was appointed Professor of Chemistry at the Royal Academy of Arts, which post he held until 1911. Church was educated at King's College, London, at the Royal College of Chemistry and at Lincoln College, Oxford. He

Arthur Church (later
Sir), Professor of
Chemistry 1862–79

Robert Warington,
assistant to Voelcker
and Church; later
Sibthorpian
Professor of Rural
Economy at Oxford
Univeristy

was a highly cultivated and distinguished man both in the realms of science and of art. Among his many writings were, *How Crops Grow*, in collaboration with (Sir) W.T. Thistleton-Dyer, and, *The Chemistry of Paints and Painting*. In fact, he became a leading authority on that subject. At Cirencester, in 1870 and 1871, he investigated the growth of sugar beet; he was the discoverer of turacin, an animal pigment containing copper from the feathers of the turaco or plaintain eater. He was curator of the Corinium Museum and wrote the guide for it. As an art collector he specialized in English pottery and in Oriental artwork. No mean artist himself, in his younger days he exhibited at the Royal Academy. He died in 1915, leaving behind a memory of, 'personal charm, wide culture and kindness', and of 'a most able and courteous gentleman'. (Ernest Armitage)

The assistant to Voelcker and to Church, from 1862 to 1867, was Robert Warington, MA (Oxon.), FRS. He taught and his laboratory notes formed the first nucleus of the *Laboratory Guide*, which was published by Church. He went on to join Lawes and Gilbert at Rothamsted and was the joint author with them of many scientific papers. In 1894 he was appointed Sibthorpian Professor of Rural Economy at Oxford University.

The third of a trio of extremely able men who, from being professors at

Cirencester, went on to high eminence in their field was George Thomas Brown, CB, who was knighted for his services to veterinary science. He was appointed Professor of Veterinary Science at the College in 1850, at the age of twenty-three. At this young age he was the first to occupy the Chair and he stayed until 1862 when he left to work for the Privy Council as Chief Adviser on veterinary matters. He was, in fact, dismissed, as we shall see later. In 1872 he became Director of the Veterinary Department of the Board of Agriculture, the precursor of the Ministry of Agriculture and of the State Veterinary Service. During his time at the RAC he founded the Veterinary Museum. Later in his career in 1881 he became Professor at the Royal Veterinary College for sixteen years, was Principal for four years and eventually a Governor. He was created CB in 1887 and knighted in 1898.

He was Consulting Veterinary Surgeon to the Royal Agricultural Society of England and his contributions to his discipline consisted mainly of articles and reports. It is said that his addresses to the students at the College were models of style, and that he was a fluent and forcible speaker, and a strong and fearless administrator.

This by no means concludes the list of men on the staff who rose to higher status. Among the others was Dr William Fream, B.Sc. (London), LLD, FLS. In 1877 he was appointed Professor of Natural History and held this post for two

William Fream, Professor of Natural History 1877–9 (photograph taken at Downton Agricultural College in 1885)

years. He is notable for his extensive writings, being editor of the *Journal of the Royal Agricultural Society of England*, and agricultural correspondent of *The Times* for twelve years to 1906. He wrote *The Elements of Agriculture*, the definitive textbook for students of agriculture which is still in publication today. He left the College to join Professor John Wrightson in founding the College of Agriculture at Downton (q.v.) and where he taught natural history. He was very much a lover of the countryside and of wild flowers. He was seen as, 'a rather portly figure in his late twenties, with a fresh face, a trim beard and moustache and balding slightly'. Some observations after his death from apoplexy in 1906 are revealing: 'An excellent and attractive teacher', 'A somewhat voluminous contributor to the agricultural press'!

Dr H. W. Lloyd Tanner, MA, (Oxon.), D. Sc., FRS, Professor of Mathematics and Natural Philosophy from 1875 to 1879, was another link with the foundation of the College. He was a prolific author of agricultural books, including *First Principles of Agriculture, Jack's Education or How He Learnt Farming* and *Holt Castle or The Threefold Interest in Land*. His father was the first student to be awarded the College Diploma.

Finally in the team was William Turner Thistleton-Dyer, the co-author of *How Crops Grow*, a book famous in its day. He was Professor of Natural History from 1867 to 1870.

A foretaste of what was to be the outcome of Constable's staff relations is illustrated by the resignation at the end of 1862 of another of this strong team of educators and researchers, Professor James Buckman. From being curator and resident professor at the Birmingham Philosophical Institution, Buckman was appointed Professor of Geology, Botany, Rural Economy and Natural History at the College in 1848. During his time he wrote *The Natural History of British Meadow and Pasture Grasses* and *Science and Practice in Farm Cultivation*. He also contributed papers to the *Proceedings of the British Association for the Advancement of Science* and to the *Geological Society's Transactions*.

Buckman was secretary of the Cotteswold Club from 1854 to 1860, one of whose members refers to a visit he paid to the College to investigate the experiments Buckman had conducted into developing vegetables for human consumption from their wild prototypes. He had a limited success with the parsnip, as the seeds were in commercial production by 1861. He carried out similar trials with oats (*Avena Fatua*). This visit must have been later in the century for the writer refers to a splendid photograph of Buckman which shows him as having 'a fine face with a snow-white beard and flowing hair'. He goes on, 'I daresay he was by no means old but these Victorian worthies are deceptive. One sees a picture of a venerable man then reads that it is Lord Tennyson at the age of forty-two. It makes me wonder, if I saw a photograph of Methusaleh at 42 what he would have looked like at 969!' Certainly, looking at the pictures of the characters of the time one draws the same conclusion – the more especially when one knows their age when at the College.

He presented collections of Roman antiquities to the Corinium Museum in Cirencester and of fossils to the College. He had thus been at the College and an active participant in his discipline for some twelve years prior to the advent of Constable as Principal. During his time he created the Botanical Gardens on the north side of the College. What led to his resignation is documented from his own papers.

In September 1862 he was informed by the Chairman of the Council, Edward Holland, that the Council had taken the Chair of Botany away from him. The reasons given were simply that he had not held it always to the 'express satisfaction of the Council, the Principals under whom [he] served and the scientific public'. Specific mention was made that this was not the action of the current Principal. It had apparently taken the Council twelve years to come to this opinion!

Behind this, however, *were* actions of Constable. He had told Buckman that he would appoint an assistant for botany, as Buckman was overworked. Buckman had heard from a friend that a new Chair in Botany was contemplated – and that negotiations had been pending for several months. Upon challenging the Chairman, Buckman eventually received a copy of a letter from the Chairman to Constable. This referred to the 'disgrace he [Buckman] has brought upon himself as an analyser of grass seeds'. This was due, it was said, to either carelessness or ignorance. Either 'is sufficient to disqualify him for the . . . position he holds. . . .'

Buckman had, in common with other professors, complained of alterations to classes and lectures apparently peremptorily ordered by the Principal. There is a hint of Constable's manner of conducting such reforms in the Chairman's letter: '. . . if there had been more of a conciliatory spirit shown by the Principal, much ill-will would have been spared. . . .'

These allegations were denied by Buckman. In a long and detailed letter of resignation he refuted the aspersions cast on his standard of work and quoted many instances of praise he had received, particularly from the previous Principal, the Revd J.S. Haygarth. He denied absolutely the two specific complaints against him by a spirited defence, maintaining unjust treatment in relation to the Professorship of Botany and misrepresentations of a highly injurious nature in regard to his scientific pursuits.

He maintained that he was 'ultimately induced to promise to the Principal to relinquish the professorship of botany'. He went on, '. . . it was not effected until worn down by mental suffering, and was the result of an interview with the Principal, the character of which I cannot trust my feelings to describe'.

He brought support from the scientific journal, the *Gardeners' Chronicle and Agricultural Gazette*, which had contained the original allegations of the matter of the grass seeds analysis: in its edition of 1 September 1860 it explained satisfactorily the differences. He answered the charge that he had 'lost caste with scientific men at the late Oxford meeting of the British Association' (June 1860) by quoting the Committee of the Association. Drs Daubeny and Lankester had sufficient confidence to support financially the researches of himself and Dr Voelcker.

Of course, we have only Buckman's version of the events leading up to his resignation; a charitable interpretation might give the Council the benefit of the doubt concerning their actions towards Buckman. But the inference cannot be avoided that Constable's reforms were implemented by him by decree rather than by consultation or persuasion, and that, being the Council's creature, they perforce supported him even though they appeared to recognize the management style that he had adopted early in his appointment. This became a recurring feature of his period of office. Constable must have been motivated in the end by malice for he ordered the Botanical Garden created by Buckman to be destroyed.

There was, indeed, at this time, yet another incident which reveals the dissension which existed then (1862) between the Principal and his staff. It concerned the departure of Brown, the Professor of Veterinary Science. At the time that he left he wrote to the *Cheltenham Examiner* to deny that he had been dismissed by the Council. It seems that the Council had peremptorily 'dismissed' him because, as he said in his letter, they had expressed the belief 'that any hopes of a restoration of good feeling at the College are not likely to be realised so long as I [Brown] remain attached to the staff'. Thus had the solicitors to the College, Messrs Charles and C.W. Lawrence, written to Brown. The Chairman, Edward Holland, had published that the Veterinary professorship was vacant.

Brown's riposte was that the Council could not have dismissed him since 'the successive prostration by illness of each member of the Council had rendered their meeting impossible up to the present time, rendering imperfect communication only practical' – according to the Council's solicitors. Brown gave notice to the Principal on 22 November 1862 that he intended to be at the College on the following Monday to perform his duties. The solicitors warned that he would be regarded as a 'wilful trespasser'! Thus was Brown dismissed; although the details of this are somewhat obscure it is clear that the dissension was acute and is further confirmation of Constable's autocratic and intemperate style of management.

Thus we can see the calibre of the men that Constable was surrounded with: undoubtedly they matched his own intellectual prowess and they were nearly all relatively young. Whether they matched his capacity for rigour in the teaching of students and whether they subscribed to his methods of discipline to achieve efficiency is hardly revealed. One can only speculate that, immersed as they appeared to be in primary research, it is unlikely that they found that atmosphere of a relaxing nature which is conducive to creative thinking. In other words, although Constable sought to emulate an Oxbridge college in the standard of entry and of achievement by setting high academic targets, it is doubtful that he was successful in creating the necessary environment of the quiet cloister and quad.

Constable was a successful manager so far as the College's finances were concerned, perhaps less so in dealing with the College farm, for it made losses from the early 1860s until the College was relieved of the responsibility in 1865 when it was handed back to the Bathurst estate. A meeting of three of the guarantors and the Hon. W.L. Bathurst, brother of Earl Bathurst, was held on 5 December 1864. Mr Bathurst indicated that due to the state of his health Earl Bathurst wished to be relieved of the guarantee he had given, and of the office of President. It was proposed that he be so relieved and that he would take back the farm into his own estate, 'and forego any claim for advances of money he may have made at any time on account of Buildings, Implements or other outlay for the farm. . . .' Furthermore the Earl was willing, on return of the farm to his estate, to make arrangement with the College for the students to have access to the farm in order to observe farming operations, the College to make an annual payment for this facility. The three guarantors, the Earl of Ducie, Mr Sotheron-Escourt and Mr Edward Holland accepted these proposals, the plan was effected and by this separation of the farm and College a loss-making liability was avoided. The first tenant was an old student, Harry Rivington, and he was succeeded by another student, Russell Swanwick, who was there until 1925.

There were forty acres immediately round the College which were retained for experimental purposes and for a small dairy herd and sheep flock of differing breeds.

By the time this had been settled pressure on the College funds had built up again. With the retirement of Earl Bathurst and the election of his Grace the Duke of Marlborough as President the mortgagees had asked for the repayment of their loan, now in the sum of £30,000. After petition to Her Majesty the Queen a Supplementary Charter was granted and at the same time His Royal Highness the Prince of Wales became Patron. The Supplementary Charter stipulated that a Committee of Management should be elected to manage the affairs of the College. It would consist of ten people, two of whom would be Mr T.H.S. Sotheron-Escourt and Mr Edward Holland. It was Mr Edward Holland, through the Principal, who had been in effective control of the College since 1848, maintaining a period of relative stability and prosperity. Now, however, another financial crisis was upon the effective Governing Body, the new Committee of Management. Four members were nominated by the bondholders: the Earl of Ducie, Sir Michael Hicks Beach, MP, Lt.-Col. Robert N.F. Kingscote, CB, MP and Mr Ambrose Lethbridge Goddard. The Council appointed four others: Mr Allan Alexander Bathurst, MP, the Revd Thomas Maurice, Mr Edward Bowly and Mr William John Edmonds.

The Committee embarked immediately on the problem of raising the money and decided to appeal to the landed proprietors of the country for a sum of £30,000. A prospectus setting out the aims of the College was published and there was to be an issue of bonds of £100 each, repayable after thirty years and with interest at 4 per cent per annum. Only £9,300 was subscribed and it was the representatives of the late Earl of Ducie and the two surviving guarantors,

Mr Sotheron-Escourt and Mr Holland who came to the rescue by making up the deficiency.

From that point onwards, the finances of the College were managed successfully. Constable increased the fees and by utilizing the surpluses that were made in subsequent years, at the end of his period as Principal the loan had been reduced significantly. However, as we shall see, in the next period it became difficult to maintain these repayments and a further financial crisis developed.

Before the end of Constable's era, some of the principal supporters and the strongest advocates of the College died, leaving behind a debt of gratitude for their faith and work in nurturing the infant College and seeing it to post-adolescent maturity through financial and personnel vicissitudes. Mr Edward Holland died apparently sometime between the shareholders' meetings held on 4 April 1874 and 3 April 1875. At the meeting of 1875 the shareholders recorded their gratitude to him for all his efforts on behalf of the College. This was certainly no more than his due and a Memorial Trust was set up to commemorate him and his work. Records of this Trust were lost in the fires at the College in 1913 and 1923, but from information gained since the Second World War a gold medal, known as the Holland Medal, was struck and is to this day awarded annually to the student who is first in order of merit on the Estate Management diploma course. It is one of the two premier medals awarded to students. It was, in 1948, endowed by $3\frac{1}{2}$% War Stock.

Mr T.H.S. Sotheron-Escourt died in 1876 and thus the last surviving original guarantors and members of the Committee of Management had departed.

Towards the end of Constable's time as Principal there occurred a notorious event resulting in the poorest of relations between Principal and staff – perhaps it was not unexpected as it is apparent that the rule established by Constable was one of a degree of autocracy not experienced before at the College. This contretemps (and it was really more than this since the schism was wide and of public concern) broke through what had been a simmering discontent.

It concerned Church, Professor of Chemistry, who had succeeded Voelcker in 1863 and who had by then developed a research reputation among the agricultural public and was, as well, a highly effective and respected lecturer. As we now know, subsequent to his dismissal (for that was the result of the public dispute), he went on to extend his reputation as an eminent national chemist and to achieve the granting of a knighthood.

The origins of the dispute lay in one of the by-laws governing the regulation of the teaching staff. This required permanent professional staff, in effect the professors, to reside within the College. We can look at this matter in some detail for there still exist copies of the original correspondence and of press cuttings of the time.

From its inception the College had maintained the rule of the old universities, though mainly abandoned by them, that staff were required to be resident in College. This was applied specifically to the professorial staff who were, presumably seen as *in loco parentis*. However, the College had only single accommodation and therefore no provision for married staff, yet Constable stuck rigidly to this rule. This was in spite of the fact that Wrightson, Professor of Agriculture, and Professors Way, Blyth, Voelcker, McBride, Traquair and Mayer had been given permission to live out of College on getting married.

At the beginning of the Spring Term 1879 Church informed Constable of his intention to get married during the next College vacation and, as he confirmed, of 'the consequent necessity for my no longer (after April 24th) living within the College walls'. Constable responded to this by accepting what he, Constable, deemed as Church's resignation. Church's response was to deny in firm terms any intention of resigning his post. Constable maintained that there was an effective resignation, which he accepted, 'tho' it is given one month too late'! From these small beginnings there blew up a storm so violent that it led to the resignation of two other professors, acrimonious correspondence, adverse publicity in the press, amounting almost to a national scandal and a resulting diminution in the reputation of the College that took many years to recover.

Church, realizing that the Principal meant what he said, now undertook a strong defence of his actions and had a look at the authority under which Constable appeared to have acted. He took as a first assumption that the decision of Constable's was that of the Governing Body of the College. He pointed out that the by-law of 1870, which vested in the Principal all future appointments and dismissals of professors, did not apply in his case. He reiterated that he had *not* resigned and said, '. . . you have several times said to me that marriage, and marriage alone, would entitle me to live out of College. . . .' He said that since he had been appointed by the Council in 1863, and under the by-laws then in force, only the Council could remove him. Constable promptly went to the Council and at a meeting on 5 March 1879, attended by both the Professor and the Principal, the following resolution was approved by five votes to two:

> The Committee of Management are of the opinion that the discipline of the Agricultural College cannot be satisfactorily maintained except by the residence of Professors within the College walls in conformity with the original by-law No.47. Being fully sensible of the services rendered by Professor Church during his 16 years residence in College they the more regret that they cannot accede to his recent proposal on non-residency, as compliance with it involving such alterations as would unduly disturb the present organisation of College Staff.

It is to be wondered just what alterations would have been necessary which 'would unduly disturb the present organisation . . .', since six other members had been given permission to live out of College, presumably without such disturbance. With only seven members voting and a majority decision it seems to have been a precipitate action, no doubt taken on the strong advice of the Principal.

So Church, a man highly regarded in the scientific world, was effectively dismissed for what, on the face of it, was an anachronism in the rules of a College based on the principles of the Oxbridge colleges, but apparently not on their practices.

The word had got out. On 17 February 1879, at the beginning of the Constable/Church correspondence, the *Mark Lane Express* reported, 'It is high time that those who are responsible for the success of the Cirencester College should enquire into its management . . . there have been a great many more changes in Staff lately than were desirable, and now Professor Church, who has probably done more for this institution than any other man, is about to leave and that not of his own free will. The question is, should he be obliged to leave to suit the caprice of the Principal, who appears to quarrel with nearly everybody he has under him?'

The *Yorkshire Post* of 20 February 1879 said, 'Mr Church has filled the chair of chemistry in the College for 16 years, during which he has done much to sustain the waning reputation of the institution, and we regard his tacit dismissal . . . as a blunder whose effects will tell seriously against the future prosperity of the College. It is well known that the Cirencester College has missed its destiny, that it is not patronised by the class for whose benefit it was established. . . .'

Strong words, indeed! This was just the start of a blast of criticism from all quarters in the agricultural world, and this was even before the date of the Committee of Management's decision to remove Professor Church. On 24 February the *Mark Lane Express* reported that the resident professors and students had decided to present the Professor with a testimonial in recognition of his services over the sixteen years. It was lead by Lloyd Tanner and Fream. There followed letters to editors of journals, many of which were, in a curious Victorian manner of concealment, signed with pseudonyms, but purporting to reveal the inside story. Were they then from members of staff, anxious not to have the wrath of the Principal and the Council descend upon them? One in particular, hiding under the *nom de plume* of 'One Who Knows', was caustic in condemnation of the Principal, and arraigned him on several counts: first for the loss of highly effective teaching staff; secondly for the change in direction from students who intended to be bona fide farmers to those not the sons of farmers; thirdly for the treatment of Professor Church; and lastly for the manner in which he held sway over the Council, which was also a criticism of the Council and its pusillanimity. These then were the four main planks for criticism and of these the press concentrated of the actions of the Council and the Committee of Management.

The *Live Stock Journal* of 28 February thundered, '. . . any Council which hands over to the Principal of a College the supreme control of everything in connection with the institution, including the appointment and dismissal of its Professors, virtually abnegates its powers as a Council, if it does not absolutely destroy its own *raison d'être*'. In comes the *Mark Lane Express* with another thrust seeking to prove that the actions of the Principal are, in fact, *ultra vires* and, knowing that the Committee of Management are to meet in a few days time, advises them, 'The Committee of Management have something to decide on Wednesday next besides the question whether the Principal is to to be censured for grossly exceeding his authority, or whether he is to be upheld and his impertinent dismissal of Professor Church confirmed. They have practically to decide whether Cirencester College shall live or die as an agricultural institution. If Professor Church is driven out of the College, he will probably not go alone. . . .'

These prognostications proved right in one sense: others did leave the College; but the College did eventually weather the storm though it was a long time in abating.

So the Committee of Management in making their decision of 5 March to uphold Constable could not have wanted for advice from all quarters. But clearly the advice that they listened to in the end was that closest to home, i.e. that of Constable who was in a sense their protegy. This was the face-saving course of action. To have denied Constable would have been to dismiss him rather than Church, for it undoubtedly would have been a resigning matter for a man of such strong principles.

The storm intensified. On 10 March, five days after the resolution, Professors Fream and Lloyd Tanner resigned. The College had lost three of its most senior staff at one go. From this point on there was nothing but condemnation, mainly of the Council and the Committee of Management, by the press and by those writing to the press. It is probable that this stung the Committee into an ill-advised resolution on 5 April, when the question of the many professors who had left the College was discussed:

> The Committee of Management having heard a statement as to the alleged dismissal of a large number of Professors during the past 16 years are of the opinion that these allegations are without sufficient foundation and that although it is true that several Professors have passed through the six Professorial Chairs of the College, these (with a few exceptions of Gentlemen who have from ill health or for reasons which have been explained to the satisfaction of the Committee) have gone on to take posts of higher emolument and of greater importance.

The Press again strongly condemned this resolution, the *Live Stock Journal* carrying an article from 'An Old Professor' which analysed the departures of staff during Constable's time and showed that this resolution 'is so devoid of foundation and so utterly opposed to facts that no apology is needed for drawing attention to its glaring inconsistencies'. The article went on to show the fallacy of the statement that those who had left had taken 'posts of higher emolument'. He showed that three-quarters of the professors at the time they vacated their chairs had no other appointments in view. They only obtained such posts *after* their resignation or dismissal. On examination of all staff who had left in the sixteen years, some nineteen out of twenty-five 'did not leave on purpose to take other posts and who at the time of leaving had not obtained any other occupation. They were either unkindly dismissed or driven to resign'. There is no reason to doubt that his stinging rebuke was correct in its facts and interpretation.

With these recriminations and others in the press of the day this unhappy episode drew to its close. Its effects were felt long beyond the departure of Constable, who, on 5 December 1879 resigned on grounds of ill health. Lest it be thought that this resignation was, like some of those of his staff, masked in intent by the 'ill health' reason, it must be noted that there are several references to the fact that he suffered from some unspecified ailment which gave him constant pain or discomfort. Such resignation was evidently compounded by the events through which he had received intense and sometimes vitriolic criticism and condemnation.

Constable's staff management, looked at over his period of office, is best summed up in the words quoted in *The Field* of 29 March 1879, remembering that the author was probably John Coleman, an ex-student and Professor of Agriculture at the College until 1862 when he became editor of *The Field* and was therefore probably the 'old member of the College' who is being quoted:

> It will be remembered by many persons that the interference of the Principal in every department was the alleged cause of Professors Voelcker, Brown, Buckman and Coleman resigning in 1861–62. The same causes have led to the severance of many valuable connections since that time; and now the last of the old class of Professors is about to leave. The wonder is that men of standing can be got to accept positions under such a regime; and it is not to be denied that of late exceedingly young men . . . have been appointed. . . . Perhaps no man, living or dead, has made more Professors than the present Principal. . . . Bayldon, Church, Wrightson, Wood, Cunningham, Dyer, Traquair, Watson, M'Nab, Murray, M'Bride, Nettleship, Hunting, Fream, Lowe, Wall, Andrew, Tanner, Mayer, Cathcart, Boulger and Sheldon have in turn occupied the various chairs during the last fifteen years. Church, Wrightson and M'Bride stand out more conspicuously than the rest . . . but what of the rest? . . . they left but little trace behind them. . . . Small remuneration and other exactions drove them away, and as a consequence, we have a College well nigh without a renowned staff of Professors. . . . Again and again have first class men been engaged. . . . Unfortunately, when a Professor seemed likely to make a reputation, some misunderstanding with the Principal was almost sure to drive him away; and thus it is that Professor Church, who has devoted his life to the

College, is, because forsooth he is about to be married, obliged to resign his position. . . .

We do not know the old student whom we have quoted; but he has undoubtedly hit the nail on the head. It is evidently dangerous to be successful at Cirencester.

The College had, in appointing Constable, chosen a man who would achieve two of the objectives that the Council had in mind: firstly to change direction from an institution as an extension of secondary school education to one paralleling the Oxbridge colleges; and in doing this to lift the entry level to one which in fact, tended to preclude the sons of yeoman farmers, the original intention of the founders. Whether this latter effect was intentional on the part of the Governing Body is doubtful, but bearing in mind the constitution of the Council and its strong connections with the landed proprietorship of the time it is probable that no attempt was made to arrest this trend. On the other objective, that of achieving financial stability, it can be safely said that Constable had a measure of success. Certainly the criticism levelled at him about the disposal of the College farm back to the Bathurst estate took no account of the parlous state of the finances at the time, and he and the Council really had no option.

But what the appointing body did not know and presumably could not anticipate, was that Constable had little or no capability as a staff manager. Though it must be said that they should have known something about him bearing in mind that he was a close friend of the previous Principal (or perhaps this worked to their disadvantage!). Not only did his ongoing management reveal the consequences of an autocratic style but his engagement of new staff appeared to be flawed. Upon the resignation of the Professsor of Agriculture (Sheldon) he appointed a young man of twenty-two who, two years ago was himself a student at the College. This was Mr Percy Cathcart, who had in the previous year been dismissed from the post of Farm Manager at Woburn Experimental Farm for the Royal Agricultural Society of England, on account of his incompentency as a farmer.

As is inevitable in disputes, sides were taken. The greater strength of support within the College lay with Church, as one would expect. Not only did two of his contemporaries take the extreme step of resigning but there was mustered an extraordinary degree of support from the students as well as the staff. Indeed, there was a farewell banquet in Cirencester and, as we have seen, a collection for a presentation. It is not idle to speculate that had this affair been conducted in modern times there would have been student protest marches with accompanying paraphernalia. In those Victorian days a banquet and a presentation was an overt protest. Externally the support was initially for Church on grounds of a peremptory decision flying in the face of equity and fairness. This quickly extended to critical and harsh words being said about the Council's actions, both in respect of Church and of the original decision of the Council to abrogate pretty

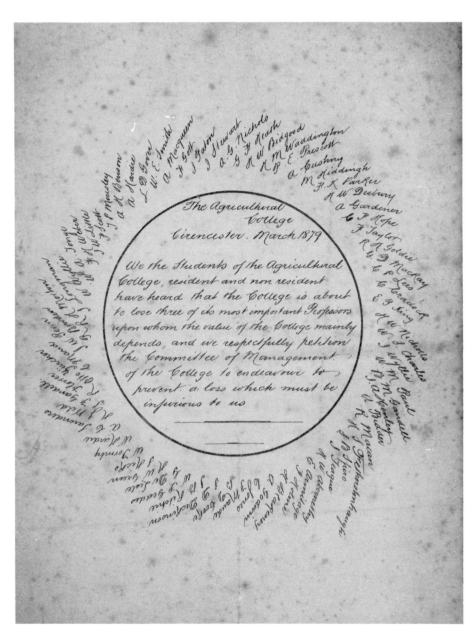

The Agricultural
College
Cirencester. March 1879

We the Students of the Agricultural
College, resident and non resident
have heard that the College is about
to lose three of its most important Professors
upon whom the value of the College mainly
depends, and we respectfully petition
the Committee of Management
of the College to endeavour to
prevent a loss which must be
injurious to us

'The Round Robin' petition by students on the resignation of three professors

well all responsibility for the running of the College. The only support for Constable came from the Council who were in any case party to the happenings and already prejudiced in his favour. All except two members voted against the infamous resolution of 5 March. We do not know who they were.

Eventually an amended set of by-laws and regulations was drawn up and staff were to be permitted to marry without the permission of the Principal and only required to live in College if it was a condition of their contract of employment. The opportunity was also taken to require that any member of staff who wished to publish any material either in the press or as a book, or give a lecture, would have to obtain the permission of the Principal. This latter change was to prevent adverse publicity, the very thing that had brought these matters out into the open. It was final stroke by a Council who, by changing the residence rule, had gone as far as it could to admitting the validity of the charges against them.

So Constable left, to become Rector of Marston Bigot in Somerset. Perhaps the final word should be with John Wrightson, a former Professor of Agriculture from 1865 to 1877, who had received much the same treatment as the others. Wrightson had been a student at the College, passing out with the Diploma in 1863. During his period as Professor he carried out extension work, becoming well known and respected for his talks and lectures outside the College and for the many articles and papers that he contributed to agricultural discussion. He maintained a strong loyalty to his College after he left. He founded Downton College in Wiltshire, which he ran on much the same academic lines as Cirencester but with greater emphasis on practical work and with a lighter touch in managing his staff.

Writing of the College as he knew it in 1862 he recalled the days when Voelcker, Brown, Buckman, Coleman and Bayldon filled the Chairs. He starts by saying, mildly, '. . . the College was rather acutely divided by internal politics. . . .' He went on:

The Revnd. J. Constable, the Principal, was a man of very kind and affectionate disposition, and was never seen to better advantage than when attending at a sick bed, where he was not only sympathetic but very helpful. He was a man of great determination of character, and of commanding appearance and socially attractive. He was a firm disciplinarian. He often suffered from a very painful ailment, and this, if it made him irritable at times, also made him considerate of illness in others. I will not criticise his management of the College, but he was entirely absorbed in the welfare, from his point of view, and worked extremely hard. He was, in fact, an excellent friend and a 'good hater'. I . . . feel sure that his errors, if any, were of judgement rather than the heart.

I always had a class at 6.30 a.m. and this early exercise was looked on by the Principal as highly important. It was a good point for the public . . . but the

Professor was hit hardest, because he must be there; . . . the classes were often extremely thin and occasionally fell through. . . .

Bearing in mind that magnanimity is a trait likely to be highly developed in one who was eventually helped considerably by Constable in setting up his own College of Agriculture, this pen picture of an autocrat rings true.

Chapter Four

CONSOLIDATION WITH McCLELLAN, 1880–90

The existing agricultural colleges . . . are all standing witnesses to the fact that . . . State Aid is needed.

Report of the Paget Commission, 1887

During Constable's time the College was visited by Charles Dickens. Dickens had been in America in 1868 and on his return he came to the College where his son Edward Bulwer Lytton, affectionately known to him as 'Plorn' was a student from February to July 1868, taking first-year Agriculture; his results were not remarkable: he got 276 marks out of a possible 600! He subsequently went sheep farming in Australia, where he joined his brother Alfred Tennyson. Dickens made a complete inspection of the College and the result was a seven-page article in *All the Year Round*, No. 4949, published on 10 October 1868.

Entitled 'Farm and College' it opened with a sentence which encapsulates the single reason for agricultural education: 'That part of the holding of a farmer or landowner which pays best for cultivation is the small estate within the ring fence of his skull.' It continued:

Let him begin with the right tillage of his brains, and it shall be well with his grains, roots, herbage and forage, sheep and cattle; they shall thrive and he shall thrive. 'Practice with Science' is now the adopted motto of the Royal Agricultural Society. Amateur farming by men whose real business lies in other trades, and who, without any true scientific training, play with a few of the results of science, cannot pay and never ought to pay. The farmer's occupation is the oldest, the most necessary, and, when rightly pursued, one of the worthiest a man can follow. Of late years it has risen to the dignity of a liberal profession, and the young Englishman may go through part of his special training for it in a well-appointed college.

This is the Royal Agricultural College at Cirencester. After fighting an uphill fight for twenty years, it stands upon higher ground than any other institution of its kind. There is, indeed, no other of its kind in England; but of institutions for the practical and scientific training of the farmer out of England; among the agricultural academies in France, Germany and elsewhere; not one, we believe, is at the same time satisfactory and self supporting. . . .

Our English College, founded six and twenty years since, not by Government, but by working farmers, when a fashion had come up for recognising the new need of scientific training to their business, has not received one farthing of public money. It had to find its own way in the world, and paid so heavily for the experience by which it profits now, that there is a charge to be met of some twelve hundred a year, interest on debt incurred in its young days. For the last twenty years the college has paid this out of its earnings, while providing liberally from the same source for the minds and bodies of its students.

Dickens went on to expound on the part played by British innovators and scientists in the development of agriculture, and showed how the advent of the application of scientific principles came with the founding of societies and institutions all at much the same time in the mid-nineteen hundreds: 'In eighteen 'forty-two a body of Mid Lothian tenant farmers started an "Agricultural Chemistry Association". . . . The Agricultural College at Cirencester originated in the same way in the same year 'forty-two. . . . The Yorkshire Society had been formed in 'thirty-seven; the Royal Agricultural Society of England . . . in 'thirty-eight; the Royal Agricultural Improvement Society of Ireland in 'forty-one; . . . and in 'forty-three the chief of the Farmers' Clubs came into life, the Central Farmers' Club. . . .' Dickens did not avoid telling of the trials of the young College immediately after its founding:

The managers of the new college were sanguine, and had all their experience to buy: there was no other agricultural college in the country by whose early mistakes they might profit; so they began, like heroes, with an offer of board, lodging, practical and scientific education, all for thirty pounds a year. What could be more desirable than that? 'How lovely the intrepid front of youth!' Experience the first showed that while each student paid thirty pounds a year for everything, he cost the college thirty-two for meat and drink alone. That being so, how was the debt on the buildings to be met? How were the teachers to be paid? Out of the profits of the farm? Aye, but that, too was managed at a loss. There was the bright ideal notion that the students should become practically acquainted with every detail of farm work – hoeing, digging, paring turnips, feeding sheep, and so forth; but that if they did field labour they gave their service worth wages, and should be credited with wages of their work. Thus it was thought that their industry might pay some part of the cost of their maintenance. And, behold, there was a book kept in which every student was credited with the wages of such work as he did on the farm. Such work! Well.

Following a reference to the establishment of Cornell University Dickens returned to the matter of manual work by the students:

When the business of the college farm required that certain work should be completed in a certain field by a particular day, the chance would be that it was not done, or done badly, if it was entrusted to the students. To the students of that day: we speak of times completely gone, of difficulties conquered, partly by the abandonment of efforts in a wrong direction; for the results of the first years of work in the Agricultural College at Cirencester were disappointing. In the year 'forty-eight the managers found that they had overdrawn their account at the bank to the extent of about ten thousand pounds. They were working college and farm at a loss, and had not much to say for the results produced. Even the art of managing the hearty, free-spirited farmers' sons, accustomed to much outdoor sport and little study, who then came to the college, had yet to be learnt. . . .

Then there was the very troublesome fact of the overdrawn ten thousand. The promoters met to consider whether the college was to be closed as a failure. The results of the discussion was that the work of the place lay before it, not the less clear for its early errors and shortcomings.

And so Dickens told of the rescue act performed by the Earl of Ducie, Earl Bathurst, Mr Sotheron-Escourt and Mr Edward Holland, describing the College as later, '. . . the best and most successful agricultural college that has yet been founded anywhere'.

Dickens's visit was by no means superficial: he went into every department and met with all the professors and the students. He even took the trouble to visit the town – notable for the livestock market – and held forth on the subject of water quality in the town and College as it happened to be the subject of research in the laboratories and of lectures in the classrooms that he attended.

He concluded: 'The English farmer cannot rise to the full height of the position made for him by the growth of science, until he receives a sound school training, valid in every part, and follows it up with a thorough training his business.' That is true today and has been so throughout the history of the Royal Agricultural College. '. . . let him go to the Cirencester College and work firmly through the two years' course. If he spends his time well he will learn enough for his purpose, although even after he has taken his diploma he will feel that the two years' curriculum was all too short. . . . It is his own fault then if he be not in his own profession . . . a duly qualified practitioner. Their day may be long coming, but of some such sort must be the English farmers of a day to come.'

This reflection back to the early days of the College is important at this juncture because it shows the period of Constable in a kinder light. Dickens visited in 1868, at the start of this period. By the time Constable left the stage, after the dramatic and powerful scenes of staff resignations and dismissals, the backdrop of a significant improvement in the finances of the College achieved by more rigorous attention to costs was revealed. It meant that the next incumbent would have a much more stable start to his occupancy of the Principal's post.

★

In October 1879, during the illness of Constable, the *locum tenens* was the Revd John B. McClellan, and on Constable's resignation in December of that year McClellan was offered the post of Principal which he accepted. Thus commenced the longest uninterrupted occupation of this post for it was held by McClellan until 1908.

John B. McClellan was another product of Trinity College, Cambridge. The *Agricultural Students' Gazette* (Vol. XIV, 1908) had this to say at the end of this long period in office:

He was born in Glasgow, and educated at St. Peter's School, York. At school he was elected to a Foundation Scholarship at the age of 13, and subsequently on leaving was elected to the School Exhibition for the University. At Cambridge he was elected Scholar of Trinity College, by competitive

The Revd John B. McClellan, Principal 1880–1908

examination, at first sitting; and in three out of four of the College Examinations was first in first class, being second in the fourth. He was also Greek Testament Prizeman, English Oration Prizeman, and Latin Prizeman of the College, one of the competitors being the late Prime Minister, (W. E. Gladstone) with whom he remained on terms of friendship throughout his life.

In 1858 he graduated B.A., Double First Class, in the Classical and Mathematical Triposes – the only double first of his year in the University: and was awarded the Trinity College Wrangham Gold Medal for first class in all College Examinations and in the two University Triposes above mentioned – an award of rare occurrence.

Truly, the Governors had struck gold in having the opportunity to appoint a man of such high academic achievement for what was a relatively small college of seventy-three pupils in that year! For those days they paid him well: in 1872 his salary was £600 per year plus capitation fees which, between 1872 and 1879 averaged £790 per year. The *Gazette* continued:

In 1859, having been Headmaster of King Edward's Grammar School, Bath, he rounded off his scholastic successes by being elected Fellow of Trinity College, by competitive examination and proceeded to his degree of M.A. in 1861. In the same year, having entered Holy Orders, he was presented to the College Living of Bottisham, in the diocese of Ely and during his tenure of the Living was twice commissioned Rural Dean and published a New Translation of the Four Gospels from a newly revised Greek text, with Analyses, Analytical and Chronological Harmony, Notes and Dissertations, etc., a work originally intended to cover the whole of the New Testament, called forth high eulogiums from Church and secular reviews and was stated by the late Bishop Christopher Wadsworth of Lincoln to have entitled the author to the gratitude of the Christian Church.

And so this very learned man came to the College to take over after a stormy period and it is evident that he quickly calmed things down. He filled the vacant professorial chairs, commenced experiments on manures and feeding stuffs on the farmland retained and sent the results achieved to the agricultural press, the local Chambers of Agriculture, Council members of the Royal Agricultural Society of England, and to the Agricultural Department of the Privy Council who published them in their periodical and reorganized and brought up to date each department of the College museum. McClellan had clearly determined to take the College back to its state of pre-eminence in the fields of research so ably started and developed in the time of Voelcker, Church, Brown and the others. Voelcker was now the Consulting Chemist to the Royal Agricultural Society of England, Church was with the Royal Society of Arts and Brown with the Royal Veterinary College, so he did not lack outside contacts to encourage him in continuing the research work of the College. It was in May 1881, shortly after his appointment, that he took on Edward Kinch to be Professor of Chemistry, that Chair whose successive occupants had brought so much distinction to the College. The contract restated the by-laws which set out the relationship between the Principal and professors. These were little altered from Constable's time save in one respect. The by-laws did not specifically require professors to reside in College. Instead they said: 'XXIV – The Professors shall be appointed by the Principal, and be removable by him, and shall be provided with board and lodging in the College during session time.' There was a note to the effect that, '. . . the Professors, except by special licence of the Principal, with the consent of the Committee of Management, are resident in College during Session in apartments assigned by the Principal. During the Vacations the privilege of board and residence is not available.' This was a much less peremptory provision than before, though the Principal still retained the right to hire and fire.

The contract, which was standard for all professors, required the delivery of lectures and practical classes not exceeding twenty hours per week, including one hour per week in the museum and the conduct of weekly, sessional, Diploma and scholarship examinations. The professor had to engage in laboratory instruction for not more than nine hours per week and was allowed to use the College facilities (which included two assistants) for private work. In return for this Kinch was to receive a salary of £300 per annum. In 1883 there was added to this a capitation fee of 10s. (50p) per student. In Kinch's case the provision that the Principal should provide board and lodging during the session was deleted and the presumption is that Kinch lived out of College. Thus, for Kinch, there started one of the longest associations of a staff member, for he retired in 1915, thus completing thirty-four years of service to the College.

One of the very first tasks of the new Principal was to present diplomas, certificates and prizes to the students. This must have been a pleasant undertaking for he found that these were highly satisfactory results. He said that, after only a very short time at the College, he had seen enough to convince him that the College offered exceedingly large opportunities for students who were industrious. The reports from all departments were of highly satisfactory work. He was evidently pleased to have got off to such a good start.

Shortly after the installation of the new Principal a testimonial was proposed to the late Principal, the funds raised to be devoted as well to the erection of a stained-glass window in the east of the College chapel. Subscriptions were called for in January 1880.

Life for the student in 1880 was recounted by one in the *Agricultural Students' Gazette*. It is clear that they were early risers for by eight o'clock the erstwhile student had been roused from his bed by a College servant, to find it pouring with rain and having donned uncleaned boots, '. . . weighing about half a hundredweight . . .', he proceeded to catch up the class with the Professor of Agriculture at the lambing pens, now soaking wet, and the shepherd, '. . . [who]

has the true British nature, is as surly as a bear, especially after a wet night, and has the most profound contempt for an enquiring mind'. There was still time for a ten-minute service in the chapel and then breakfast, followed by lectures with the first one over by 9.45 a.m. It was off then to the Veterinary Hospital and a lecture on pathology and he was quite lost in a plethora of diseases. A quarter of an hour's break followed (our student spent this rendering the *Bonne Bouche Polka* on the piano), and then a lecture on geology. At twelve o'clock he was back to the Veterinary Hospital to see a post mortem examination. Dinner was followed by another start at two o'clock. But he cut the drawing class and with a fellow student traipsed over to the farm ostensibly to gain practical knowledge; tiring quickly of this they decided to go into town. Here they ordered books, only to have to rush back for evening chapel, and to join the choir! Then he went to his room for evening study at seven o'clock but succumbed to the temptation of attending a charity amateur theatrical performance on the excuse of supporting charitable works. In bed by lights out at eleven o'clock he continued by candlelight. The student of 1880 apparently worked hard and played hard: not a bad formula, but this may have been somewhat of an exception for the Principal's diary is later peppered with disciplinary cases, many of which were about drunken and disorderly behaviour. It was in that year that McClellan agreed to the creation of a 'Students' Committee', the origin of the Students' Union that was to come in future years.

A revisit by a student (John Ruffle, MRAC) who had left in 1862 was combined with attendance at a Congress organized by the new Principal on 4 June 1880. He arrived at the College down the main avenue to find that twelve years previously it had been planted with lime, pine, fir and chestnut trees. He recollected his days at College with Constable, who '. . . for weal or woe, has . . . guided the institution earnestly. It is hoped his successor may develop the good plans began under him, and learning by the failures of the past, avoid the many pitfalls which lurk around a man in a prominent position. . . .'

The Congress, the first of its kind, was launched by inviting old and present members, and past and present professors, with the intention of repeating it annually, triennially or quinquennially. Its purpose was to hear of and discuss the latest advances in agricultural science. The Congress was addressed by Professor Buckman on the natural history of meadows in connection with the diseases of animals. He was followed by Professor Henry Tanner on Agricultural Research and Experimental Stations. This Congress was a gathering of distinguished gentlemen associated with the College such as Professors Mayer (Professor of Veterinary Surgery at the College), Harker, Brown, Church and McBride.

One of the early achievements of the Principal, with the Committee of Management, was to obtain official recognition of the title of the College. Although known as 'The Royal Agricultural College', this was not so in the original and Supplementary Charters, the reference there being to 'the Agricultural College'. The use of the title 'Royal' came about because of the continuing royal patronage of the College. In 1881, following a petition, the Queen was graciously pleased to command that in future the College would be known as the 'Royal Agricultural College'.

By April 1881 student numbers had increased to eighty-six. The course syllabus was amended and comprised Agriculture, Agricultural Law, Chemistry, Mathematics, Bookkeeping, Engineering, Surveying, Physics, Botany, Geology, Drawing, Veterinary Surgery, Pathology, Therapeutics, Practical Carpentry, Lathe and Smith Work, Saddlery and Harness Work. This was a true amalgam of technical subjects with practical skills. Later in the year Estate Management was included.

This inclusion of estate management was no new departure. From the outset, the syllabus had included estate management subjects, such as the design and construction of farm buildings, surveying and levelling. But Estate Management as a subject to form a separate syllabus had not existed; the need became apparent with the continuing entry of sons of landowners as well as those setting out on a career as land agents of country estates. This introduction of the new course leading to the College Diploma was a significant step for the College and the start of what, from 1932 onwards when extended by Boutflour the then Principal, was to become the major teaching department of the College. It led to the close association that the College has with the profession of the land.

Special instruction was devised for those many students wishing to make a career in the colonies. The connection was strong, especially with India, for the Bengal Government created six scholarships of £200 per year, two annually and tenable for $2\frac{1}{2}$ years and open to certain native Indian graduates of the University of Calcutta. The first two joined the College in 1882. During this period in the history of the College the *Agricultural Students' Gazette* had frequent reports from old students describing their experiences in the overseas possessions of the Empire ruled over by Queen Victoria.

McClellan made arrangements for lectures to be given by well-known scientists, many of whom were past professors of the College such as Voelcker and Buckman. One of these notable people who came to give lectures was Miss Ormerod. Eleanor Anne Ormerod (1828–1901) was an economic entomologist who, from her childhood, cherished a love of flowers and from this began a lifetime study of insects. She gradually built up a national and then an international reputation and was, in 1882, appointed Consulting Entomologist to the Royal Agricultural Society of England. From October 1881 to June 1884 she was special lecturer at the College and delivered six valuable lectures on insects. She also lectured at the South Kensington Museum and at the Farmers' Club. In 1900 the University of Edinburgh made her their first honorary woman Doctor of Laws. It is well known that Miss Ormerod, although giving valuable and well-attended lectures was not over fond of that task, being happier in devoting her time to her incessant work. In a letter of 11 June 1897 to a Mr Cecil Hooper she said: 'I never lecture now. I never did like it, and in the course of my life I do

Eleanor Anne
Ormerod, special
lecturer at the
College 1881–4

not think I have given as many as 20 lectures.' Written when she was sixty-nine, she added, '. . . I am writing against time, leaving . . . so much work'. It was written of her that, 'Probably the most characteristic feature of Miss Ormerod was her thoroughness. If an absolute stranger wrote to her on a point on which she considered she could help him, not one but four or more sides of note paper would reward the querist; and all in Miss Ormerod's hand, for she disdained a secretary.' The College was fortunate to have engaged the services of this eminent and busy researcher.

One of the early changes made by McClellan concerned the Diploma of Membership. He drew the attention of the Committee of Management to the fact that as the Diploma answered to an 'honours' degree there appeared a need for something in the nature of a 'pass' degree which should be within the reach of those students whose work at the College merited recognition. The Committee of Management passed the following resolution:

That whereas the Diploma of Membership answers to a Degree in Honours and it is expedient to establish a Pass Degree, authority is hereby given to the creation of such a pass Degree under the style of Associateship and that the Principal be and is hereby instructed to draw up conditions for such Associateship and submit them to the Committee of Management for consideration.

The Principal made such recommendations and the award of Associate Member of the RAC was henceforth adopted. It was later dropped around the turn of the century when the Diploma was divided into classes which have remained to the present day.

As an adjunct to the improved syllabus a biological laboratory was established in 1882. As described it was 'a most commodious room . . . furnished after the modern style followed in Continental laboratories'.

The number of students was steadily increasing: in 1879 there were 73, both in-students and out-students; in 1880, 82; in 1881, 86; in 1882, 90; in 1883, 94; and in 1884, 102. In fact, casting ahead, during McClellan's time the highest was 106 in 1885 and the lowest was 70 in 1902. The receipts from students in the year ending 31 December 1884 were: in-students £10,492 and out-students £2,630. This was the first time the income from in-students had topped £10,000.

During the 1881/2 session two members of the Committee of Management died: the Revd T. Maurice and Mr Edward Bowly, the latter having been one of the original founders of the College. His obituary, by Professor Wrightson, Principal of the Downton College of Agriculture, printed in the *Journal of the Royal Agricultural Society of England*, Vol. XVIII p. 353 said of him:

> All breeders of Shorthorns, all old Cirencester students, all sportsmen who have hunted through Braydon Forest and the Vale of the White Horse country, and all frequenters of our great Agricultural Shows, will have heard with

The biological laboratory in 1885

regret of Mr Edward Bowly's death. . . . he was especially beloved in and
around his home, and in his own neighbourhood and county. His genial and
unaffected manners, straightforward, if somewhat old fashioned opinions, and
his genuine respect for his 'brother farmers', won their esteem and love, so that
no man was more respected and liked than he on the Cirencester market. . . .
we see in him an improver of cattle and sheep, a promoter of agricultural
improvements, and of technical education as bearing on agriculture.

He was one of the earliest promoters and most constant supporters of the
Royal Agricultural College, Cirencester, and was one of its Governors. He
was tall and very thin . . . erect and distinguished in appearance, very
courteous, friendly and jocose in his manner, and hearty in his laughter.

Edward Bowly was, in fact, the chairman of that meeting of the Cirencester
and Fairford Farmers' Club in 1842 which first considered adopting and
supporting Robert Jeffreys Brown's proposal for an agricultural college.

It was in 1882 that Herbert J. Little was appointed External Professor of
Agriculture and Rural Economy and on 29 May he delivered his first lecture.
Professor Little came from Coldham Hall, Wisbech and lectured at the College
for eight years until his death on 30 January 1890. He was regarded as one of the
most highly valued and distinguished agriculturalists. A highly cultured man he

Herbert J. Little,
External Professor of
Agriculture and
Rural Economy
1882–90

conducted his affairs with ability, courtesy and genial dignity. In his own county he was a Commissioner of the Peace and an alderman.

The holder of the Chair of Agriculture, as a full-time post, was Professor Robert Wallace, appointed in the same year as Little. It seems strange that, in a College of only some ninety students, it was necessary to have two professors of agriculture, albeit that one was part-time. It seems to have been the practice to employ external lecturers who may have only delivered a few lectures a session.

Robert Wallace was twenty-nine years of age when appointed (many of the professors in the early days of the College were under thirty). He had been educated at Edinburgh University where he had attended lectures given by John Wilson, the Professor of Agriculture, formerly Principal of the College until 1850. After three years at Cirencester he saw opportunity for advancement when Wilson retired and vacated the Chair, and was successful in gaining appointment. It is said that he was disenchanted with the College (he was no exception from some of his predecessors!); at Edinburgh he widened the scope of teaching, establishing new degree courses in agriculture, and from his experience at Cirencester he knew that the intake could be widened as well by attracting future land agents and farm managers. Wallace's career at the University saw the expansion of its Department of Agriculture both physically and in the comprehensive nature of its teaching and in its influence in the developing colonies.

In this same year of 1882 the names of all diploma men since 1847 were enscribed on the walls of the dining hall. The design was by Professor Waller, the College architect, and the practice was continued up to the outbreak of the Second World War.

After three years in post McClellan was highly pleased with progress; following the turbulent end of Constable's tenure it must have been with some satisfaction that he wrote at the end of the 1882 session: 'Most agreeable and successful – new Professors Little, Wallace, Garside and Thomson – all succeeded well and the whole staff for the first time in harmony with the Institution and the Principal and efficient; also harmonious as regards the students.'

★

Each year since its formation the Royal Agricultural College Club had met for dinner, once in the summer and once in the winter. This club for old students, the beginnings of an Old Students' Association, was originated by an old student, Jacob Wilson with Professor Coleman and one or two others, in 1858. In recounting this at the summer dinner held at the Queen's Hotel in Reading on 12 July 1882, Jacob Wilson, in the chair, said that the College was fuller than it had been for many years and that 'therefore all that its detractors can say against it seems to have very little effect'. This is confirmation that McClellan had clearly recovered the College from the effects of the adverse publicity aroused during the Constable/Church affair. He also added, 'When I tell you that the Royal Agricultural College has sent out two hundred diploma men you will have a fair idea that it must have sent out some thousands of students . . . you will realise that those could not have lived at the College and gone forth from it without carrying with them some benefit throughout the world generally.'

At the annual dinner in 1882 there was among the guests one Captain Boycott, noted as a gentleman whose name had attracted considerable attention in connection with Irish affairs! Captain Boycott, in responding to the toast of 'The Guests', said that he considered Ireland was a very good country to live 'out of'!

As an indication of the role of the College in those times, an article in 1884 by Professor T.J. Elliott condensed the requirements for teaching into three elements – 'the three l's' – landowners, land occupiers and land agents. Having identified the historical nature of the inheritance of the landowner, he concluded, 'Although the landowner suffers more or less from all the ills that farming is heir to, and receives . . . not more that $2\frac{1}{2}$ per cent interest on the . . . value of his property, he enjoys the sport and pastimes of a rural life. . . .'

What he had to say about the second 'l' is a reflection of the conditions of farming in the 1880s. 'Since the repeal of the Corn Laws in 1846, the English land-occupier has been compelled to compete with a large and constantly increasing import of corn, the effect of which has been to lower very considerably the value of English produce. To meet this the . . . farmer must increase the produce of his land, and this can only be acquired through the expenditure of extra capital. . . .' His conclusion was that only high farming could support the fresh capital that was necessaary. Professor Elliott concluded by suggesting that the land agent should, with the benefit of the College education, be able to secure tenants for the landowner with the capital and ability to develop the land and ensure that the tenant was provided with the necessary aid from the owner to enable him to make farming pay. What must be remembered is that in those days by far the greater part of agricultural land in the kingdom was farmed by tenants of the great landowners.

Times were not easy for farmers then: Professor Little reported that the 1883 winter wheat harvest was extremely poor due to quite unfavourable conditions for putting it in. Other cereal and pulse crops were yielding average results. He had to say that agriculture had not emerged from the cloud in which it had for some years been enveloped and that he envisaged a reduction in rental values being inevitable.

Despite increasing competition elsewhere in the country and the unfavourable conditions, the College continued to flourish and the Principal succeeded in persuading the Committee of Management that extra accommodation was needed. These were to comprise a bailiff's lodge and a working dairy. Coincidently with this a special Professorship of Practical Dairy Farming was to be instituted. The bailiff to be appointed had a wife who was 'a good Dairy

The dairy and
bailiff's lodge

Woman'! In addition, opportunity was taken to provide a 'large and commodious
room' for out-students.

The site chosen was at the entrance to the College drive on the Cirencester/
Tetbury road. The bailiff's house of four bedrooms and the dairy, with three
main compartments for cooling and settling of milk, for separation of cream and
for cheesemaking, were all built of local stone with Broseley tiles in keeping with
the main structure of the College. The furnishing and utensils of the dairy were
obtained on loan under a special agreement with the Aylesbury Dairy Company,
while the other equipment and building materials were obtained at very much
reduced cost. The out-students' room was erected in a space previously occupied
by the old fives court and gymnasium, on the north side of the quadrangle
between the chapel and the chemical laboratory (the tithe barn). This room has
had many uses: at one time it was a drawing office and it is now the Senior
Common Room.

At the same time two new fives courts were erected in the field near to the old
cricket pavilion: they consist of an Eton court and a Rugby court. However,
McClellan was not always willing to adopt new ideas for recreation: he refused,
in 1886, permission for the creation of a golf course on College land. Lord
Bathurst did agree to one being started in his deer park. And the request to
McClellan for the students to hold a dance in the out-students' room was very
firmly denied! The total cost of these additions and improvements was about
£3,000. Other alterations and improvements were made to the homestead
buildings and the veterinary hospital.

★

Students' don
race c. 1887

Life at the College at this time was not all dull, comprising detailed lectures and getting up before 6 a.m. In 1886 the athletic sports lasted for two days and in the evening of the second, on 7 April, the sports dinner was held. This account of the dinner possibly does more to reveal some part of the social life of the College than any other report of extra-mural activities:

THE ATHLETIC SPORTS DINNER

In the evening the usual dinner was held. Among the guests were Lord Bathurst, Lord Apsley, Major Chester Master, Captain Lindsell, and others. After dinner the usual loyal and patriotic toasts were given. The rising of the

Principal to propose the toast, 'Her imperial Majesty the Queen,' was the signal for an amount of rapturous applause, which, however flattering it might be to the proposer of the toast, was – well, to put it mildly – perhaps a little too pronounced. We think that it is a mistake to call in the assistance of plates, and we commend as an antidote, to the notice of those in authority, the softening effect thereon of the experiment of the destructive distillation of tobacco. The next toast was that of 'The Army, Navy, and auxiliary Forces.' Commander Thomas replied in one of the speeches of the evening. He pointed out, we fear in the captious spirit of an out-student, that the College had no right to fly the ensign which waved during the day from the tower, but naturally he had not then seen what the Principal had during the day stated at Gloucester. His remark that he had known many naval officers who wished to become agriculturalists, but never an agriculturist who wished to become a naval officer, was loudly cheered. Captain Lindsell and Mr. Colin Campbell also responded to this toast. In a speech of some length, which was received at some points with dubious applause, Mr. Ellett proposed 'Success to the R.A.C.' The Principal responded. 'The Staff of the College' was proposed in a sympathetic speech by Lord Bathurst, and was responded to by the different members in the order they were vociferously called for. Mr. Ohm's remarks were that he only answered for himself, and thought the other Professors would like to answer for themselves. The Professor of Agriculture was next on his legs, and was evidently nervous, for we were unable to catch the remarks that he made. The next speech was that of Mr. Kinch, who brought down the house with the highly apposite remark that though he could not hope that tobacco of good quality, as Mr. Ellett hoped, could be grown in England, he was able to point out that the tobacco question presented itself at that moment in a far more pressing shape; he alluded to the process of destructive distillation, with which experiment he believed most Students of the R.A.C. to be thoroughly conversant. Messrs. Harker and Garside were next on their legs, and then Professor Thomson, who seemed to be much impressed by the enthusiastic drinking of the R.A.C. Students. We then were treated to a rollicking speech from Mr. Robinson, who described his encounters with the fugitive atoms of the wily molecule. The boisterous hilarity of the two Chemistry Professors and their jokes, indicated that there must be far more in the laboratory atmosphere than its ordinary condition would suggest. Then followed the toasts of 'The Winners of Events,' 'The Sports Committee,' 'Cricket, Football, and Lawn Tennis,' proposed by Major Chester Master, Rev. J.H. Bluck, and Mr. Sewell, and responded to by Messrs. Cave, Fowler, Cheney, Oakley, Mackenzie, and Steedman. Mr. Fowler's health was accompanied with musical honours. An attempt, but too successful, was made by Mr. Paget to improve upon the authorised programme, and the final toast of the guests was responded to by Dr. Hooker.

The 'Bosses' of the high table then retired, and Prof. Harker having been

The College cr[...]
1st XI in 1885

voted into the chair, a number of highly select songs, &c., were given by various professors and students. It is invidious to single out anything special when all were so good, but we must award the palm to Prof. Harker's recitation of the Lorelei, or the adventures of the Knight with the maiden 'who had nothings on.' Prof. Ohm's and Prof. Garside's songs brought down the house, as also did those of Messrs. Occleston and Cheney, the hiatus in the song of the latter being much deplored. The proceedings wound up with a most happy and sympathetic speech from Mr. Mackenzie, proposing the health of Prof. Garside, who is leaving the College. It is needless to say that the retiring Professor's health and success were drunk, in the absence of any liquid, with musical honours and repeated cheers. Mr. Garside in reply said how much he felt leaving the College, where his relations with everyone had been so delightful, and gave in his best style 'Sally in our alley' as a farewell song. Thus ended the Sports Dinner of 1886, and a jollier, pleasanter evening no student could wish to spend.

(From the *Agricultural Students' Gazette*; Vol. 2, No. 6, April 1886, pp. 180–1)

Unless the dinner started earlier than supposed, it is to be wondered at what time it concluded! By count, there were eight toasts with responses from nine of the diners. In addition there were nine other speeches! And all this before the

The College Rugby football 1st XV in 1885

entertainment for the evening. Finally another toast of Professor Garside who was leaving the College and a reply. That makes a total of twenty-eight! The Victorians were certainly fond of speechifying as a means of social activity!

The Rugby Football Club, too, had its moments. The sport was so well established that the 1st XV were playing such noted first-class clubs as Gloucester and Cardiff. The College team were not necessarily holding their own but were in 1886 giving as good as they got. By 1887, however, these leading clubs were getting too strong for a team of students to hold them. On 15 October the College played Gloucester at home and lost by three tries and two goals to nil (ten points to nil). Seven days later they played Cardiff at home and were beaten by two tries and eight goals to a try. The match report said, '. . . the College forwards played well to the end, and by sheer dash, pluck and good backing up made a much better match than the score appears to relate'. Considering that the Cardiff team contained seven internationals this was an extremely good effort. However, it was the last match against Cardiff to be played.

★

McClellan continued with the general expansion of the facilities offered by the College. In 1887 he introduced an entirely new course: a special one-year course

THE ENTRANCE

THE VETERINARY HOSPITAL

THE DAIRY, EXTERIOR

THE BOTANIC GARDENS

THE PRINCIPAL'S HOUSE

THE COLLEGE, SOUTH FRONT

GENERAL VIEW OF THE BUILDINGS

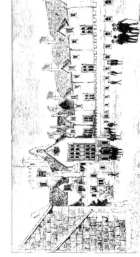

THE QUADRANGLE

THE COLLEGE FARM

THE CHURNING-ROOM IN THE DAIRY

THE VETERINARY SHOP

THE MUSEUM

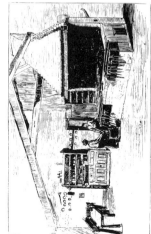

THE FORGE

THE ROYAL AGRICULTURAL COLLEGE, CIRENCESTER

VISITED BY THE BRITISH ASSOCIATION DURING THEIR MEETING AT BATH

intended for out-students not proceeding to the Diploma, and mature men who were only able to devote one year to study. In addition to the introduction of the Associateship as a lower class in the Diploma examination he brought in a Certificate of Proficiency in Practical Agriculture or Estate Management alone. The final examination for the Diploma and gold medals was placed on a wider and more satisfactory basis by extension of the range of efficiency on the part of the candidates, and by the introduction of additional external examiners. At the request of the Government of India a special extra veterinary course was included in the course syllabus for Indian students.

However, from 1886 onwards, student numbers started to diminish because of competition from other agricultural educational establishments. From one hundred and six students in 1885, the next year showed a drop to eighty-nine, and this trend continued throughout McClellan's time, levelling off at about seventy to eighty. The Principal drew the attention of the Committee of Management to the extension movement gathering momentum in certain counties, and to correspondence he had had with the Board of Agriculture suggesting that the College might with advantage cooperate by becoming a centre for Gloucester and other neighbouring counties.

It was at this time, in 1887, that the Government had set up a 'Departmental Commission on Agricultural and Dairy Schools', chaired by Sir Richard H. Paget. This body was appointed for the 'purpose of enquiring into and reporting upon Agricultural and Dairy Schools in Great Britain, which may properly receive Government Grants, and to advise as to the Department which should be charged with the administration of such Grants'. It was the first government commission ever appointed to consider agricultural education and that alone. Evidence was given by McClellan as well as by Professors Wrightson and Fream, both former members of the College staff and now at the Downton College of Agriculture, Wrightson being the Principal.

On 2 November 1887, when McClellan gave his evidence to the Commission, his information about the College was:
– The College had an average number of ninety-two students.
– The age of admission was seventeen to twenty-one, with out-students being mainly over twenty-one.
– There was no entrance examination: a good general standard of education was looked for.
– The pupils were 'sons either of nobility, of army, navy, church, bar, merchants, land agents and some farmers'.
– There were some Indian students.
– The fees were £135 per year.
– For a private room the extra cost was thirty guineas.
– The length of the Diploma course was two and a half years.

f the British ation, *The* *, Saturday 8 aber 1888, no. ol. XXXVIII

– The College farm comprised five hundred acres leased from Lord Bathurst with thirty acres under the College's own management. The tenant of the farm was Mr Russell Swanwick.

– Experimental work was carried out and the results disseminated by papers from the professors.

– The College administration was by a public company and there were no endowments.

The financial situation was 'always precarious' and at that time the income did not pay all expenses because of expenditure on buildings. McClellan said, 'A capital of £30,000 was raised to start with . . . shareholders became insolvent . . . under a new charter bondholders took over. When all bonds are repaid, shareholders return to their original rights.'

In giving evidence his opinion was that there was a need for agricultural education for labourers and tenant farmers. He would acccept government aid for the Royal Agricultural College in the form of grants for scholarships and for professorships and he advanced arguments in favour of this. The Commission examined McClellan on the standard of teaching at the College and this was acknowledged as very high. In fact the Commission, in its conclusions, confirmed this opinion:

> The existing agricultural colleges, namely the Royal Agricultural College at Cirencester . . . are all standing witnesses to the fact that . . . State Aid is needed; [they] are . . . obliged to charge fees far beyond the capacity of tenant farmers.
>
> We recognise the excellence of the course of instruction at the Royal Agricultural College . . . but in view of the fact that the expense of education at these colleges is so high as to absolutely preclude them from being of any value to the ordinary farming class, we have not thought it right to deal further with them in our Report.

The Commission made nineteen recommendations in all, of which the principal ones were:

1. State aid was needed to establish 'Virtually a new system since very insufficient provision exists for agricultural teaching'.

2. The intention was to expand on existing schools (except for a 'Central School of Agriculture' to be provided and maintained by the State).

3. Provision was to be made for labourers as well as tenant farmers.

4. Seven 'District Dairy Schools' were to be established, endowed and grant-aided by the State.

5. There should be one central school for Great Britain, totally financed by the State, to teach all facets of agriculture, forestry and horticulture. The location suggested was to be near Rugby. It should not enter into competition with already established colleges such as Cirencester, Downton etc.

6. There should be one or two 'Middle Class Endowed Schools' to be grant-aided.

7. There was a minor provision to be made for research, and all administration was to be by the Department of Agriculture.

The immediate result of the Commission was the allocation by the Treasury for the year 1888–9 of a sum of £5,000 in aid of agricultural and dairy schools, which was increased to £8,000 in 1891. The distribution of this money was entrusted to the Agricultural Committee of the Privy Council which one year later was merged in the Board of Agriculture. Gradually the scheme of agricultural centres was set up, to exist at the Universities of Wales (Aberystwyth and Bangor), Newcastle, Leeds, Nottingham, Reading and Cambridge. Similar centres were set up in Scotland.

The significance for the College was that, not for the first time, there would be no State assistance because the Government was not prepared to assist the finances of a college which it acknowledged provided an excellent standard of teaching – but not to those whom the State felt obliged to assist, i.e. the tenant farmers and labourers. The essential dilemma, to be faced many times in the future relations between the College and the Government was that, to provide the necessary standard required a stricter financial regime which inevitably meant that obtaining an excess of income over expenditure was only possible with external help in the form of grants or benevolent supporters willing to finance such deficits. For the College to have accepted government aid would have meant changing the whole *raison d'être* for which the College was created – not the original intention of providing education at a very young age for sons of tenant farmers – but as an independent national and international agricultural college. To have accepted the sort of terms that the Government required would have meant reducing the College to a county institution.

Chapter Five

'A PRIVATE ENTERPRISE FOR A
PUBLIC OBJECT', 1891–1908

*At the time of its Jubilee the College was at the zenith of its prosperity and
prestige, despite the prevailing extreme agricultural depression. . . .*

Lord Bledisloe, 1946

McClellan had failed to obtain government assistance and the College was not to
pursue this again until the end of McClellan's tenure in 1908. In giving evidence
to a second Commission on Agricultural Education (the Reay Commission)
McClellan referred to the College as never having been 'a private venture for
profit'. It was, he said, 'A private enterprise for a public object'. Since the College
had run at a loss for the greater part of its existence the first statement was
nothing if not true in practice. One supposes that the originators, though imbued
with the noble intention of providing an institution for the education of the rising
generation of farmers where none existed before, would not have wanted it to be
run at a loss and to an extent had hoped for a profit if only for the purposes of
expansion.

As to whether it was 'a private enterprise for a public object' this too can be said
to be true, though the public bodies that examined the College with a view to
supporting it financially regarded this object as limited since education was not
being provided by the College for 'the ordinary farming class' i.e. tenant farmers
and labourers. It may be regarded as true in the sense that the standard of teaching
was acknowledged as excellent and therefore it set an example to the colleges,
institutes and agricultural departments of universities on methods of teaching, in
that it had conducted original research and was continuing to do so, and finally in
that the products of the College were, in the coming years, to perform public
service both at home and abroad. The College was to provide many who served
their country in the colonies, not only in the agricultural field but in the
administrative and diplomatic services. Furthermore it was educating students
from the colonies, especially from India. The College was performing a role
clearly understood in those Victorian days of the zenith of the British Empire. It
had never quite forgotten its duty to the erstwhile colonies to provide agricultural

education for students from what was to become the Commonwealth, nor to lose the links thus forged. It was during this second period of McClellan's time as Principal that this wider outlook of the College was developed.

★

Following the Paget Commission and the failure to obtain direct government assistance, attempts to secure a more stable basis continued. The discussions that the Principal had with the Board of Agriculture did lead to a meeting between the Chairman of the Committee of Management and Her Majesty's Inspector of Agricultural Education, Mr Brooke Hunt, MRAC, MRASE. He was a former student of the College and for many years Chairman of the Agricultural Education Association. It was emphasized that nothing could be undertaken at the expense of the College or which would interfere with its present work, thus probably losing to some extent the confidence of the public. The Principal did, however, draft a scheme for submission to the Chairmen of Gloucestershire and Wiltshire County Councils and others, setting out how the College would be willing to assist them in promoting an extension of agricultural teaching throughout the counties. The scheme was submitted to the various county councils and though acknowledged by them, no definite action had come about by April 1892.

By December 1891 the majority of the counties of England and Wales had had twelve months' experience of the working of the various technical education schemes set on foot by their various councils. Thus some of the recommendations of the Paget Commission had come about: it is of note that a considerable number of the various directors, lecturers and instructors were graduates of the College. Locally, the professors of the College were giving lectures to assist the local authority.

On Saturday 29 July 1893, the Rothamsted experiments celebrated their jubilee. A large gathering of agriculturalists, scientists and government representatives met at Rothamsted to congratulate and honour Sir John Lawes and Dr Gilbert on completion of fifty years' collaboration in the world-famous experiments conducted there. In the absence of the Principal, Professor Kinch presented an address from the College, and, in a short speech, thanked Sir John and Dr Gilbert for their unvarying kindness to the staff and students of the College on their excursions to Rothhamsted, and for the lectures given, containing accounts of original Rothamsted work. These lectures, published in the *Agricultural Students' Gazette*, were often the first published accounts of Rothamsted work. The address by the Royal Agricultural College was reprinted in the *Agricultural Students' Gazette*, Vol. VI, No. 1 August 1893, p. 107 (*see* Appendix VIII).

On 19 December 1894 a highly respected member of staff, Professor Harker, died at the relatively young age of forty-seven. He was in fact in the prime of his

Left: Sir John
Bennett Lawes
right: Dr Joseph
Gilbert of
Rothamsted w
lectured at the
College

career. Harker was appointed to the Chair of Natural History in August 1881, to succeed Dr Fream when that professor left to go to Downton College of Agriculture. He resided in college until his marriage in the summer of 1885 to the only daughter of a Mr John Watson of Gloucester, when he took up residence in the town. Harker suffered from a long, drawn-out illness eventually warranting surgery which did not prove successful. A 'Harker Testimonial Fund' had already been started during his illness and was continued for the purpose of the education of his two young sons.

He was held in high regard by students and staff, not only for his lectures but for his manner of conducting them, for he was a genial and amiable character. He devoted his spare time to his research studies and his work was not limited to his duties at the College. He was a Fellow of the Linnean Society, Vice-President of the Cotteswold Naturalists' Field Club, and Consulting Botanist and Entomologist to the Newcastle Farmers' Club. He developed a high reputation for his knowledge, scientific and practical, of all the subjects of his department at the College – botany, geology and zoology.

He was succeeded by Theodore T. Groom, BA (Cantab.), B.Sc. (Lond.), FGS, late scholar of St John's College, Cambridge, and Lecturer and Demonstrator at the Yorkshire College, Leeds. Groom had conducted valuable researches and had published many scientific papers.

The year 1895 was to mark the jubilee of the Royal Agricultural College. Early in that year the Council of the College had set up a committee to organize the celebrations which would take place in the Summer Term. The committee comprised, with Professsor Kinch in the Chair, Professors Ohm and Blundell, together with Messrs West, Talbot, Gurney and Waterfield (in-students),

Charles Bathurst,
later Lord Bledisloe

C. Bathurst, Eaton, Day and Goldstand (out-students), and Swanwick, Dugdale,
Gay Roberts, Gaisford and Ross Hume (old students) with Mr E.B. Haygarth,
the College solicitor and Lecturer in Law. The first decision made was to hold a
dinner in the town on Friday 26 July, preceded by a conversazione on 25 July.
When eventually and successfully held, the conversazione attracted nearly 500
people and 120 sat down at the dinner, consuming 163 bottles of champagne, 14
of sherry and 22 of claret!

To commemmorate the jubilee a register of students and staff from the
inception was commenced, mainly due to the initiative of Charles Bathurst, later
Lord Bledisloe. This was paid for by subscriptions and sales. This proved to be a
difficult task owing to lack of information on past students. However, it was
completed and published under the editorship of Charles Bathurst and Professor
Kinch in 1897. It is of a remarkably comprehensive standard and is now located in
the College library, historical section.

The highlight of the celebrations was a visit by HRH the Prince of Wales,
Patron of the College. This comprised a reception and luncheon on the jubilee
day, Thursday 25 July 1895. On Sunday 21 July a special Commemoration
Service had been held in the College chapel, the sermon being preached by the
Principal.

The visit of the Prince of Wales, who also visited the town of Cirencester, was
a splendid affair, marred only by heavy and persistent rain throughout the day. On

arrival at the railway station, the Prince travelled by royal carriage to the College down the road lined by the 2nd Volunteer Battalion, the Gloucester Regiment and with the band of the Regiment playing 'God Bless the Prince of Wales'. Such pomp and ceremony, typical of the period, was carried on throughout the day. At luncheon all the staff and representatives of the students were present together with the Governing Body, supporters of the College and VIPs from Parliament and the Government as well as from the agricultural world.

★

At the luncheon, following the speech of the Prince of Wales in praise of the College, the Principal responded:

> It was intended, and was the first movement in the way of establishing a College for the promotion of a specific education for those who were to be engaged in agricultural pursuits. After a time the Royal Agricultural Society of England offered prizes for the purpose of encouraging scientific and practical studies in connection with agriculture, but those prizes were first proposed by one of those connected with the Governing Body of this College, the suggestion met with very little approval. By perseverance, however, the Royal Agricultural Society was enabled to see that our method of adopting the principles of science and endeavouring to apply them to the practice of agriculture in this country was one that ought to be be encouraged, and very soon were established those series of prizes which have continued to the present day. . . .

This was a strong claim – perhaps borne out by the work of Voelcker and others in the early days.

At the dinner in the Corn Hall on 26 July 1895 some of the speeches revealed the spirit of the College at that time. W.T. Thistleton-Dyer (not then knighted):

> Having been a Professor myself, it is a melancholy thing to see that the College was once in the predicament of having a Professor who could not lecture . . . [He did not say who this was!] . . . as I belonged to [the College] it was then a remarkably efficient institution. But there was a certain monastic austerity about it which it is singular I miss now, I suppose the College has come to that period of life when we all desire a certain measure of ease and comfort . . . and . . . I am delighted to see in the College a certain comfort, a certain elegance, I might almost say, a certain luxury.

The Principal, in replying to the toast of the College: 'We are not founded, as some Colleges are, for the purpose of putting money into the pockets of the promoters. On the contrary, we were rather founded for the purpose, as I know we have done, of taking money out of the pockets of our promoters.' McClellan could hardly have uttered a truer word: without the philanthropy of the early founders, especially Edward Holland, and of the later benefactors, especially the Earl of Ducie, the College would have quickly folded.

There were references to discipline which indicate that the students were not necessarily hard working and diligent in their studies. Col. Chester Master, a Governor: 'Do not . . . think that the Governing Body were responsible in any way for the discipline of the College.' He was quite aware he was touching on a somewhat tender subject: 'They were all boys and youths once, and whatever punishment they might have received no doubt they had all reaped the benefit of it.' A fine Victorian response! The Principal: '[He] knew that on some occasions . . . [he] might have been called in to exercise that discipline . . . which was solely confined to the Principal . . . if there was any student whom he had in any way been called upon to visit with any severity, it had been against his own private feeling, and only in obedience to the sense of duty which he owed to the College itself.' A somewhat schoolmasterly attitude! But there is ample evidence in the Principal's diaries to show that the students of that day could be an unruly, drunken and disorderly lot.

★

At this time the Governors sanctioned the striking of twelve jubilee medals to be awarded to the Principal and professors. Later in the year an old student, Leon F. Goldstand, himself a gold medallist in 1894, generously offered £200 for the institution of three silver medals. He was a wealthy and able Polish landowner, whose chief amusement in his vacations was shooting wolves and who, during the First World War, was Consul-General for Poland in London. He wrote to the Principal on 20 September 1895:

I have thought over our last examination results and come to the conclusion that their [sic] is a certain amount of unjustice [sic] in the fact that my friend Mr Chamberlain being only 23 marks behind me, did not receive any distinction. It seems to me rather bad luck on a man not to get a medal only because he happened to come a term later, but such are the rules of the college and we students must obey them.

If I have written all this Mr McClellan is for the reason – I want to put at your disposal the sum of 200£ the interest of which sum should be destined to buy three silver medals a year, which would be awarded to diploma students acording [sic] to your own decision.

If you accept this offer I should request that the medals be called . . .
The McClellan   )
The Harker   )   silver medals
The Goldstand   )
I hope that you would award the first of them to Mr Chamberlain who has

always been a model student and a very hard worker. My address will be Wiesbaden . . . and I should be very pleased if you are kind enough to answer this letter. If the sum of 200£ seems to you to [*sic*] small I shall be pleased to increase it.

I remain dear Mr McClellan yours very respectfully

Leon F Goldstand

★

The time of the jubilee in 1895 was a highpoint in the College's fortunes and of its reputation. Writing in 1946 in *Country Life*, Lord Bledisloe, then President of the Royal Agricultural Society of England, said: 'At the time of its Jubilee the College was at the zenith of its prosperity and prestige, despite the prevailing extreme agricultural depression, and these it continued to enjoy, with fluctuations of fortune, until the first world war, when, as practically all its staff and students of militay age joined the armed forces, it was left empty.' In Lord Bledisloe's time as a student, as Charles Bathurst, there were many contemporary with him who, after leaving College, went on to high status or office in different fields. He wrote:

> I shared lodgings in the old mediaeval town with my dear friend, Christopher Turnor, the future Lincolnshire model squire and eminent agriculturalist, and Charles Foxcroft, afterwards M.P. for Bath. Among my fellow students were Lord Charles Kennedy (now Marquess of Ailsa), Archibald Weighall (afterwards Governor of South Australia and Chairman of the Royal Empire Society), Hugh Lord Emlyn (afterwards fourth Lord Cawdor), and Leon Goldstand. . . . Among my fellow students were Counts Peter and Paul Bobrinskoy from Russia and Count Gulinelli from Italy, Robert Holland-Martin (afterwards Chairman of Martins Bank and of the Southern Railway) and E.L.T. Austen, 'the Scarborough Giant', whose chief pets were snakes and chief sport fox-hunting. This, however, he conducted on foot, as no hunter could carry his great weight. No one knew better the habits of the fox . . . he was a great walker. . . . I walked with him from my home near Monmouth to his home at Scarborough: it took nine consecutive days.

Maybe many of these students did have the silver spoon in their favour but nevertheless these contemporaries of Bledisloe were illustrative of the class of student at Cirencester in the late nineteenth century and they achieved their subsequent positions by some degree of merit developed from their stay at the College. The influence of the College staff was recognized by Bledisloe:

> Among the very competent professional staff during my studentship were three whom I regarded with much affection and valued both as instructors

and personal friends. They were Professor Blundell (Agriculture), Kinch (Chemistry) and Harker (Natural History). They opened my eyes to the environment and secrets of the British countryside, and made for me rural life, at home and abroad, the intensely interesting experience which it has since proved to be.

Another example of a student who rose to high office was Basil S. Cave. In the New Year's Honours List of 1897 the CB was granted to him, as HM Consul at Zanzibar, in recognition of his brave and able management of affairs in connection with the bombardment of the usurping Sultan's palace, the deposition of the usurper and the enthronement of the lawful successor to the Sultanate. Cave was one of the many students in those Victorian days who sought his life in the colonies of the British Empire and is an example of one of many who won honours. He took the College Diploma in April 1886, was appointed HBM Vice-Consul to the Sultan of Zanzibar's dominions in 1890 and promoted to Consul in 1894. He was, it is believed, the youngest man who had received the honour of the CB. He later (1903) was promoted to the rank of Consul-General. In 1892 he had married Mary McClellan, the youngest of the three daughters of the Principal.

★

In 1898 Bacteriology was included in the course syllabus and in 1901 a number of illustrated exhibits of the College and its work were sent to the agricultural section of the Paris Exhibition, following which, at the request of the French Under-Minister of Agriculture the prospectus and several photographs of the College were forwarded to him for inclusion in his report to the Minister of Agriculture. Complete copies of the experiments undertaken by the College during the past ten years were sent to the British Board of Agriculture.

In 1897 Henry Tanner, MRAC, FCS, died, the very first student to take the Diploma of Membership, which he did in 1847. His is the first name on the College rolls enscribed on the walls of the dining hall. Henry Tanner was at one time (1858) Professsor of Agriculture and Rural Economy at Queen's College, Birmingham. For about a year (1880–1), at the invitation of the Principal, he was lecturer on the Principles of Agriculture at the College and was very largely instrumental in setting up and organizing the Royal Agricultural Congress of 1881.

★

The propensity for professors to leave the College for reasons other than the more acceptable ones of betterment or retirement was continued with the departure in July 1898 of Professor Hugo Ohm after nineteen years' service, 'because the rules of the institution do not admit of a Professor of Physics being

Hugo Ohm (seated),
Professor of Physics
1879–98

married'! The marriage of professors and their subsequent residence was thought to have been settled with the departure of Constable and the revision of the by-laws and the new contracts of employment, as evidenced earlier by that of Professor Kinch; and Ohm was appointed in 1879 at the very time of the turmoil about professors and their employment rights following marriage. But the relaxation was only for two of the professorial posts, Agriculture and Chemistry, the remainder had this residential restriction and the Professor of Physics was one of those. It meant that application had to be made to reside out of College; it was not a bar against marriage as such but that was what it could be in practice. So Ohm was refused and the Governors said, '. . . [it is] not consistent with the requirements of the College to have three professors non-resident . . . at least four Professors should reside in College for disciplinary purposes'. It may be that they were influenced by the fact that Ohm had been in trouble with his Principal in 1881 over 'serious breaches of duty as a resident Professor'. He tended to return to College late at night – or so the Principal regarded coming in at midnight or just thereafter. McClellan said in his diary, 'I fear his being a habitue of the King's Head', and threatened him with dismissal for repeat performances! Ohm subsequently went off to become a schoolmaster – Headmaster of the Hereford County School.

★

This matter of discipline exercised McClellan regularly: there are frequent reports of disciplinary action in his diary. It seems that some of the students were a wild, unruly bunch and as a whole given to demonstrations and protests from time to time. Certainly there were often cases of drunk and disorderly behaviour with students returning from town much the worse for drink. One notorious incident involved three students who were sent down for bringing two prostitutes from Cheltenham to Cirencester for 'immoral purposes'! Naturally the Principal had to take immediate action and as a result there were violent demonstrations by students who, with the three culprits, rampaged through the town and the Principal's garden 'shouting, hooting, breaking windows and singing, "Britons never will be slaves" '! McClellan described this as, 'One of the most disgraceful,

Diploma group of 1901. *Seated left to right*: Professors West, Locke, Blundell, the Principal J.B. McClellan, Professors Kinch, Paton and Wooldridge

wanton, shameless and outrageous demonstrations ever made by the students'. It ended by a deputation of students attending on the Principal with apologies, but there was no mercy for the culprits whose sending down was confirmed.

★

The turn of the century saw frequent lists of old students serving at the front in South Africa in the Boer War. In 1901 in another development King Edward VII became Patron of the College.

Forestry had been included in the syllabus since the 1880s and had gradually assumed more importance, so that in 1903 a Chair of Estate Management and Forestry was created and F.C. McClellan, the son of the Principal and a student in 1886, was appointed to the post. In the same year Dr W. Schlich, FRS, was appointed an Honorary Professor of Forestry. He was closely connected with the establishment of Alice Holt and Bagley Woods. Lord Bathurst kindly made his woods available for practical classes and set aside and fenced off an experimental forest garden. F.C. McClellan must be credited for forming the forest garden which was laid out at the western extremity of a tract of Lord Bathurst's parkland known as Rough Hills on the Cirencester/Stroud road. Lord Bathurst financed the whole undertaking.

On 17 November 1903 Dr Schlich delivered a comprehensive lecture on the world supply of timber and the prospects for British forestry. Attending was the President of the Board of Agriculture, the Earl of Onslow, together with College Governors. At this time the Earl of Ducie was still Chairman of the Governing Body, but just prior to this, the death of the Duke of Richmond and Gordon had created a vacancy in the office of President of the Council and this was filled by the Earl Spencer, KG.

One of the outstanding members of staff during the time of McClellan was the Professor of Agriculture and Rural Economy, Edward Blundell. Born in 1842 he became Professor at the College in 1891. He was also Practical Instructor on the College farm and responsible for Practical Dairying. Blundell was an assiduous traveller in search of knowledge and, until his retirement, managed great distances by bicycle. He became a close personal friend of Charles Bathurst, whom he taught, and stayed many times at Lydney Park, the home of Bathhurst. Among many of his cycle rides were trips to the opening in December 1895 of the South-Eastern Agricultural College (Wye College) and, in 1900, to Harper Adams College; to the Forest of Dean and then on to Pontypridd, by daily stages. With Professor Duncan, Head of Veterinary Science, he cycled in 1898 by moonlight to Devizes and Stonehenge. All the while he was accumulating knowledge of the current state of agriculture as well as indulging in botanical studies. During many of these trips he played golf – it's not revealed in his diaries just how he transported his clubs!

In 1901 he acquired a car, a gift from a student named Aspinall, and before this

Edward Blundell,
Professor of
Agriculture and
Rural Economy
1891–1908

his only alternative to the bicycle was a pony (named 'Dreadnought') and trap. In 1908 he retired from the College at the same time as McClellan, and a few years later he resigned from the Golf Club (presumably Cirencester, though the College did have its own course in the Deer Park), 'on account of their having commenced Sunday play'.

In his later years he was still active in the interests of the College for he wrote to Lloyd George and Lord Ernle in 1919 about the need for the College to reopen after the First World War. In 1920 he celebrated his golden wedding with his wife, Jessie, and died at the age of ninety in 1932. The College was indeed fortunate to have on their staff such men as Blundell, prepared to devote their lives to the education of their students and to take part, as he did, in organizing and supporting many of the social activities.

★

In 1907 the Board of Agriculture set up a Departmental Committee to report on agricultural education under the chairmanship of Lord Reay. It took evidence from 30 April 1907 to 30 February 1908 and produced a wide-ranging report of 648 pages. McClellan gave evidence as he had done before to the Paget

Dining hall at
turn of the ce

Commission. This time the situation was different: there had been agricultural depression through the nineties due to adverse weather conditions and heavy falls in product prices. In fact the state of agriculture was so serious as to cause the Government to set up a Royal Commission on Depression in 1893.

Competition from State-aided and county-aided institutions had become increasingly severe: agricultural colleges were set up at the South-Eastern College at Wye in 1894, at Sutton Bonington in 1895, at Newport, Shropshire (Harper Adams) in 1901 and at Seale Hayne, Devon, in 1903. In order to alleviate the problems of finance, the Governing Body looked hard at the possibilities of some conjunction with a university. Oxford seemed to be the logical choice, for had not the College been modelled on this near neighbour, both in the design of its campus and in the construction of its syllabus? Constable, in particular, had looked eastwards in his contemplation of what the first agricultural college should be and do. McClellan, no less, sought to emulate the teaching and ethos of the premier university so near. Oxford, however, had other ideas and looked to Reading as a University Extension College. Bristol University seemed to be a possibility.

By 1907 the Governors were offering entrance exhibitions in order to attract students. Three of £50 each were offered by the Chairman, by Lord Bathhurst and one by the College. Gloucestershire County Council also offered a special scholarship of £100, tenable either at the College or at Reading. But no applications were received. Student numbers continued to drop and the annual accounts were showing deficits. In 1904 receipts had been £9,870; in 1905 they were £9,032; in 1906, £7,969 and in 1907, £7,494. The numbers of students had slipped from seventy-nine to sixty-five.

McClellan had, in fact, carried out a remarkable job in persuading the Governors to continue to make up the deficits over the years (in fact from 1898 onwards it was the Earl of Ducie who had made up the greater part of the deficits by contributing some £3,123 up to 1907), but the time was bound to come when a fresh effort had to be made to see if State aid could be procured on terms likely to be acceptable, and which would maintain the College at the same level and allow it to educate the same class of student in terms of age and attainments on entry. However, it was realized that the Government was unlikely to accept the then constitution of the College as a purely private institution and that it would have to be such that it would be acceptable to the Board of Agriculture. In effect the College had to be owned and managed by a limited company incorporated under the Companies Acts, 1862 to 1907.

With the setting up of the Reay Committee the Governors realized that this would be an opportunity to obtain State aid and thus recover from the worsening financial position. So there began a time of intense activity in seeking to influence those who would be likely to support the College in its endeavours to find a new role in the context of the now burgeoning agricultural education sector of the country.

One of the most ardent protagonists of the College and a supporter of its search for a legitimate and accepted place in the developing environment was J.C. Medd. Medd lived in Stratton, Cirencester, farming there, and had for many years taken a positive interest in agricultural education. He was a member of the Committee of Management and prominent in public service in the county and locally. He was already in the thick of the general discussions about this subject which was exercising the minds of leading agriculturalists and administrators. Several meetings had been convened in the late nineties, many of them at the College. In 1898, in particular, a private meeting was held at the Royal Agricultural College, attended by leading landowners and farmers; a Committee, of whom Medd, Kinch and McCracken of the RAC were members, was formed to urge that steps be taken to:
1. Secure systematic and efficient instruction, both theoretical and practical, in agricultural subjects.

2. Diffuse a more thorough appreciation of the advantages of instruction.

The Committee resolved that agricultural and rural education should be administered by the Board of Education, which was then a newly formed department. It made many other detailed recommendations about the administration of schools in the country. But this primary recommendation about the Board of Education being responsible for agricultural education was, to some extent, flying against current thought in favour of it being in the hands of the Board of Agriculture.

J.C. Medd had advanced views on the subject. He suggested that:
1. The Board of Agriculture should have total responsibility for all agricultural education.
2. There should be a consultative council to oversee the development of such education.
3. The country should be divided into districts with government inspectors in each.
4. Counties should be grouped around a collegiate centre. He instanced cases where this might happen using the then established university departments.
5. Intermediate agricultural and horticultural schools be established.
6. There should be demonstration stations in each county.
7. Knowledge should be disseminated by regular reports.
8. The Board of Agriculture should be provided with larger funds.
These propositions were far-seeing. It requires little effort of imagination to see that these proposals contained the elements of the agricultural education and advisory services which developed in the years to come.

By October 1907 the Committee of Management of the College had reached the stage of resolving that the constitution be changed in order to meet the requirements of the Board of Agriculture and thus make it acceptable for the receipt of grants. A meeting was planned for 16 October 1907 at which Medd would put resolutions to meet this:
1. That the Royal Agricultural College at Cirencester should in future be administered under a scheme to be approved by the Board of Agriculture.
2. That a majority of the Governing Body will in future consist of representative members nominated by local and other authorities.
3. That the College should be open to inspections by the Board of Agriculture and be subject to the regulations of the Board.
4. That steps have been, or are being, taken to give immediate effect to these resolutions.

Medd's suggestion was that the whole property should be conveyed to three trustees, whom he later nominated as the Earl of Ducie (the then Chairman), Lord Moreton and Lord Bathurst. He wanted 'something of this kind' to be sent to Lord Reay, 'otherwise Cirencester will be completely ignored, as it is obviously ineligible for grants as at present constituted'.

He conveyed these views in letters to E.B. Haygarth, the Secretary to the

Governors, and in his next letter he said that his own position was 'a somewhat delicate one, and I am anxious to avoid any appearance of interference'. No wonder, for he was a member of Lord Reay's Committee! In addition he was a member of the Agricultural Sub-Committee of Gloucestershire County Council. So he had to operate behind the scenes and was clearly a powerful influence in these matters. In fact in October 1906 the Principal had asked him to make definite suggestions for the future management of the College so as to comply with the requirements of the Board of Agriculture and to secure a grant.

On 3 August he wrote again to Haygarth: he discussed what the Departmental Committee might do, especially Lord Barnard, a member of the Committee and in the chair taking evidence. He suggested that he would get the Reay Committee to recommend that the RAC became a collegiate centre for Gloucestershire, Wiltshire, Somerset, Hereford and Monmouth.

Suddenly, on 5 August he changed to another tack. He mentioned the constitution of Swanley Horticultural College for women and sent papers about this to Haygarth. Swanley College was in receipt of grants from the Board of Education and Medd thought that it might be more effective to approach that Board rather than go through the reconstruction necessary to satisfy the Board of Agriculture. He gave contacts in the Board of Education for Haygarth to follow up.

Now nearing the vital meeting of the Committee of Management, Medd sent another letter; it is plain that anxiety was creeping into his mind, let alone that of the members of the Governing Body. He says that the Committee should pass resolutions, 'expressing their readiness to reorganise the College so as to bring it into conformity with the regulations of the Board of Agriculture'. He thought that this would induce the Reay Committee to recommend that the RAC 'be treated in respect of grants upon terms of equality with other collegiate centres'. Without this, he said, Cirencester will be 'wholly ignored'.

In this long letter of 13 October he outlined the manner in which the College could work with Gloucestershire County Council and suggested that the Council might be willing to fall in with a scheme whereby the monies which the Council was allocated for agricultural purposes might be channelled through the College for distribution upon work then carried out by the Agricultural Sub-Committee of the County Council. In other words, as he put it, 'The College would merely be the conduit through which the money passed, but the effect would be to place the total grant upon the credit side of the College balance sheet.' He felt that, as a member of that Committee, he could persuade them of his views. This seems to have been something of a last resort, for it only really had presentational merit, and did not bring actual financial relief.

Next he turns to the matter of a link with Bristol and reveals that Professor Lloyd Morgan, the Principal of the University College, Bristol, still aimed to cooperate with Cirencester and thought that it might be connected with his Agricultural Department or that it might be affiliated to Oxford University as soon as the School of Agriculture was established.

So, on 16 October 1907, the critical meeting of the Committee of Management took place and after lengthy discussions the resolution passed was:

1. That the Royal Agricultural College at Cirencester is in urgent need of financial support by Grants from Government and Public Authorities similar to those accorded to other Agricultural Institutions in this Country.
2. That if such Grants can be secured the College shall in future be administered under a Scheme of Reconstruction to be submitted and approved of by the necessary authorities.
3. That under such Scheme the Governing Body shall in future consist of persons nominated by Local and other Authorities and that the College shall be open to inspection by the Board of Agriculture, and that these Resolutions be forwarded to the Chairman and Secretary of the Departmental Committee now sitting upon the subject of Agricultural Education and to the Board of Agriculture.

These resolutions were not dissimilar to those proposed by Medd but were not couched in such peremptory terms. But they were confirmation that the Governors were prepared to see the College as a very different establishment if it was to survive.

★

During this time and throughout 1907 up to February 1908 the Reay Committee on Agricultural Education was sitting. Principal McClellan was in the process of giving evidence while the College Governors were deliberating. He started before Lord Barnard, as Chairman, by outlining the history of the College and the financial background. He was explicit in saying that the College 'has never been a private venture for profit. It was a private enterprise for a public object.' The numbers of students were declining, said McClellan, due to competition from the state-aided colleges. As a consequence the College had been running at a loss for some considerable time. The deficit had been made up by private contributions. This was 'not satisfactory'! He felt that they could not increase fees in the face of competition from the aided institutions and the fees had, in fact, been increased from what they were originally. 'It is also certain that without assistance we cannot go on for very much longer.' He made the point that students went to the State-aided institutions who could afford to go to Cirencester but who used public money instead.

In discussing the costs of maintaining the College he had this to say: 'The present financial position is extremely precarious. It can scarcely, I think, be expected that the Committee of Management . . . can carry on a college from year to year at a loss: therefore, without financial assistance, sooner or later, the College will necessarily be closed, that is my opinion.' He concluded by saying that the College would be prepared to submit to State inspection, to have a representative governing body, to act as a collegiate centre for Gloucestershire and to be affiliated to a university department if one is established at Oxford.

From the resolutions passed on 16 October by the Committee of Management the intention was to devise a scheme of reconstruction and a small committee, consisting of Lord Bathurst, Lord Moreton, Sir Nigel F. Kingscote, Sir John Dorrington, Col. Curtis Hayward, G. Bazley and J.C. Medd, produced an interim report on 22 November 1907. One of their immediate recommendations was that under the new cirumstances the Principal should be a layman and an active member of the teaching staff, and at their meeting on that day the Committee of Management accepted the proposal that a new Principal should be sought.

This would have come as no surprise to McClellan for on 12 November he had submitted a long and detailed report to the Governors on the method for reorganization of the College. *Inter alia* he had said, 'Personally, I have now held my own position for many years and . . . I am aware that the time must come . . . when either myself or the Governing Body may deem it prudent that a new Head should undertake the responsibilities of the Principal's Office under new conditions. I am not anxious to desert my post in the time of distress, but if . . . the severance should arrive sooner rather than later, I shall welcome relief from my responsibilities.'

He himself raised the points about the duties required of the Principal asking whether the Principal should be one of the teaching staff and whether this would lead to economies in administration. He did not agree on either point: he gave cogent reasons. He maintained that the Principal was effectively undertaking the duties of Director, Bursar, Secretary (Collegiate), Dean of the chapel and Chaplain, with responsibility for the discipline of students, selection of staff, arrangement of studies, and supervision and control of every department. He reckoned that the sharing of duties must interfere with the responsibililty of professors of departments. His general view was that the Principal should not be a specialist but that a classical education was the most valuable attribute onto which could be grafted the scientific studies. It would seem, therefore, that the Sub-Committee took little notice of McClellan's advice. His report also recommended a change in the Chair of Agriculture; granting that though the then occupant, Professor Blundell, was thoroughly competent with practical experience, he was lacking in scientific training and could not therefore carry out experimental and research work that was necessary in that post.

And so the stage was set for radical changes in the College: a new constitution and a new Principal to carry out the reorganization necessary. McClellan had been Principal for twenty-nine years, the longest serving Head of the College since it was founded. The parting was with no acrimony: McClellan said in his acceptance of the end of his contract,

> . . . this [the official notification of the resolution of the Governing Body] is
> very welcome. The strain of carrying on the College as it is has been too great

and I would have tendered my resignation some time ago but for the reflection that, when Lord Ducie was so nobly struggling against fate, it would have been ungrateful obviously to add to the difficulties before steps could be taken to alter the cause of the strife. I shall be sorry to part with old friends, but it is of absolute necessity and I should not have been willing to place myself under the new conditions which must now arise.

The long-time supporter of the College was also nearing the end of his positive association. Lord Ducie was contemplating giving up his Chairmanship of the Governing Body. In a letter to the Secretary he expressed his regrets at the impending departure of McClellan, saying, 'I must bow to the unanimous verdict of my colleagues and others as regards Mr McClellan. . . . Have they considered the difficulty of finding a substitute? Will a substitute be found to take a position that must be of an uncertain sort? I undertake to pay the deficit for 1907 . . . after that I decline to pay any longer. . . . My position must pro tem be considered neutral although I cannot oppose the wish of my colleagues.'

The Earl of Ducie did resign at the meeting of the Governors on 4 April 1908 and generously placed, in addition to his last contribution to make up the deficit, a further £1,000 in the names of Lord Moreton and Earl Bathurst as an emergency

The 3rd Earl of Ducie, Chairman of the Committee of Management, 1908

fund. Each in their own way, Ducie and McClellan, had seen the College through progressively difficult times, the one financially and the other in maintaining the standard of education in the face of growing and strong competition from the newly created agricultural institutions helped by State and local authority support.

It was at the meeting on 4 April that the draft Scheme of Arrangement was approved:

> . . . That the Secretary be directed to summon an Extraordinary General Meeting of the Shareholders for the purpose of passing the following Resolution:
> (a) That the Royal Agricultural College be dissolved.
> (b) That the following members of the Management Committee, namely, The Rt. Hon. Lord Bathurst, The Rt. Hon. Viscount Cobham, The Rt. Hon. Lord Moreton, The Rt. Hon. Sir John E. Dorington, Bt., Col. T.W. Chester Master and Col. J.F. Curtis Hayward be authorised to present a Petition to the High Court of Justice for an Order for the winding-up of the College under the Companies Acts 1862 to 1907 with a view to the subsequent submission to the Court of a Scheme of Arrangement (to be sanctioned under the Joint Stock Companies Arrangement Act 1870) providing for the Transfer of the undertaking and assets of the College to a Company limited by Shares to be incorporated (by licence of the Board of Trade and with such permission as may be required for the use of the title 'Royal') as the Royal Agricultural College.

An Extraordinary General Meeting of the shareholders was held on 23 April 1908 when the action of the Special Committee and of the Management Committee was approved.

This was acted upon and a liquidator appointed. To complete the reorganization, application was made to the Chancery Division of the High Court of Justice for the new company to be registered, under which it was proposed that the existing bond debt of £12,000 alone would be the bond and share capital of the institution in the proportion of £10,800 debenture bonds and £1,200 ordinary shares, and that the original share capital raised when the institution was first founded, amounting to £20,060, be finally written off and expunged. The original amount of the bond debt was £30,000; of this sum £11,600 had been paid off out of profits, £6,000 discharged by voluntary surrender (a generous act by some of the bondholders) and this left £12,000 still undischarged.

The reorganization was sanctioned by order of the High Court of Justice, dated 29 July 1908. A Certificate of Incorporation was issued on 11 August 1908, permission being granted by the Board of Trade for the word 'Limited' to be omitted from the name, and His Majesty the King agreed to the retention of the prefix 'Royal' and to continue as Patron. Thus the Royal Agricultural College became a limited company incorporated under the Companies Acts of 1862 to 1907.

The memorandum and Articles of Association were prepared and approved, and the first Directors and Ordinary Governors of the new company were The Rt. Hon. Earl Bathurst, the Rt. Hon. Viscount Cobham, the Rt. Hon. Lord Moreton, Sir John Dorington, Bt., Col. T.W. Chester Master, Col. J.F. Curtis Hayward, H.J. Bailey, A.F. Somerville, JP and Col. W.E. Carne Currie.

The full new Governing Body comprised: an Hereditary Governor, Earl Bathurst, and the Ordinary Governors; of the Representative Governors three were appointed by Gloucestershire County Council, one each by the County Councils of Herefordshire, Monmouthshire, Somerset, Wiltshire and Worcestershire, the University of Oxford, the Royal Agricultural Society of England, and the Bath and West of England Agricultural Society, and one by the University of Bristol and West of England.

★

The College Governors had, after intense discussion and with bankruptcy looming over them, reconstituted the College and taken up a stance which would enable it to be eligible for aid from the State and to work in close cooperation with the local education authorities, as well as leaving the door open for affiliation with either Oxford or Bristol Universities. As McClellan put it, on Prize Day 29 July 1908, the 'Old College' came to an end. He retired with honour, following a final Governors' meeting and a dinner and presentation from the staff and students. The possibility of a long period of stability with expansion beckoned.

Chapter Six

A FRESH START THEN CLOSURE, 1908–22

From 1845 till now the R.A.C. has carried on . . . without any assistance from government . . . [which] has placed [it] at a great disadvantage. . . .

Letter from the Governors to the President of the Board of Agriculture, 1908

On 27 January 1908 a public meeting had been held at the King's Head Hotel Assembly Rooms, Cirencester, to tell agriculturalists of the district of the arrangements then in progress for the reorganization of the College in order to secure recognition by the Board of Agriculture and to obtain grants from that department. Earl Bathurst, CMG took the chair.

The meeting was addressed by J.C. Medd, who must have had a sense of satisfaction that his efforts had reached fruition given the cooperation of the County Council and the impending changes. His address gave a clear account of the situation of the College leading up to the very necessary reorganization:

The facts are simple. For many years the Board of Agriculture have been endeavouring to place the agricultural education of the country upon a systematic and organised basis. With the exception of the Western counties, of which Gloucestershire forms one, this is being gradually accomplished. . . . More definite steps were taken last year by the appointment of a Departmental Committee, which is still sitting, to inquire into and report upon the whole condition of agricultural education. . . . As at present constituted, the Royal Agricultural College, being under private control, is ineligible for any financial aid from the Board. It alone of the great agricultural colleges had never received one penny of public money, a fact which those familiar with its splendid record, covering a period of more than sixty years, can hardly credit.

In reality, those familiar with the financial record of the College would certainly have credited it!

Medd then went on to set out the scheme of reconstruction and said,

> [The] scheme has been prepared, submitted to and approved by the Board of
> Agriculture. The Board has characterised the scheme as a 'good' one, and did
> not desire its modification in a single particular. In effect, the sole organic
> change introduced by that scheme is to create a representative Governing
> Body. . . . No suggestion has been ever made, or even hinted at, by which the
> social and educational status or the prestige of the College can be lowered in
> the slightest degree. . . . The intention is, and the result will be, to strengthen
> its position, to increase its usefulness, and to widen its sphere of influence.

Medd extolled the virtues of the teaching at the College in comparison with
other colleges, noting the financial assistance they received in relation to the
numbers of students taught, and drew the conclusion that Cirencester was well in
the van.

While the speech was somewhat eulogistic, this was probably not without
foundation, for those responsible for the negotiations with the County Council
and with the Board of Agriculture – the retiring Chairman of the Governing
Body, the active Governors, the retiring Principal and Medd – had effectively
achieved all that they had set out to do and had done so without altering the
standards of the College teaching, nor of the entry qualifications. Essentially they
had rescued the College from collapse and closure. More than that, by establishing the association with the County Council, 'the benefits of the Royal
Agricultural College were to be placed within the reach of the sons of Gloucestershire farmers', said W.H. Tremaine, a member of the County Agricultural
Committee. This would, to some extent, return the College to its original
objective to provide training for the sons of tenant farmers.

Concurrent with the work of the reconstruction scheme, the Governors had
the vital task of selecting a Principal to replace McClellan. This time there was no
immediately suitable candidate, either on the staff as in the case of the
appointment of McClellan or, as in the case of Constable, someone known to the
outgoing Principal and out of the same stable.

So the Governors, for the first time, decided to advertise. On 25 January 1908
an advertisement was placed in most of the leading agricultural journals. The
terms were simple and straightforward:

'1. The New Principal must be an active member of the Teaching Staff, and fully
qualified as such.' This restated the strongly held view of the Governors that the
Principal should teach as well as manage; it was the cause of the disagreement
with McClellan.

'2. The salary will be a fixed sum of £600 per annum with capitation fees, in
addition, of £3 for each In-Student amd £1 for each Out-Student respectively,
reckoned on the average numbers per annum. Residence provided rent free, with
up-keep of garden, gas, rates, and taxes.

3. The Appointment will be subject to a written agreement, containing ordinary conditions in such cases.'

In answer to this advertisement thirty-one candidates applied for the post. This was whittled down to nine to be invited for interview. There was a high standard of academic attainment among these, and it is worth noting that there were five members of Trinity College, Cambridge, in the selection list. So it looked as though the long-enduring association with this college might be continued. Most of the candidates had first-class degrees, though the selection committee did include two qualified as land agents and one as a veterinary surgeon. For the majority the principal disciplines studied and practised were scientific. This was indeed a change from the disciplines held by the previous incumbents.

The post was offered to James Richard Ainsworth-Davis, the Head of the Zoology and Geology Departments at the University of Wales, which post included the teaching and direction of work in the Department of Agriculture. He was also Examiner in Natural History to the College of Preceptors and a member of the Court of Governors, Council and Senate of the University of Wales. Ainsworth-Davis had received his scientific education at the Royal School of Mines and had graduated from Trinity College, Cambridge. At South Kensington he had studied Biology under Professor Huxley, and Geology under Professor Judd, and obtained First Classes in both subjects in 1880. At Cambridge

James R. Ainsworth-Davis, Principal 1908–15

he obtained First Classes in both parts of the Natural Sciences Tripos, 1882 to 1884, Zoology and Geology being his special subjects. He had been head of the departments at Aberystwyth for twenty-four years, and for ten years was also responsible for the Department of Botany. He had as well been Dean of the Faculty of Science for the previous three years. The College had indeed appointed a man of very high academic standing, in keeping with the appointments made since the earliest Principals and, once again, a product of Trinity College, Cambridge.

Professor Ainsworth-Davis was the author of a large, popular work, *The Natural History of Animals*, of *A Text Book of Biology*, of *An Elementry Text Book of Physiology* and many other books and translations of German books. He came with glowing references. His spare time activities included raising and command-ing a University Company in the 5th Volunteer Battalion of the South Wales Borderers. He was forty-six when appointed, married with two children.

In accepting the offer of appointment Ainsworth-Davis had many immediate suggestions to put forward: these ranged from comments about the recon-struction scheme, including the composition of the Governing Body (he thought that the Principal should be an ex-officio member and that the representation should be extended to the University of Wales), and that he should not be overburdened with teaching at the expense of the necessary administrative duties. He wanted to push ahead as soon as possible with the possible association with the proposed University of Bristol and sought authority to negotiate with Principal Lloyd Morgan.

An intriguing facet of the applications for the post was that an application was received from M.J.R. Dunstan, who was not selected because he was only willing to be a candidate upon condition that the salary was raised! He was then the Principal of the South-Eastern Agricultural College at Wye and eventually did become Principal of Cirencester in 1922.

★

The first meeting of the Governors of the reconstituted College was held on 26 August 1908, when Lord Moreton was elected Chairman and the Secretary, E.B. Haygarth, was instructed to write to the public bodies to seek the appointment of Representative Governors. He was also instructed to seek an interview with the President of the Board of Agriculture by a deputation asking for grant aid.

The letter sent to the President of the Board of Agriculture, the Rt. Hon. Earl Carrington, set out briefly the situation of the College and the reasons for applying for grant aid:

My Lord
  We, the undersigned, being either Governors of the Royal Agricultural College, Cirencester, or persons desirous of seeing that College as useful a

centre of instruction in Agriculture, Forestry, and allied subjects as possible, beg respectfully to adduce for Your Lordship's consideration the following statement, upon which we base a claim for participation in the annual grant made by Parliament for the aid of Universities, Colleges, and other institutions providing instruction in the subjects before mentioned.

(1) The R.A.C. was founded by Royal Charter in 1845 with a capital of £24,000, afterwards increased. H.R.H. the late Prince Consort was the first patron, and acquired the first five shares. Since then the College has been successively under the patronage of the late Queen Victoria, H.R.H. Prince Albert Edward of Wales, and H.M. King Edward VII. In March 1880 H.M. the late Queen Victoria was graciously pleased to command that the Institution be styled the 'Royal' Agricultural College.

From 1845 till now the R.A.C. has carried on its work without any assistance from government or other public funds, and the foundation during the last 20 years of numerous state-aided Agricultural Colleges and University Departments of Agriculture has placed the R.A.C. at a great disadvantage, private generosity alone having saved it from complete collapse.

During the years 1845–1908 several thousands of students have been educated at the College, and many of these occupy, or have occupied, prominent positions in the United Kingdom, the Colonies, the Empire of India, and elsewhere.

(2) Your Lordship's Department was recently approached by the Governors of the College with the view of obtaining a grant in aid. They received the answer that as an Institution ostensibly designed for the profit of shareholders such a grant was impossible, but that if reorganised and placed under public control the College would cease to be technically disqualified.

(3) The College has now been reorganised, and by a Memorandum under the Companies Acts 1862–1907 has become a Limited Liability Company trading without profit, under the name of the 'Royal Agricultural College, Cirencester,' the word 'Limited' being omitted by license of the Board of Trade, and permission being accorded by the Home Office to retain the prefix 'Royal'.

A copy of the said Memorandum dated 11.8.08, is submitted with this Memorial.

(4) There are at the present time 67 students classified under the following headings:–

United Kingdom	52
Empire of India	8
Dependency of Egypt	3
Friendly Powers	4

Of these 28 are freshmen representing the largest winter entry since 1883, with the single exception of 1899.

(5) Among the chief advantages offered to students of the R.A.C. are –

(a) The position of the College in an area noted for high farming and stock-keeping, in immediate proximity to the extensive woodlands within the park of the Earl Bathurst.

(b) The possession of over 50 acres of land, upon which experiments of various kinds can be and are being carried out.

(c) The existence of a College Farm of about 500 acres of which the tenant is an old student, Mr Russell Swanwick, who is under covenant to afford all reasonable facilities to the students of the College for the study of modern methods of farming. The students are therefore able to see how farming can be carried out at a profit, and Mr Swanwick has a well known reputation as a breeder of Cotteswold sheep, Berkshire swine and thoroughbred horses.

(d) Possession not only of the usual scientific laboratories and museum, but also a botanic garden, a Kitchen garden, a properly equipped dairy, all available for instructional purposes.

(e) Unique facilities for the study of Forestry, in the form of a Forest Nursery, a Forest Garden, and the privilege of studying forestry opera-tions on the estates of the Earl Bathurst, the Earl of Ducie, the Marquis of Bath, the Lord Fitzhardinge, Colonel Holford, and crown property in the Forest of Dean.

(f) It may be added that the social life of the College is strongly developed in all directions.

(6) The RAC sets before itself the following programme, but the extent to which this can be carried out will entirely depend upon the funds available:–

(a) Research in all applied subjects, also upon Heredity, Variation, Mendelism and other matters which have both a theoretical and practical bearing.

(b) It is hoped and expected that the RAC will be fully recognised by the University of Bristol, now in course of foundation, as the College of Agriculture and Forestry for that University, where degree courses in these subjects will be given.

(c) Continuance of the work in Agriculture and Forestry for students of the land-owning class, and those desiring to become estate-agents, or to take up the various positions in the colonies and the Empire of India. Such students may either take a Diploma Course of 7 (or more) terms, or may pursue a short curriculum, according to their special requirements. Students of the kind indicated necessarily play a prominent part in determining the destinies of Agriculture and Forestry in the United Kingdom, the colonies and the empire.

(d) Co-operation with the County Councils of Gloucester and such other adjacent counties as may choose to be affiliated in local experiments and classes, and in the education of county scholars and short course students. Two Gloucestershire county scholars have already been admitted as out-students on favourable terms, and the winter course initiated this year for the sons of tenant farmers will be repeated in 1909.

(e) The establishment of Saturday and summer classes for the benefit of teachers, more particularly in connection with the important movement in regard to Rural Education, which is now held to be of primary value.
(f) The establishment of a Bureau of Information for the benefit of those concerned with Agriculture and Forestry in the West of England.

We are confident that Your Lordship will give full weight to the above statement, details regarding which will gladly be furnished, and we venture to hope that grants in aid will be made to the R.A.C. under three separate headings:

1. Agriculture.
2. College experimental area and College Farm
3. Forestry

We have the honour to remain,
My lord,
Your Obedient Servants,

Ducie
Bathurst
John E. Dorrington
J.F. Curtis Hayward
Edward Currie
Henry J. Bailey
Moreton
Cobham

J.W. Chester Master
Arthur F. Somerville
R.D. Cumberland-Jones
J.R. Ainsworth-Davis
E.B. Haygarth

★

This resulted in an inspection by officials of the Boards of Agriculture and Education at the beginning of 1909. They expressed satisfaction at the progress made since reorganization and at their request the financial year was changed to correspond with the academic year. Eventually application was made for grant aid and the Board of Agriculture intimated their intention of making regular grants to the College as from July 1909. This turned out to be an annual grant of £1,200, the first payment being made in 1910. So at long last the College had received its first support from public funds. Another Special Forestry Grant was obtained from the Treasury; £1,000 per annum from the Development Fund for Scientific Research Instruction and Experiments in Agriculture and Forestry.

One other result of the reorganization scheme which was very necessary was the granting by the Earl Bathurst of a new lease of ninety-nine years of the College buildings and the forty acres of land still held by the College at the same rent as then paid, namely £225 per year, in place of the existing lease which had about thirty-six years to run, but at the expiration of the period of that lease the rent would be increased to £400 per year. He also renewed the covenant

presided, and was supported by Mr Edward Holland, the Hon. C. Carnegie, M.P., Professor (afterwards Sir) George Brown, Professor Coleman (diploma 1848, Professor of Agriculture at the College from 1856 to 1862 and honorary secretary of the Old Students' Club), Professor Buckman, Mr R. Grenfell, Mr Henry Tanner (the first diploma student of the College), Mr Jacob Wilson, and Mr Edmund Ruck. The reason for this large gathering was probably the fact that the College was going through a somewhat exciting period. About $2\frac{1}{2}$ years before, the former Principal, the Revd J.S. Haygarth, had died, and had been succeeded in 1860 by the Revd John Constable, whose policy had aroused some friction both among staff and students. Indeed, there was a general change in the staff about this time, Professors Voelcker, Coleman, Buckman and Brown all left soon after the Chelsea dinner, although Dr. Voelcker's resignation was the only one alluded to in the speeches as actually imminent. . . .

This very mild reference to the dramatic events of 1860 to 1879 confirms the fact that matters had now passed into the history of the College and the effects had now vanished.

The report continued: 'In proposing the toast of the College coupled with the name of Mr Tanner, Dr Voelcker stated the aims and objects of the Club. He said:– "The object of these annual gatherings is plain and simple. It is to enjoy ourselves once a year, to see each other's faces, and to exchange a hearty welcome." '

Much of the rest of this report concentrated on the lives and work of Henry Tanner and of the Principal before 1860, the Revd J.S. Haygarth, also mentioning Allen Harker, one time Professor of Natural History, all of whose lives and times are described in earlier chapters. From this time onwards the dinners were continued, for many years there being two a year, one at the time of the 'Smithfield Show' and the other in 'Royal Show' week, the former being in London and the latter moving around as the 'Royal' then did. Once the 'Royal' settled at Park Royal in London for the time being the Old Students' club dinner also settled in London and only one dinner was held, in Smithfield Week.

★

During the later period of McClellan's time and throughout the Principalship of Ainsworth-Davis one of the outstanding members of the staff was Professor Edward Kinch, a successor to the many eminent holders of the Chair of Chemistry. He was appointed to the post in May 1881 and held it until 1915. His association with the College was, however, longer than this for he was Chief Assistant to the Professor of Chemistry from 1869 to 1873. So his time at the College spanned three Principals – Constable, McClellan and Ainsworth-Davis. He was one of the two (McBride was the other) from Cirencester who went to

Edward Kinch,
Professor of
Chemistry
1881–1915

Japan following the visit of Professor Tajori Tamita in 1870. He died in 1920 aged seventy-one.

One of Kinch's first assistants, from 1890 to 1893, was James Kendrick. From the College Kendrick went on to Aberdeen to be appointed in 1911 to the newly created Chair of Agriculture at the University, which he occupied for thirty years. He was another who, along with Wilson and Wallace, left the College to become a leading figure in Scottish agricultural education.

While Kinch was Professor of Chemistry there was appointed to the post of Assistant to the Department of Natural History one Reginald George Stapledon. Stapledon was to become the pioneer of grassland development in the United Kingdom and in New Zealand and was more responsible than any other man for the greater prosperity of the hill farming areas through better strains of grasses and utilization of the natural grasses upon which so much of the livestock production of the country depended. His name is synonymous with the Welsh Plant Breeding Station at Aberystwyth. Shortly after his appointment Ainsworth-Davis had split off Botany from the Department of Natural History to form a new Department of Botany and put Stapledon in charge. It was then that he began an association with Kinch which was to become the start of his interest in grassland. This association is described in the *Biographical Memoirs of Fellows of the Royal Society*, Vol. 7, November 1961:

Reginald G.
Stapledon (later Sir),
Assistant to the
Department of
Natural History

Years afterwards Stapledon said that he owed the beginning of his interest in grasssland to Kinch, the outstanding figure on the staff at that time, and the type of man to whom Stapledon would certainly be drawn. He was a native of the region, born 61 years earlier at Faringdon, only 18 miles away, soaked in knowledge of country lore and much else – 'ask Kinch' was usually the answer to a difficult question – 'a fascinating companion on a country walk' as one of his pupils, Lord Bledisloe, described him, also a keen gardener. Mellowed by a great sorrow in early days, when after a year of happy marriage he had lost his young wife, he was deeply interested in his students and young colleagues and always ready to help them. He had first come to the College in 1869 as Assistant in the Chemical Department, but left four years later for a short spell in London; then in 1876 he went to Japan as Professor of Chemistry at the Imperial College of Agriculture, Komaba, Tokyo. Westernisation was only just beginning: he had known the old Japan and had brought back with him some examples of Japanese art and crafts which he delighted to show his visitors. He had returned to Cirencester in 1881.

He was well versed in the Rothamstead investigations and had in 1888 started a repetition on a smaller scale of the Park Grass experiments on the manuring of permanent grass for hay, the same treatment being given year after year to each plot so that the effects were cumulative. At Rothamstead not only weights of hay were taken, but the botanical analyses were made also. Hitherto this had been impracticable at Cirencester and Kinch now asked Stapledon to undertake it.

This was the beginning of [Stapledon's] association with grassland.

From this Stapledon extended his studies of Cotswold pastures and of the effects of environment in determining the vegetation type. In his stay at Cirencester he classified grass types and searched for hardy, indigenous plants. The *Biographical Memoirs* continue:

He [Stapledon] was obviously happy at Cirencester. He was much liked by the students and mingled with them a good deal, joining in their Tennis, concerts and other activities: 'he seemed too young,' one of them wrote, 'to be regarded as a don to be revered'. He would put up a notice to the effect that on Sunday afternoon he was going for a country walk and any student that would like to join him would be welcome. These walks became very popular and the students were greatly impressed by his power of keen observation, 'with his eyes on the ground to identify every blade of grass, even when not in flower'.

He stayed three years at Cirencester: they were crucial years of his life: it was there that he found his life's work. He had been a late starter, but he came within the spirit of his old Headmaster's well-remembered dictum and was one of the best enders.

Stapledon left to become a botanical adviser at the University College of Wales at Aberystwyth, under Professor C. Bryner Jones. His experimental work prospered and he became the first Director of the Welsh Plant Breeding Station at Aberystwyth. Stapledon's acknowledged pre-eminence in the field of grassland improvement has been more fully described elsewhere.

The association with Kinch was clearly a fruitful one and Kinch can be credited with giving this hard-working and brilliant young man encouragement and his head. The reference to Stapledon's relation with students must apply equally to Kinch. No less popular for inculcating in the student mind the need to deploy the critical faculties, notable in the powers of observation, he, too, took an active interest and participation in the sporting activies of the College. For practically the whole of his time he was the Chairman of the Sports Committee, using his influence to obtain facilities for the many burgeoning games and sports. Kinch was virtually a one-man extension service, his advice being sought by practitioners from near and afar. 'Ask Kinch' was indeed a by-word during his time.

How lucky were the students at the turn of the century to have men such as Kinch and Stapledon to guide them!

★

By the initiative of Ainsworth-Davis a summer school was held at the College starting on 14 August 1911 and lasting for three weeks. This innovation was for the benefit of secondary schoolteachers in Gloucestershire and other counties. It followed a very successful series of lectures on Nature Study by Ainsworth-Davis. That these teachers were prepared to give up their time during holidays when other other outdoor occupations were more attractive demonstrated the popularity of the lectures. Ainsworth-Davis's motive behind the summer school was his belief that there was a need for the various elements of rural education to complement one another, especially those relating to farmers' sons, the greater number of whom were educated in the rural elementary schools. Since the elementary schoolteachers were scattered over the counties and had little opportunity to meet to discuss methods and to achieve some degree of correlation, to bring them together at a summer school would go some way towards achieving his objectives. In fact, Ainsworth-Davis had made a close study of rural education, seeing it as an essential groundwork for further education for those who would enter farming.

College Beagle
c. 1910

His first lecture to the summer school students gave a wide-ranging résumé of the present situation of British agriculture, having first told his audience that, 'the College staff hoped to learn as much from the summer school as they taught, for it was extraordinarily interesting to come into close connection with men engaged in important teaching duties in different counties, and those present could rest assured that his colleagues and himself would pump them for all they were worth'. His speech made reference to the amount of foodstuffs that Great Britain imported and to the stiff competition that the farmer faced in the market place for the sale of his produce. He expounded on his ideas about rural education, emphasizing that as Principal of an agricultural college it was important that he did not operate in a watertight compartment. They were all there at the summer school in the interests of, to use his word, 'correlation'. It was necessary that they should work together. He was pleased to see that the attendance came from nine counties: Wiltshire, Gloucestershire, Somerset, Worcestershire, Buckinghamshire, Warwickshire, Derbyshire, Norfolk and Sussex.

A significant development in rural education came in January 1912 when it was announced that the new scheme for administering the money devoted to agricultural education would allow the whole control to pass to the Board of Agriculture instead of being divided between that Department and the Board of Education. Ainsworth-Davis commented in public that this was the most important and sensible thing that had appeared for a long time in connection with agricultural education. Others, too, welcomed this new arrangement. It was not unnatural that those concerned with the teaching of agriculture and related subjects should welcome that the responsibility for financial support from the government should be handled by one instead of two departments, though whether Cirencester would ultimately benefit remained to be seen. For other institutions, for example, the South-Eastern Agricultural College, Wye, there might be little change. As the Principal of that College, M.J.R. Dunstan, said at the time, the College was maintained by the County Councils of Kent and Surrey for agricultural education and research work, and also affiliated with London University and therefore already came under the supervision of the Board of Agriculture. But, he said, it would at least simplify the procedure regarding applications for a grant from the Development Fund. For the RAC the move would probably be an advantgeous one since the Board of Agriculture would not be under the restrictions it had suffered and which had caused the College to make separate applications to each of the government departments.

Later on, in 1913, a full inspection of the College was made by inspectors of the Board of Agriculture and Fisheries. This comprehensive report was one of the first since the College became eligible to receive the government grant. It outlined the history of the College and set out the aims and objects of the reorganized College:
1. To train, as heretofore, landowners, estate agents, surveyors, and intending colonists in agriculture, forestry and allied subjects.

2. To provide instruction for county council scholars in the above subjects.

3. To give short courses for sons of tenant farmers.

4. To inaugurate classes for teachers in nature study and similiar subjects.

5. To cooperate with the associated county councils in their educational and experimental work.

6. To serve as a bureau of information for the agriculturalists of the West of England.

7. To prosecute original research in agriculture, agricultural chemistry, forestry and allied subjects.

These aims and objects were, then, the outcome of all the negotiations that had gone before, pursued by the Governors with J.C. Medd taking a leading role, in order to rescue the College from extinction by obtaining money from the government in exchange for a different constitution of the College and a wider role within the sphere of county council rural education and extension. Also, one can detect the hand of Ainsworth-Davis in item four.

In general the inspectors were well satisfied with the administration, the standard of teaching and the facilities provided. Their criticisms were moderate. They wished to see the Governors taking a more active interest in the working of the College and that the Finance and Emergency Committee should hold regular meetings and exercise a more active control over the finances of the College. So far as the educational accommodation was concerned they wished to see rather more equipment, though what was there was adequate. The residential accommodation was also noted as convenient and comfortable with one exception: the heating. This applied also to the lecture rooms and laboratories. One visualizes the students and their teachers well protected in thick, woollen clothes – indeed, a glimpse at the photographs of the time reveals the Norfolk jackets, waistcoats, breeches and leggings for the students and the frock coats and beards for the staff! The College has, throughout its time (or at least until very recent times when an efficient central heating system has been installed) had a reputation for operating in winter at the fringe of discomfort and visitors were usually advised to wrap up well! Perhaps successive Principals have believed in reproducing the conditions of the bleakest farm as part of the practical training!

No criticisms were to be made of the farm and of the forestry training: they were obviously regarded as entirely adequate. Some minor improvements to the numbers of staff were suggested and the courses were accepted as satisfactory except for the regulations governing the curriculum for students given exemption as intermediate degree holders from the first year of the Diploma course.

Considering the very detailed nature of the report it was to be regarded as a highly satisfactory acceptance of the College as an agricultural teaching establishment and, when the extreme difficulties with which the College was faced since the turn of the century are noted, it can only be to the credit of McClellan in setting the foundations for improvement and of Ainsworth-Davis in implementing all that was required to achieve this recognition, not forgetting the resolution of the Governors in turning round the constitution of the College.

In 1911 the Principal reported, at the RAC Old Students' Club dinner, that compared with an entry of between forty-six to forty-eight students in 1908, before the reconstruction, there were now some eighty in College and that the College had entered upon a new lease of useful and vigorous life. There was now a substantial annual grant-in-aid from the Board of Agriculture, and there was the expectation of benefiting to an appreciable extent by the establishment of the Development Fund. Over two hundred students had received instruction, or were receiving instruction since 1908. They had come from thirty-one English counties, from Wales, Scotland, Ireland and many foreign countries. He felt that the College was both a local and imperial concern. About 75 per cent of the students had been the sons of landowners, farmers, land agents and others connected with the land, and about 90 per cent of them had engaged or purposed to engage in the management of land. He said:

Though the bulk of the valuable research work of the College was done in the palmy days of the past it was hoped there would be a recrudescence of it in the future . . . of course the College as now existing and equipped was not equal to the requirements of the extended work we were now doing and had in contemplation, and a building scheme for erecting a new block of modern lecture rooms, laboratories, and departmental museums, and for improving the veterinary hospital and workshops was now being promoted, and an advance from the Development Fund had been asked for that purpose. A sum of at least £10,000 was necessary for building and equipment. . . .

The Governors commenced an appeal for donations to the Building Extension Fund, as the Development Commissioners had promised to advance £5,000 and another £5,000 was needed. The funds promised were on condition that the College worked in conjunction with the University of Bristol under a scheme approved by the Board of Agriculture, and that the balance of the sum required to complete the buildings should be obtained by subscriptions and donations from outside sources, and not be raised by the College itself as a loan. We shall see this limitation being applied again in 1935 when the then Principal, Boutflour, sought to obtain grants for new laboratories. By April 1913 some £2,548 had been given or promised and the Appeal Committee, consisting of Lord Moreton, Earl Bathurst, Mr H.J. Elwes, Mr F.W.B. Cripps, the Principal and the Secretary, was redoubling its efforts, for the target was now not just the £5,000 to supplement the money promised by the Development Fund but was to be enough to build a new wing. It was hoped that enough would be donated to enable the erection of a large hall – suitable for public meetings, to serve as a gymnasium and drill hall (in connection with the Senior Officers' Training Corps) – and a library.

A meeting was held at Crewe House, Curzon Street, Mayfair, by invitation of the Marquess of Crewe, to raise money for what was now called 'the Extension and Equipment Fund'. By far the bulk of support came from old students and from Governors. Since its foundation there were now many of those students who had either risen to high office or to inherited wealth and there were many from the countries of the British Empire who had similiarly acquired status and wealth. As Mr C. Bathurst (later Lord Bledisloe) said, 'He hoped the Principal would perservere with his suggestion for endowing some of the chairs of the College, and that he could find some rich former students who might help in that work. He often remembered with amusement that during his own College days an Indian student to whom he gave some slight assistance in work offered to present him with seven villages in India as a reward for his help. He hoped that it would be possible to trace that Indian student and secure those seven villages as a contribution to the present effort.'

But it is clear from the papers relating to this appeal and to the speeches in support, that the predominant motive for supporting this plea for financial help was that of loyalty and fondness for, as it was so often referred to, 'the dear old College'. Perhaps it was the Victorian propensity for somewhat overemphasized sentimentality that lingered on in the days of the new century, but it is without doubt that, ever since its foundation, the Royal Agricultural College had generated this spirit of loyalty.

By August 1913 the Appeal Fund had reached £3,329, and a Special Committee of old students issued a special appeal to supplement that of the Governors. By July 1914 this figure had increased to £4,147.

The annual show of the Royal Agricultural Society of England was held at Bristol between 1 and 5 July 1913 and the Governors took the opportunity to send a deputation to present a loyal address to the Patron of the College, King George V. This referred to the proposed building extension. Prompted, no doubt through the right circles, the reply included consent for the College to name the new wing 'King Edward's Wing' in commemoration of that monarch's visit to the College in 1895. Needless to say, this gracious gesture was made public to encourage support for the Appeal!

★

Mention was made earlier of the long-serving records of some of the staff, notable among the professors, at least after the wholesale dismissals in the time of Constable. This characteristic of the College was maintained at lower levels. In 1913 there was reported the death of William James at sixty-eight years of age and a member of the staff for forty-nine years. He entered the chemistry laboratory as second assistant at the time that Dr J.C.A. Voelcker left the College, i.e. in 1862. He remained as an exceedingly able and trustworthy assistant and friend to succeeding professors, namely to Church for sixteen years, and afterwards to Dr

E.W. Prevost, and then for thirty-one years to Kinch. His obituary notice in the *Agricultural Students' Gazette* read:

> To many generations of students (to the earliest he was known as 'Tom') he endeared himself by his invariable courtesy and inexhaustible patience in explaining difficulties and helping students out of troubles, as well as by his all round knowledge of his subject. . . . His loss will be long felt not only by his near relations but by many friends, and by generation of R.A.C. students and members of the Staff. He owed most of his preliminary training in manipulation and analytical processes to the late Robert Warington, F.R.S., to whom he was an apt pupil, and he became an accomplished and conscientious analyst.

A Memorial Fund was raised and a sum of £289 collected. This was vested in trustees for the benefit of the family; a typewriter was bought for one of the daughters (he had eight children), the rent of his house paid for the time being and the remainder invested. One supposes that in those days no pension as such was paid and it seems a modest recompense for long years of devoted service.

★

In November 1913 a fire broke out in the College and seriously damaged the West Wing. It was described many years later (in 1948, in fact) by A.C. Duncan, one of the longest serving of the College academic staff:

> It arose in a private room at the top of a small staircase at the north end of the west dormitory corridor, and was first discovered by a cleaner.
> These cleaners . . . were all women, and presumably, like the 'bedders' in certain Oxford colleges, were appointed for being 'women of evil countenance'. However, the truth of this was not easy to discover because they wore on all occasions vast sun bonnets which tended to obscure their faces. On this occasion the cleaner who attended the room found the door locked, and smoke issuing from underneath it. As the occupant was missing it was feared that his charred remains would be found inside, so the door was burst open, when flames and smoke prevented any attempt at rescue . . . the occupant was not inside but had made up a large fire before going into town.

The Agriculture and Physics lecture rooms were completely destroyed, together with practically all the engineering and physical apparatus, drawing boards and materials, building construction diagrams and the Agriculture and Forestry lecture diagrams. In addition, the in-students' common room and billiard room were rendered uninhabitable. The fire endangered the chemical

The aftermath
1913 fire in whi
now the Landr
Room

laboratory (the tithe barn) and threatened the out-students' room and the chapel but was brought under control in time. The conflagration, for such it was, happened in the evening when the students were at dinner. In addition to the Cirencester Fire Brigade four other brigades were summoned, from Tetbury, Gloucester, Stroud and Malmesbury and all were needed to put out the flames, together with the willing assistance of the students. It must have been a very dramatic event and one can visualize the students and firemen milling around the scene. One student spied a looter making off with his spoils and chased him with a forestry axe! Fortunately he dropped the stolen property before suffering the descent of the axe!

Coming at the time when the College was appealing for funds in order to extend it was essential that the costs of restoring the buildings damaged were met by insurance. In the event this was so and the restoration works included a new laboratory for Zoology and Veterinary Sciences.

By July 1914 the total sum received for the Appeal was £4,147, still short of the £5,000 necessary in order to claim the Treasury £5,000 and make a total of £10,000, and far short of the larger figure that the Principal was hoping for. But the rebuilding after the fire had nearly been completed and would be ready for the Michaelmas Term.

But with the threat of war becoming prevalent students numbers began to drop. From the small but flourishing Officers' Training Corps students were joining the Forces and potential students were responding to this need to serve their country. By December 1914, with the War in progress since August and four months after a dedication ceremony of brasses in the College chapel to honour the memory of two benefactors and two students (one of the latter had fallen for his country at Isandhiwana, in the South African War), there was talk of another memorial fund which would be needed to honour the names of students and staff fallen and who were to fall in the new, greater war. The July 1915 issue of the *Agricultural Students' Gazette* had in it a Roll of Honour with 307 names of past and present students serving with HM Forces. It included four Governors and four members of staff. The majority, by far, were junior officers in infantry-line regiments and we know now that the casualty rate would far more than decimate the ranks of these volunteers. Already there were twenty-one notified as killed in action or as having died after being wounded.

Among those killed was Lieutenant Russell Kenneth Swanwick, the third son of the tenant of the College farm. The Professor of Veterinary Science, A.C. Duncan (he who had ridden by bicycle with Edward Blundell in moonlight over Salisbury Plain!), was now a lieutenant in the Army Veterinary Corps. M. Kershaw, 2nd Lieutenant, 1st Battn., Gloucester Regiment, who had been a lecturer in Physics and was OC of the College OTC, had been posted missing in November 1914 and was reported by the German Red Cross as dead. Several Governors were serving: the Earl Bathurst (Hereditary Governor), Charles Bathurst as a captain in the Royal Monmouth RE, F.W.B. Cripps, and the Hon. Hicks Beach in the Royal Gloucestershire Hussars Yeomanry and J. Penberthy. They were all to be the first of many students, staff and Governors who volunteered to serve their country.

Because of the fact that students were mainly recruited from the classes which supplied the bulk of officers to both of the services, the numbers at the College and of those who might enter the College in the future was quickly down by about 60 per cent. The development proposals for the construction of King Edward's Wing had to be postponed.

The financial position was, as it had so often been in the past, rendered immediately critical by this inexorable falling off of students and potential students as well as of the younger staff. At the commencement of the 1914/15 session a meeting of the Governors was attended by a Mr Bruce of the Ministry of Agriculture who explained that the Treasury had definitely consented to provide financial assistance to the College, in difficulty because of the war. It was decided to carry on for at least another term and to ask subscribers to the Building Fund if their subscriptions could be used as a guarantee to the bank until it was known to what extent the Government would assist, or whether it might be used to pay off the College debts.

A sum of £1,500 was eventually received from the Treasury's Emergency Fund, but the College was informed that the annual grant of £1,200 would not be paid. This was indeed the final straw and on 3 July, at a meeting of the bondholders, the Chairman, Lord Moreton reported that the number of students had fallen from seventy to twenty, that the finances were such that the current assets of the College would be sufficient to discharge the current liabilities on receipt of the £1,500 and that Lord Bathurst would waive payment of the rent during the closing of the College. He therefore put forward the proposition that the College be closed for the duration of the war. All bondholders were written to obtain authority for the closure.

Since the foundation of the Royal Agricultural College it had faced and overcome many crises of funds and of confidence and it was now only due to the overwhelming external circumstances that the doors were closed to those seeking agricultural education.

The July 1915 issue of the *Agricultural Students' Gazette* recorded the melancholy fact of closure:

> It is our painful duty to inform our readers that since it has been decided to close the College until the termination of the war, it will be necessary to suspend the issue of the *Gazette* during this period; and this is particularly unfortunate as our Magazine is just celebrating its fortieth year of existence.
>
> The *Agricultural Students' Gazette* was started . . . in April 1875, the originators being the Hon Roger Gordon Molyneaux, Mr Pierce Mahoney, and Mr J. A. Macononchy. Their object as stated in the 'Prefatory' was – 'to awaken more than a transient interest in some few, at least, of the many who look with favour on an institution in which the motto of "Practice with Science" has been adopted with considerable success.'

This last edition contained also the sad facts of the deaths of E. B. Haygarth, the Secretary of the Royal Agricultural College, and of Sir Arthur Church, the Professor of Chemistry dismissed by Constable.

Edward Brownlow Haygarth was actually born at the College on 26 April 1854, his father being John Sayer Haygarth, the Principal from 1851 to 1859. Haygarth had qualified as a solicitor, returned to Cirencester as partner to his relative, Charles William Lawrence, and succeeded him as Secretary to the College. It was he who had helped to steer the College through the legal thickets of the reorganization and the obstacle course of obtaining government assistance, ultimately so successfully. Haygarth was a staunch supporter of the College, not only professionally, but also on the sporting and social side. Field sports were his first love and he was also a keen and proficient player of team sports, football and cricket, as well as golf. He maintained the reputation of the College for producing sportsmen of high standard for he was an international at Association Football and captain of the Cirencester Cricket Club from 1891 to 1889; he also played for

Gloucestershire. He was a founder member of the Cirencester Golf Club and captain for several years. He took part in local affairs being Chairman of the Urban District Council for many years. He helped in the establishment of the Bingham Public Library in Cirencester.

★

Winding down the College involved letting off the thirty-three acres of farmland to Mr Stewart, the Dairy and Poultry Manager, for the duration of the war at a rent of £70 per annum. The sale of live and dead stock realized £676 which was invested in war loan. The College itself, together with the Principal's house, the kitchen garden, cricket field, outbuildings and grounds, including the Stroud road lodge, was let to a girls' school, Milton Court College, needing to move away from the south coast. The rent paid was £500 per annum.

The staff were disbanded; in the last issue of the prospectus, the 1914/15 War Issue, the staff were:
1. Principal –
   Prof. J.R. Ainsworth-Davis, MA (Trin. Coll. Camb.), FCP.
2. Agriculture, Dairy Farming and Poultry Farming –
   Prof. Drysdale Turner, MSEAC, PASI.
   Also Prof. of Agriculture at the University of Bristol.
3. Dairy and Poultry Manager and Lecturer –
   Charles D. Stewart NDD.
4. Estate Management and Forestry –
   Prof. H.A. Pritchard, FSI.
5. Chemistry –
   Prof. E. Kinch, FIC, FCS.
6. Land Surveying, Estate Engineering and Drawing –
   Prof. W.A. Thain, AMICE.
7. Botany –
   C.B. Saunders, B.Sc.
8. Veterinary Science and Bacteriology –
   Prof. A.C. Duncan, FRCVS (Dean of Residence).
There was a vacancy in Physics and Applied Mathematics – as mentioned M. Kershaw had joined the Gloucestershire Regiment and was killed in action in 1914. In addition fifty old students were killed in action.

Ainsworth-Davis left to become an instructor in the Army. He rose to Major and was Chairman of the Central Civilian Advisory Board at GHQ. He did not return to the College: from 1919 to 1920 he was Assistant Secretary to the Service Students' Bureau at the Board of Education and later became a lecturer in Biology at the Middlesex Hospital Medical School. He was examiner, presumably external, in Rural Economy at Oxford and in Zoology at the Universities of Edinburgh, Aberdeen and Wales. He died in 1934.

The College was in suspension: the Board of Governors met regularly during the war in anticipation of reopening as soon as possible after hostilities had ceased. In fact it was before the Armistice, on 11 March 1918, that the Governors decided to approach the Board of Agriculture to ascertain their intentions towards the College. They hoped for an early reopening, but these hopes were to be dashed.

Chapter Seven

REBUILDING WITH DUNSTAN
AND HANLEY, 1922–30

*. . . negotiations had been commenced with the University of Bristol with the
view of starting an Agricultural Degree . . .*

M.J.R. Dunstan, 1922

Reopening the College after the First World War was entirely dependent on
raising the necessary finance, for the College's assets were solely the properties on
leasehold land: the College buildings, the Principal's house, kitchen garden,
cricket field, the farm and outbuildings which had been let during the closure.

Bearing in mind that at the outbreak of war it had been seriously considered
that the College should go into liquidation, the only way that it could be opened
in 1918 was by the provision of sufficient capital for re-equipping and of income
for maintenance beyond that which student fees and farm rents would provide.
Even this might not manage the debenture debt of the College which was of the
order of £10,000.

There were only two practical means of obtaining the money. One was by way
of grant-in-aid from the Government and the other was by an appeal to debenture
holders, old students, friends and the general public.

The Governors had kept up regular meetings during the war and in March
1918, even before the Armistice and probably with the prospect of demobi-
lization in the immediate future, they decided to initiate discussions with the
Board of Agriculture.

A deputation attended at the Board which indicated that it might take over the
College for two or three years for disabled officers' training. However, the Board
decided that this would be too expensive and the idea was dropped. They did,
however, say that they were prepared to ask the Treasury for an increased grant
of £2,000 a year for two or three years and possibly a loan for capital expenditure
if the Governors were prepared to reopen the College. This was carefully
considered by the Governors who came to the conclusion that it would need
£13,000 a year to run the College in addition to the Treasury grant of £2,000 and
on a minimum of sixty students at £200 a year. They asked the Board if they

would be prepared to make a grant of £2,000 a year for a period of at least two years and guarantee the Governors against loss during the same period to the extent of a sum not exceeding £2,000, subject to their having additional representation on the Governing Body and such control over expenditure as they felt necessary. This suggestion was not accepted by the Board.

So it became necessary to look at the alternative. Lord Bledisloe took over the chairmanship at this juncture from Lord Moreton.

Charles Bathurst, later to become the first Viscount Bledisloe, (1867–1958), was a student at the College from 1893 to 1896 where he obtained his Diploma and was awarded the Ducie Gold Medal. He was editor of the *Agricultural Students' Gazette* and helped in the compilation of the students' register. (This register contained details of all staff and students from the foundation to 1897. It was subsequently maintained by Blundell up to his death in 1932, and is a very valuable document of the history of the College.)

At the time of the celebration of the jubilee of the College he was a member of the organizing committee which arranged the visit of the Prince of Wales. It was the start of a fond association with the College which lasted for his lifetime and which is cherished in the memory of the College, not just by the award of the Bledisloe Medal to distinguished old students and by the naming of one of the buildings of the College, but by the many occasions on which Lord Bledisloe

Lord Bledisloe,
Chairman of the
Governing Body
1919–29

came to the rescue of the College in hard times and by the manner in which he promoted the cause and reputation of the College throughout the world.

Bathurst practised as a Chancery barrister and conveyancer and in 1910 became Conservative Member of Parliament for the South or Wilton division of Wiltshire. His lifelong preoccupation was with agriculture: he was a founder member of the Central Landowners' Association (now the Country Landowners' Association) and he 'fathered the modern concept of landownership as a profession useful to the community, demanding specialised training to meet changed conditions'.

He was Parliamentary Secretary to the Ministry of Food from 1916 to 1917. He was appointed KBE in 1917 and created a baron in 1918. This was followed by a term as Parliamentary Secretary to the Ministry of Agriculture as a consequence of which he had to resign his chairmanship of the Governing Body. He accepted an invitation to remain an Honorary Governor.

In 1930 he was created GCMG and appointed Governor-General of New Zealand: this was the peak of a very successful career when he was accepted by the people of that predominantly agricultural country as a man who understood their needs. He was much admired, respected and liked in New Zealand for his qualities of farming knowledge and experience, his ability to communicate and his charm and diplomacy.

In the year after his arrival there was a severe earthquake, causing devastation and loss of life in Napier and Hastings. He was quickly on the spot to offer support and consolation to the victims. When the general depression of the 1930s resulted in deductions in salaries of public officials he gave up 45 per cent of his salary to share in the economies. One particular act brought gratitude from New Zealanders. He purchased privately the house at Waitangi, North Island, where the treaty of 1845 between the settlers and the Maoris had been signed, and presented it to the nation.

In 1935 he was created Viscount and travelled extensively, especially within the Commonwealth. He was honoured by many agricultural associations and societies both at home and abroad, and received an honorary D.Sc. from Bristol University and an LLD from Edinburgh University. In all his travels he never forgot to keep in touch with his old College, to promote its virtues and to extend its educational principles to all who would listen.

In 1946 Lord Bledisloe had recounted his memories of the situation the College had found itself in after the First World War:

> At the time of its Jubilee in 1895, the College was at the zenith of its prosperity and its prestige, despite the prevailing extreme agricultural depression, and these it continued to enjoy, with fluctuations of fortune, until the first World War, when, as practically all its staff and students of military age joined the armed forces, it was left empty and taken over by a Nonconformist Girls' School, driven by fear of invasion from East Anglia. The greatest crisis in its

history was reached after that War, when, in competition with other more modern colleges receiving Government and County Council grants, and faced with higher maintenance costs, and a diminution in the flow of students from other countries, it appeared hopeless to re-open and carry it on as a self supporting 'economic proposition'. The Government of the day regarded it as disentitled to any grants from the public purse, as having failed to 'democratise' itself and (as a Company) having private shareholders and debenture holders, although none of them had ever received a penny in return for their investment.

Lord Bledisloe was one of the staunchest supporters that the College ever had; without doubt he was responsible for the enhancement of its reputation, and instrumental in rescuing it after the First World War. He stands with Edward Holland and the Earl of Ducie as one of the saviours of the Royal Agricultural College and his memory is kept in the naming of a medal and of a hall of residence.

★

At a meeting of the Governors held on 11 November 1919 it was decided to make an appeal to the public and to old students and others to assist in reopening the College. Lord Bledisloe recalled: '. . . as then Chairman of the Governors and with the invaluable support of four old students (the late Marquess of Crewe, Mr Christopher Turner, Sir Beville Stanier, M.P. and Sir Archibald Weighall), I made a stirring appeal to all old 'alumni' of the College to help pay off the debenture debt. The response was generous, the debentures were redeemed and the College launched on a new more democratised lease of life. . . .'

One of the responses to this appeal came from Professor Malcolm James Rowley Dunstan, OBE, MA (Oxon.), FRSE, the Principal of the South-Eastern College, Kent, (now Wye College, University of London) who put forward a firm plan for re-establishing the teaching on modern lines.

Dunstan's proposals certainly intended a break with the past, remembering that there had been a gap of seven years since the College closure and fourteen years since the major reorganization had rescued the College from potential bankruptcy. Even by then the research on which the Royal Agricultural College had developed an international reputation and on which practical science was taught to students, had diminished. Dunstan realized that knowledge of science could be gained at universities and his proposed plans were based much more on practical application of scientific principles.

He suggested a two-year course with a year's work on a farm. The course was intended to give students a thorough, progressive knowledge of the land and an intelligent and active interest in the development of estates. The subjects were to be comprehensive: Agricultural History, Economics, Local Government and Village Organization, Report Writing at Public Meetings, Plans of Houses, Farm

Accounts, History of the Agricultural Industry at Home and Abroad, English and French History, Land Tenure, Buying and Selling, Farm Bookkeeping, Valuations, Landlord, Tenant and Labourer, General Estate Management, Surveying, Allotments and Smallholdings and Rating and Assessments. A formidable list with the apparent duplications, certainly to modern eclectic eyes. In addition students would have visits to farms and estates. Entry was to be at eighteen or nineteen years of age – a long way from the early schoolboy entry at fourteen or fifteen of fifty years ago. Successful students would be awarded the College Diploma and gone was the continuous assessment by tests of the Constable and McLellan eras.

Dunstan planned for six lecturers, a modest number for the initial intake of fifty-six students. Fees for tuition were to be £80 to £90 a year. Education and Domestic Departments would deal with educational training and accommodation with an Administrative Department to handle rent, repairs and maintenance, salaries of staff, fees for instruction and the cost of College upkeep. He envisaged a Bursar and a Secretary appointed to handle these departments, and a member of the teaching staff to be Warden.

Dunstan expected to run on a balanced educational budget provided that the inclusive charge to students was £150 per annum. Total income would be £8,400, cost of salaries for the first year £4,000, the balance to pay the Principal and Education Department. It would still need a capital sum for reopening and an annual sum for ongoing costs. The Governors estimated that a minimum sum of £25,000 would be required.

Perforce they then had to return to both alternatives – i.e. help from the Government and funds from private sources. The debenture debt of the College was £10,800 and an appeal to debenture holders obtained waivers of payment to the tune of £5,295. A special appeal to residents in and around Cirencester realized £4,846. This demonstration of local support illustrates the generosity of neighbouring landowners and others ever since the formation of the College. The remaining £959 required to pay off the balance was advanced, under guarantee, by the bankers to the College.

Off went the Chairman, Lord Bledisloe, on a second attempt to secure government funding and he received a sympathetic response from Sir Arthur Boscawen of the Ministry of Agriculture and Fisheries, who felt that Dunstan's proposals could be supported and put into action. He convinced the Treasury, and an offer came to the College of a grant of £15,000 together with a maintenance grant of £2,000 per annum, for the period terminating 31 March 1927 – not much different from the previous request by the College in 1918. The offer was accepted and Dunstan, who had been invited to become Principal when he had presented his scheme, was formally appointed and the College opened on 23 October 1922.

★

Dunstan had been Principal of the South-Eastern College since 1902 when, at the age of thirty-two, he had succeeded (Sir) Daniel Hall. Before this he had been Director of the Midland Agricultural and Dairy Institute from 1896 to 1902, and Director of Technical Instruction, Nottinghamshire, from 1891 to 1902. So by 1922 he was a man of considerable experience in agricultural education. At Wye he had been very successful in building up the college, both in respect of numbers and in reputation. His interests were broad and he was involved in developing work on hops and horticultural products. He was very much involved with the setting up of the Fruit Research Station at East Malling and with fruit marketing, as at Ashford with its annual Fruit Shows, both prior to the First World War.

He maintained his connections with Wye to the end of his life, attending meetings of the Old Students' Association, the Agricola Club, and was much in demand as an after-dinner speaker.

Dunstan was not without experience of the financial difficulties in running an agricultural college and this was to stand him in good stead in the coming years at Cirencester. When he was at Wye a 'financial scandal' hit the headlines in 1909 and this led to questions in the House of Commons. The difficulties were such that staff salaries could not be paid for some months! Dunstan was accused of 'milking' the funds and the perquisites of office. However he survived what was evidently a *cause célèbre*. This seems in no way to have prejudiced his acceptance of the principalship of the College.

Malcolm J.R. Dunstan, Principal 1922–7

It is probable that he had a strong desire to go to the College for, at the time of the retirement of McClellan in 1908, he answered the advertisement for a successor. He was not, however, short-listed. The reason for this is likely to have been the fact that in his application he stated that he would require a higher salary than that being offered – £600 per annum. Considering that he was already a Principal with some years experience this does not seem to have been unreasonable.

As to his character, references in the publications of *Agricola* indicate his popularity with the students and certainly with the past students, with whom he maintained a strong connection. There may have been a certain haughtiness and arrogance in his manner. The story is told of his meeting with an old student of Wye during the First World War: this was on the Lees at Folkstone where he met a private in the Canadian Expeditionary Force. The only comment Dunstan made was to the effect that he expected Wye men to hold commissions! This certainly rankled with the emigrant who had returned to help save the Empire from its foes! Perhaps this is no more than indicative of the peremptory nature sometimes usual in successful men, as well as of a devotion to the institution for which he was responsible.

When Dunstan took over at Cirencester, agriculture in Britain was at a point where the three years of high prices since the end of the War had come to an end. Towards the end of Dunstan's tenure at the College it is plain that the period was one of agriculture recovering only very slowly from a severe depression. By 1922 many landowners had proceeded to sell their estates. The high price of produce in the previous three years had induced many to bid for the land, and the sitting tenant had either to outbid or be dispossessed. As an owner he had frequently to pay more in interest on loans and mortgages, as well as having to maintain the fixed equipment which formerly the estate had done. This put them in a far worse position than the farmer of 1821 in the slump after the high prices of the Napoleonic wars. Add to this the import of cheaper grain from overseas and British farmers were having to turn to livestock production. Those who could not produce grass cheaply were in a sorry state. The post-war progression to this depressed state of agriculture in 1922 must have been reflected in the intake of students, and Dunstan, who had seen the intake at Wye grow from thirty-one to two hundred, no doubt wondered if he could ever increase the student numbers at the College.

Immediately he implemented plans to install central heating, a hot water system and electric lighting at a cost of £10,560. The money raised from an appeal in 1912 towards the provision of additional lecture rooms and laboratories, which was not proceeded with because of the War, totalled £4,261. £1,500 of this had, with the consent of the donors, been used to pay existing liabilities at the time; the remainder was used as working capital. A house for the Bursar was provided by making alterations to the stables at a cost of £650.

The manner in which the funds had been realized necessitated the reconstruction of the Governing Body. At an Extraordinary General Meeting held on

4 October 1922 the number of Ordinary Governors was increased so that there would be not less than eight and not more than twelve. Representative Governors were appointed by: the Ministry of Agriculture and Fisheries, the University of Bristol and West of England, the Royal Agricultural Society of England, the Bath and West and Southern Counties' Agricultural Society, the National Farmers' Union, and Cirencester Urban District Council.

Invitations were extended to, and accepted by: the Marquis of Crewe, KG, The Hon. Edward Strutt, CH, Mr Christopher Turnor, Sir Archibald Weighall, KCMG, Mr Alexander Goddard, CBE, Sir John Oakley, Professor E. Blundell, and Mr W. Scotford Harmer. The previous Governors who remained were: Lord Bledisloe, KBE, Earl Bathurst, CMG, and Major F.W.B. Cripps, DSO.

In his first report to the Governors the new Principal said that, owing to delays in completing the alterations, the opening had had to be postponed, from 9 to 23 October. A start was made with an entry of fifty-six students, of whom thirty-seven were to take the two-year course and nineteen to take the special one-year course arranged on the suggestion of the War Office for officers of both services who were being compulsorily retired. The Departments of Agriculture and Dairy Farming, Agricultural Machinery and Engineering, Bookkeeping and Estate Management, Farm Business and Economics were ready and fully staffed. Others were in process of organization.

The farmland comprised fifty acres (ten in foul and poor condition and forty in grass, of which five acres were needed for a sports field). This restricted practical farm work and the two-year students had to wait until their second year to gain the greater part of their practical farm work experience. Russell Swanwick, who was still the tenant of College farm, had offered land on terms to be agreed.

There was, indeed, still a lot to be done. Without proper facilities cheese-making could not be started, work was still needed to convert the loose boxes into a smithy and carpenter's shop and the implement shed was not yet erected. Funds were short for the purchase of tools for the Engineering Department and the farm buildings needed painting and repairs done.

Life at the College for the students must have been somewhat spartan for the central heating was then not yet satisfactory, the steam boiler for generating steam for cooking not yet working well and water supply for the lavatories was insufficient! But at least there were beds and blankets! Worship in the chapel was not possible since the roof and organ had not been repaired and the cricket pavilion and fives court still awaited repair. The lodge on the Stroud road and dairy cottage were nearly ready but not yet occupied and other cottages were awaiting repair.

The impression gained from this first report is of heroic efforts being made to open the College as soon as possible after the inordinate delays since becoming available following the end of the First World War. Dunstan forecast a small financial loss after the first year, a not unexpected result in the light of the financial strictures imposed by the limited funding. He was 'quite confident that when we get our full complement of two year students we shall be able to keep our expenditure well within our range'. He reported that the social and sports life of the College had resumed with a Rugby football fifteen in the field.

Significantly he reported that, 'negotiations had been commenced with the University of Bristol with the view of starting an Agricultural Degree, and the preliminary proposal is that a four year course will be instituted, the whole of the scientific instruction in the course being given in two years at the University, followed by two years' technical instruction in agricultural subjects at the College, successful candidates being awarded the degree of Bachelor in Agriculture. B.Agr.'.

This proposal would follow closely Dunstan's own ideas, expressed in his original proposals for the curricula to be followed by the College, i.e. that the teaching of agricultural science was best left to the universities and that the College should teach the practical application of that science.

Agreement was finally reached for a five-year course; the extra year over Dunstan's proposals to be spent on a selected farm where commercial management and practical work would be studied and the student would submit a written report. The first two years were to be spent at Bristol and Long Ashton (the Agricultural and Horticultural Research Centre) where the subjects of Chemistry, Botany, Zoology, Geology, Physics, Agricultural Chemistry and Agricultural Botany would be dealt with. In the second two years at the RAC the subjects taught would be Agriculture in all its aspects including Veterinary Science, Engineering, Bookkeeping, Cost Accounting, Surveying, Forestry and Agricultural Economics. Exemption was to be granted for the first two years to graduates in science at other universities.

Dunstan's views on this major development for the College were:

> The length of the Course is greater than that of existing degree courses at other Universities and due consideration had been given to the effect that this will have on the number of students who will probably take the course, but the opinion is that it is unnecessary to constitute another degree on the same lines as at other Universities which aim at training a candidate in the more scientific aspects of agriculture – this Bristol degree will attempt the training in the more commercial and economic aspects of the industry, giving at the same time a thorough preliminary scientific training.

It was intended that the first candidates would be admitted in October 1923.

Much of the work needing to be done when the College had been opened on 23 October 1922 had been completed by the time of Dunstan's report to the Governors in March 1923; indeed there was an incentive, for their Majesties King George V and Queen Mary had graciously consented to visit the College on 12 April of that year. In his own words, 'it is hoped to get the College and grounds into a presentable condition by . . . the date of the Royal Visit'. By now there were sixty students, of which forty-two were resident in College. The chapel was restored and the services of a Chaplain, the Revd A. Thornley, MA, FES, FLS had been secured. Since he was a distinguished entomologist he could become a consultant to the College. He was also to undertake the duties of Librarian – a very useful acquisition!

The official opening took place on 12 April 1923 with a royal visit. King George and Queen Mary arrived at the College in incessant and penetrating rain, to be met by Lord Bledisloe, the Chairman of the Governors, having been received at the railway station, Cirencester, by Lord and Lady Bathurst. After presentation to the Governors, the Principal and staff, their Majesties toured the College and planted two commemorative trees on the sports ground. Indicating the grim weather conditions of the visit, *The Times* of 13 April 1923 reported: 'The site for this [planting] ceremony was between the pavilion and the fives court, and the rain so heavy and the grass so wet that the distance, although only some 200 yards, was covered by motor-car. . . .' As he planted the oak the King jokingly remarked on the sticky character of the soil, and Professor Dunstan replied that he must blame Lord Bathurst for that, for he was the owner of the land. It was the second royal visit that had been rained upon: the conditions for the visit of the Prince of Wales in 1895 had been much the same!

★

The year 1923 was a year of significance not only for the advent of a degree course and a visit by royalty but less agreeably for an outbreak of fire, the second one in the history of the College. It broke out in the clock-gable roof on 13 March and was discovered at about 3.30 a.m. Thanks to the timely assistance of members of staff and of students, and to the absence of wind, the spread to the main buildings was prevented. The main staircase, gable-end roof and one room in the tower were seriously damaged by fire and adjoining rooms were subjected to flooding by water. The fire brigade was unable to assist for some time owing to the suction hose being too short to reach the underground tank and the mains had to be broken to afford a water supply. For future eventualities alterations were subseqently made to the tank. The damage amounted to £1,787.10s.0d. recovered by insurance. An unrecoverable loss was that of the College archives, a handicap to the production of a College history!

Another restriction being identified by the Principal at that time, in addition to the limited accommodation, was reflected in the need for more farmland for practical demonstration. There were, in 1923, only ten acres under the plough and this was quite insufficient for teaching purposes. As he said:

The teaching of the details of practical manual work is of course best accomplished on a commercial farm and only takes secondary place in the College curriculum, (the intention of which is to train practical heads rather

Plate 1   The College shield and crest

Plate 2   Front view of the College, *c.* 1860

Plate 3 Robert Jeffreys Brown, the originator

Plate 4 Rear view of the College, *c.* 1860

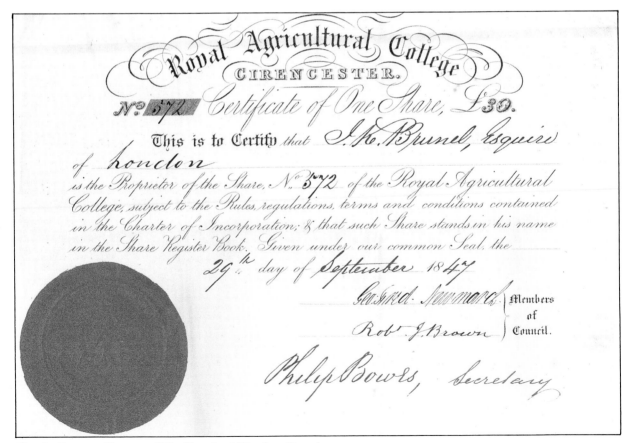

Plate 5 Share certificate no. 572 of Isambard Kingdom Brunel

Plate 9   John Blyth, Professor of Chemistry 1847–8

Plate 10   George T. Brown (later Sir), Professor of
Veterinary Science 1850–62

Plate 11   James Buckman, Professor of Geology, Botany,
Rural Economy and Natural History 1848–62

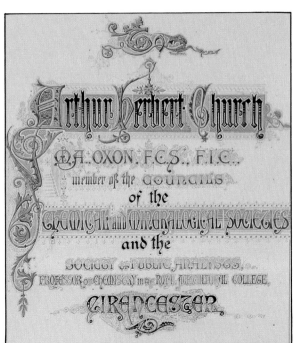

We the undersigned past and present **Professors** and **Students** of the **Royal Agricultural College**.

desire to offer you our sincere congratulations on your approaching Marriage, and our hearty good wishes that a long and happy life may await you and your bride

We desire to place upon record the intense regret with which we regard your severance from the COLLEGE, where for a period of sixteen years you have performed the duties of your office with such marked success, and to assure you that the remembrance of your work will long be a source of deep satisfaction to each one of us

May we express a hope that SCIENCE will be still further enriched by the continuance of those researches which have already made your name illustrious both at home and abroad, and which have tended so much to the advancement of the CHEMISTRY of AGRICULTURE.

With this expression of our esteem we beg you to accept the accompanying

Service of Silver Plate

as a token of our regard, trusting it will often recall to your mind those by whom it was presented.

Plate 12 The illuminated cover and address presented to Arthur George Church by the staff and students of the College

Plate 13 Allen Harker, Professor of Natural History

Plate 14 Lord Bledisloe, Chairman of the Governing Body 1919–29

than hands) but with sixty students who must be taught the elements of practical work in small classes of 6–8 at a time, our present area of plough land does not afford sufficient opportunity even for this preliminary teaching, and students complain, not unreasonably, of the absence of opportunity.

Regarding accommodation the Principal pointed out that the entry for the coming October would be mainly of students under twenty-one years of age who should live in college or in a properly supervised hostel in the town. He had thoughts about converting the library (over the dining hall) into nine bed-sitting rooms, and to transfer the library to where a 'recreation-entertainment hall' could be created as well. The old laboratories could be utilized for these purposes.

Dunstan concluded that the satisfactory solution would be the provision of a hostel. He could not see this being provided otherwise than by the College since a private individual could not run an enterprise which would be unoccupied during the vacations and in any case under private management the College could not be certain that the discipline would be satisfactory. He had spotted a vacant house in Cirencester which with some alterations would be suitable. The fallback position if such a hostel were provided and then proved to be unnecessary or unsuccessful was that it could be let furnished or unfurnished.

In this account to the Governors, Dunstan concluded that the sports and social side of the College was now becoming more active. A May Ball had been held; the first of many held annually with few interruptions up to the present day.

As a result of the Principal's need for more accommodation and of the conclusion arrived at by the Governors that the number of in-college students which would make the College an economic proposition was seventy, a deputation of the Governors, consisting of Lord Bledisloe and Major Cripps, visited the Ministry of Agriculture on 6 March 1924. They were introduced to the Parliamentary Secretary by Sir Thomas Davies, the member for Cirencester. They sought further financial assistance for the provision of accommodation for an additional twenty in-college students. Plans had been prepared by Mr Lawson, who had carried out the repairs and re-equipment of the College in 1922. The estimated cost was £5,000.

The deputation was informed that it was very unlikely that the Treasury would depart from the decision in their letter of 20 May 1922, that £15,000 was the limit of capital grant and that £2,000 per annum was the maximum annual grant, which might be on a descending scale until 1927 when the question of grants to agricultural colleges would be reconsidered.

With this Dunstan put forward possible courses of action:
1. To remain *in statu quo* when the College would be run at a loss for a year or two and then at a small credit balance.
2. To increase in-college accommodation by eight bedrooms ready for occupation in October 1924.
3. To increase in-college accommodation by twenty bedrooms by the same date.

He accompanied these possibilities with separate budgets showing costs and anticipated revenue, utilizing the available government grants. He recommended the adoption of the second scheme as viable because he did not anticipate much difficulty in raising the numbers by eight or ten at once, whereas the addition of twenty rooms could be difficult to fill at once and income would immediately drop by up to £1,250. In the then state of the agricultural industry he did not think it wise to count upon a large increase in the numbers of agricultural students. It would be possible to extend at a later date should this prove desirable. Then the effect of increased fees would have been ascertained. The chance of obtaining money from the Treasury would, of course, be less later on.

The Governors decided to accept this course of action and negotiated an overdraft of £2,000 with the bank to cover the cost of the additional rooms and a house for the Bursar. This scheme was never carried out. Successive reports by the Principal to the Governors showed a worsening financial position. The 1922/3 session showed a deficit of £2,763, due to some capital expenditure being included in the annual expenditure, and the 1923/4 session ended with a deficit of £555, due to increased cost of food, heating, lighting and general repairs.

By the end of 1924 Dunstan was saying, 'Next session should provide the test as to whether the College can be carried on as a satisfactory financial proposition, and if our expenditure cannot be kept within our income, the situation must be seriously considered. The entry of students is rather disappointing, but I have hopes that our fee income will be as great as last year.' He made some economies in staff salaries and in lighting, heating and office expenses. However, he had to tell the Governors that he could not see that it would be prudent to embark on the expenditure to provide the eight extra bedrooms, for the following reasons:
1. It would not be possible to keep within the overdraft limit of £2,000.
2. The number of entries was not large enough to be certain of filling the rooms.
3. Students occupying the larger rooms had no objection to sharing, so eight more could be taken if necessary.
4. A threatened builders' strike made completion before the next session uncertain.

This was a very unfavourable time, not only for the College but for all similar institutions. Agriculture was in a state of depression with an unsettled outlook. Indeed the whole country was in the throes of the late-twenties' depression. Although there were many enquiries from parents and guardians about the College courses, many considered the fees too high. (These had been raised from £150 to £160 per annum, which was only slightly more than when the College had reopened in 1922, but which was considerably higher than fees at other grant-aided colleges.) Lack of confidence in the future profitabillty of farming was also the cause of withdrawals.

The 1925/6 session commenced with only forty-three students, as against fifty-two in the previous term. In an effort to increase the intake fees were reduced to their previous level of £150 per annum for in-students and £85 per annum for out-students.

Aerial view of the
College in about
1925/6

A further reason given by the Principal which militated against larger numbers
applying was the small area of the College farm. Dunstan had drawn attention to
this in earlier reports in concluding that practical tuition was handicapped by this
fact. He presented a report drawn up by the College staff (Robert Howie,
Vice-Principal, and W.R. Thompson) with proposals for improving the teaching
of practical farming and for meeting these objections by the possible acquisition
of College farm. This recommended that if the College had a teaching farm it
should be run on strictly commercial lines, not on experimental or demonstration
lines. The authors said:

> In our opinion a college farm which does not 'pay' does not serve the purpose
> for which it is intended. It may serve as a training centre for manual operations

(in which a student can however gain real proficiency only by continued practice and experience on a commercial farm) but it is not the object lesson in successful management which it should be if it is to be of use to the College. If the farm is typical of the district and is a paying concern it may be of great value not only to College students but to the agriculturalists of the district – if it is not a paying proposition it ceases to be of use to the students and attracts farmers only by appealing to their critical faculties.

The report then outlined the history of the Royal Agricultural College farm from being under its direct management from 1846 to 1865, to being let by the owner, Lord Bathurst to tenants. Mr Russell Swanwick, the tenant for many years, had just died and it was anticipated that the farm would be vacant in some months' time. The report recommended that, if the opportunity occurred, the College should lease it directly, and run it as a mixed farm typical of the district. An arrangement such as that which had been obtained since the College gave up the direct lease in 1865 was not regarded as of much value.

Although this did not come about and the College has not since then had any arrangement regarding this farm, it is worth noting that this general philosophy of the College only having a farm for teaching purposes if it is run on straight commercial lines has been adopted up to the present day. As we shall see it reached full exposition in the era of Boutflour, and has continued since then.

In March 1925 Lord Bledisloe resigned from the Chairmanship, for health reasons, and was succeeded by Earl Bathurst.

The finances of the College continued to cause concern and the Ministry of Agriculture was once again approached for financial help. On 24 March 1925 Dunstan wrote to Sir Thomas Davies, the local MP, to ask him to tell (Sir) Kingsley Wood, Parliamentary Secretary of the Ministry of Agriculture, of the position of the College. He asked for assurance that the government grant of £2,000 per annum would be continued for a period of six years from March 1927, saying that the College can 'provide education of the right standard for the students who are undoubtedly of a better standard with each entry'.

He was concerned about the reputation on the part of the College for no work and 'this reflects on parents who pass it on and therefore it attracts the wrong kind of student'. He intended to corrrect this. (Apropos of this alleged reputation, Dunstan wrote at the same time to Lord Bathurst turning down a request to give the students more time for hunting!) He went on to say in this letter that:

> . . . if the grant is not to be continued at its present amount we should know before we enter into any arrangements with the staff and students for the next session. . . . It may be that the Governors will wish to carry on the College in

spite of the insecurity of the grant but I am afraid that it will have to be with another Principal.

It would be a pity if the £22,000 (£15,000 Government Grant, £7,000 local and other monies) spent on the re-opening of the College were thrown away. . . .

He said that he did not want to increase the fees as this would attract the class of student 'who can be catered for at Cambridge or Oxford . . . – there would be a falling off of sons of people of moderate means'.

Kingsley Wood visited the College on 1 May 1925 but this evidently was not sufficient to persuade him of the need to support the College at the same level for a further period though the Ministry was prepared to make a grant of £1,000 for the 1927/8 session, during which period the whole question of agricultural education in the West would be considered. This implies that the Ministry did not see the College as a national centre for agricultural education, which, since its foundation it had patently become. It is probable that the long gap of closure since 1914 did much to induce such an impression.

There was a suggestion that the Development Commission would pay a maintenance grant. It is not known whether this refers to the Ministry offer of £2,000 for the 1927/8 session or was in addition. It was mentioned in a letter by the Principal to the Secretary of the Ministry of Agriculture and Fisheries in June of 1925, stating that it was not sufficient and that the Governors wanted a promise of a grant to the end of the academic year 1927 or 'they may not be able to carry on the College'. In an effort to supplement income the College was let to outside bodies during the vacations.

On 3 June 1926 the Governors called a special meeting to pursue the negotiations with the Ministry. As a result a letter was approved for despatch to the Secretary of the Ministry of Agriculture and Fisheries and a deputation nominated to attend an interview. This deputation consisted of: Earl Bathurst, Lord Clinton, Major F.W.B. Cripps, Sir Thomas Davies, MP, and the Principal. This letter took note of the Ministry's offer of the grant of £2,000 to be made, but only to March 1927, and thanked the Government for the help which had enabled the College to open and carry on since October 1922.

But it went on to say, '. . . the Governors have unanimously come to the conclusion that the College cannot be continued without some outside financial aid. . . .' The financial situation was outlined. The accounts showed:

1922–23, a deficiency of *£2673 –6 –1* (due in part to the inclusion of some capital expenditure in the annual expenditure),
1923–24, a deficiency of *£555 – 14 –1*,
1924–25, a surplus of *£634 –15 –11*.

The financial result of the present year – 1925–6 – will not be available until September 30th, but the Governors do not anticipate such a satisfactory situation as that obtained in 1924–5, owing to the withdrawal of provisionally entered students on account of the unsettled and depressed condition of the Agricultural industry which has caused many parents and guardians to seek other futures for their sons or wards. The annual intake of new students in this as in other similar Colleges depends very largely on the immediate outlook for agriculture without much reference to a longer view of the possibilities of agricultural prosperity.

The re-opening of the College after a period of eight years inactivity has been a difficult matter and the $3\frac{1}{2}$ years during which the College has been open are not sufficient to establish it on a self supporting basis. . . .

The letter went on to state that the support by the Ministry was evidence that 'the College was intended to fill a place in the agricultural education organisation of the Country. . . .'

It was envisaged that the College would be included in the Scheme of Agricultural Education for the South Western Province, having missed out through being closed for eight years.

Since the Governors did not consider that the College could become self-supporting for some years they felt that in the absence of outside financial assistance it would have to close. Such closure would be a calamity, 'in view:–
(1) of the improving stability of the agricultural industry which will result in a greater demand for the kind of instruction offered by the College,
(2) of the sacrifice of the whole of the capital expended on re-equipment,
(3) of the contracts entered into with students for the completion of their term of education.'

The Governors asked for a renewal of the grant for at least a term of years to enable them to carry on the work of the College, 'which has now been in existence *80 years* and in possesssion of a Royal Charter, the work of which they consider has been and will be of great importance to those either managing their own estates or in carrying the industry of farming'.

Unfortunately there was a negative response to this appeal and as a consequence Dunstan tendered his resignation as Principal, to take effect at the end of the session. It needs little imagination to see that this was a frustrated man who was inclined to take upon himself the responsibility for the failure of the plans he himself had put forward for the restart of the College after the War. What is apparent is that his budgets, in order to meet the cost of rehabilitating the College physically and to meet the running costs both of the necessary staff and domestically, had necessitated setting the fees at a level which was uncompetitive with other institutions (which probably received greater subvention from the government and local authorities than did the College). In addition, the fees at such levels did not attract the type of student that Dunstan had in mind. This compounded the situation, for such students did not give the College the impression of a hard-working institution producing the future practical farmers for the nation. And so the very parents for which Dunstan had designed his plans, as he said, 'of moderate means', were discouraged from sending their sons. The better ones went to Oxbridge and yeoman farmers could not afford the fees for their sons.

In 1927 there was published the report of the Departmental Committee of the Ministry of Agriculture and Fisheries on, The Re-assessment of Annual Grants to Institutions providing Higher Agricultural (Including Veterinary) Education in England and Wales, under the Chairmanship of Lord Bledisloe. It looked at all such institutions and in particular said of the Royal Agricultural College:

> The Governors explained to us their firm conviction that they would not be able to keep the College open after (March 1928) without some government grant; . . . they urge that the annual grant since 1922 was given to enable the College to 'stand on its own feet' and that five years is too short a period for that purpose. In a few years they believed that it would attain a position of reasonable security; if not, they would themselves propose to close it. Incidently we may remark that the College, which at one time catered solely or mainly for the land-owning class has now among its students only a minority of that class; the origin and type of its students can no longer be urged as an objection to Government assistance.

It is interesting to note firstly that the financial position of the College was truly serious enough to warrant such statements to the Government: there is little doubt that the Governors meant what they said. Also it is worth noting that the statement about the class of student hitherto accepted reveals another reason behind repeated refusals or hesitations of the Government about grant aid. Indeed, casting forward, it is possible that this statement was not enough to dispel such views in future by successive governments.

The report went on: 'It must find its future in becoming a local rather than in seeking to remain a national institution; for this purpose it is eminently desirable that it should be linked up with County Authorities. The Governors . . . sympathise with these views. The Principal has conferred with the officers of the various Local Authorities and of Bristol University . . . with a considerable measure of success.'

In fact, in March 1927, a meeting of the Advisory Council of the local authorities concerned in agricultural advisory and research work in the counties of Gloucestershire, Wiltshire, Somerset, Worcestershire and Herefordshire had been held, as foreshadowed in the Ministry's reply in March 1925. The matter of the College being included in any scheme was considered and suggestions were made for the development of the College on lines which would make it more useful to the district. It was suggested that there should be a collegiate centre in the western province linked up with county work in the same way as in other districts. These suggestions were put to a committee consisting of the agricultural organizers of the counties, the Vice-Chancellor of Bristol University, the Director of the Long Ashton Research Station and the Agricultural Advisory Officer attached to Bristol University. This committee met at Cirencester and it was suggested that the College could be of service by running a short course of varying lengths, assisting in county lecturing and advisory work in certain branches of agriculture, holding conferences on matters of agricultural importance and in carrying out trials of manuring and crops in the vicinity of the College. The representation of the College on the Advisory Council was also proposed so that the College would take an integral part in all the agricultural educational and research activities of the province. This scheme was approved by the College Governors and the county organizers of all the counties, with the exception of Somerset which had its own Farm Institute. The Ministry of Agriculture gave its blessing to the scheme and promised to make a grant to the College extending over a period of five years if it proved successsful.

This was, in effect, a rescue operation for the College although probably the others in the scheme may not have seen it as such since the College was in a unique position to help with agricultural advice and development in the West, having the facilities and the staff to accomplish this. Furthermore, after a long period when little or no research or extension work had been carried out since the halcyon days of Voelcker et al., this was an excellent opportunity to resume the extended role and thus to re-establish the reputation of the College. At the same time the material support of the Ministry would put the finances on an even keel and enable the original intentions of the reopening plans to be achieved.

Dunstan intimated that he wished to withdraw his resignation – a not surprising move since there was now the possibility that his plans for the College could be implemented and the hard work he had put in brought to fruition without the continual worry of making ends meet. However the Governors thought it in the best interests of the College to accept his resignation, to take effect at the end of the session and thus to give a new Principal a free hand to carry out the suggested scheme for cooperation with the counties.

There is little doubt that Dunstan performed a vital task in tackling the reopening of the College after the war. Restarting after a closure of eight years with little or no financial resources to tap is difficult in itself but coming after the haemorrhage of the First World War when there would be unlikely to be any returning staff or students made it a task of Herculean proportions. Dunstan's presentation must have been very convincing and the Governors' faith very strong for all of them to have embarked on this enterprise. Plainly it was highly dependent on the support by government, which on reflection would appear to have been barely sufficient. Parsimony can be a characteristic of governments and it must be judged to have been somewhat short-sighted because stronger support might well have obviated the need for the fees being set at a level which ultimately prejudiced the intake, both in quantity and in type.

In 1927 the College journal was revived – the *Agricultural Students' Gazette* – as a quarterly publication which it had been from its foundation in 1875. The first of the new issues (Vol. XVIII, Spring Term, 1927) contained an introduction by Lord Bledisloe, then Parliamentary Secretary to the Ministry of Agriculture, Fisheries and Food. He said:

> In days when Agricultural Colleges were few . . . the Journal of England's oldest and most famous centre of Agricultural Education had a recognised and established position in current Agricultural Literature, comparable with . . . the journals of the Royal Agricultural Society and the 'Bath and West', and its original articles by my old friends, Sir John Bennet Lawes and Sir Joseph Henry Gilbert of Rothamstead, Sir William Thistleton-Dyer of Kew, Messrs Kinch and Allen Harker (our much loved Professors of Chemistry and Geology) and other great lights in the firmament of Agricultural Science. . . .

This praise is evidence that the reputation of the College in the field of agricultural science was not forgotten, though we may perhaps understand his unstinted praise since he was, as we know, a lifelong supporter.

In that same issue is plenty of evidence that activities had resumed to much the same degree as before the closure. The College farm was in constant use. It was said that, 'the farm, along with the estate of which it is a part, is the main structure round which the whole work of the College is co-ordinated. It is the chief laboratory of the College. It forms a complete and constantly changing mass of illustrations on which all the teaching is based, allowing the latter to be thoroughly practical in its character.' All the major sports had been revived, the annual Beagles Hunt Ball took place in the tithe barn, a discussion society had been formed in the previous year and the Principal had advocated the resurrection of the RAC Students' Club.

There was a different view of these activities. A former student, G. Sandwith, wrote of his time there, 'In 1927–28 the College under Professor Dunstan was more like a comfortable country club than a seat of learning. Some students devoted themselves to hunting, point-to-points, racing, beagling, shooting, fishing, sports cars, motor-cycles, pubbing – or whatever!'

And so Dunstan's time as Principal came to a close; it had been a period not only of revival of the College but also one in which the farming industry had suffered one of the severest depressions for decades. Even in 1927, as Dunstan himself said in an article on 'Farming in England':

> . . . [it] is in transition and . . . not in an entirely satisfactory condition. Since the great drop in prices in 1922 . . . there are signs of a revival, slow, it is true, but prices are on an upward trend. It is useless to expect capital to be attracted to the agricultural industry unless a fair return, of some permanancy, can be assured and it is not easy today to secure such a return on either landlord's or tenant's capital. . . . Landlords are too impoverished to give much assistance

. . . farmers have no ready money to spend and must see that every penny that is spent is expended wisely on production. . . .

Dunstan concluded his survey in 1927 of British agriculture by asking that, 'A better understanding by the townsman of the countryman's position and importance might lead to an improved situation, but the farmer will, probably, then have to fight his battle alone, (or in co-operation) – the government keeping the ring and seeing fair play for him.'

The following issue of July 1927 contained an appreciation of the Principal and outlined the parlous state to which the College had arrived in 1922:

. . . the very life of the old institution depended on the finding of a Principal, endowed with the personality, ability and energy to enable him to reconstruct the R.A.C., and instil new vigour into it.

As a lecturer, his facility and elegance of expression, added to a natural eloquence and obviously profound knowledge, commanded a hearing and created an interest in what might very well be dull subects. His colleagues on the staff will long remember his genial rule, guided by the principles – *Suaviter in modo, fortiter in re.*

★

By the time a new Principal was due to be appointed to replace Dunstan there was a strong team of lecturing staff, gradually built up by him since the reopening in 1922. In addition to a Vice-Principal, Robert Howie, B.Sc. (Edinburgh), co-author of the report on the possible acquisition of the College farm, there was now a Warden, P.S. Brown, NDA and these two, togther with the Principal, were responsible for the Agriculture Department along with W. Biffen, B.Sc., NDD and A.V. Gifferd, NDA, NDD, BDFD (Hons.). The Principal also taught Agricultural Economics. The Veterinary Science and Forestry Departments were in the hands of two men who would eventually give long service to the College, A.C. Duncan, FRCS, and A.D.C. Le Sueur, FSI. Some others doubled up, namely W. Biffen taught Agricultural Science and A.V. Gifferd, Dairying and Poultry Management. The Secretary and Bursar was J.N.L. Jones. Bearing in mind that the numbers of students during the period varied at about the fifty-five mark, the teaching ratio was reasonable. By 1927 there were the following courses:

A one-year course designed for the sons of farmers and others to gain a practical education in the main subjects of Agriculture, Agricultural Economics, Veterinary Science, Bookkeeping, Forestry, Poultry Management, Horticulture and Agricultural Engineering, with practical instruction.

A two-year course including all the subjects in the one-year course together with Estate Management, Surveying, Building Construction, Farm Costings and Applied Science.

A degree course in conjunction with the University of Bristol extending over four or five years.

A short course of about six weeks duration. This was intended for farmers' sons who could not be spared for the longer courses.

The syllabuses were very comprehensive and included practical work, but not manual work. Students were familiarized with farm operations and were instructed in farm management by means of 'visits to farms of repute in the neighbourhood where good management prevails, or to an estate which offers special points of interest . . .' (College Prospectus, 1927). They were expected to have spent one year continuously on a 'good commercial farm'. Those completing the two-year course satisfactorily were awarded the College Diploma.

These then were the resources awaiting the appointment of a new Principal who would be expected to carry out the new scheme for cooperation with the counties.

Having decided not to accept Dunstan's withdrawal of his resignation the Governors took on the task of finding a successor. It seems to have been a somewhat arbitrary decision for logic appears now to point to the need not for change but for continuity with the very man who had seen the College through the extremely difficult time of restarting, holding the line so far as finances were concerned and marshalling limited resources. He had initiated and conducted the negotiations for the new scheme with the western counties and in addition to that he had landed the plum of the university degree course and had been instrumental in setting it up. Whether there was pique in the action of the Governors following the first offer of resignation by Dunstan, which he had obviously regretted when in sight of the successful outcome of the proposed new scheme, or whether there was a genuine belief that the College would be best served by a change of management is not known. But on the face it, Dunstan might have claimed to have been hard done by.

To find a new Principal the Governors charged a committee with this task. It consisted of the Earl Bathurst, Sir Archibald Weighall, Major Cripps and Professor Barker. Wisely, the Vice-Chancellor of Bristol University was co-opted on to this committee, which commenced enquiries immediately, having decided not to advertise in the first instance.

Of the various names thus thrown up one stood out. This was Dr J. A. Hanley, Chief Advisory Officer in Agriculture at Bristol University and the University's representative of the Board of Governors at the College. If the Governors were to offer him the post, not only would this be the appointment of a man familiar with the College, the vicissitudes of its history and its requirements for the future, but it would cement the link with the University. On 2 May the Governors offered the post to Dr Hanley and he accepted. A basis for his acceptance was that he would continue to act as Chief Advisory Officer in Agriculture at Bristol University but that he would reside at College. His salary and emoluments were shared by the College and the University and though no

Dr J.A. Hanley,
Principal 1927–30

term was fixed for the appointment it was hoped that it would continue for at least five years. This seems to have been a less than formal arrangement and as such could have been the seed for difficulty in the future but it was not so and in the event the appointment lasted for the five years as envisaged.

So Hanley took up residence at the College during the summer vacation of 1927. His was the job of implementing the new scheme and particularly of making connections with the counties as well as linking up the College as the teaching centre for higher agricultural education in the province with the Research and Advisory Centre at Bristol. As Dr Hanley said, 'Fortunately or unfortunately . . . the teaching centre . . . is separated by 36 miles of passable road, and a still greater length of excellent but meandering railway line from the University which serves as the Research and Advisory Centre.'

One of the first steps he took was to introduce from the beginning of the 1927/8 session a short course in farming. His objective was not, as he said, 'to convert the College into a "Farm Institute" ' but to see that 'the College merely falls into line with other well-known colleges which provide short courses for men who cannot spare the time for a full course on Agriculture'. This course would be of eleven weeks duration and was intended for students from the counties of Gloucestershire, Wiltshire, Worcestershire and Herefordshire. The fees were £25 per term for students from these counties and £35 per term for those from elsewhere.

Thus, in addition to the degree course and the Diploma course, the two main planks of education at the College, there would be this new short course, a short vacation course on Practical Dairying and Poultry Management and special short courses for students who wished to concentrate on certain branches of agriculture or estate management, such as, for example, Estate Forestry. One other significant alteration was the decision by the Governors that the age of admission to the College should be reduced from eighteen to sixteen years. This can be seen as a consequence of the new link with the counties in the scheme for provincial agricultural education.

Concurrent with the change of Principal there were staff changes. Senior staff leaving in 1927 were Howie, Vice-Principal, Biffen and Gifferd. In their place came: J.H.F. Thomas, B.Sc., NDA, Vice-Principal and Lecturer in Agriculture who had been an agricultural lecturer on the Wiltshire County Council staff for two years and was before that a lecturer in Agriculture at the Monmouthshire Agricultural Institute, Usk; H.E. Wells, NDA, NDD, Lecturer in Dairying and

Hanley, staff and students. *Seated, front row, third from left*: P.S. Brown; *right of the Principal*: J.F.H. Thomas and A.C. Duncan

Poultry Husbandry; H. Dale, NDA, Lecturer in Surveying and Bookkeeping; and E.P. Weller, PASI, Lecturer in Estate Management and Economics.

However, Dale and Weller left shortly afterwards in March 1928, the latter to take up the post as Head of the Estate Management Department at Cambridge University and at that same time the Bursar, Jones resigned through ill health. He had been Bursar since 1992. P.S. Brown was appointed as Bursar as well as Warden. This created a more important post which covered the entire internal management of the College. Other appointments were made to strengthen the lecturing staff.

In spite of the more stable financial arrangements as a result of the scheme agreed with the Ministry, the University and the provincial counties, the financial estimates for the 1927/8 session anticipated a deficit of about £1,300, necessitating an increase in the bank overdraft to £3,500 with the lease of the College as collateral. Unfortunately the number of students remained stuck at the levels throughout the period since 1922, even slightly lower. At the beginning of 1928 it was reported that there was a record number of students, seventy-two, of which sixty-seven were resident in College, but this large number was accounted for by the presence of forty-three students who attended a special course in Grassland Management which was held during the first four weeks of the term. The report at the start of the summer term 1928 revealed 'the smallest number of students on record since the re-opening of the College in 1922'. Thus there were probably only around thirty-five to forty students on the longer, full-time courses. It must have been that the newly introduced short courses were money spinners for otherwise the College would have been in financial straits that matched those of the very early days. Indeed, such short courses would prove to be a financial rescue service in many instances.

In addition there was some sponsorship. The Grassland Management course was supported by Nitras Ltd who provided funds for scholarships to young farmers or farmers' sons resident in Great Britain and Ireland. Because applications for the course were so numerous they increased their original offer from £500 to £600.

Further short courses of about six weeks duration were held during January/February and April/May. These were also for farmers' sons. The newly introduced short course was extended to admit students of Bristol University holding scholarships at a fee of £105 and non-scholarship students at £120. An extension of this course permitted successful students to qualify for the College Diploma by completing a further four terms, making seven terms in all. A silver medal for the one-year course was presented by Mr Scrutton, a wealthy Governor.

Soon after his appointment in December 1927 Thomas reported on the state and management of the College farm and, bearing in mind that the agricultural depression was in full spate, he prefaced his comments: 'There can be no such thing as the wholesale salvation of British Agriculture, the industry being so

Left: J.F.H. Thomas,
Vice-Principal. *Right*:
P.S. Brown, Bursar
and Warden

varied in the number of systems followed in different localities, that no given set of mitigating factors can be expected to operate with general success . . . we must analyse carefully our own particular systems and methods, with a view to discovering those changes which should be introduced to develop the profit earning capacity of the holding.' Thus we see a continuance of the farming policies outlined by Howie and Thompson in their earlier report just after the reopening of the College, that is, the presentation to students for their education of a successful commercial venture.

Because of the limited area of land available to the College, Thomas recommended the adoption of intensive methods 'to achieve the highest possible production per acre'. Having had an extremely unfavourable season, cash arable crops were low yielding, but forage crops more than sufficient. Hay was ruined. So the abnormal growth of grass was ensiled and, to the chagrin of the students, the Eton fives court was turned into a temporary grass silo! The farm management offered that '. . . it is not intended that this flagrant act of vandalism shall be established as a precedent . . .'! The numbers of livestock were down, barren cows, store bullocks and store sheep having been sold off. Thomas intended to develop an intensive system of grassland management, with the use of active nitrogenous fertilizers on small areas, coupled with heavy stocking and rotational grazing. He looked to increasing the dairy herd and young cattle for baby beef production. A small flock of ewes was to be retained, and pigs and poultry increased to maintain the intensive production.

Throughout 1928 and 1929 Thomas worked hard to convert the mixed, low-intensity farming system to the more intensive methods and, in spite of some very adverse weather conditions in both years, by the end of the 1928/9 session he was able to report that the intensive grazing plots were established and proving satisfactory, that the small dairy 'had acquitted itself well, and is now a source of steady revenue by the sale of liquid milk'. The sheep flock was proving profitable but the small herd of breeding pigs was nearly all but lost by sale or burial owing to an unexplainable outbreak of a contagious disease. The cash crops had been poor.

★

In the winter term of 1928 the Block Grants Assessment Committee visited the College; in their report they had stated that it would be the greatest pity if the College were lost to agriculture and they backed up their opinion by increasing the grant by £1,000 a year for the next two years. In addition, following their recommendations, Gloucestershire and Wiltshire County Councils were invited to nominate two representatives each on the Board of Governors.

In December 1929 Lord Bledisloe resigned as a Governor on his appointment as Governor-General of New Zealand. The Governors asked that his name remain on the list, ex-officio as it were.

At last the introduction of the short courses by Hanley was beginning to show favourable results. Applications for entry to the various courses continued to improve and both the 1928/9 and 1929/30 sessions commenced with a full complement of students. As a result the College finances improved and, by the end of the 1929/30 financial year, showed a credit balance of £2,195, and an electric lighting plant had been installed at a cost of £424.

In October 1930 Hanley was offered the Chair of Agriculture at Durham University, which he accepted, and so ended his period as Principal at the College for he necessarily had to offer his resignation. So the second of the two Principals who had taken the College through its most difficult period and the nadir of its fortunes came to leave. Taken together Dunstan and Hanley might be regarded as successful Principals: Dunstan had to reopen the College in adverse conditions and on a limited budget, set up the curricula, engage staff and organize the domestic administration; Hanley to develop the rescuing scheme and establish courses that would show a profit in order to return the College to its original purpose of being a self-supporting institution for national agricultural education. But there was considerable difference in their styles. The ex-student who commented on life at the College under Dunstan as being, '. . . like a comfortable country club . . .' continued:

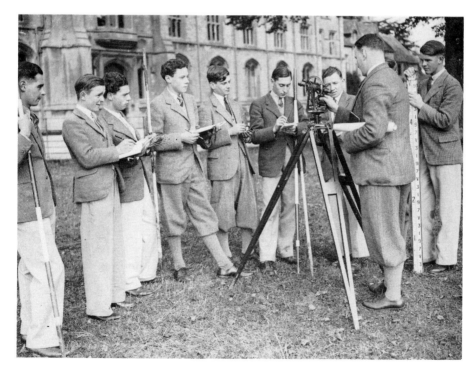

A surveying class,
c. 1930

But, in 1928–29, there was a severe shake-up under the scientist, Dr J.A. Hanley, and his energetic Vice-Principal, Thomas (a practical Wiltshire sheep farmer). Except for (Warden) Brown, Le Sueur (Forestry), Major Duncan (Veterinary) it seems there had been a purge of the staff. No doubt Dr Hanley would have liked to purge some of the students; but, then, there were so few of us in those days! (Although, we always fielded a combative rugger XV, cricket XI, tennis team, etc.) Dr Hanley was a good lecturer, as well as a soil and grassland expert. He introduced . . . the Hohnheimer (Dutch) intensive system of grazing on the College Farm with astonishing results. Also, in his time, students were coming to the College on Government grants, for the first time, I think. Those students *wanted* to work! Dr Hanley's enthusiasm for science was infectious; in one way or another, we all benefitted during our second year. [George Sandwith]

The College was by now just about in balance and able to stand on its own feet but still needing, as the other colleges in the country needed, an amount of government support. It had achieved a series of attractive courses, with a competent and keen teaching staff who encouraged, by their own example, enthusiasm for the acquisition of knowledge. What kind of Principal did it need now? The potential was now there for the College to expand and develop if the right man could be found to exploit this: a character to lead the College in the forefront of agricultural education and applied research.

Chapter Eight

THE FIRST BOUTFLOUR PERIOD, 1931–45

The most progressive and outstanding young man in agricultural education.

Lord Bledisloe, 1930

With the impending departure of Hanley, the Governors of the College set about the search for a new Principal in their usual manner, by the appointment of a small committee. This consisted of the Earl Bathurst, Major Cripps, Col. Fuller, Mr Scrutton and Mr Scott. Their first instruction was to discuss possibilities with Bristol University and they were given full authority to select and to appoint Hanley's successor. However, the University was not prepared to combine the post of Chief Advisory Officer in Agriculture at the University with that of the Principal of the College, as Hanley had been. But it would agree, if an outstanding man were found, to the joint appointment of Principal of the College and Professor of Agriculture at the University. This would give a seat on the Senate and on the Science Board. The College would in this way be very securely tied to the University – certainly to a stronger extent than at anytime in the past. It would, of course, mean the continuation of the teaching of the degree course and would enhance the status of the College.

Before taking further steps the Governors asked Hanley for any recommendation he could make of a suitable candidate to fill the post. Hanley certainly did have a person in mind: he was Robert Boutflour, the National Director of Dairy Husbandry who was based at Harper Adams Agricultural College. Hanley knew him well – indeed this man had already made a reputation for himself in his work as Organiser of Agricultural Education in Wiltshire. He had revolutionized the feeding of dairy cows by propounding hitherto unused scientific methods and startling the farmers in that county by his forthright and determined advocacy. To continue this work he had been made the National Director of Dairy Husbandry with the aim of promoting the greater efficiency of dairy production. Hanley first wrote to Boutflour to find out if he would be interested. He was: based as he had been at an agricultural college for a short time prior to his evangelizing work in Wiltshire, he felt that he could indeed extend his experience to the preparation of students for their careers in the rapidly developing industry of agriculture. He was invited to attend for interview.

This took place in November 1930. It must have been a foregone conclusion: the Governors knew well the work and character of the man they were considering for appointment. The College had had many different Principals, mostly of an academic bent and all of conventional outlook in terms of agricultural education. Now they were about to appoint an iconoclast fresh from his barnstorming campaigns in Wiltshire and from being the first National Director of Dairy Husbandry. He accepted the post of Principal and expected to be appointed Professor of Agriculture at Bristol; after all, that was what Bristol had agreed to. But the University got cold feet; it seems that they did not consider his academic qualifications were sufficient (he had a first degree from Durham University obtained in 1911) and so he was offered a Readership only, with the promise that if he proved satisfactory eventually he would be offered the Chair. Looking back at the high academic qualifications of Principals appointed before the First World War it was a significant contrast that this new appointment was of a man qualified essentially by experience in the giving of agricultural advice. Furthermore he was a brilliant and effective communicator.

Hanley left at the beginning of 1931 and Boutflour took over the reins. He anticipated a very different job from that which he had been doing; it would mean, he hoped, a respite from the constant travelling to give lectures, a chance to have a more settled home life and above all a new opportunity, with the management of the teaching and guidance of students, to extend and expand his influence in the developing dairy industry.

★

Born in 1890 and brought up on farms in Durham, Robert Boutflour, son of a master mariner, a Captain in a windjammer in the China tea trade, was subject to maternal influence because his mother ran the farm in the absences of her seaman husband. A determined woman, she decided that her second son (there were also six daughters) should have a second string to his bow in addition to farming in order to provide greater security. So she pressed for him to go to university and in 1908 he had obtained a scholarship to the Armstrong College in the University of Durham. By 1911 Boutflour had graduated as Bachelor of Science in Agriculture.

Appointed in 1912 as a lecturer in agriculture at the Tamworth Agricultural College he had an initial task of handling students, some quite mature. Small in stature, but of blocky build, he was quite capable, both physically and in courage, of standing up to some of the lazier and older students who tried 'getting at' this novice lecturer. Boutflour earned their respect; he would do exactly the same with the hard-bitten farmer audiences he was to meet and conquer in the coming years.

In 1914, at the outbreak of war, he obtained the first of the posts which matched his talents: lecturing to students at the Harris Institute, Preston, for Lancashire County Council and, significantly, starting advisory work to farmers. Though he was on war service shortly after starting, his experience in dealing with farmers reluctant to and fearful of carrying out a 'ploughing-up' campaign helped to prepare him for the major advisory struggles to come.

His entry into full extension work came in 1919 with his appointment as a district officer of the University of Leeds for the Craven district of Yorkshire. It was here that his interest in dairy farming was aroused. After a period in the Lindsey division of Lincolnshire as Agricultural Organiser to Lincolnshire County Council, he landed the plum post of Chief Agricultural Officer and County Land Agent to Wiltshire County Council, in 1922, not without some opposition to this appointment of a young man.

It was here that he built a national reputation by his advocacy of the application of scientific methods to the management and feeding of dairy cows. Built during those Wiltshire years, it was based on the adoption of methods that allowed high-yielding cows to achieve their potential and survive. He quickly became an effective communicator. He took the scientific principles of animal nutrition then established and by unorthodox means translated them into terms easily under-stood by the working dairy farmer. He was unorthodox because his method of communication was face-to-face contact with farmers at evening gatherings and personal meetings on the farm, and because he used down-to-earth language, often shocking his audience, insulting them, amusing them, but always prepared to put his ideas to practical examination – and to be proved right! Nobody had ever talked to the agricultural community in such a forthright manner before.

Boutflour set out to show that cows needed to be fed according to yield, that once their basic food requirements for maintenance were met, then concentrated balanced rations could be increased at the rate of $3\frac{1}{2}$ lb to the gallon and the bulk home-grown foods (roots, stray, hay) could be reduced accordingly. In fact he claimed that he could get more milk without roots than with them, that they were not necesary to feed to a cow and that they had no place at all in the ration of a high-yielding cow. Little wonder he was called 'No Roots Boutflour'.

His ideas came from a lecture that he attended at Reading University given by Professor James Mackintosh, who also advocated feeding a dairy cow for milk production before she was due to calve (later called by Boutflour 'steaming up' – which came from his experience as a boy in charge of getting steam up in traction engines). These startling ideas (as they were regarded then) shook the farming community of Wiltshire; their effects rippled away to other counties. There was opposition, of course, from those too blinkered to see the merits of change unless it was clearly demonstrated to them and from those whose interests were threatened.

For example, Boutflour told farmers to make up their own balanced rations by buying 'straights', i.e. the separate feeding stuffs, and then mixing them up in recommended proportions. This would produce a cheaper and more effective product than that sold by the feeding stuffs' manufacturers. He had, in fact, done the same kind of thing in Lincolnshire where he had raised the wrath of the fertilizer companies by recommending the purchase of straight fertilizers; the farmers could then get the equivalent amount of plant food of purchased compound fertilizers by a mixture of ammonia for nitrogen, superphosphate for soluble phosphate, steam bone flour for insoluble phosphate and muriate of potash for potash. He was blunt and said, 'You have paid £7.10.0d [£7.50p] a ton for manure that is only worth £2.10.0d [£2.50p]'. Here's a memory of Voelcker who was saying much the same thing over fifty years before!

The feeding stuffs' manufacturers were quick to change: as a result of their increased sales Boutflour had lasting good relations with them especially with British Oil and Cake Mills Ltd which was to be reflected in the financial support that they subsequently gave to the College.

Boutflour's methods were successful. They were indeed so highly successful that he was in demand as a lecturer to the extent that he found it difficult to respond to all the demands. His assistants at Trowbridge were similarly worked off their feet in this extension work. His first was Roger Sayce, B.Sc. (Agric.) who had brought from Leeds University the essential data on the starch and protein equivalents on which the balanced rations depended. With Boutflour he developed advisory techniques for the dissemination of such information. He was followed by W.T. Price (later to become the Principal of Seale Hayne Agricultural College) and J.F.H. Thomas, who eventually joined the College as a senior lecturer. These men, with others of their time, were the forerunners of the National Agricultural Advisory Service (NAAS), founded in 1946.

His work so impressed the Ministry of Agriculture that in 1926 he was made National Director of Dairy Husbandry, a unique post specifically designed with Boutflour in mind. It was based at Harper Adams Agricultural College, Newport, Shropshire. From here his influence could spread nationwide and it did. With Dr Crowther, the Principal of that college, he established a small, experimental dairy herd, given by the British Friesian Society. Boutflour lectured all over the country and his travel schedule was formidable. By now he had assessed the value of publicity in promoting his ideas and had harnessed it to his benefit. He was regularly reported in the agricultural press, he broadcast on the wireless and took part in the 'Brains Trust', a popular show on the BBC that drew a listening audience of millions. The press always expected the unusual from him, not to say outrageous statements designed to shock either through exaggeration or insult. On the other hand his humour was equally reported and in this way he tempered his sharpness to his audience. His lecture halls were invariably full: some came as opponents, most left as converts. Unfortunately he made some enemies in high places; unorthodoxy often does. But what he preached became, in time, accepted practice.

In addition to his pronouncements on balanced rations for cows he now turned

≡

" *If*
Camels
gave
More
Milk
than
Cows

—*we should keep them in spite of their humps*
and goose-rumped tail-settings! "

says Mr. Robert Boutflour.

" **Performance versus Pedigree in**
the Breeding of Dairy Cows "

is the title of an ADDRESS which will be given to

THE NORFOLK LIVE STOCK CLUB

by

MR. ROBERT BOUTFLOUR, B.Sc.,

at the ROYAL HOTEL, NORWICH,

On Saturday, April 1st, 1933, at 4.30 p.m.

Membership of the Club is open to any person interested in the Livestock
industry on subscribing the small annual sum of 5/- to THE HON. SEC.,
NORFOLK LIVE STOCK CLUB, NORFOLK AGRICULTURAL STATION,
SPROWSTON, Norwich.

Mr. Boutflour writes regularly in " The Dairy Farmer."

Notice of an address
by Boutflour to the
Norfolk Live Stock
Club, 1 April 1933,
on 'Performance
versus Pedigree in
the Breeding of
Dairy Cows'

his attention to the breeding of dairy cows and following a visit to the United States of America he became convinced of the need for progeny testing and the development of the 'proven sire'. He castigated breed societies and poured scorn on the shibboleths of 'Like begets like' and 'By type and pedigree you'll get good cattle'. This hardly made him popular with breed societies or with the Ministry of Agriculture and their livestock officers who were judging the potential productivity of bulls by their conformation.

He consistently drove this home, as he wrote in an article in 1933:
'I hope I have demonstrated to you three facts:
(1) That you cannot select cows on appearance for performance, and therefore show ring inspection wins are of very little guidance.
(2) That you cannot select cows on appearance for constitution.
(3) That like begets like only sometimes, and at other times like does not beget like; pedigree is no sure guide and therefore buying on pedigree alone is gambling.' (*Dairy Farmer*, April 1933)

★

This then was the man that Dr Alec Hanley suggested to the Governors of the College should take his place. He must have been aware that he was asking the Board to take a relatively extreme act of faith to appoint as Principal someone at a considerable remove from those previous occupants of the post. Iconoclasts are not necessarily the best people to guide and instruct young open minds: they may inculcate ideas that make the new recruit unacceptable to conservative employers!

But Hanley knew his man well for he had supervised him in his early days. It is an interesting fact from which wrong deductions may be made that it was Boutflour who had put forward Hanley (his former superior at the University of Leeds) for the newly created post of Agricultural Information Officer at Bristol University, from which job Hanley was appointed to the Chair of Agriculture. They were always close working colleagues and family friends.

There was only one competitor for the post and he withdrew. So Boutflour became Principal on 5 December 1930 and took up residence on 1 February 1931. There was certainly surprise among agriculturalists particularly those who could not see this very public man, with a national reputation for stirring up and convincing farming audiences, settling into the closer, quieter, academic world of teaching students. But they did not see it as Boutflour did. For him the College could be a vehicle through which he could continue his campaigns, but with the added bonus of influencing the young men who would pass through his hands. He could train them in scientific methods of farming and land agency and mould them into becoming critical thinkers, just as he himself had done.

But he had the strength of his supporters: none more so than Lord Bledisloe who had received advice on his farm from Boutflour and had expressed the view that he was 'the most progressive and outstanding young man in agricultural education'.

★

The Governing Body at this time consisted of Earl Bathurst (Chairman), Mr C.P. Ackers, Viscount Bledisloe (he was by now Governor-General of New Zealand and therefore a nominal member only), the Marquis of Crewe, Major F.W.B. Cripps, Sir Thomas Davies, Mr Alexander Goddard, Mr W. Scotford Harmer, Mr J.H. Scrutton, Mr Christopher Turnor, Sir Archibald Weighall, Lord Clinton, the Hon. Claude Biddulph (Representing the Royal Agricultural Society), Mr T. Loveday (Vice-Chancellor of Bristol University), Mr A.L. Hobhouse (Representing the Bath & West Agricultural Society), Professor B.T.P. Barker (Representing the University of Bristol), Mr G.G. Harris and Mr J.M. Scott (Representing Gloucestershire County Council), Major G.J. Buxton and Col. W.F. Fuller (Representing Wiltshire County Council) and Mr E.G.H. Massey (Representing the National Farmers' Union).

On his arrival Boutflour found that his senior staff were: J.F.H. Thomas, M.Sc., NDA, Vice-Principal; P.S. Brown, B.Sc. (Agric.), NDA, College Warden, Secretary and Bursar; H.E. Wells, B.Sc. (Agric.), NDA, NDD, Agriculture; A.C. Duncan, B.Sc. (Agric.), FRCVS, Barrister at Law, Veterinary Science; A.D.C. Le Sueur, B.Sc. (Agric.), FSI, Dip.For., Forestry.

Shortly afterwards, in 1931, Boutflour appointed Dr G. Redington, M.Sc. (Leeds), D.Sc. (Aberdeen) to take charge of Agricultural Science, and E. Shaw, B.Sc. (Agric.) to join him. Dr Redington had been Lecturer in Agricultural Botany at Armstrong College, Newcastle and Lecturer in Plant Physiology at Aberdeen University.

Boutflour must have been well pleased to take over an experienced and capable staff but he found that in other respects the College was in a parlous state. Firstly the numbers of students had dropped alarmingly: upon opening in October 1931 there were only some fifty students enrolled. This number was achieved only because a number of overseas students arrived at the last moment. There were certainly not enough to ensure a break-even income for the College, let alone show any surplus which might be devoted to carrying out improvements to the facilities. Secondly there was a lack of laboratory facilities and equipment, and the provision of a botany laboratory was one of the first priorities to match the appointment of Redington. Lastly the resources for practical teaching were quite inadequate. As Boutflour said, 'There were only about forty-eight acres of land, out of which roughly twenty-two acres were used for sports fields. There were nine nondescript cows, three sows and half a dozen sheep. The only farming implements were some haymaking tackle, a model of a Ransome plough 18in.

According to Mr. R. Boutflour, Principal of the Royal Agricultural College, Cirencester, a cow is better milked to a lively tune.
We seem to know that cow!

A political cartoon
1933, based on
Boutflour's ideas

long, and a couple of draught horses.' What a situation for a former National Director of Dairy Husbandry!

Boutflour's logic told him that it was imperative to increase the numbers of students if a satisfactory income was to be achieved and that the way to do this was through greater publicity for the College. That publicity could be achieved by exploiting his own reputation and so, with some degree of reluctance, he decided to continue his lecturing campaigns throughout the country and to write for the agricultural press. In this way the name of the College would be constantly in front of the public; not just the name, for Boutflour realized that the type of student he wished to attract and no doubt the parents who would be sending their sons, would be expecting more than a dry-as-dust academic institution. He deliberately set out to put before the landowning fraternity the prospect of a College with extra-mural attractions, particularly country pursuits and sporting activities. He revamped the College prospectus in order to create this better presentation. The trick worked and applications started to flow in. Boutflour was not above pulling the wool over people's eyes – he was known to have advertised in the *The Times* that the College had no vacancies and thus to receive even more requests for places!

The success of these methods brought in their train another problem: as the numbers increased the need grew for more residential accommodation. This was later to be solved by the construction of the King George V Wing and the Cedar Hostel. In the meantime every available corner of the buildings was used to house students.

To increase the area of farmland negotiations were opened with Messrs Phillips and Young, the tenants of College farm, with a view to taking over part of this farm by the surrender of part of their lease. This would have equipped the College better for the practical instruction of students, an improvement on the limited arrangement for the use of College farm. These negotiations failed because the terms of compensation were never agreed: they were thought to be excessive. However, in 1934, Captain Bruce Swanwick offered to let his farm of 157 acres at Coates (Fosse Hill Farm), to the College on a five-year lease at a rent of £1 per acre and an ongoing valuation of between £1,200 and £1,500. Fosse Hill Farm had rather more than half of its land under arable cultivation and was well situated at only one mile from the College. There were more than adequate buildings and although the layout and equipment were designed mainly for light horse breeding and mixed livestock and not for dairying there was no doubt that they could be easily adapted for cows. The intention then was to convert the College holding, i.e. that surrounding the College proper, to a grassland dairy farm and to run Fosse Hill Farm as a mixed enterprise on a strictly commercial basis. It was not long before a herd of Ayrshire dairy cows was established there.

One of the earliest actions of Boutflour was to open the College chapel. It had been closed for several years and he was conscious of the necessity of providing for the spiritual needs of the students. He managed to obtain the services of the vicar of Cricklade, the Revd Dr S.W.L. Richards, OBE, MA, DCL, Hon. CF, as visiting chaplain. The chapel opened for services on Sundays. He also had daffodil bulbs planted beneath the trees on either side of the main avenue and, despite harsh treatment from Army tanks parked under the trees after the retreat from Dunkirk, these still flourish in springtime, sixty years later.

So far as the curricula were concerned, the College was still offering the Bristol degree course and, after revision by a special sub-committee of the University, the students were to spend the first five terms at the University and the last four terms at the College. The syllabus of the one-year farming course for sons of Gloucestershire and Wiltshire farmers, established by Hanley, was revised and the course opened for students from outside those counties at a fee of £50. The College also ran the University's fruit preservation course in the College kitchens for three weeks in the summer vacation.

In 1932 Boutflour established the course that was to become the largest and most successful up to the present day. There had always been some element of estate managment in the curriculum of the College and McClellan had created a Chair of Estate Management and Forestry in 1903. What Boutflour started was a Diploma in Estate Management. It was a logical progression from his policy of encouraging the sons of landowners to enter the College, itself a result of his successful attempts to increase numbers by making the College environment attractive to these very people. The object was to train intending land agents to manage the estates of the landowners (the greater part of the agricultural land of the country was still let to tenant farmers, mainly by the larger estate owners), to train the sons of such landowners to manage in their own right and to enable the successful students to obtain qualification from the professional institutions as surveyors and land agents.

The course was an immediate success and one of the reasons for this was that being trained at an agricultural college, rather than by pupillage or at a non-agricultural institution, meant that the would-be surveyor and land agent had a sound basic knowledge of, and practical training in, scientific agriculture. This enabled him to run lands in hand, of which there would be, in the coming years, a greater area as landlords began to seek the benefit of direct farming profits rather than relatively static rents. This became an even greater influence in the post-war years. Probably Boutflour was one of the few to see, as early as 1932, that contrary to the general expectation that there would be a lessening in demand for land agents because of the gradual break-up of the larger landed estates on account of inheritance taxation (regarded even then by many as punitive), the profession would, in fact, expand to meet a demand for estate management by public authorities, by owner-occupiers and by corporate land-owners.

★

The College was still receiving support from the Ministry of Agriculture. In May 1931 the Agricultural Block Grants Re-Assessment Committee met at the College and the grant allocated to the College for the 1931/2 session was £1,900. However the 1932/3 session commenced with a drop in student numbers and as a result the attention of the Ministry was drawn to the fact that the name of the College had been omitted from their publication *Education for Agriculture*, which had given rise to a rumour that the College had closed down. The Ministry apologized for the omission, and an advertisement was placed in the national press. This appears to have been another instance in the hot and cold relationship that the College had with the Ministry; it was to be followed by others. It is probable that the only consistency in this relationship lay in the fact that the College always tried to be staunchly independent as a privately launched and maintained institution, and had only sought the assistance of government funds when in dire straits. It was not helped by the fact that Boutflour, in spite of previously holding the Ministry appointment of National Director of Dairy Husbandry, was regarded as a 'wild card'. The reaction of civil servants becomes understandable.

Indeed another instance occurred later on in this first Boutflour period. In 1938, when the College applied for a 50 per cent grant for the provision of extra student accommodation and laboratories, the Principal, after protracted correspondence ending with a refusal by the department, had to win the support of the Minister to have the decision overturned. This hardly made him more popular with the civil servants!

★

By 1932/3 things began to take a turn for the better as Boutflour's endeavours to increase the student numbers were beginning to show results. In order to develop the Estate Management course two new members of staff were appointed in October 1934; they were to have a long association with the College.

A. Noble, B.Sc. (Lond.), Est. Man. (Gold Medallist), NDA, joined from Seale Hayne Agricultural College where he had been Lecturer in Agriculture for eleven years, following his training at the same college. H.N. Jacobs, NDA, PASI, came from Messrs Hewett Lee, Land Agents of Farnham.

The staff and students in 1934

Gloucestershire and Wiltshire County Councils offered grants to the College in return for free places for their students, at an annual value of £75 each, on the one-year farming course. These grants amounted to some £300 to £600 per year.

In 1935 the Block Grants Committee paid another visit to the College and a grant of £2,500 was allocated for each of the next five years. This, together with the monies to be received from Gloucestershire and Wiltshire County Councils, enabled the arrangement with Captain Swanwick for the lease of Fosse Hill Farm to be confirmed. The occupancy of this farm has been maintained to this day and has proved an invaluable asset in the practical training of students. Thus Boutflour had succeeded in the third of the objectives he had set himself.

This improved financial position enabled him to set about increasing the student accommodation – a real necessity – for he was in fact accommodating them in his own residence as well as in any reasonable empty space in the main building. He told the Governors at their meeting on 20 March 1935 that the College could only accommodate fifty students, whereas there were sixty-one students attending courses that term and entries for the next session exceeded that number. He estimated that a new wing, together with equipment, would cost £8,000. He anticipated that the Ministry would make a grant of half the cost and he had been promised £2,356 from various sources.

In his application on behalf of the College for a grant from the Ministry of Agriculture he reported that there would be seventy-one students, including those from Gloucestershire and Wiltshire, and that the cost of maintaining the College was between £8,000 to £9,200 per annum. The total cost with tuition was about £170 to £175 per student; since the fees charged were £150 per annum there would be a shortfall. He pointed out that the arrangements with Gloucestershire and Wiltshire were that sixteen free places were to be provided in return for which there was a contribution of £600 from each county.

On 1 November 1935 the Ministry approved a grant towards the much needed accommodation of £4,000 on a pound for pound basis. Thus he was able to tell the surprised Governors that he had, in effect, got the money. He produced architectural plans for a new wing to match the style and facade of the College, to be built in stone, to extend the College on the south-west side and be directly connected. This would provide individual rooms for twenty students on the first and second floors, and on the ground floor a lecture room and a common room. The Governors approved the plans and instructed the architect, Major Stratton Davis, to proceed. The tender was eventually let to R.A. Berkeley, builders of Cirencester, at a cost of £7,997.

However, all did not proceed smoothly: there were problems over the interconnecting corridors (eventually the plans were modified to omit such corridors above ground level) and as a result there had to be a supplementary grant of £1,000 – this did not highly please the Ministry which accused the

Left: Mr Cecil
Leveson-Gower with
right: Robert
Boutflour, in 1935

Students in 19
off beagling!

College of bungling. Whether this influenced the Minister of Agriculture, the Rt. Hon. Walter E. Elliott, MC, MP, who declined an invitation to open the new wing is not known, but it was completed and opened on Tuesday 26 November 1936 by Mr Herwald Ramsbotham, OBE, MC, MP, Minister of Pensions (formerly Parliamentary Secretary to the Minister of Agriculture). It was named the King George V Wing.

This must have been of great satisfaction to Boutflour. He had rescued the College from financial insecurity to the point where, without recourse to loans and with the assistance of the Government, the essential fresh accommodation had been provided in an elegant extension of the College buildings in keeping with the Gothic design so boldly projected by the original founders.

The year saw the death of HM King George V and the accession to the throne of HM King Edward VIII, who later abdicated and was succeeded by HM King George VI. The new king graciously consented to become Patron of the College.

★

Boutflour's efforts to increase student numbers continued to reap success to the extent that even with the new wing there was not enough accommodation to meet the demand. By the beginning of the 1936/7 session the College was full with ninety-nine students, some still overflowing into the Principal's house. A hostel was built very quickly – it was put up between August and October – to house a further twenty. This, to be known as the Cedar Hostel for the obvious reason that it was constructed in durable cedar wood, was located at the back of the College opposite the new King George V Wing. It cost £2,000 and a grant was obtained from the Ministry of Agriculture of 50 per cent. The hostel still stands today, in good order and in full use, fifty-six years later.

There were problems over the grant from the Ministry. Boutflour was in too much of a hurry to wait for formal approval and by the time P.S. Brown, the College Secretary, wrote on 10 August 1937 following a visit from C.H. Harper of the Ministry, the contract had been let! But the Principal, in his contacts with the Ministry, had defined the building as temporary. He probably did not realize that this would rule out any chance of a grant. Nonetheless, after further inspection and a meeting on 11 November 1937 of two of the civil servants, Nathan and Harper, with Boutflour, Thomas and Brown, the grant was approved retrospectively on the basis that the building could be classified as semi-permanent. It seems that Boutflour's powers of persuasion had triumphed again!

What the Ministry had said, in a letter dated 3 February 1937 to the Treasury from whom consent had to be sought, was that if the grant was not paid the cost would all have to be met out of income '. . . and will necessitate, *inter alia*, deferring desirable increments in the salaries of lower-paid members of the staff'. It went on, '. . . additional laboratory and teaching accommodation is urgently needed at this College, in respect of which the College authorities contemplate making shortly an application for grant. . . . This project, the realisation of which is very desirable in the interests of efficient teaching at the College, would also have to be deferred if the grant . . . is not made.' This need for laboratory accommodation had been noted in a report by Major Garnsey, an official of the Ministry, when he visited in connection with the application for a grant for the new wing. He regarded it as most urgent. He said, '[The Science Laboratories] . . . are much as they were when the College was originally built in the early days of the 19th century. They are antiquated and totally inadequate.' Nathan, too, had noted this need when he visited in November 1937. So Boutflour still had problems to face.

★

The 1937/8 session started with one hundred and six students and this number increased to one hundred and twenty by the next session of 1938/9. So Boutflour had at last exceeded the previous maximum number of students which had been reached as long ago as 1908. Yet another insufficient resource now stood in his way – the lack of laboratory space as well as lecture halls. Following his success in persuading the Governors and the Ministry to finance semi-permanent buildings he decided to seek approval for four laboratories to accommodate seventy students, and two lecture theatres for ninety students, together with the necessary preparation rooms. He put the plans, estimated to cost some £6,000, to the Governors and sought a 50 per cent grant from the Ministry on the same lines as for the Cedar Hostel. The Governors approved but instructed that this was subject to obtaining the government grant or at least a firm assurance that this would be forthcoming.

So off went the plans and estimate on 6 April 1938 to the Ministry of Agriculture and in return the Principal received a letter dated 29 April 1938 requesting alterations and improvements as well as financial statements. It included the statement, 'The Ministry would be prepared to consider . . . an application. . . .' It was asked that the plans be by a registered architect. Instructions were given to the architect to make the amendments to the plans and to obtain tenders.

The requested details were sent and in his letter of 2 May 1938 Boutflour said that the College's cost would have to come out of revenue and a short-term loan. He pointed out that the present conditions were not tolerable: staff shared sitting rooms, they were taking classes in duplicate, they had no billiard room as it had been turned over to students, they lived in tiny bedrooms, three in attics in the Principal's house and seven rooms in that house were used by staff and students. Salaries, with two exceptions, were below normal. External lecturers had no room at all and the students had no recreation room. He went on that this had gone on for four years, that since 1931 when there were forty-six students the numbers had increased to one hundred and twelve and that entries would have to be closed before commencement of the session. This painted a picture of a College bursting at the seams.

It seemed that the Ministry was now disposed to approve the application if it could be shown that the funds that the College had to provide as the balance over and above a grant would come from outside sources and not from revenue. On 17 September 1938, A.R. Whyte, who was dealing with the case at the Ministry, urged Boutflour, in a personal letter, to make an effort to find the funds from outside. Boutflour replied that he had, indeed, tried. He said:

> The attitude of quite a number of men I have approached is that agricultural education is a public service and that their income tax should meet the requirements. Mr J.H. Scrutton, who for years was Hon. Treasurer of the College, and who knew its requirements, refused on these grounds to either give or leave money to the College in his will, and he was a millionaire.

The difficulty is that one cannot make a public appeal for £3,000. If a public appeal is to be made the time has to be opportune and the amount large. I propose to make a large public appeal on the occasion of the College Centenary, either in 1942, the anniversary of its inception, or in 1945, the anniversary of the beginning of its work.

The Ministry letter quoted 'new money'. Boutflour asked, '. . . were not increased fees amounting to £6,000 per year, "new money?" ' He continued, 'the need for the laboratories is urgent. The present accommodation has been seen by the Minister, Mr Ramsbotham, Mr Dale, Mr Nathan, Dr Wilkins, the late Maj. Garnsey and yourself [Mr A.R.Whyte]. For 112 students there is laboratory accommodation for 12 and bad accommodation at that. . . . the College had been seriously overcrowded with a view to getting extra fees to enable us to meet our share of the cost of extra buildings and equipment.'

On 7 October 1938 Whyte replied: 'We cannot put the case forward'. In effect the grant was refused. On the next day Boutflour responded: '. . . we were given to understand that the Ministry would pay a grant'. He referred to the letter of 29 April but it is possible that he read too much into such an official letter, though we do not know whether verbal assurances were given. In view of the successful application for the Cedar Hostel, which was of similar construction to the proposed laboratories, and the request for more details and the expense to be incurred on architect's fees, it was a not unreasonable assumption by Boutflour that a grant would be forthcoming. He was also probably bolstered up by knowledge of the previous reports made by Ministry inspectors which recognized the extreme and urgent need for these buildings.

He replied that the College could not now go back: plans had been made, put out to tender and prices obtained. Arrangements had been made for eight degree students to occupy the premises for 50 per cent of the time: 'These committments cannot be met without the laboratories, and as we cannot get rid of the committments we must have the laboratories by some means or other.' He asked for a loan and for repayment of the architect's fees of £300 since the Ministry had instructed that an architect be appointed. He finished, 'The College opened on Tuesday with 123 students.'

He was quite put out by this seemingly arbitrary decision of the Ministry. What happened next was typical of Boutflour's bulldog, but astute, attitude to a seemingly intractable problem. He set off to London on 9 October 1938 to make a personal appeal to the Minister, according to his own account of the affair, which continued, '. . . but on Kemble Station I saw W.S. Morrison [the Minister of Agriculture and MP for Cirencester] board the train. I had hoped I would run into him and I was lucky. I travelled up to London with him and the first thing he said on seeing me was "Have you got the grant for the laboratories yet?" I told him exactly what had happened. "So, they think I am the office boy", he remarked, looking far from pleased, and his parting words to me were, "Don't despair, you will get your laboratories." I did not go to the Ministry but caught the next train home to await events.'

The result of this encounter was that, on 10 October 1938, the Minister dropped a note to the Permanent Secretary, Sir Donald Fergusson, saying, 'Boutflour spoke to me about this in a state of considerable anxiety yesterday. The refusal of the grant apparently puts him in a hole for the course now commencing. About £3,000 is involved and they have gone ahead expecting it.'

This plain note must have concealed Morrison's annoyance that the decision had been taken without consulting him for, at the opening of the Cedar Hostel, he had said, publicly, 'I firmly believe there is still need for more accommodation, particularly laboratory and lecture room accommodation. To any potential benefactors who may be here – or to whom my words may carry – I say, if they were prepared to assist in this direction they would be bestowing their benevolence on a very worthy cause. That is a good story, and we hope it is to be "continued in our next"! . . . It is the combination of self-help and Government assistance, which is the happy marriage required to ensure the survival of our vital industry.' The College could not have asked for a much clearer indication that the Minister supported their application.

By this date there had been minutes in the official files sympathetic to the RAC case and suggesting that a grant be paid either at £3,150 or a loan without interest of £3,150.

On 11 October Whyte wrote a minute saying that the Treasury had asked departments to refrain from putting up proposals for new expenditure unless they could not be abandoned or postponed within the public interest. He felt that the College could put up with overcrowding and that the Principal must limit entries! He said, 'he has been unwise to raise the number to its present level for . . . the College is not equipped . . . for so large a number'. He pointed out that the Development Commission (who would provide the money on Treasury authority) would not accept the College share out of income for 'the money is indirectly passed on to the Ministry to pay'. He then suggested a half grant, half loan of the total amount.

The matter was now on its way to the Permanent Secretary and the next civil servant, Houghton, found that, within the Treasury guidance rules, it *could* be approved since, though the proposal could be postponed without detriment to the public good, he conceded that the laboratories were not a 'new' service. So he would not have opposed it. But he said, '. . . it seems desirable that some action should be taken to restrain the Principal from admitting an excessive number of students to Cirencester, which, I understand, means taking students that would otherwise go to another agricultural college'. This idea of the College being too full of students was first broached in Whyte's minute of 11 October – seemingly without any investigation, survey or external evidence. The Secretary appeared to agree with this.

A mollifying letter was then written to Boutflour couched in sympathetic terms and seeking to persuade him to postpone until 'times are more favourable'. But the underlying reason for the suggested postponement, which was effectively a refusal, was not given, i.e. that the College was taking students at the expense of other colleges. It was now beginning to be clear that the refusal was not for the reasons originally given.

Boutflour replied that he was at his wit's end. He understood that there was to be a scheme put forward for the balance of the cost to be taken as a loan scheme. It must be remembered that so far as Boutflour was concerned this matter of the balance of the cost was the only reason for refusal. He went on to suggest that the Permanent Secretary should come to the College and see for himself. He wrote that he could not postpone the works and that it was impossible to carry on without the finance.

As a consequence of this emphatic response by the Principal, Sir Donald Fergusson told the Minister that, after all, it could be recommended for inclusion in the estimates – but he still made the point about the Cirencester increase reducing the intake of other colleges – 'there is vacant accommodation elsewhere'. The Minister agreed.

This evidence casts new light on the account given in Boutflour's biography: it shows that the very success he had in building up the College from a low start, and in developing its potential was met in the Ministry, not with the help that would ensure the creation of a first-class institution to serve the agricultural community, but with a stultifying misunderstanding of Boutflour's aim to bring the College up to modern standards. The essence of the matter was contained in the report by Major Garnsey that the facilities at the College were 'built in the early days of the 19th century. They are antiquated and totally inadequate'. This should have overridden the proposition developed late in the discussions that the success should be curbed since it was apparently affecting other colleges, a proposition not shown to be valid by any investigation. It smacks of wanting to slow Boutflour down for any plausible reason.

The account about Boutflour's meeting with the Minister may be embellished by the anecdotal story from contemporaries that in fact he had found out that the Minister was going to be on that train and had 'arranged' the fortuitous meeting! If true it reflects his determination and astuteness!

★

The grant arrived: it was for £3,150, half the cost of the building and an offer of a loan for the remaining £3,150 repayable over ten years. The Governors accepted the offer and the tender of R.A. Berkeley Ltd of £6,300 was accepted.

By 1937/8 additional staff had been appointed: B.J. Fricker, NDA, NDD, Lecturer in Agriculture; R. Holliday, B.Sc., Lecturer in Botany; H.L. Knapp, B.Comm., Lecturer in Accounts and Asst Bursar; C. Tyler, B.Sc., Ph.D., Lecturer in Chemistry; and G. Williamson B.Sc.(Agric.), Lecturer in Agriculture.

At this time the fees at the College were £75 per year for tuition and £150 per year for tuition and board. For degree students the fees at the University were thirty guineas per year for tuition.

★

During these years Boutflour was engaged in writing articles (a chore he hated) on dairy farming and continuing his general campaign to lift the level of milk production by the adoption of modern scientific feeding methods. He still lectured throughout the country and organized conferences at the College, many supported by the British Oil and Cake Mills Company. All this exposure to the farming public reflected on the College and there is little doubt that its reputation was improved by such activities. Never before had the College had a Principal with such a clear understanding of the value of publicity and presentation. His own reputation extended beyond the shores of the United Kingdom.

An example of Boutflour's talent for publicity was that, in 1933, he advocated the playing of music to dairy cows in order to increase yields. He got wide coverage, as far away as New Zealand and South Africa, much of it in a humorous vein. The *Hawkes Bay Herald*, on 14 November 1933, reported:

> The Principal of the Royal Agricultural College, advising farmers in Ashby-de-la-Zouch on milking, said that cows liked human company and music. They should be treated to lively ditties and not to such strains as 'Art Thou Weary, Art Thou Languid?'

This particular talk even got into the *Musical Times*! It was the subject of much merriment by the cartoonists of the day, but it achieved Boutflour's purpose in gaining public notoriety for himself and for the College – maybe his tongue was in his cheek!

From America came a response to his many arresting articles: it was from a Mr Parmalee Prentice, a retired lawyer and millionaire whose wife was the daughter of the first John D. Rockefeller. He had an deep interest in the breeding of dairy cows. This was the start of a correspondence about the merits of bull recording, the value of which Boutflour had been pressing for several years. Prentice had established the Mount Hope Bull Index and had introduced progeny testing in the United States and other countries. Boutflour had, in 1933, invited Dr A.L. Hagedoorn of Leiden University, Soesterberg, Holland, a recognized geneticist, to come and give talks on his work in this country.

This regular correspondence with Parmalee Prentice continued right up to his death at the age of ninety-two in 1955, and three visits to Mount Hope were made by Professor Boutflour and his wife Mary. They became firm friends.

★

186

In the time of Constable and McCellan it had been the practice to invite men eminent in their field to lecture at the College: examples were Lawes and Gilbert, the Rothhamsted scientists. Boutflour resumed this practice and in his turn invited at one time or another many of the noted agriculturalists of his day either to lecture or to give papers at conferences. Not only that, but to widen the interests of students, speakers on a variety of subjects were invited. John Masefield, the Poet Laureate, and Peter Scott, the ornithologist, were among those who came and held their audiences fascinated.

★

Boutflour's Cow Management Chart was hung in dairies throughout the country and packed in the briefcase of all graduating students. It summarized the basic principles of his methods and provided a simple ready reckoner for the cowman. It was, in a sense, in the agricultural industry, a best seller.

During the Easter Term, 1934, in an issue of the *College Journal*, Vol. XX, Part 3, the following lighted-hearted verse was printed in praise of Boutflour's principles and of his chart:

THE MILKY WAY

Behold, my child, the Boutflour Chart,
See Rationing as the finest art!
No longer does our farmer groan
At undue prominence of bone;
No longer does the breeder wail
At elevation of the tail.
Nor need the modern cow feel shame
If she in all her legs be lame.
We tolerate her lumps and warts
If they increase her daily quarts.
A coat that's groomed to shining silk
Is not conducive to good milk.
But Boutflour's Chart points out the way
To seven gallons every day.
Beware the wicked roots, my child,
For roots make Boutflour very wild.
Control her hay, he advocates,
As for the rest . . . feed concentrates.
And don't forget that if you 'Steam'
Your cow increases milk and cream.

GIN.

★

THE ROYAL AGRICULTURAL COLLEGE

Clean Milk Production

REMEMBER. METHODS COUNT, MORE THAN ELABORATE EQUIPMENT.

1. FIRST ESSENTIALS (Milk and Dairies Regulations 1949)

(1) Clean sheds, adequately lit, good ventilation, hard floors and walls rendered smooth, efficient drainage. A proper dairy for cooling essential.
(2) Clean cows, hind quarters clipped and regularly groomed.
(3) Clean utensils in sound condition. Properly sterilised by steam or chemical means, stored free of dust.
(4) Clean milkers, with proper overalls, any person suffering from infectious disease must not be employed at milking.

2. HELPFUL EQUIPMENT

(1) Wash hand bowl and towel in cowshed, brushes and curry comb.
(2) Strip cup and udder cloths.
(3) Proper washing up 2 compartment trough in dairy.
(4) Steam sterilising chest or washing racks for milking machines if sterilising by chemical means.
(5) Hot water raising equipment.
(6) Efficient cooling by water or by refrigeration.

3. METHODS TO FOLLOW

(1) Remove all dung from shed, swill down to prevent dust.
(2) Wash the udder in warm water (120°F) with clean udder cloth, take fore-milk by strip cup, examine for mastitis " clots."
(3) Attach teat cups or start to hand milk within 2 minutes of washing the udder. Milk quietly and quickly, machine strip as soon as air bubbles appear in " sight " glass.
(4) Remove milk to dairy and cool immediately.

"Good milking is quick milking"

COW RATIONING & MANAGEMENT CHART

THE ROYAL AGRICULTURAL COLLEGE, CIRENCESTER.

Calf Rearing Information

1. USING WHOLE MILK FEEDING CHART

	WARM MILK per day	BOX FOOD (see meal mixtures opposite)	HAY (Good Quality)	WATER
1st week,	4 quarts	—	—	—
2nd ,,	4 ,,	—	—	—
3rd ,,	4 ,,	—	—	—
4th ,,	4 ,,	offered	—	—
5th ,,	3½ ,,	Then give from 1 lb. to 1½ lb. daily as cleaned up.	offered	offered
6th ,,	3 ,,		Then gradually increase in small quantities	
7th ,,	2½ ,,			
8th ,,	2 ,,			
9th ,,	1 ,,			

FEED IN THREE MEALS DAILY.

Typical Meal Mixtures

1. 6 parts linseed cake (broken). 4 ,, bean meal. 5 ,, oats or barley (crushed). 4 ,, flaked maize. 1 ,, fish meal.
2. 3 parts linseed cake. 4 ,, crushed oats. 2 ,, maize meal. 1 ,, fish meal.
3. 4 parts linseed cake. 3 ,, crushed oats. 2 ,, barley meal. 1 ,, fish meal.
4. 8 parts linseed cake. 4 ,, crushed oats. 4 ,, flaked maize. 3 ,, sharps or middlings. 1 ,, fish meal.
5. Or a calf meal made by a reputable firm.

2. USING MILK SUBSTITUTES

(1) Proprietary milk substitute foods now available, used to replace whole milk, 1½ lb. of substitute in 1 gallon of water replaces 1 gallon of whole milk. Start substitution after 3 weeks of age.
(2) If separated milk available can be used to replace whole milk if extra dry food such as crushed or whole oats given as a fat substitute with a vitamin A and D supplement. Fed after 3 weeks of age.

REMEMBER :
(1) Best quality hay only, allowed ad-lib. to calves.
(2) Do not wean too soon.

MAINTENANCE REQUIREMENT

To determine this take live weight in cwt., subtract 1 and multiply by 2. This gives maintenance requirements in lb. of hay per day—e.g., 12 (cwt.)—1 = 11. 11 × 2 = 22 lb. for a 12 cwt. cow.

TYPICAL STANDARDS for -	Friesians	Shorthorns	Ayrshires Red Polls	Guernseys Jerseys
In Pounds of Hay daily - -	22	20	18	15

HAY REPLACEMENT—

3 lb. silage = 1 lb. hay
4 lb. kale = 1 lb. hay
2 lb. brewers' grains = 1 lb. hay } Up to half the quantity of total hay fed can be replaced by these foods.
1 lb. straw = 1 lb. hay (This substitution is not recommended for high-yielding cows).
3 lb. roots
¾ lb. sugar beet pulp (dried) = 1 lb. hay.
4 lb. beet tops = 1 lb. hay.
¾ lb. dried grass (Medium quality) = 1 lb. hay.

AMOUNT OF DRY FOOD

Only a limited amount can be dealt with efficiently. To determine this quantity, take normal live weight in cwt., subtract 1 and multiply by 3. This gives cow's capacity in terms of lb. per day of hay and concentrates—e.g., for an 11 cwt. cow—11—1 × 3 = 30 lb.

TOTAL DAILY CAPACITY FOR	Friesians	Shorthorns	Ayrshires Red Polls	Guernseys Jerseys
In Pounds of Hay daily - - -	33-36	30-33	27-30	20-25

In the case of each breed heifers should receive 3 lb. less daily.

PRODUCTION RATION STANDARDS

The mixture of concentrates fed should have a starch equivalent value of 65—70 per cent., and a digestible protein content of 15 per cent.

Amounts of Concentrates to be Fed Per Gallon of Milk Yielded		
	For Friesians, Shorthorns, Ayrshires and Red Polls	3½ — 4 lbs.
	For Guernseys and Jerseys	4 — 4½ lbs.

FEEDING CHART

Special attention must be given to the necessity for actual reductions in the amounts of hay fed, in proportion as the milk yield increases.

DAILY YIELDS	FRIESIANS		SHORTHORNS		AYRSHIRES RED POLLS		GUERNSEYS JERSEYS	
	Hay LB.	Concentrates LB.	Hay LB.	Concentrates LB.	Hay LB.	Concentrates LB.	Hay LB.	Concentrates LB.
1 gallon	30	—	27	—	25	—	24	—
2 gallons	30	3½	27	3½	25	3½	16	8
3 ,,	22	10½	20	10½	18	10½	13	12
4 ,,	20	14	18	14	14	14	9	16
5 ,,	18	17½	14	17½	12	17½	5	20
6 ,,	14	21	12	21	9	21	3	24
7 ,,	11	24½	8	24½	6	24½	—	—
8 ,,	7	28	5	28	3	28	—	—
9 ,,	4	31½	—	—	—	—	—	—

Cows giving yields higher than those above require SPECIAL MANAGEMENT.
Cows losing milk should have teats sealed with collodion.

MINERAL MIXTURE

To each cwt. of concentrates add 1 lb. common salt ; ½lb. ground chalk 1lb. sterilised bone flour.

EXAMPLES OF BALANCED RATIONS FOR PRODUCTION

HOME-GROWN FOODS.

Beans - - - 1 part (by weight)
Oats - - - 1 part ,, ,,

PARTIALLY HOME-GROWN FOODS.

Fish Meal	1 part	Decorticated Groundnut	1 part
Oats	4 ,,	Oats	2 ,,
Barley	1 ,,	Barley	1 ,,
Wheat	1 ,,		

HIGH-YIELDING COWS. Cut out all hay and concentrates one p.m. meal each week and feed instead—5 lbs. bran, 2lbs. linseed cake, 1 tablespoonful sulphur, ½ teaspoonful saltpetre. (Feed as mash).

TYPICAL PURCHASED RATION

Decorticated Groundnut Cake 1 part
Flaked Maize or Maize Meal 3 ,,
Palm Kernel Cake - - - 2 ,,

(Or use a good balanced dairy cube made by a reputable firm).

For the last gallon of a high yielding cow—
2 lbs. Whole Linseed.
½ lb. Fish Meal.

STEAMING-UP BEFORE CALVING

FEED DAILY EITHER PALM KERNEL CAKE OR BALANCED PRODUCTION RATION as follows :—

3 lb. daily during 6th week before calving.
4 ,, ,, ,, 5th ,, ,, ,,
5 ,, ,, ,, 4th ,, ,, ,,
6 ,, ,, ,, 3rd ,, ,, ,,
7 ,, ,, ,, 2nd ,, ,, ,,
9 ,, ,, ,, 1st ,, ,, ,,

Heifers during this time should have their udders massaged night and morning for ten minutes.

Any heifer or cow coming to her milk during this time should be milked regularly as if calved.

During last 14 days increase gradually up to 75% of what you estimate the cow will require after calving.

IMPORTANT

The day before the cow is due to calve drench with ½ lb. glauber salts and 1 tablespoonful of ground ginger in 3 pints of tepid water. Repeat this drench directly after calving.

Compiled by R. Boutflour, C.B.E., M.Sc., Principal.

FOOD VALUES

To obtain a balanced production ration, mix the foods so that the starch equivalent is five times the protein equivalent.

Home Grown Conc'trates	Protein Equivalent %	Starch Equivalent %	Succulents	Protein Equivalent %	Starch Equivalent %	Purchased Concentrates	Protein Equivalent %	Starch Equivalent %
Oats	8	60	Fodder Beet	¼	12	Undecorticated Cottonseed Cake	17	42
Barley	6	71	Kale and Cabbage	1¼	9	Coconut Cake	16	77
Wheat	10	72	Beet Tops	1½	9	Palm Kernel Cake	17	71
Beans	20	66	Mangolds	½	7	Maize Gluten Feed	19	76
Peas	18	69	Swedes	½	7	Malt Culms	16	43
Linseed	18	116	Grass Silage	1½-2	9-12	Bran	10	43
Dried Grass 20% C.P. or over	15	55	**Purchased Concentrates**			Weatings	11	63
16%–19% C.P.	12	51	Decorticated Groundnut Cake	41	73	Dried Brewers' Grains	13	49
12%–15% C.P.	9	47	Soya Bean Cake	37	69	Maize Meal or Flaked	9	84
Sugar Beet Pulp (dry)	5	65	Linseed Cake	25	74	Maize Germ Meal	10	79
			White Fish Meal	53	59	No. 1 Dairy Cake	13	60
			Decorticated Cottonseed Cake	37	70	Grain Balancer Cake	21	62
						High Protein Cake	30	68

Swedes, cabbages and sugarbeet tops should be fed AFTER milking.

ORDER OF FEEDING FOR THE DAY

Twice Milked Herds

5.0 a.m. Half Concentrates
5.30 ,, Milk
7.0 ,, After Milking Half Hay
7.30 ,, Water

3.0 p.m. Half Concentrates
3.30 ,, Milk } Half hour later if practicable
5.0 ,, Half Hay
5.30 ,, Water

Three Times Milked

5.0 a.m. One-third Concentrates
5.30 ,, Milk } Half hour earlier if practicable
7.0 ,, One-third Hay

1.0 p.m. One-third Concentrates
1.30 ,, Milk
3.0 ,, One-third Hay

7.30 ,, One-third Concentrates
8.0 ,, Milk
9.30 ,, One-third Hay

Water should be laid on for high-yielding herds.

SHORT CUT TO BALANCING DAIRY COW RATIONS

Fish Meal — Meat Meal — add 6 of Cereal Group

High Protein Cake, Decorticated Ground Nut Cake, Decorticated Ground Nut Meal, Decorticated Cotton Cake, Decorticated Cotton Seed Meal, Soya Cake, Soya Meal, Extracted Soya Meal — add 3 of Cereal Group

Undecorticated Ground Nut Cake, Maize Gluten Meal — add 2 of Cereal Group

Grain Balancer Cake, Linseed Cake, Beans, Maize Gluten Feed, Undecorticated Cotton Cake — add 1 of Cereal Group

Coconut Cake, Palm Kernel Cake, Palm Kernel Meal, Weatings, Bran, Dried Brewers' Grains, No. 1. Dairy Cake — add no Cereals

CEREAL GROUP Maize, Barley, Oats, Wheat, Rice-Bran, Flaked Maize, Locust Beans, Maize Germ Meal, Tapioca Flour

ILLUSTRATION

Assume you have on hand

1 ton Fish Meal	× 6	6 tons
3 tons Decorticated Ground Nut	× 3	9 tons
2 tons Linseed Cake	× 1	2 tons
3 tons Beans	× 1	3 tons
2 tons Coconut Cake	× 0	0 tons
1 ton Bran	× 0	0 tons
3 tons Undecorticated Ground Nut	× 2	6 tons
Parts Cereal to add		26 tons

Say—
Oats — 10 tons
Barley Meal — 6 tons
Maize — 5 tons
Rice Bran — 5 tons
} or any other combination of Cereals amounting to 26 tons.

SHORT CUT FOR ESTIMATING QUANTITIES

32 weeks — 224 days   10 lbs. per day for 32 weeks = One ton

SUMMER FEEDING

CONTROL OF GRASS— 1½ hours good grazing morning, 1½ hours good grazing afternoon, Remainder of time outdoors on a bare pasture. or Strip grazing by means of electric fence.

All cows going out to GOOD GRASS should receive 4 lb. hay per day.

In May — — feed production ration for all gallons over four.
In June — — ,, ,, ,, ,, ,, ,, three.
In July, August and September ,, ,, ,, ,, ,, two.

AUTUMN GRASS IS NOT A FIT FOOD FOR A HIGH-YIELDING COW UNLESS CONTROLLED IN FEEDING.

Particulars of Courses from:—The Warden, Royal Agricultural College, Cirencester.

HUGHES & SON, LTD., PRINTERS, THE GRIFFIN PRESS, PONTYPOOL, MON

The Cow Management Char[t] as developed by 19

The Spring Term of 1935 saw the celebration of the ninetieth anniversary of the College. On Sunday 25 March a thanksgiving service was held in the College chapel of St George the Martyr, when the Right Reverend Dr A.C. Headlam, Lord Bishop of Gloucester, gave the address to a large congregation which filled the body of the chapel and the gallery. Governors and staff attended in full and the service was conducted by the Chaplain to the College, the Revd S.W.L. Richards.

Two days later Countess Bathurst planted a golden cedar in the new arboretum to commemorate the silver jubilee of the College Patron, King George V, and the ninetieth anniversary.

In addition to the opening of the Cedar Hostel by W.S. Morrison, the Minister of Agriculture and Fisheries, in 1937, and in contrast to this modern development, the College had a reminder of the past on Sunday 17 June, when a memorial tablet to the Revd John B. McClellan, the Principal from 1879 to 1908, was dedicated in the College chapel. As the *College Journal* stated, 'He was . . . responsible for the destinies of the College during a long period, which from the agricultural viewpoint was largely one of depression. In spite of this it was a

Service of thanksgiving in the College chapel for the ninetieth anniversary in 1935

189

period of prosperity for the College; we have to go back to Mr McClellan's time to find student numbers at all comparable to the present state of affairs.' What the writer did not say was that the College was maintained thus only through the financial life-saving acts of Lord Ducie. Under Boutflour no such benefactor was available, as he had revealed in his correspondence with the Ministry.

Present at this ceremony was Lady Cave, the daughter of McClellan, who had married the student who had become the Consul-General of Zanzibar and had been knighted for his work there. There was, too, another connection with the past, indeed with the very origins of the College. In 1847 the first Diploma of the College was awarded to Henry Tanner, the only student to gain the honour in that year. From 1875 to 1879 his son, Dr H.W. Lloyd Tanner, MA (Oxon.), D.Sc., FRS, held the post of Professor of Mathematics and Natural Philosophy at the College, and was the first man to be awarded the D.Sc. by the University of Oxford. In October 1937, one of the new students who entered the College was W.R. Tanner, great-grandson of Henry Tanner.

The year 1937 was certainly an eventful one for the College in other ways, too. Dr Hagedoorn, the renowned Dutch geneticist, paid a second visit to lecture on 'Plant and Animal Breeding'. This was part of Boutflour's aim of bringing distinguished lecturers to the College just as had been done in earlier days. It was Hagedoorn's seminal work on breeding that had provided him with the material for his campaigns on the breeding of dairy cows.

At the Fourth International Grassland Conference held at the College on 15 July that year, Professor Stapledon was welcomed back, as also was Professor Johnstone-Wallace of Cornell University.

A final item of significance, though on a different note, during this year, was the success of Dr Cyril Tyler, Lecturer in Agricultural Chemistry – not, however, in his chosen discipline, but in achieving fame on the cricket field. On his fifth appearance for Gloucester as a fast off-break bowler, he took five wickets against Middlesex at Lords. His victims included Patsy Hendren and H.G. Owen-Smith, the South African Test player and English Rugby Captain.

★

Early in 1937 the Vice-Principal, Thomas, resigned to go farming and his place was taken by Roger Sayce, who came from Suffolk, where he had been Organiser of Agricultural Education since 1930, and who had been with Boutflour in Wiltshire before that and was no stranger to his methods. Thomas had been at the College for eleven years. He had, in addition to being Vice-Principal, been Lecturer in Stock Husbandry and had taken responsibility for the management of the College farms at Fosse Hill and at the Steadings. His particular specialism had been the management of sheep and on this he had built his reputation. As he said on leaving he hoped to achieve a secret ambition to own and manage one thousand sheep.

Dr. C. Tyler B.Sc., Ph.D, A.I.C.

GLOUCESTERSHIRE'S SUCCESSFUL BOWLER WHO LECTURES at the ROYAL AGRICULTURAL COLLEGE CIRENCESTER ON ANIMAL NUTRITION

Born Ossett Yorks. 1911 Was at Leeds University First Club RAWDON.C.C. Self. taught – bowls fast med. off spinners varied with surprise leg.breaks.

Capt G D Maxhin DFC. 33 Fleet St 1938

Dr Cyril Tyler, Lecturer in Agricultural Chemistry and Assistant Bursar – and cricketer!

191

When Boutflour had been appointed to his post he was made Reader only at the University of Bristol. Now, at last, the University appointed him as Professor and a more effective liaison was achieved between the College and the University by a complete reorganization of the syllabus for the degree course, whereby the intermediate examination was to be taken after one year at Bristol and the final one after two full years' study at the College. According to Boutflour's biographer, his relations with the Vice-Chancellor (Dr Thomas Loveday) were not good. For a start there was the matter of the attitude that the University took in advising students of the degree course at the RAC. Boutflour had discovered that a prospective student had been advised, when interviewed at Bristol, that the degree at the College was not highly thought of. An assurance was received from Loveday that this would not happen again. But the two were of very different characters, the one ebullient and outgoing, the other a man of few words and with, as the biography says, 'a face of granite immobility'. There were clashes with the University over staff matters, but Boutflour had kept on good terms with the staff of the University. Even so, it was a pleasant surprise for him to receive the promotion. It did mean that the College had at last one professor on the staff after the many such posts held up to the turn of the century, and that the University had kept its word.

★

During 1938 and into 1939, following the Chamberlain/Hitler Munich agreement, the sense of impending war hung over the College. As the editorial in the *College Journal* for the Autumn Term 1938 said, 'It seemed strange to settle down again to lectures, and labs. and farm classes, after that hectic week of martial preparation, the talk of A.R.P. [Air Raid Precautions], the fitting of gas masks, the anxious waiting of news of the Chamberlain visits to Germany, hope, despondency, and then the elated excitement of the Prime Minister's last homecoming. . . . So began a term which was noteworthy for the fact that no less than 120 students came into residence. . . .' The optimism expressed about the events at Munich was short-lived. The journal of the Summer Term 1939 was the last for many years until the College reopened in 1946.

The closure, when it came, was at a time when the College was more active and more successful than it had ever been. The examination results showed a high pass rate in all the College diplomas, in the external examinations for the National Diploma in Agriculture and in the examinations of the professional bodies, the Institution of Chartered Surveyors and the Land Agents' Society. Accommodation for residence and for teaching had been increased to cope with the record number of students, teaching had been augmented by the acquisition of highly trained and experienced staff, and the prowess of the students at the numerous sports now offered was at a high level. The Rugby fifteen was beating Oxford colleges and in the Spring Term did not lose a match. There were strong debating and dramatic societies, and the Beagles Hunt was going strong.

Aerial view of the
College in 1938, the
laboratories and the
Cedar Hostel in the
left middleground

Academically, current and previous members of the College were winning
awards and speaking on public platforms. Roger Sayce was appointed as
Vice-Chairman of the Cirencester branch of the National Farmers' Union and
was the chief speaker in the BBC Midland programme in a discussion on
sugar-beet. N.D.G. James, who later became a lecturer at the College, won the
gold medal in the Chartered Surveyors' Institution Special Diploma in Forestry,
an award that had not been made for about twenty-five years. Stapledon,
Director of the Welsh Plant Breeding Station and a former Professor of
Agricultural Botany at the College, received a knighthood for services to
agriculture.

There were some staff changes. H.N. Jacobs, who was Lecturer in Poultry
Husbandry and in Surveying was appointed Senior Lecturer at the National
Institute of Poultry Husbandry, Newport, Shropshire. Later he was to return to
the College. The staff were joined by K.L. Robinson, B.Sc. B.Agric. (Belfast) as
a lecturer in Chemistry and Geology. P.A. Tucker, B.Sc. (Lond.) (Est.Man.),
PASI, arrived to be Lecturer in Surveying and Building Construction, having
been with the local firm of Hobbs and Chambers. J.R. Clapham, B.Sc.
(Dunhelm), NDA, NDD, took over as Lecturer in Dairy Husbandry from
G. Williamson, B.Sc. (Dunhelm), NDA, NDD, who left to join the Scottish
Department of Health in Edinburgh.

As the outbreak of war appeared imminent the Governors met on 2 September
1939 to consider the future of the College. The Principal had reported that he had
reason to believe that the College would be taken over by the Office of Works,
though he could not say for what purpose. It was agreed that no decision as to the
future could be made, and it was left in the hands of the Chairman, Sir Frederick

Cripps, Sir William Harris and the Hon. Claude Biddulph to take action in the event of the College being requisitioned. Following the declaration of war on 3 September 1939, at a meeting of this sub-committee, the Principal reported that the College had been taken over by the Office of Works. He had notified all students and parents that the College would not open for that term. He had also written to Sir Patrick Duff, the Secretary of the Office of Works, explaining the financial position of the College, but had had no reply other than an acknowledgement of his letter.

And so the College closed down for the second time in its history, due to a cause outside its control, and again at a time of rising success.

In spite of the fact that on the day after war had been declared the Office of Works arrived to take over occupation of the College, Bouflour made a late attempt to obtain the release of the College from the requisitioning. He had contacted the Ministry of Agriculture who had promised to get in touch with the Office of Works to see if the College could be released. Other colleges had been reopened to train members of the Women's Land Army. He had received some seventy-five applications for entry from prospective students and he felt that the College could continue without loss, provided the Ministry grant was continued. But the Ministry would not guarantee that the grant would continue to be paid. Lord Bledisloe expressed surprise that the College had been closed whereas other colleges had been reopened. The difference was, however, that the College had been taken over by the Office of Works; other colleges had been closed or kept open by order of the Ministry of Agriculture. Boutflour saw a connection between this and the episode of the grant for the laboratories.

So, the College closed for the duration of the war as far as agricultural education was concerned. In June 1940, following the withdrawal of British troops from Dunkirk, it was occupied by the Royal Ulster Rifles, then by a smaller number of the Royal Army Service Corps. For the remainder of the war it was occupied by 27 Group Headquarters of the Royal Air Force.

The staff were, of necesssity, given notice by the Principal and he, the Vice-Principal and the Bursar, received similar notices from the Clerk to the Governors. The staff found other jobs or went into military service and Boutflour moved out of the Principal's residence into Dairy Cottage at the Tetbury road entrance. In a very short time he was asked to be the Executive Officer to the Gloucestershire War Agricultural Executive Committee; he remained with his wife in the cottage for the duration.

The Steadings Farm was let to J.R. Clapham who occupied the cowman's cottage. Mr Phillips, of the College farm, took over the Fosse Hill Farm at a rent of £75 per annum for the first year and £100 per annum thereafter, eventually increased to £125, to be handed back to the College after the war.

The College had, of course, a claim for compensation in regard to the requisition and for this purpose the Bursar was kept on and continued to reside at the College after the expiration of his notice. In fact, the Governors instructed

Messrs Gerald Eve and Son to prepare the claim for compensation and, after negotiations with the Office of Works, it was agreed on the basis of a compensation rent of £1,650 per annum from 7 September 1939 to 31 March 1941 and £1,900 per annum thereafter. Expenses of £2,600 were paid.

The Governors continued to meet during the war: at these meetings the matter of the Treasury loan was dealt with. In November 1940, £2,500 received was invested in $2\frac{1}{2}$ per cent Conversion Stock and in 1943 the first instalment of principal and interest was paid.

★

This closure came at a time when the Royal Agricultural College was riding on the crest of a wave, created by the most dynamic Principal it had ever had. There is little to dispute this: no other Principal had increased the intake of students to such a degree, had carried out such an ambitious programme of expansion and had so boosted the reputation of the College in the sphere of agricultural education. There was a strong connection with Bristol University, enabling the College to offer an agricultural degree and the emphasis on the estate management teaching had resulted in the creation of a diploma which was acceptable as preparation for the final examinations of the professions of the land. Financially the Governors could be grateful to the Principal they had so boldly appointed for securing the income to match the increased expenditure that the expansions had required.

In Boutflour's period the College accounts showed that from 1935 onwards there had been a modest excess of income over expenditure and with the compensation from the Government the College remained solvent during the war years. This was a healthy change from the times of losses and yet it covered a period of major expansion. The College had added considerably to its assets, without incurring liabilities by borrowing: the King George V Wing, the Cedar Hostel, the laboratories and the squash court had all had been added since 1931. To see this put into abeyance must not have been easy to accept with equanimity, but at least the prospect of restarting with the advantages of the improvements was there for contemplation during the dark days of war.

Chapter Nine

THE SECOND BOUTFLOUR
PERIOD, 1946–58

*On any assessment he is one of the great men of British Agriculture: of the
company of Hall and Stapledon.*

R. Trow-Smith, 1955

The outbreak of war in 1939 brought the College to a stop as it had done in 1914: agricultural education took second priority to winning the War in spite of the fact that home production of food was to be a vital component in the struggle. The reason for closure seemed the same as in 1914: potential students would be serving in the armed forces. However, it was not quite the same because Boutflour had, in seeking to avoid requisitioning, noted that he had at least seventy-five applications and this would have meant that the College could have operated on a restricted basis. He would, nevetheless, have had difficulties in keeping or finding staff for they too went off either into the services or on to essential wartime work.

For how long the College would close, no one could forecast. What would be the state of agriculture and what would be the demand for agricultural training were unanswered questions. For the Governors, managing an institution closed for the duration of hostilities for its primary purpose became an act of faith with the objective of seeing that the College would be in a financial position to reopen and that it would not have the same struggle as it had had between 1918 and 1922.

The staff had left; Boutflour remained present in the Dairy Cottage but without the post of Principal for he was now working to increase wartime food production as the Executive Officer to the Gloucestershire War Agricultural Executive Committee. At the outbreak of war he had not known what the future of the College would be nor whether he would be able to resume the Principalship: it might well go to someone else. If it did, the new incumbent might welcome some briefing in order not to start blind, so Boutflour thought. He therefore sat down and wrote a letter addressed to 'The Principal upon Re-opening' and left it sealed for the post-war Principal, whoever that might be.

Dated 3 September 1939, it opened, 'War is upon us and my duties here will soon end. In the event of the College re-opening under someone other than myself, namely you, I thought my last job should be to give some guidance.' He went on,

> You have not got any easy job, as you will find if you study the history of the College . . . you will find that for most of this time the College has been badly managed, and when things go wrong the Principal bears the brunt, as you will read:–
> The 1st and 2nd Principals were dismissed.
> The 3rd died at 49 years.
> The 4th, 5th, 6th, and 7th were virtually dismissed.
> The 8th resigned, and
> I am the ninth.

These comments that Boutflour made at that time must be read with acknowledgement of his propensity for hyperbole and bluntness – which served him well in his communication with farmers. But though there is some degree of correct judgement in saying that four were 'virtually dismissed' it surely would not apply to McClellan, who recognized that he had reached a natural end to his occupation of the post when the reorganization in 1908 was being discussed, nor to Ainsworth-Davis who left upon closure of the College in 1915.

Boutflour said, 'I do not wish to infer that the Principals have been inefficient (some have done their job as well as it could have been) and I do not wish to infer that the Governors have been harsh or unreasonable. Such happenings are due to the type of management from which the College is administered.' In this Boutflour was right: some of the Principals who had left not necessarily of their own volition had been the victims of financial circumstances over which they had had little control. The cyclical nature of the College's finances had resulted in frequent crises warranting some reconstruction scheme. McClellan survived as long as he did because there was a generous benefactor as Chairman. But in the end a recasting of the corporate basis of the College, as in his case, and of the teaching policies in Dunstan's, led to the appointment of a new Principal.

Boutflour put down his thoughts on the Governing Body, since the relationship between it and the Principal was, in his eyes, the key to efficient management. He pointed out that with only four meetings a year, one in London and three at the College, many Governors could not be expected to know much about the running of the College. He advocated abandoning the London meeting and advised the Principal to present only soundly worked out schemes to the Governors, and to keep details of day-to-day management, especially of staff and student control, away from them! He said, '. . . you must always have in mind that the success of the College entirely depends on you, and that you . . . only can know what should be done, and that this can only be done with the consent of the Governors, so that you must get their confidence, and you must get your own way'. This extract surely reveals a secret of Boutflour's success and certainly expresses succinctly his philosophy of management.

He was undoubtedly proud to be the Principal of a College which, as he said:

> . . . is the oldest, has the greatest tradition. It has more of the public school about it than any other place. It draws its students from the public schools, and parents expect to pay at least public school fees; (many are surprised at the lowness of the fees). If the fees were higher than other places it would give the College a higher standing, in fact it would stand distinct and alone, and I have felt we would get students more easily if the fees were higher, for a very large percentage of people gauge a place by its cost, (I presume that is why Eton and large and expensive hotels are always full). It need not be raised a great deal either, 160 guineas or £180. . . .

Boutflour was nothing if not commercial in his attitude towards filling the College with students. His marketing strategy has much in common with many companies aiming at the top bracket and fixing charges at the level that those in that market can afford rather than at a rate relative to the services provided, allowing for a reasonable profit. It seems to have been a successful policy in pre-war days but we shall see that after the war it was to be changed and a more comprehensive spread of students achieved. His advice to the next Principal was expressed in very pragmatic terms, in his characteristic manner:

> You should get your students from the public schools. Keep in touch with headmasters and with the secretary of the Headmasters' Conference. Once full, print a list of names of students with their school and circulate with all prospectuses. Most applicants will find the name of someone they know and this will attract him. This practice has done more than any other in getting our students.
>
> Be firm and refuse any nit-wit or any other person that you would not be proud of introducing as an old student, even though they come from a good school or family. When they leave they are more obvious than others and do the place no good. Keep as far as possible to British White people, I took over with over 25% coloured. For the last five years I have had no more than 1%.
>
> When you interview parents of a good student realise the fees you are after equal your salary for three months, and as to whether you earn your salary primarily depends upon you landing him, fully realising if you didn't get him others will.

No wonder the people at the Ministry had been worried about Boutflour's ability to increase the numbers of students at the Royal Agricultural College at, as they presumed, the expense of other colleges! Yet he was aiming at a fairly exclusive market. It wasn't until after the war that the acceptance of students became more eclectic. Another change deriving from this period was the reduction in the numbers of overseas students: the days of providing qualified

Robert Boutflour,
Principal 1931–58

land managers for the Empire were over. This was particularly apparent from 1922 onwards and those coming from overseas were from the Commonwealth countries seeking to train their own people rather than to receive trained Britons sent out to manage the colonies. It must be realized, however, that prior to Boutflour's time, the College receipts were augmented by fees from these overseas students and they were very essential in keeping the College afloat. But Boutflour's success in recruiting students from Britain obviated the necessity of relying on overseas fees.

His letter touched on internal matters. His instructions on discipline were simple and to the point:

Scrap as many rules as possible.

Have sets of rules only for people who have not respected trust.

Let your Warden only be responsible to you for discipline.

Let the lecturer be the last word in discipline in his own lectures and classes and thereafter no authority, and do not give him the right to appeal to you, or the Warden.

Do not have the staff living on the same floor as students; when staff live with students they get enjoyment in making a row, if no staff there they only annoy one another and B quietens A.

How different were these simple rules from the days of Constable and his autocratic regime! It reflects the gradual change over the years from social relations and mores of the Victorian era. Even more changes were to come in post-war times.

No mention is made of his unique methods of appointing, promoting or maintaining staff. He was no believer in long, drawn-out procedures with applications, short-lists and detailed interviews. Once he had made contact with a potential member, his mind was immediately made up, relying on his instinctive ability to judge a man's character and capabilities. He also looked for sportsmen. Many were surprised to be offered the job on the spot and asked to start immediately! Perhaps these methods were not to be passed on to another Principal. But they were effective: very few unsuccessful choices were made. For this reason he did not often have to exercise the unpalatable right to fire anyone; when he did little time was wasted.

Another indicator of such change lay in the social side of College life. The Students' Club, which had been in existence since the early days and which had concentrated mainly on sports activities, had always been chaired by a senior staff member. In fact Professor Edward Kinch was the longest serving Chairman from 1897 to 1915. He was followed by the Principals, Dunstan and Hanley. But Boutflour had presided over only eight meetings before he proposed that the Chairman of the Club should be a student. His subsequent advice in his letter was to see that the right man was elected and to keep in constant touch with him. Thus he initiated the relative independence of the Students' Union, as it was to become.

His final words of advice were:

> The most important building in the College is its Chapel. Do have a Chaplain, and have regular services, for whilst you may not get large attendances, the influence is great and good. Whereas to have a Chapel and not to make full use of it the influence is bad.
>
> I wish you luck and success. It is a great life. I have enjoyed my eight and a half strenuous years, may we meet in happier days.
>
> P.S. Live your life day to day with the students. I always told my students I knew what they were going to do before they did it.

Boutflour's priorities were clear.

★

The Governors continued to meet during the war: there was some residual management to be carried out. By 1944 there were thoughts of reopening the College. The Bursar, the Revd P.S. Brown, who had been retained to look after College interests, reported that he was receiving applications for entry from many sources. The current Chairman of the Governors, Earl Bathurst, had died in that year and Major Sir Frederick Cripps was elected Chairman to succeed him.

So it was decided to make application to the Office of Works for early repossession of the College. Professor Boutflour, who had been reappointed as Principal in March 1944, had reported that all other agricultural colleges were open and full and that, in addition to the applications already received, a number of pre-war students who had not finished their courses were anxious to return after the war. He believed that a government grant could be obtained though he considered that the College could carry on without outside assistance.

Application was made to the Ministry of Agriculture and to the Office of Works for the lifting of the Requisition Order and for the property to be returned to the occupation of the College in time for it to be opened by Michaelmas 1944. This was not possible: not until 24 October was a letter received from the Office of Works to say that the Air Ministry would make arrangements to vacate the College on 31 March 1945. The Principal was instructed to contact the old staff to see if they could return to their duties.

Some could return, some could not. The Revd P.S. Brown, wished to accept the living at Duntisbourne Abbots and so resigned but carried on as College Chaplain. Brown had been appointed Lecturer in Agriculture and later as Bursar and Warden. It was while at the College that he had studied for the priesthood and had been admitted to Holy Orders in 1936. He eventually became Rural Dean.

Roger Sayce, who had been Executive Officer for the West Suffolk War Agricultural Executive Committee, decided to stay there and became County Agricultural Officer. H.L. Knapp, C. Tyler and R. Holliday all had other jobs they wished to stay in. But there were many of the old staff who were able to return: Le Sueur (Forestry), A. Noble (Estate Management), P.A. Tucker (Estate Management), G. Redington and K.L. Robinson (Agricultural Science), and Major A.C. Duncan (Veterinary Science) were all gladly received back to resume their work. Two important posts needed to be filled quickly. One was that of Bursar and Warden and the other that of Vice-Principal and Director of the College Farms since these were to be surrendered at Lady Day 1945 (the Steadings) and Michaelmas 1945 (Fosse Hill Farm).

So advertisements were placed in the national press for a Vice-Principal and Farms Director. Eventually Kenneth N. Russell, B.Sc., NDA (Hons.), NDD (Hons.) – a gold medallist in both examinations – from the West of Scotland Agricultural College was appointed. This appointment was to prove highly successful and was another example of Boutflour's ability to pick the right man for the job.

The post of Bursar and Warden was filled by an ex-serviceman, R.E. Meyler. In 1946 he resigned to follow a career in Kenya and was replaced by Harry Bailey, another ex-officer. By the time the College was able to open for the 1945/6 session additional staff had been recruited: C.H. Merivale (Animal Husbandry), D.E. Singleton (Crop Husbandry), E.H.R. Parsons (Agricultural Law), C.D. Anderson (Bookkeeping and Accounts) and D.M. Barling and R. Hill

Boutflour with academic staff in 1946. *Back row, left to right*: R. Hill, P.A. Tucker, C.H. Merivale, C.D. Anderson, G. Redington; D. Singleton, D. Barling, the Revd J.G. Sutton, A.C. Duncan. *Seated, left to right*: A. Noble, K.L. Robinson, K.N. Russell, R. Boutflour, H. Bailey; E.H.R. Parsons, Dr J.H. Grove-White

(Agricultural Science). The Revd J.G. Sutton was appointed as Chaplain and Dr J.H. Grove-White as Medical Officer.

At the opening of the College the members of the Governing Body were: Major Sir Frederick Cripps (Chairman), His Grace the Duke of Beaufort, the Rt. Hon. Viscount Bledisloe, the Marquis of Crewe, Lady Apsley, Lady Cripps, the Hon. Claude Biddulph, Brigadier E.B. Hankey, Sir Arthur Hobhouse, Col. W.F. Fuller, Lt.-Col. D. Macleay, Major G.J. Buxton, Sir William Harris, Professor M. Skene, Professor T. Wallace, Professor G.E. Blackman, Mr F. Peter, Mr J.P. Terry, Mr C.P. Ackers, Mr S.J. Phillips, Mr A. Goddard, R.R. Ware, Mr C.W. Whatley, Sir Archibald Weighall and Mr B. Swanwick.

★

There was a potential major hurdle to be overcome before any reopening could be considered. The Minister of Agriculture and Fisheries, the Rt. Hon. Tom Williams, had, in July 1944, appointed a committee under the chairmanship of Dr T. Loveday to: 'Consider the character and extent of the need for higher agricultural education in England and Wales and to make recommendations as to the facilities which should be provided to meet the need'. The report was drastic. It plumped for graduate courses leading to degrees in agriculture and agricultural science, as well as in estate management. It threw out two-year and lower than degree courses at universities and wanted the three independent colleges, the Royal Agricultural College, Seale Hayne and Harper Adams, to concentrate on two-year diploma courses, not to attempt to teach to degree standard and to give up one-year courses to farm institutes. It proposed that each of these colleges should specialize: the College on a two-year Estate Management course, Seale Hayne on agricultural teaching, and Harper Adams on Poultry Husbandry.

Thus the committee envisaged two types of agricultural education: the university degree course of three years (four years for Estate Management) and only two-year courses at the agricultural colleges. This was based on estimates of: an annual output of one hundred and fifty agricultural degree students, and of five students per year for the public service and ten for the private practice of estate management, but there was no estimate for the two-year courses. We can see now that this was a sadly low estimate. The three independent colleges had, it seems, capacity for three hundred students.

This report, had it been adopted, would have reduced the colleges to a level so far below that of the universities that they would have been little more than farm institutes. It said of the College, in paragraph 224: '. . . there is no reason why an agricultural college should be aided from public funds if admission is effectively restricted to a small section of the community that can afford to pay high fees. The Ministry of Agriculture and Fisheries is therefore entitled to require the college, in exchange for its maintenance grants, to reserve a substantial proportion of its places for scholarship holders.' The final words, in paragraph 229, were: 'The output of the system (of agricultural education) needs to be improved in quality rather than increased in quantity. The task is one primarily for the Universities, which must raise the standard . . . in order to put agricultural teaching on as high a plane of scholarship as any other branch of vocational education.'

This must have come as a severe shock to Boutflour; not unnaturally he opposed it strenuously. The consequences, if it were to be adopted by the Government, would be to relegate the College and the other two colleges, to a second or even third-class role. Considering that in pre-war times the College had offered the Bristol degree, and remembering the difficulties he had had with Loveday in those years, his opposition was implacable. This was not only on account of the lower place proposed for the College but because the forecasts of demand were so wildly inaccurate in his eyes; he foresaw a strengthening demand, especially from returning servicemen, and a lifting of the standard of the courses to be offered, virtually the opposite of the Loveday recommendations.

However, a maintenance grant of £14,000 per year was recommended for the College as well as for Seale Hayne and Harper Adams. In the event the College got only £10,500, the same as it had received before, and carried on unfettered by the Loveday Report, maintaining its independence. Time eventually proved Loveday wrong.

★

Ever since the foundation of the College the property had remained on the leasehold land belonging to the Bathurst estate. The Governors now felt themselves in a sufficiently strong position to make a bid for the purchase of the freehold of the College. Negotiations were opened with the estate which included also the tenancy of another farm, known as Field Barn Farm, of 205 acres. However, the trustees of the estate were not prepared to consider an offer of less than £50,000 for the College, so negotiations were broken off. The bid for the farm tenancy was more successful: it was agreed at a rent of £250 per annum.

The College opened in October 1945 with eighty-four students, a few of whom were pre-war students returning to complete their courses. The association with Bristol was not resumed which meant that the degree course was not offered. This is not surprising bearing in mind the recommendations of the Loveday Report so strenuously opposed by Boutflour and the lack of any meeting of minds between the two men concerned.

Basically there were three courses available: the 'A' course in Agriculture leading to the College Diploma and the National Diploma in Agriculture; the 'B' course in Estate Management leading to the College Diploma and to exemption from intermediate examinations of the Royal Institution of Chartered Surveyors and of the Chartered Land Agents' Society; and the one-year farming course. The ending of the association with Bristol meant that Boutflour now longer held a chair and could no longer term himself 'Professor'.

★

Before the war Boutflour had been contemplating the celebration of the College centenary. This anniversary fell in 1945 but clearly circumstances were against it being marked in that year. A celebration was therefore arranged for May 1946 subject to the invitation to Their Majesties King George VI and Queen Elizabeth being accepted. Once more the College was to be highly honoured by another visit by the reigning monarch. Their Majesties toured the College and took lunch in a marquee erected in the garden of the Principal's house (now the Bathurst Wing).

For the first time during a royal visit the weather was clement and a very splendid affair ensued; it was, after all, no ordinary occasion and Boutflour was determined to make sure that the College got the recognition it deserved. Many

The royal visit in 1946. *Far left*: HM Queen Elizabeth with Robert Boutflour. *Right*: Lord Bledisloe (*far right*) with the Rt. Hon. Tom Williams, the Minister of Agriculture

distinguished guests were invited to the luncheon and the press was there in force to record the day. Their Majesties were introduced to the Governors by the Chairman, Sir Frederick Cripps: among these were Viscount Bledisloe, PC, GCMG, Sir Archibald Weighall, KCMG, and Mr Alexander Goddard, CBE, all of whom had been gold medallists when students at the College.

At the luncheon the King, in responding to the toast of his health, referred to the many and continuing links between the monarchy and the College. He said:

As you know, the association of my family with this College goes back to its first beginnings, one hundred years ago. And, looking through its records, I notice that the visits of my forbears and myself have taken place at regular intervals of almost exactly a quarter of a century. This may be a coincidence, or it may be the magic application by the College authorities of the system of crop rotation. Whatever the case, I hope the association may continue to be as close as it always has been. My great-grandfather, my grandfather and my father all took a real interest in this College, and so do I. . . .

He paid tribute to Lord Bledisloe: '. . . I read the account of the festivities of 50 years ago. At the dinner . . . the Chairman said, "I was looking . . . at that very admirable journal, the *Agricultural Students' Gazette*, which Mr Charles Bathurst edits with such marked skill and assiduity." . . . this Mr Charles Bathurst is one and the same person as our old friend Lord Bledisloe . . . he is a farmer who has done as much for British agriculture as any man alive. . . .' Both Tom Williams,

Minister of Agriculture and Fisheries, and Lord Bledisloe, made reference in their speeches to the fact that at around the same time three great institutions of agriculture were celebrating their centenaries: the Royal Agricultural Society of England; Rothamsted, the first agricultural research establishment; and the College.

Boutflour, responding, drew a pen-picture of the changes in agriculture since the foundation of the College: '. . . the greatest invention of the past century was agricultural education . . . had [it] not come into existence 100 years ago half the white people now alive could never have been born. The amount of food produced in the world at that time was very low. The amount of food produced in the world in the last 100 years has more than trebled – the result of education.' He also pointed out that whereas the College had been built to take 152 students it was only in October 1947 that the intake would exceed that number. He emphasized the need to increase the output from the limited acreage of agricultural land in the country. This was a necessary injunction for, in the very newspaper

The full party du[ring] the royal visit in 1946.

reporting this event (*Wiltshire and Gloucestershire Standard*, Saturday 25 May 1946), there was a notice by the Ministry of Food telling the general public where to get their new food ration books!

After their tour of the lecture halls and laboratories Their Majesties planted beech and copper beech trees on the side of the cricket field.

★

To commemorate the centenary, an appeal was launched and circulated to the joint-stock banks, to City Guilds, agricultural organizations and to prominent residents in Gloucestershire and neighbouring counties. A Development Fund was established for the following purposes:
1. The improvement and extension of the College buildings with a view to adding to the number of students.
2. The further modernization of laboratory equipment and the provision of facilities for research.
3. The provision of additional modern agricultural buildings.

The objective was to raise £70,000 to mark the centenary year. The appeal was not successful: the reasons for this failure are not known but it was probably due to the timing and to the manner in which the appeal was conducted. Immediately after the War the country was in a state of relative economic exhaustion and against such a background an appeal would have had to be conducted with a high degree of professionalism for it to achieve its objectives. This was certainly the case with an appeal launched later on in the 1980s. In the event, by February 1947 only about £5,000 had been subscribed.

In 1946/7 there were 179 students, the bulk being the ex-service entry. During the previous session Boutflour had run mainly refresher and revision courses for the students who had managed to return earlier than most from their military service. It must have been hard going for the staff, many of whom had just returned from their wartime duties and who, in common with the early arrivals, had to bring themselves back to their teaching standards. It was typical of Boutflour, at the beginning of the Summer Term 1946, that he persuaded the staff to lecture in that term the whole of the year's work for the benefit of the students who were only too keen to catch up on their lost years. Even in the evenings lectures were given in most of the lecture halls, only finishing late at night.

In spite of the failure of the centenary appeal the College managed to purchase further student accommodation, now so vital if the influx of ex-servicemen was to be housed. A large private residence very near to the College buildings came on to the market in 1947 and it was purchased for £13,500. This house, Bartonbury, had at one time been the residence of Robert Jeffreys Brown, the original founder. In order to finance this, the Ministry of Agriculture was persuaded to offer a grant of half the cost, subject to the College raising the balance from external sources as a gift. It seems that relations with this

Trent Lodge,
acquired in 194
through the
generosity of
Pure Drug Co

department were on a much better footing than had been so before the war. One result of Boutflour's lecturing was that he was able to ask the Boots Pure Drug Co. Ltd, to whom he had given a series of lectures before the war, to contribute the balance. Included in the purchase was a cottage known as Ammonite Cottage. The additional accommodation was opened that year by Lord Trent, the Chairman of Boots the Chemists, and renamed Trent Lodge. It added housing for forty students and Ammonite Cottage was available as staff accommodation.

Now that he was back at the College with the future expansion plainly evident and with a Farms Director appointed, Boutflour could set about the College farms and put into practice his long cherished ambitions for dairy herd management. He was determined to establish a high-yielding herd at the Steadings and, with Kenneth Russell established, the policy of running the farms primarily as commercial units. This was, in effect, a continuation of the principles laid down as far back as McClellan's time that propounded that the best way to teach students practical farming was to show the results at first hand of College farms run for profit and not as demonstration farms. The farms were to be operated as follows:

1. The Steadings Farm (68 acres) would be run as a specialized, high production dairy farm with some fattening of pigs, and with potatoes as a cash crop.
2. Fosse Hill Farm (156 acres) would be an arable/dairy farm with milk production on more extensive lines, the aim being to maximize labour output.

3. Field Barn Farm (205 acres) would be an arable farm with poultry, store cattle and a flock of Kerry Hill ewes.

Twenty cows were purchased and under Boutflour's direction and Kenneth Russell's management high yields were soon being recorded. The Steadings's herd was costed by the Economics Department of Bristol University, and by 1948 the herd had shown profit of almost three times the average of all other herds costed by the University. This Friesian herd attained an average of over 2,000 gallons, with one cow, 'Beauty', reaching 10,000 gallons over three lactations.

The feeding and management techniques soon attracted the attention of the British Oil and Cake Mills Ltd (BOCM), who held many conferences and demonstrations at the College and produced a film of the Steadings herd entitled 'Cowmanship'. The publicity given to the College herd and farms by these conferences and demonstrations resulted in the farms becoming the venue for many visits by the farming community from all over the world. Under the control of Russell they began to show satisfactory financial results and the loan granted by the Treasury towards the cost of the new laboratories was finally discharged.

★

By the start of the 1948/9 session there were 387 students and the fees were £210 per annum. This big increase was due mainly to more returning ex-servicemen but also to the awakening demand for education in agriculture and estate management. There had been some staff changes: Messrs Robinson, Anderson, Merivale and Singleton had resigned, and among the newcomers were Dr W.E. Chambers BA (Oxon.), Ph.D. (Lond.) and J.A.R. Lockhart, B.Agric. (Belfast).

★

The sports and social activities of the students had been resumed and in 1946 the Rugby and hockey clubs were flourishing and were already making a success of their matches with their pre-war fixtures, both maintaining a high standard. Cricket, too, had started off well in spite of adverse weather conditions but as before the war, the College managed to have a county cricket player, Sir Derek Bailey, in their team. He was, in fact, Captain of Gloucestershire. The College Beagles had to start again from scratch because the pack had been lent to the Royal Gloucestershire Hussars and very little of the original pack were left at the end of the war. Under N.D.G. James as Master and Russell Freeland as Secretary they got going once again and eventually Freeland took over as Master.

★

In 1947 Lord Bledisloe offered to present and endow a gold medal, to be awarded to an old student who had made a contribution to agriculture after leaving College, another illustration of his abiding interest and support in his Alma Mater. The offer was gratefully accepted by the Governors, and Lord Bledisloe vested in the Charity Commissioners of England and Wales, under a Declaration of Trust, the sum of £1,000, the income from which was to provide the gold medal.

DECLARATION OF TRUST

I, the Right Honourable Charles, Viscount Bledisloe, P.C.; G.C.M.G; K.B.E.; M.R.A.C., being desirous of paying, with the authority of the Charity Commissioners for England and Wales, to the Banking Account of The Official Trustees of Charitable Funds at the Bank of England the sum of one thousand pounds sterling in order that the same may be invested in the purchase in their name of one or more of the stocks funds or securities (other than mortgages of real property) authorised by law for the investment of trust funds and that the income derived therefrom may be applied by the Managing Trustees hereinafter appointed to the Charitable purposes hereinafter declared DO HEREBY DECLARE that the said sum of One thousand pounds sterling is proposed to be paid by me to the said Official Trustees, under Order of the said Commissioners, UPON TRUST that the income accruing from the aforesaid investment may be remitted by the said Official Trustees unto or in accordance with the direction of the Governing Body for the time being of the Royal Agricultural College, at Cirencester, in the county of Gloucester, as Managing Trustees of the Charity intended to be hereby created (hereinafter called the Trustees) UPON trust to be applied by the Trustees for the benefit of the rural community in Great Britain or any other part of the British Commonwealth and Empire in providing a gold medal (to be called the Bledisloe Medal and to be a diameter of not less than two inches and of a weight of not less that two and three quarters ounces) to be awarded to a former student of the said College, who in his after career has, in the opinion of the Trustees, done work of outstanding excellence in improving the standard of husbandry or of any of its allied arts or sciences or otherwise in promoting the economic or social welfare of the said rural community. And I direct that the first award shall be made within six months from this date and that subsequent awards shall be made at such intervals as the Trustees shall think fit but that in any event within a period not exceeding five years from the date of the last preceding award. And it is my desire that the Charity intended to be hereby created shall be called the Bledisloe Medal Charity, IN WITNESS whereof I have hereunto set my hand this 15th day of September 1947.

[Signed] BLEDISLOE OF LYDNEY.

The first award was made on 13 May 1948 to Sir Archibald Weighall, Bt.,

KCMG, DL, JP, MRAC, and it was presented by Sir John Russell, OBE. In subsequent years the Bledisloe Medal has been awarded as follows:

1948 Mr Alexander Goddard, CBE, MRAC
1950 Sir John H. Milne Home, DL, JP, MRAC
1955 Mr J.Á. Arnold-Foster, OBE, FRICS, MRAC
1962 Sir Wilfred de Soysa, MRAC
1965 Mr (now Sir) Derek Barber, MRAC
1970 Major N.D.G. James, OBE, MC, TD, MA, FRICS, MRAC
1975 His Excellency Hossein Sepehri
1978 Sir Emrys Jones, B.Sc., LLD, D.Sc., F.I.Biol., FRAgric.S
1989 Major G.B. Heywood, MBE, FRICS.

Special permission was granted to permit the award to Sir Emrys Jones, who was not an old student, but the five-year clause (i.e. that the awards should be made within a period of five years from the date of the last preceding one) seems not to have been rigidly observed!

★

At this same presentation Sir John Russell presented the first medals to be awarded to students after the war. The recipients for 1947 were: Ducie Gold Medal: B.A. Shepherd; Holland Gold Medal: A.K.J. Quinney; Goldstand Silver Medal: J.O. Gaze; Harker Silver Medal: R.B. Sayce; McClellan Silver Medal: R.N. Cardwell; Haygarth Medal: H.R. Fell.

Boutflour was highly delighted with the results that the students were achieving in external examinations. He had, as mentioned before, set up the Estate Management course for students who would eventually qualify as surveyors, land agents and auctioneers by taking the examinations of the Royal Institution of Chartered Surveyors, of the Land Agents' Society (later the Chartered Land Agents' Society) and of the Chartered Auctioneers' and Estate Agents' Institute (the latter two now amalgamated with the Royal Institution of Chartered Surveyors). These bodies had made concessions for the ex-service students whereby they could take a special ex-service final examination, and so the Estate Management course had been extended into a third year. A little later they were to agree that the award of the College Diploma would grant exemption from their final written examinations. On leaving the college the successful student therefore only had to pass the practical examinations that the professional bodies imposed before achieving full professional qualifications and corporate membership. The first students to be entered for these examinations all achieved high places and this included the Percy Wilkinson Prize of the Land Agents' Society awarded for the first in order of merit won in three successive years. Students taking the National Diploma in Agriculture of the Royal Agricultural Society of England were also achieving satisfactory results.

★

By 1949 the numbers of students had risen to 414 and extra student accommodation was once again a pressing need. By good fortune a property came on the market which would help to solve this problem. Coates Manor Estate, sited about three miles from the College, comprised a manor house, a farm of about 270 acres let to Messrs S.J. Phillips and Sons, and fourteen cottages. The College negotiated the purchase from the owner, Mrs A.P. Payne, and secured it for £28,000, half the cost being met by a grant from the Ministry of Agriculture.

The manor house was sufficient to take seventy students from October 1950. The property had an unusual history. Formerly known as Hams Hall it was built in 1760 at Lea Marston in Warwickshire. The interior was burnt out in 1890 and although only a shell remained it was rebuilt within a year exactly as before. The present building is the top two storeys of what was originally a three-storey house. From 1760 to 1905 it was owned by the Adderley family, Mr Charles B. Adderley and Sir Charles Adderley, who later became Lord Norton and who had a long and distinguished political career extending over sixty-four years (thirty-seven years in the House of Commons and twenty-seven years in the House of Lords). He was an associate of Sir Robert Peel, Lord John Russell, Disraeli and Gladstone. Sir Charles Adderley also helped to found the Canterbury Colony in New Zealand in 1848, and it was at Hams Hall that the New Zealand constitution was first drafted. Between March 1919 and December 1921 Mr Oswald Harrison, a shipping magnate, built the present house with material he brought from Hams Hall, retaining the first and second floors in much the same form except for two bay windows which had been part of the last manor house. Mr Harrison was followed by Mr and Mrs Firth of Firth's Stainless Steel and then by their daughter, Mrs Payne.

It was therefore fitting that the opening ceremony should be performed by Lord Bledisloe, former Governor of New Zealand, on 24 May 1950 (Empire Day) and that he should rename it 'Bledisloe Lodge'.

When Coates Manor had come on the market, Boutflour had immediately applied to the Ministry of Agriculture for a grant to finance the purchase. He probably anticipated a long, drawn-out battle of wills remembering what had happened before the War concerning the laboratories. However, in March 1949 he persuaded the Governors that the College ought to possess a small estate which would complement the teaching of Estate Management by practising the principles being taught, in the same way that the College farms functioned. He wrote to the Ministry on 7 March 1949 putting forward the proposition that the Ministry should help to finance by a 50 per cent grant the purchase of an estate at a cost of about £60,000 to bring in an income of £3,000 per annum. Shortly afterwards a meeting to discuss this was held with the Director of the Agricultural Land Service, R.R. Ware, and two senior administrators, R.G.R. Wall and F.M. Kearns. They invited Boutflour to put forward a proposition on these lines. When Coates was available at an asking price of £40,000 the Ministry obtained a

Plate 15 Sir Archibald Weighall, Governor of the College

Plate 16 Alexander Charles Duncan, Professor of Veterinary Science 1905–56

Plate 17 The Bathurst Wing

Plate 18   Bledisloe Lodge, opened by Lord Bledisloe on 24 May 1950

Plate 19   Bledisloe Court, erected in 1983

Plate 20 The Boutflour Hall, erected in 1959

Plate 21 The Hosier Library Reading Room

Plate 22   The College chapel, showing the Boutflour memorial window in the east end

Plate 23 Professor Robert Boutflour, Principal 1931–58

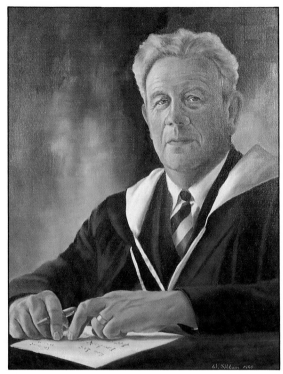

Plate 24 Frank Garner, Principal 1959–71

Plate 25 H.V. Hughes, Principal 1979–90

Plate 26 Professor Arthur Jones, appointed Principal in 1990

Plate 27   The visit of the Prince of Wales in 1989

Plate 28   The College in the summer of 1990

Plate 29 Watercolour painting of the College

valuation from the District Valuer of £28,000 and offered a grant of pound for pound with this valuation as a maximum purchase price.

They accepted that this was to be a start in building up 'the Estate', but they made the grant conditional on the student numbers not dropping below one hundred and seventy. In this event, it was required that Coates be resold! Armed with this Boutflour was able to obtain the property at £28,000, with the prior agreement of the Chairman of the Governors. He then asked the Governors for the balance from the College reserve funds and got it! And so, for the first time, the Principal was able to extract a substantial capital grant from the Ministry without a long argument; it was ironic that this time the department wanted him to guarantee, in effect, the increase in numbers whereas, in pre-war negotiations they wanted him to hold back! Such were the vicissitudes of dealings with official bodies.

There were some other improvements carried out during this period of expansion of the College up to 1953: in 1950 the old disused veterinary hospital at the Steadings was converted into a lecture hall with a turntable for animal and machinery demonstrations; the College drive was resurfaced; the major part of the College was re-roofed; a hostel for twenty domestic staff was built at the back; twelve new garages were added and the chemistry and botany lecture room was extended. The total cost of these was about £12,000 and grants of 50 per cent were given. It is of interest that in the five years to 1955 in which these improvements were carried out the College received no more than its contemporaries, Seale Hayne, Harper Adams and Studley Colleges, in fact rather less since the rates of grant for them were in some cases more than 50 per cent and up to as much as 90 per cent.

★

Boutflour's success with the dairy herd at the Steadings, in taking the production yields up to as high as 3,000 gallons a year, gained national recognition. Conferences and meetings were being held regularly at the College and elsewhere, which he arranged and at which he spoke, many of them sponsored by BOCM. This firm had realized the potential of his work when he was carrying out his advisory campaigns in Wiltshire and had watched the progress of his ideas about animal feeding stuffs. He had been condemning the traditional feeding of linseed and undecorticated cotton cake to dairy cows and had substituted more simple concentrated foods in balanced rations. BOCM changed their production and began to sell these balanced compounds. Other firms were able to benefit from his advice but it was BOCM which repaid the College for the benefits they had gained by following this advocate of modern feeding methods. As we shall see later on, their recognition of this remarkable man took the form of a generous financial contribution to the College for the erection of the Boutflour Hall.

★

In 1950 the Bursar, Harry Bailey, died after a short illness. He had been a well-liked Bursar and Warden with many friends and was a vital cog in the wheel of expansion. Boutflour needed a replacement of equal calibre and was able to persuade Neil Jacobs, his son-in-law, to take the post. He had been at the College in pre-war times on the Estate Management staff and had been Director of the National Institute of Poultry Husbandry at Harper Adams Agricultural College from 1938 to 1940. He came from the post of County Agricultural Officer for Worcestershire. Another change, early in 1951, was the appointment of D.M. Barling as Head of the Agricultural Biology Department, occasioned by the death of Dr Redington, whose portrait hangs today in the tithe barn.

★

Over the period of the development of successful dairy farming methods by Boutflour, he had never committed these to paper – continuous talks, demonstrations and lectures since his pioneering efforts in Wiltshire had flowed, but no definitive work had been done setting all this down. However, this was remedied by Kenneth Russell, the Vice-Principal, who, in 1950 wrote *Making Money from Cows* – a publication with a most apt title, for that was just what Boutflour had constantly sought to do. It was said that he had put thousands of pounds into farmers' pockets and millions into the pocket of BOCM. The publication continued a long line of books written earlier on agricultural subjects by distinguished members of the College staff.

A reviewer said of Russell's book: '[It] covers all phases, the science, the practice, and the economics of milk production. It shows not only how to manage cows for high yield but also for high profits. It is written by a man who is just as much at home in the cowshed as he is in the lecture room, for he is a man of great scientific knowledge and who has an ability to farm equal to the very best of practical farmers.'

★

In spite of the fact that the 1951/2 session, with 490 students, saw the increase in the use of the College in vacations for courses organized by outside bodies, (this was an initiative of the new Bursar, Jacobs), the accounts for the earlier years showed a deficit. The Governors had always been reluctant to increase fees to a realistic level; it was only as a result of pressure from the Principal and Bursar that fees for resident students were therefore raised for the next session to £250 per annum and for non-resident students to £130 per annum.

It was in this year, 1952, that Queen Elizabeth II succeeded her father, King George VI, and graciously consented to be Patron of the College, and Boutflour was honoured by being created CBE in recognition of his service to agriculture.

★

There were changes to the Governing Body over the next two or three years. A reorganization took place in 1951 consequent on the deaths of R.R. Ware, the Director of the Agricultural Land Service and representative of the Ministry of Agriculture, and of Sir Archibald Weighall, Bt.

Lt.-Col. Sir Archibald Weighall, Bt., KCMG, DL, JP, MRAC (Gold Medallist), had been a student at the College in company with Lord Bledisloe at the end of the nineteenth century and had been a Governor since 1923. Writing in the *College Journal* (Vol. XLII, 1952/53) Lord Bledisloe said:

> There has been no better human advertisement for the Empire's oldest and greatest centre of agricultural training. He was a man of amazing energy, versatility and inspiring initiative and comradeship. . . . He was a fine sportsman, a born leader (always in the van of progress), blithe, lovable, impeccably smart in his attire, and a humorous, impressive and forcible speaker, in spite of his characteristic and incurable stammer. He attributed his successes in life mainly to the R.A.C. It never had a more loyal, faithful or popular 'Alumnus' . . . he never lost the common trust.

In his distinguished career he served as an army officer in the South African and First World Wars, he was Governor of South Australia from 1921 to 1922, President of the Royal Agricultural Society of England in 1946 and President of the Land Agents' Society in 1934.

In 1953 Major Sir Frederick Cripps resigned as Chairman of the Board of Governors and was succeeded by the Rt. Hon. Earl St Aldwyn. Opportunity was taken to increase the responsibilities of governors and to involve them more closely with the work of the College by creating Finance and General Purposes, and Farm and Academic Committees with Earl St Aldwyn as Chairman of each. One of the first acts was to invite the attendance of the Chairman of the Students' Union. One important decision, which subsequently proved to be very much to the benefit of the College was to place the responsibility for the investment of surplus College funds in the hands of the Chairman and the Bursar.

The Farms Committee met on the 27 July 1953 to inspect Coates Manor Farm. This was to be taken over from Messrs S.J. Phillips and Son from that Michaelmas on terms agreed for the surrender of £1,500 compensation, tenant right valuation of stock and crops and no claim for dilapidations. The shooting was retained by Mr Phillips at one shilling per acre.

It was decided to run it as an arable and beef stock-rearing farm with a flock of Clun ewes and a pig-fattening enterprise. The buildings were adapted for these purposes. During the year the College won the first prize for the most productive farm over thirty acres in the county and third prize for the best managed farm. The Steadings herd won the BOCM milk yield competition for the highest yield of a team of eight cows, the Challenge Cup of the National Milk Recording Society for Gloucestershire for a herd of over fifteen cows with the highest butter fat yield and the same Society's Challenge Cup for the best managed herd of under twenty cows. During the year some 850 people visited the farms. They also won the Gloucestershire Root, Fruit and Grain Society's prize for the best cultivated farm over two hundred acres.

The farm profit for the year was approximately £3,451 while the excess of income over expenditure for the College as a whole was £14,984. As a result the annual grant from the Ministry of Agriculture and Fisheries was ended and from that time onwards no grants, apart from capital grants, were received from government sources.

This excellent performance by the farms is attributable in large measure to Kenneth Russell, the Vice-Principal and Farms Director. He had put into practice the Boutflour principles of dairy-herd management. Unfortunately the College was to lose this outstanding man at Easter 1955, when he was appointed to the post of Principal of the Yorkshire Farm Institute at Askham Bryan. Boutflour said of him:

> On the re-opening of the College, he, at the age of twenty-nine, took over and restocked the pre-war farms of the Steadings and Fosse Hill, together with the newly acquired farm, Field Barn – a total of 430 acres, and he had farmed them with outstanding efficiency and high profitability. He has won cups for the best managed farm, highest production farm, best managed livestock, highest milk yields; but what is more important is that the Costings Accounts kept by the University of Bristol shows his farming to be the most profitable on the larger acreage farms. In September, 1953, his farming operations were extended by the taking in hand of Coates Manor Farm of 260 acres.
>
> Mr Russell's farming operations, however, were only a means to an end, that is, to supply demonstrations to students of successful farming. In a lecture room he can have few equals, for he is clear-thinking, fluent, and can be heard, and there is no doubt that the 2,200 students who have passed through his hands will have a considerable influence on the agriculture of the country, by putting into operation his great teachings.

Kenneth Russell followed the tradition of many of the eminent teachers at the College who down the years had so effectively passed on their knowledge and experience by demonstration of scientific methods, thereby gaining reputation not just for themselves but for the College and for the benefits that could be bestowed on all who came seeking an agricultural education. What is more, he was a man for his time for he complemented his Principal, Boutflour, by executing the principles of farming the Boutflour way. They were a contrast. Russell achieved his goals by sheer hard work. In fact he overworked to his own detriment. Boutflour set about his tasks with flair, persuasion and eloquence and as a master of communication.

A contemporary who was a student at this time and who attended the lectures

Kenneth N. Russell taking a livestock class

of both men said, 'With Russell in the lecture hall you never stopped writing. It was all intense and full of detail, set out methodically; you really needed no text book – it was all there. With the Principal you never took a note; but one thought or fact was driven into your head for ever! A visitor standing outside the lecture room could identify who was in there. If it was quiet it was Russell; if the period was punctuated by laughter and raised voices it was Boutflour. Students were never so lucky as those who were taught by both men.' The old library over the dining hall is now the Kenneth Russell Memorial Room and from this splendid start the College farms have, save for in 1960, never failed to show a profit.

When Russell resigned in 1955 the Board decided not to make a joint appointment of Vice-Principal and Farms Director. The post of Farms Director went to Henry R. Fell, MRAC, an old student of the College who was managing for Mr Clifford Nicholson. Unfortunately Russell departed under something of a cloud. For one thing he had not informed Boutflour prior to his application for the post at Askham Bryan; for another, the farms, although showing above-average performances, had lacked attention to maintenance and Fell had a first job of repairing fences and other equipment. Perhaps this may be attributed to Russell's single-minded aim of achieving high figures in the farm accounts; it should not be allowed to detract, except to a minor degree, from the praise showered on him by his Principal who invariably supported his staff to the outside world.

★

A further change in the Board of Governors had to be made during the year when the Earl St Aldwyn was appointed Parliamentary Secretary to the Ministry of Agriculture and so had to resign as Governor and Chairman. He was succeeded as Chairman by Col. W.A. Chester Master. On the academic staff H.V. Hughes left to become Vice-Principal of the Leicestershire Farm Institute.

★

In 1954 plans were being made for further building developments. The College had registered developments for the next five years with the Ministry of Agriculture and it had recommended:

	Estimated Cost £
Conversion of rooms at Bledisloe Lodge	2,000
Two pairs of cottages for the domestic staff	8,000
New dining hall and kitchens	16,000
Total:	26,000

These had been agreed but it was decided that a new assembly hall was of greater necessity than a new dining hall. The Ministry were willing to substitute the one for the other but only at a limit of £16,000 against an estimated cost of £30,000 for the hall. They would pay a grant of 70 per cent. The Principal reported that the British Oil and Cake Mills had offered £10,000 as a seven-year covenant towards the hall. So the position would be that the Ministry would contribute £11,200, BOCM £10,000 and the College would have to find £8,800. There was, however, an inevitable condition attached to the Ministry grant. They wished to have a firm assurance from the College that the student numbers would be reduced to three hundred over the next two years.

A meeting was held on 15 June 1954 of a ministry committee on government grants for agricultural education, chaired by Dr Keith Murray, Chairman of the

University Grants Committee, with Mrs Assheton, G.A. Nott, Professor H.G. Sanders and Brigadier F.R.W. Jameson. The last two represented the Ministry of Agriculture and the Principal and the Bursar attended for the College. The meeting discussed the proposal that the numbers be reduced to three hundred and it turned out that the College *wanted* the numbers to be reduced to this figure because of the strain on facilities and staff following the influx of ex-service students. There must be doubt as to whether Boutflour had assented to this: it was probably more the idea of the Governors. At that time there were 410 students, the previous year there had been 465 and before that 491. There was accommodation for only 220 in residence. Their plans envisaged an intake of 100 for the Agriculture Diploma course, 40 for the Estate Management course and 40 for the one-year course. The Principal opposed the idea of increasing the fees – in his opinion they were already dangerously high compared with universities and farm institutes and they got 80 per cent of their income as grants whereas the RAC got nil!

The committee interviewed the then Chairman of the Governors, Earl St Aldwyn, who reckoned it would take three years to get down to three hundred. The Vice-Principal, Russell, reported that the farm profits were about £8–£10 per acre. The committee concluded that the grant could be approved. They also added that Russell was doing too much in running seven hundred acres with no bailiff and no foreman and that he might crack up! There was little doubt that he *was* worked to excess and this perhaps explains the doubts expressed at his departure about the state of the farms.

On 13 April 1955 the Ministry offered a grant for the coming five years of 70 per cent of £26,000. This included the £16,000 estimated cost originally allocated for a new dining hall but now to be attributed to the proposed assembly hall. But the amount was to be reduced by half the estimated trading profits for the five years, i.e. £7,500.

But by June 1955 Boutflour still had his doubts about the wisdom of accepting that the numbers ought to be reduced. He wrote to Manktelow, then Deputy Secretary of the Ministry, on 27 June and said that of ninety students examined by Sir James Scott Watson and Ralph Sadler, eighty-nine had passed. 'May I ask,' he said, 'will we get better results by reducing numbers? Would it not have been a pity if we had only trained 45 instead of 90 seeing there is no other place where the other 45 could have gone to?'

The Ministry referred Boutflour's concern about reducing numbers to Dr Keith Murray, who said that the College, 'has no intention of reducing numbers below 300 . . . this [is a] deplorable situation'. The Ministry recommended to the Treasury that the condition be removed but that the grant be reduced to £8,000 from £11,200. Murray also considered that the retention of 'an excessive number of students' would have, 'consequent ill-effect on the standard of education'. The matter was referred to the Parliamentary Under-Secretary but the outcome was that the condition was not removed and what was offered for the five-year period from October 1954 was:

1. Capital grants of £18,200 (70 per cent of £26,000).
2. Non-recurring maintenance grants of £4,500–£5,000 per year starting in 1956/7.
3. A reduction in student numbers to three hundred.

In effect this was no different from the original offer. Boutflour must have had a feeling of *déjà vu* since this argument of too many students had followed him from the start of his relations with the Ministry.

By now Boutflour realized that the demand was such that far from the intake diminishing naturally it would increase and that he had rather make provision for accommodating it. So, though originally apparently (though reluctantly and most likely as a tactic in order to secure the grant) in favour of reduction, he now objected to the condition. He realized that if student numbers were not reduced he would not get the maintenance grant since the extra fees would make it unnecessary but that he did need to acquire the capital grants. He told the Ministry so, but the Murray Committee insisted on keeping to the original recommendation. Dr Keith Murray said of Boutflour, 'he is a very difficult person to argue with'.

Writing to the Ministry on 25 February 1957, Jacobs, the Bursar, said that the Governors had decided that the limit on numbers would be 470! They had also decided to accept the offer by BOCM to pay towards the new assembly hall one half of £25,000 over seven years – the College would have to find the rest out of reserves. Other members of the corn and feeding-stuffs trade were to give approximately £8,500, but the other half had to come from the Ministry. He asked once again, on behalf of the College, for the grant.

★

Running throughout all this correspondence and communication with the department there appears a general criticism started by Murray that the educational standards at the College were not as high as they should be for an institute claiming to be one of higher agricultural education. This comment was made in 1958 to the Parliamentary Under-Secretary. The criticism seems to have been arrived at by reference only to the results of students taking the National Diploma of Agriculture. There was no mention of the results of the Estate Management Diploma and the external examinations of the Royal Institution of Chartered Surveyors and the Land Agents' Society.

On 24 March 1958 the Parliamentary Under-Secretary (Lords) of the Ministry of Agriculture, Earl St Aldwyn, wrote to the Acting Chairman of the Governors, Major P.D. Birchall (who had been appointed Deputy Chairman when, earlier in the year, Col. Chester Master had been taken ill), 'as friends with long-standing informal ties with the College'. He referred to the Murray Committee on numbers and standards of teaching and noted that the numbers were then four hundred and seventy and the staff had been increased from twenty-one to twenty-five. This was not enough. The aim should be:

1. A teaching ratio of 1:15 with the number of one-year students greatly reduced.
2. Stricter entry standards to be set and enforced.
3. To be an institution of *higher* agricultural education.

The reply given by the Governors was that they were aware of and would face up to these failings especially regarding the one-year course. The Parliamentary Under-Secretary accepted that the one-year course could be kept but that it should be tightened and a higher entry standard enforced to keep the numbers low! During this exchange the grant was still being considered but the condition was never removed and in the end the College financed the balance of the cost of the new assembly hall out of reserves.

In spite of the argument and counter-argument there was no sign of animosity. When the time came to open the new hall a request was made to Buckingham Palace for the Queen to accept an invitation to visit. When consulted about this the staff at the Ministry gratuitously mentioned their unhappiness with the standard of education but still cleared the request. In the event Her Majesty could not accept because of a very full diary. It had been, possibly, left too late.

That the officials at the Ministry did find Boutflour difficult to deal with is apparent from a minute on 4 November 1955 by W.C. Tame, one of the senior officials who dealt with the case: 'Had this been any other College I would have suggested asking the Principal to come and talk matters over with us in the hope that we should be able to persuade him to come some way to our views. . . . such a meeting would not produce any useful result and might even make matters worse.'

It is difficult not to come to the conclusion that there was a failure on both sides to understand each other's viewpoint, allied to a certain amount of obstinacy. On the Ministry side the greatest influence was that of Dr Keith Murray, who judged the College in the light of university standards and demanded the equivalent. The criticism based on the results of the National Diploma of Agriculture examinations, for which only a handful of students sat, was very narrow. In 1955, in the examinations of the Land Agents' Society, which gave a qualification regarded in the professions as the equivalent of a university degree, the College won three of the top prizes awarded, the Hugh Cooke Prize, the Percy Wilkinson Prize and the Talbot Ponsonby Prize. The required reduction in numbers, the ultimate stumbling block, was borne of a desire to bring the College into line with other establishments, as well as an appreciation of the anticipated demand. For his part, Boutflour did change his view when he saw that the demand would not diminish; in any case a Principal whose College did not rely on continuous government subvention for its financial stability as other colleges did would not take kindly to being asked to reduce the possibilities of achieving such stability from the market. So Boutflour was fighting for the maintenance of the College's independence and this was to be the outcome of his own battle to rescue it from bankruptcy in his early days and of the background of history. Prickly and obstinate he was, but he would have said that this was in the interests of his College.

★

During the summer vacation of 1955 Professor Boutflour (although the connection with Bristol was severed he seemed to retain the appellation of Professor) visited Australia at the invitation of the New South Wales Milk Board and toured the Perth, Melbourne and Adelaide areas. He spoke at the opening of the Milky Way Exhibition and the Milk Industry Convention as well as to many groups of farmers. This was a highly successful tour gaining much publicity for him and his message. He went down well with Australians who took to his bluntness and his humour. He never forgot to publicize the College and made it and his home 'open house'. The year 1955 was a peak: he was awarded the Thomas Baxter Trophy, a gold medal. This was for his services to the British dairy industry. He appeared on a nationally popular BBC wireless programme, 'The Brains Trust', which although bringing more recognition, was never an exposure he enjoyed. Boutflour's strength lay in face-to-face contact with his audiences.

In that year the Board of Governors became more representative and had thirteen members representing leading agricultural organizations as well as central and local government.

★

Gradually the College admissions were approaching the target figure of 470. In 1955/6 the numbers were 413 and in 1956/7 they had gone up to 456. Fees were increased from £250 to £285 per annum for resident students and from £130 to £150 per annum for non-resident students as from October 1956. In this year once again the College took most of the prizes on the Estate Management side. In the Royal Institution of Chartered Surveyors examination students of the College won the Driver Prize for first place and the Beadle Prize for the highest marks in Agriculture. In the Land Agents' Society examinations a student of the College won the Hugh Cooke Prize for first place and four other students gained distinctions in Report Writing and one in Agricultural Buildings. Not too bad for a College supposedly low in educational standards!

On the farm the College was still winning distinctions. The Steadings herd was for the third time in succession the highest yielding in the whole county for herds over ten cows with an average of 20,569 lb per cow. It was also top of the herds for the three year average with 20,055 lb. Boutflour's aim of teaching by example was being achieved.

In addition to the proposal for a new assembly hall the Governors were considering the provision of a car park and new houses for the Principal and the Bursar, one to be in the grounds of Trent Lodge and one in what was the

Principal's garden. These were very necessary: the old house for the Principal, which had been the original farmhouse when the College was erected, was far too rambling for modern residential accommodation and there was no house for the Bursar at all, who ought to be living near to the College main buildings as he was the Warden as well. Furthermore, a new house for the Principal would release room for extra student accommodation, a perennial problem while the College was expanding. A sick-bay and more room for domestic staff would be gained. The Principal reported that as far as the houses for the Principal and Bursar were concerned he had been promised generous gifts amounting to £8,449 and that Mr Bailey of E.H. Bailey Ltd, of Matlock, had suggested that he might make a grant of £5,000. With a generous offer from BOCM, and with the assurance from the Bursar, who was managing the College's investments, that such investments would not be sold at a disadvantageous time, the Governors could authorize these developments, in spite of the lack of government support.

It will be remembered that the College did not own the freehold of its land and property: it was held on lease from the Bathurst estate. Consent for the erection of the assembly hall and the Bursar's house had to be obtained from that estate, under the Landlord and Tenant Acts of 1927 and 1954, in order to preserve the right to claim compensation at the end of the lease. Lord Bathurst was willing to cooperate in this and meetings were arranged between him, his agent Mr Lloyd, and the Chairman of the Governors. Meetings were also held with the solicitors of both sides. There was difficulty in reaching agreement about compensation: the landlords argued that the improvement was unreasonable and that consent must be withheld under the lease in order to be protected against the possible compensation claim. In the end the Governors agreed that the College would not make any claim for compensation at the end of the lease but that consent would be given to the erection of the new hall and the Bursar's house on terms that their value would not be taken in to account in assessing a revised rent of the College premises. In the case of purchase by the College both parties would be free to negotiate terms without regard to the amounts spent by the College on improvements.

The works were carried out in 1956. The work for the assembly hall was contracted at an estimated cost of £23,026, excluding architect's fees. For the Bursar's house the lowest tender, which was accepted, was £6,591. The new car park of 4,200 sq. ft. cost £2,700.

So the Principal had shepherded though another major development of the College, necessitated by his success in increasing the numbers of students and thus achieving financial stability. In addition his persuasive skills, so effective with farmers in improving their profitabiity and so effective in teaching students, were put to another good use: that of raising money for the College. Under any other circumstances it would probably have been necessary to mount an appeal with no guarantee of success. Credit must go also to the Bursar, Neil Jacobs, who, having in 1951 been instructed to build up funds, was now handling the

College investments with acumen and, by shrewd judgement, took advantage of the rising stock market of that time. In coming years, his skill in this direction and in the prudent management of expenditure was to prove of great value to the College. He was firmly supported by Boutflour who had an abhorrence of waste and wasteful spending.

★

Changes took place in the Governing Body and in the academic staff. The Ministry of Agriculture representative Governors changed: Professor G.E. Blackman and J.S. Hill were replaced by Professor A.N. Duckham and D. Christy. Five staff left and among those appointed were H. Catling (Agricultural Engineering) and G.A. Cragghill (Agriculture).

It was in 1956 that one of the very longest connections with the past history of the College was severed: Major Alexander Charles Duncan retired, having served the College faithfully and well for over fifty years. He had been appointed Professor of Veterinary Science in late 1905. He was then aged twenty-nine, having been born in Dublin on 25 January 1876. He was one of the first four students to enrol at a newly started veterinary college in Ireland. He was a gold medallist in Veterinary Medicine and Veterinary Surgery. His entry into education was as research assistant to the Principal of the Dublin Veterinary College, Professor A.E. Mettham, FRCVS. It was while he was there that he obtained his Fellowship of the Royal College of Veterinary Surgeons. He carried on his research work at the Royal Agricultural College. There was a break in his service with the College when, like many others, he served his country in the First World War. He was Veterinary Officer to the Gloucestershire Yeomanry and acted in the same capacity to the Wiltshire Yeomanry. He went overseas with the Gloucestershire Yeomanry and became Assistant Director of Veterinary Services with the Egyptian Expeditionary Force; this led him into contact with General Allenby with whom he became a personal friend.

His talents were such that before the war he had studied law and just after the end of it he was called to the Bar and became a barrister-at-law. In these pre-war days he had been College Warden for a while and thus was only too involved with the major fire on the College premises in 1913. After 1918 he had set up in practice as a veterinary surgeon in Cirencester, while continuing to lecture at the College. He had been one of the strongest protagonists for the opening of the College in the difficult days between 1918 and 1922, particularly in rallying local support in Cirencester. Duncan was a prominent Freemason and a practising Christian, regular in his attendances at the College chapel and at the Parish Church of Cirencester.

Duncan (more familiarly known to all as 'Dunky') was the editor of Thompson's *Elementary Veterinary Science* and a man with a sense of humour and a kindly way with students. His portrait, painted by Cadogan Cowper, RA, hangs in the tithe barn alongside that of one of his colleagues in later years, Dr George Redington. Duncan died, at the age of eighty-five, on 13 December 1961.

★

A tutorial system was introduced, to start at the beginning of the 1956/7 session, for both the Diploma courses. This innovation would bring the College more in line with university practice and would result in closer contact between students and staff with a fuller appreciation of students' difficulties and an early assessment of their work. For the first time weekend tours were arranged: one by J.A.R. Lockhart to Leicestershire, Norfolk, Suffolk and Essex to show these types of farming, and the other by W.H.A. Lockhart to study forestry in Shropshire, Herefordshire and North Wales. These tours continued for fifteen years.

★

Students were now being drawn from many parts of the world. Among the 462 students in 1957 were those from Kenya, South Africa, Southern and Northern Rhodesia, Tanganyika, Australia, Cyprus, Egypt, Finland, Iran, Argentina, Brazil, Ceylon, Malaya, Saudi Arabia and Spain. This very wide spread of recruitment indicated the degree to which the reputation of the College had extended beyond its traditional catchment area of the British Commonwealth. It had also gone far beyond Boutflour's injunction at the beginning of the war to his possible successor to keep to white students.

However, this year, which was a manifestation of all that Boutflour had striven for during his time, was to be marred by tragedy. In May of 1957 he had been struck down by cerebral thrombosis, as a result of which his left side was partially paralysed, though his speech was only slightly affected. Though thus disabled he carried on but inevitably his vigour diminished. Constant visits to hospital drained him and the illness brought on frequent bouts of depression. He could only walk with the aid of a stick and although his health improved sufficiently to enable him to get about, the medical officers were of the opinion that it was doubtful whether he would recover his health and strength sufficiently to resume his duties as Principal. He took this advice and resigned his post as from 28 February 1958 to end one of the most remarkable periods of the College's history.

For twenty-eight years he had fought to lift the College from near bankruptcy to be a large, thriving, nationally and internationally recognized agricultural College of excellence, and had been successful beyond any dreams that he might have had in those days of the early 1930s when he first took the bold plunge from pioneering advisory work into teaching young men the elements of agriculture.

The College was now financially secure for about the first time since its foundation. It had facilities to match any equivalent institution and its academic standards were at last recognized as being at university level for its Estate

Management courses. There was still progress to be made to raise the other courses up to this standard and to rid the College of the residual element of reputation as a place for the well-endowed, mostly engendered by the short course (not dropped because it was such a money-spinner). There can be little doubt that had Boutflour not been so cruelly taken out of commission he would have tackled these deficiencies with his acknowledged determination and single-mindedness.

Boutflour's character and the picture that he presented to the world outside the College, and the basis on which his reputation as an iconoclast was built was summed up by the closing paragraph of an article in 1955 in the *Farmer and Stockbreeder*, celebrating the award to him of the Thomas Baxter Trophy. R. Trow-Smith wrote:

> On any assessment he is one of the great men of British Agriculture; of the company of Hall and Stapledon. There may be other back-room boys as eminent; but Boutflour would never have made a back-room boy. He would for ever be putting his head out of the window to cock a snook at the passers-by, and they, looking at his still cherubic face and impish grin, would no doubt love it. For he is irrepressible, and irrestible.

Nearly three thousand students, all of whom affectionately referred to him as 'Bobby', had passed through the College during his time, more than had done with any other Principal throughout its previous one-hundred-year history. As C.H. Coad (later to become the Chairman of the Governors) wrote in the *College Journal* of 1961/2: 'BOBBY – not Professor Boutflour or 'The Prof' or 'the Principal' or 'The Old Man', but just plain 'Bobby', and known as such by thousands of students and hundreds of thousands of farmers. His name will live in history as that, and be as great a memorial to him as any man could wish for.' This testimonial to a great Principal reveals in a nutshell the character of the man – so well known throughout the agricultural industry in this country and the world over that he needed no more than a family name to be instantly recognized. There still is no other 'Bobby' to all who are associated with the College.

Upon his retirement, in recognition of his long and distinguished service to agricultural education, he was elected an Honorary Life Member of the Royal Agricultural Society of England in March 1959 and an Honorary Fellow of the Institute of Corn and Agricultural Merchants Ltd in 1961. British Oil and Cake Mills Ltd gave a lunch in his honour in 1958 at the Grosvenor House, under the chairmanship of Mr Guy Chipperfield, CBE.

Boutflour died in 1961 at the home of his daughter in Cirencester as a result of another massive stroke, having lived out his short retirement with his wife, Mary, at the home of his son in Essex. In May 1959 he had been able to return to the College for the opening of the assembly hall that he had planned and found the funds for. He made a speech, even though he had to fight through his disability. It has been described as the best he had ever made. Arthur Noble, a long serving member of his staff, described it: 'The old wit, the old drama and the old feeling were all there, and impromptu as of old.'

There is a plaque in the Boutflour Hall in recognition of his efforts to raise funds for the Hall and the Old Students' Association placed a stained glass window in the chapel. The window, which was designed and made by Mr Paul Quail, was dedicated on 29 September 1963. A final quotation may serve to précis the qualities of Boutflour: '. . . the most capable, colourful, eloquent and forceful character that ever adorned the fields of agriculture'. (Guy Chipperfield, CBE)

Chapter Ten

DEVELOPMENT UNDER GARNER, 1959–71

He pursued his objects with a rock-like determination, with the result that his achievements often confounded those around him.

Sir Emrys Jones, 1971

By the time of Boutflour's retirement the College had resumed its place as the premier agricultural college and its reputation was world-wide. An era had ended. How then should the Governors start the new period? Should they seek to maintain the same impetus created by Boutflour or take a more conservative line and look for a Principal who would consolidate the gains that had been made in the post-war period? If they did seek the same impetus where could they find a successor of the calibre, character and style of Boutflour? Wisely, they decided to take their time over the decision and a special committee consisting of Major P.D. Birchall (who had been appointed Deputy Chairman when, earlier in the year, Col. Chester Master had been taken ill), Professor A.N. Duckham and S.J. Phillips was set up. Their job was to consider which policy to adopt (the last appointment of a Principal was twenty-eight years ago), invite applications, select a short-list and recommend candidates to the main body for interview. In the meantime the Bursar, H.N. Jacobs, was appointed Vice-Principal to carry on the day-to-day running of the College.

The result of world-wide advertising was that by 19 June 1958 forty-nine applications had been received and it looked as though a decision could be made by July. The Governors made slow progress. They felt it better to let the College run in the capable hands of Jacobs for a little while longer to ensure that they got the right person. The sub-committee was given powers to choose and appoint the new Principal. On 20 November it reported to the main body that they had selected Mr Frank Garner, MA, M.Sc., a Cambridge graduate and at that time the manager of a large agricultural estate in Cambridgeshire. The Governors approved the appointment and that he would take up the post on 1 January 1959, though in the meantime he would attend Governors' meetings and visit the College as often as possible. The choice was of an essentially practical man with wide experience and the right academic qualifications. The Governors hoped that with these qualifications they had picked someone who would be prominent in promotion.

Garner was a busy man: his work in his previous post had prevented him from being present at the College for more than a few days during the Autumn Term of 1958. But in these visits he concentrated on the work and activities of the students.

Born in Wiltshire in 1904 on his father's farm, Frank Garner had entered Cambridge University in 1921 with a Senior Agricultural Scholarship and on leaving there three years later with a First Class BA he was appointed Assistant to the Director of the University farm. In 1925 he had been awarded a Ministry of Agriculture Scholarship and had entered the National Institute for Research in Dairying at Reading. Later he went to the School of Rural Economy at Oxford University and took a BA by incorporation. He had a spell in the United States and took an M.Sc. at Minnesota University, returning to Cambridge to take up appointment as a University Demonstrator and subsequently Lecturer in Agriculture. During the Second World War he had worked for the War Agricultural Executive Committee and later as County Agricultural Organiser in East Suffolk. In 1944 he was appointed General Manager of Hiam Farms, Ltd, and

Frank Garner,
Principal 1959–71

Ponsonby Prize for Practical Agriculture and the Pendlebury Prize for Forestry. In addition, an old student of the College won the Royal Agricultural Society of England Medal for Practical Agriculture. How pleased the previous Principal would have been and what a good start for the new incumbent! Furthermore there was the security of the improvement in the College finances, for the liquid assets at that time amounted to £75,000 all in invested funds. There was to be a continuing story of growth in the College assets while the investment management was in the hands of Jacobs, the Bursar.

★

The number of students in 1959 had slightly reduced to 449. Major Anthony Biddulph and Mr Ivor Morris accepted invitations to become Governors and to serve on the Finance and General Purposes and Farm Committees respectively. This year saw another visit by the Keith Murray Committee (the Minister of Agriculture's Committee on Agricultural Colleges). The result was little different from the last time: the Committee wanted changes in the College's policies that were unacceptable and which would not only change the character of the College's teaching but would certainly necessitiate a change in the financial policies. The Committee's terms of reference were:

> To review and report on the work of agricultural colleges. To make recommendations as to Grants to be paid in the quinquennium beginning October 1959. To consider and make recommendations about the place of Agricultural Colleges in the Future structure of Agricultural Education.

The Principal had suggested to the Governors that they should accede to the informal request that had been made for the Committee to pay a visit to the College. The Governors agreed, the invitation was issued and the Committee asked for details of the College's progress in the last five years. This included information on the results of internal and external examinations, academic plans for the next five years, a 'class history' of the 1955/6 intake of students, the academic staff with their qualifications and subjects taught, the College's views on the place of the agricultural colleges within the agricultural education structure, academic entry standards and whether any revision of them was anticipated and the subjects passed in the GCE examinations at 'O' or 'A' Level by first-year students of the 1957/8 intake. In other words this was to be a thoroughgoing and comprehensive examination of the College's teaching. Not only that but the Committee wanted to see the College finances for the four years 1954/5 to 1957/8.

Armed with this prior information the Committee visited the College on 30 April and 1 May. The report was not received until February 1960. The result was that the Committee:

1. Expressed satisfaction at the progress made during the previous five years, but

although improvement had been made in the educational standard they felt that there was still room for further advancement.

2. Felt that although the staff/student ratio had been reduced to 1:20 a ratio of 1:14 would be more suitable.

3. Considered students should be given more encouragement to read more widely, and to develop their powers of self-expression by being required to write essays during their courses.

4. Commended the practice of the College in keeping in touch with prospective students during their practical year.

5. Recommended that the College should concentrate to a greater extent on Diploma and Post-Diploma teaching and reduce the number in the one-year course to not more than thirty and recommend others to go to a farm institute.

6. Recommended that the College should insist on all students taking the examinations at the end of their courses.

7. Expressed disappointment that the College farms were run on purely commercial lines, but were pleased to know that some demonstration plots were being provided in the future.

The report concluded:

> While present conditions persist, we would not be prepared to recommend any financial assistance from the Ministry if the College applied for a Grant. If however the College were to adopt our recommendations and were able to show that it would thereby incur a deficit in its recurrent income and expenditure account or find itself unable to finance essential capital development, we think the Ministry should be prepared to consider sympathetically any application for Grant aid that might be made.

The Governors and the staff considered the report and concluded:

1. That the staff/student ratio of 1:20 was adequate provided the increased tutorial facilities were available. The Principal would advise whether staff should be supplemented and, if so, in what subjects.

2. Further development of the tutorial system would afford ample opportunities for the writing of essays.

3. Difficulty was experienced in finding farms for students' practical experience. This should be investigated to see if there was a remedy.

4. It was regretted that no advice had been received on advanced courses, for which guidance had been asked.

5. The one-year course was both essential and unique and was doing a good service. The course differed from the Farm Institute course and catered for a different section of the community.

6. The current entrance standards of five 'O' Level passes, including science, should be enforced.

7. The farms should be run primarily on commercial lines, and demonstrations be such as those of a progressive farmer.

As a result of this report and the response, the College did not receive, and has not since received, any annual grant from the Ministry. The conclusion must be reached that the Keith Murray Committee judged the College to be a state-aided institution rather than an independent body catering to a particular part of the agricultural industry, including estate management. There seems to be no acknowledgement of the fact that the College was satisfactorily answering the need for land agents and agricultural surveyors at a level virtually equivalent to a degree. This Diploma course was certainly a major part of the College's output; the Committee seems to have considered the College as answering the same need as a higher farm institute teaching agriculture and agricultural science only. Perhaps this is why there was no attempt to give the College any guidance on advanced level teaching.

However, there was one outcome of significance: new examination regulations were introduced. This was to be the first of the improvements that Garner was to introduce early in his time, designed to stiffen the standard and in keeping with his first mild admonition that he expected the students to work harder. The College Diploma was divided into three classes and the student, in order to succeed, had to obtain the following standards in his final examinations:

Class 1 – An average from all exams exceeding 70 per cent
Class 2 – An average between 55 and 70 per cent
Class 3 – An average between 45 and 55 per cent
Certificate – An average between 40 and 45 per cent.
The new regulations imposed a minimum on passing the first-year examinations before proceeding to the second year.

The opportunity was taken to allow students on the short course who obtained significantly higher than a pass (60 per cent instead of 40 per cent) to proceed, if they wished, to the second year of the Agricultural Science course. This opened the door for them to take the Diploma and the National Diploma of Agricultural subject to the regulations of the Royal Agricultural Society of England. The effect of these regulations was to give the short course respectability, to improve the standard of the Diploma courses and, in the case of the Estate Management Diploma, to give greater exemption to the qualifying examinations of the Royal Institution of Chartered Surveyors and the Chartered Land Agents' Society.

It was in the next session that these professional bodies agreed that the obtaining of the College Diploma in Estate Management would grant exemption from:
1. Part II of the examinations of the Chartered Land Agents' Society.
2. The Intermediate Examination of the Royal Institution of Chartered Surveyors.
This was to be subject to:
(a) Passing the College examinations above a standard to be agreed.

(b) The standard of setting and marking the Diploma examination papers being put on a level with the corresponding examinations of the two bodies.

(c) The two bodies having adequate control over the selection of examiners for the College Diploma.

(d) The syllabus for the College Diploma being modified if necessary so as to cover competely the syllabus of each of the bodies up to the standard of their examinations to which exemption was to be granted.

(e) All candidates for exemption having achieved the standard of general education necessary for entry to the professional bodies.

(f) Exemption fees being paid on a scale which would recompense the bodies for the diminution of numbers sitting their examinations.

Later on we shall see the Principal in a more ambitious frame seeking to extend the teaching of Estate Management up to degree standard and to secure full exemption from all the professional examinations. This is the keynote running though Garner's tenure of the Principalship – the aim of raising of academic standards of teaching at the College to put it on a par with the universities. It was very much due to the pressure by Noble, with the backing of the professional bodies, that these standards were made the target and that the College eventually became the premier teaching establishment for land agents and agricultural surveyors.

★

The physical needs were not to be overlooked. Improvements to Trent Lodge, the erection of a garage at the Stroud road lodge, improvements to the Tetbury road entrance to the College, a new pig-fattening house for 120 pigs costing £3,000 and the conversion of a stone barn at Coates Manor to a machinery maintenance workshop at a cost of £400 were all carried out during 1958/9. Further work was to be considered through a building development plan. All this was achieved because the College now had a substantial reserve of funds, a situation never before achieved in the College's history and undoubtedly due to the post-war expansion of the student numbers, profits from commercial farming (little wonder the Keith Murray Committee's advice was ignored for the teaching benefitted more from the policy of commercial farming than it would have done otherwise) and the prudent investment of the surpluses achieved.

It also enabled the College to go ahead with the new house for the Principal: architectural plans were drawn up again and estimates obtained showing that the cost would be about £10,000 – a substantial figure in 1959. The cost could not all be borne by the College. It was fortunate that the trustees of the Ernest Bailey Charitable Trust made a gift of £6,000 towards it and all they asked in return was that it should reflect the name of the Trust. It was completed at a cost of £11,000. In the event the Trust very generously paid for the whole project. It was opened on Tuesday 21 June 1960 at a visit by two of the Trustees, G. W. Fordham and

B.C. Orme, the former officially opening the house and naming it 'Bailey Lodge'.

The most important of this series of building improvements came in 1959 with the completion and opening of the new assembly hall, planned in the days before Boutflour's retirement. It was decided unanimously by the Governors to name it 'The Boutflour Hall'. It was to be a very fitting and lasting memorial to Boutflour who happily was present with his wife, Mary, to enjoy the opening ceremony on 21 May 1959. This was performed by the Rt. Hon. W.S. Morrison, PC, MC, QC, MP, the Speaker of the House of Commons, and a long-time friend and supporter of the College from pre-war days. The Hall was dedicated by the Bishop of Gloucester.

★

During the year, in May, Major Sir Frederick Cripps, a Governor of long standing, died and his place was taken by Major Sir Charles Cooper, Bt. There were some staff changes too. W.H.A. Lockhart left at the end of July after eight years as Lecturer in Forestry to take up a full-time appointment as Forestry Consultant with Messrs Jackson Stops & Staff at Northampton. Familiarly known as 'Paddy' he had been Warden of Trent Lodge in addition to his other duties. The Revd E.A. Dixon, who had been College Chaplain since 1953, resigned from the incumbency of Coates on being appointed to the living of All Saints, Gloucester.

Appointments included C.E. Hart (Forestry) who came to the College from the Huntley Manor Estate where he had been the agent. He also took over lectures in Estate Economy and Finance, and Business Management. The Revd J.E. Tillett became the Chaplain and A.J.L. Wiseman was appointed to Agriculture.

Another change was the departure of H.R. Fell, the Farms Director, to take the tenancy of a 1,400 acre farm in Lincolnshire. Henry Fell, NDA, MRAC had returned to the College in 1955; he had been a prize-winning student, being awarded the Haygarth Medal. He had not only managed the College farms to a high standard but had gained first prize for the best cultivated and managed farm of over three hundred acres in the county, first prize for Leys and second prize for livestock in the competition arranged by the Gloucester Root, Fruit and Grain Society. Following the industrious Kenneth Russell, Fell had certainly improved the College's reputation for setting high standards in commercial farming.

This was and, indeed, is, a vital weapon in the College's armoury. It was advertised and three applicants were interviewed by a committee of the Finance and General Purposes Committee and the Farm Committee. The post was offered to H.V. Hughes, B.Sc., (Hons.) (Wales), a graduate of the University College of Wales at Aberystwyth. For the previous five years he had been Vice-Principal of the Leicester Farm Institute at Brooksby Hall. He was no stranger to the College for he had been Lecturer in Animal Husbandry from 1950 to 1954. It was, in the event, a future Principal of the College that had appeared on the premises. Ever since the early post-war days the College has been fortunate, or consummately skilful, in its choice of Farm Directors – Russell, Fell, Hughes and Limb, a small number for a period of forty-five years and all of whom in their different ways brought credit to the College and enabled it to be counted among the top echelon of farmers in the area.

★

In 1959 there died one of those associated with the College who will be long remembered not only for his character but for his love for the College and devotion to its best interests. Readers who are old students from the post-war years will know just who 'Chris' was. Like Boutflour he was and will be remembered by the shortened derivative of his name. He was, in fact, Derrick Christopherson. The year after he joined the College as a student on its reopening in 1946 he was elected Chairman of the Union Club. One suspects that the hand of Bobby Boutflour was behind this for it was an inspired choice. In an Appreciation in the *College Journal* written by Hugh Birley, Vice-President of the Royal Agricultural College Association in 1959, it was said of 'Chris': 'This was a job after his own heart and he gave it all he had, radiating enthusiasm and helping to re-establish that corporate College spirit on which all ability to function depends. He left a mass of written evidence of his zeal to guide his successor, but could not impart that flair for guiding the deliberations at the Annual General Meeting along lines predetermined by himself!'

He had come to the College, like many others, on being demobilized from the Army. He had served in the Bays, a mechanized cavalry unit, in North Africa and Italy. Before that, after his upbringing in South Africa, he had had a varied career in farming and in gold mining. 'Early in 1950 he was given the post of Sub Warden of one of the hostels of The Fellowship of St Christopher; this is a charitable organisation providing home-life for London boys who have no satisfactory homes. He is remembered there with affection. The College connection with the Fellowship is still maintained by the fact that the R.A.C. Association holds its December meeting at this London hostel every year.'

But he hankered after his old College: he was active in promoting the connections with old students and in 1951 suggested an annual reunion. That year Boutflour offered 'Chris' the job of Warden of Bledisloe Lodge and College Librarian. This offer was made not only in the interests of the College but also in the interests of Christopherson, who had been suffering personal difficulties. It is not too far fetched to say that Boutflour rescued 'Chris' from a depressing period in his life.

It was then that he gave his greatest service to the College, for, based on the register of old students that he had first started when in London, he was instrumental in founding the Old Students' Association. Proposed by Lord Bledisloe, the most distinguished of all old students, he was elected Secretary. He remained in this post for eight years until his death and so performed the three functions of Warden, Librarian and Secretary of the Association as well as many other duties such as finding vacational employment for students, arranging outside accommodation for those not resident in College, and finding rooms for NDA students for their examinations in Leeds. He still made time for the College sports, especially his favourite, Rugby, at which he was an official referee.

His character is best summed up by another extract from the Appreciation: '. . . one of the most familiar sounds was Chris's laugh: a bubbling, infectious laugh which was utterly characteristic of its owner: a laugh full of merriment and joie de vivre: a laugh, like its owner, just a little eccentric. For Chris, like his laugh, *was* different from other people. He had, however, a great affection for his fellows and an all embracing enthusiasm in all his varied activities.' His memory is honoured by a memorial in the College chapel.

★

The year 1959/60 commenced with 462 students. There were changes in the Governing Body and in the academic staff. Mr Francis Peter, representing the Royal Institution of Chartered Surveyors, the Hon. W. Holland-Hibbert, representing the Land Agents' Society, Professor A.N. Duckham, representing the Ministry of Agriculture and Col. G.P. Shakerley, representing Gloucester-shire County Council resigned from the Board of Governors and were replaced by Col. G.R. Judd for the Royal Institution of Chartered Surveyors, Sir Randle Baker Wilbraham, Bt., for the Land Agents' Society, Major E.S. Dobb for the Ministry of Agriculture and Lord Banbury of Southam and Major P.S. Morris-Keating for Gloucestershire County Council. Mr Peter, the Hon. W. Holland-Hibbert and Sir Robert Rae were appointed Ordinary Governors.

After Christopherson's death his duties were taken over by W. Heatherington as Librarian, G.A. Cragghill as Warden of Bledisloe Lodge and by S.R.A. Medd as Secretary of the Old Students' Association, in addition to their normal lecturing committments.

★

It was in this year that the Principal started on his programme of building development in order to accommodate the higher number of students, to provide more teaching and demonstration rooms as well as meeting the domestic needs of kitchens and dining room. His ten-year programme presented to the Governors comprised:
1. A new demonstration block for Estate Management and Forestry.
2. A machinery block on the College site.

The College c
from the west

3. A new science block, or modification of the existing science block.
4. Additional student accommodation.
5. Reorganization of the kitchens and dining hall.
6. New changing rooms.

The Governors considered the Principal's draft programme and decided that the provision of a new science block was unnecessary at that time and that the existing one should be modified and enlarged to give additional accommodation for staff and preparation rooms. It was also decided to leave additional student accommodation and the kitchen and dining hall reorganization for the time being in order to limit capital expenditure. The provision of a demonstration hall for Estate Management and Forestry, a machinery block on the College site and new changing accommodation was authorized.

At the same time improvements and additions to the buildings at Fosse Hill were carried out. Increased space for housing cattle and silage, a new dairy and room for the rearing of calves were provided. The costs were met in part by a grant from the Ministry of Agriculture. Later on in the year work started on the new changing accommodation and the necessary alterations to the Principal's old house, which was later named 'The Bathurst Wing'. It involved enlarging the dining room by incorporating the breakfast room/study and panelling it in oak. Further alterations created a clinic and four bedrooms as an isolation block. The net result was to increase student accommodation by ten plus one member of staff. This released room in the main building to give additional office space and an interview room.

Between 1960 and 1964 plans for the new machinery block were drawn up, approved, put to tender, contracted and completed. The first plans in 1961, put forward by the Principal, were of three options and the most modest one was chosen. It would give 8,000 square ft of floor space and include a demonstration hall, a lecture room, a store, offices and toilets. The site chosen was to be at the rear of the laboratories. It was estimated to cost between £20,000 and £30,000 and the Principal reported that he had received a generous gift towards this cost from R.A. Lister & Co., Ltd, in the form of a seven-year covenant which would yield in the region of £7,000. Application for grant aid was made to the Ministry of Agriculture but no satisfactory answer was received.

It was decided to approach other agricultural engineering firms for help. The managing director of Massey Ferguson, Mr Hunt, visited the College in 1961 and as a result his Board approved a donation of £3,000 towards the cost. In fact, as the donation was by way of a seven-year covenant, it yielded £6,249. The College agreed that the Massey Ferguson Butler standard building should be used as a basis for the new block. The International Harvester Company of Great Britain, Ltd made a donation of £1,000. The balance came from College funds, augmented by contributions from agricultural feeding-stuffs firms.

The machinery block was constructed by Donald Cameron Ltd on a tender of £28,940 and the landlord's consent was granted on the same terms as for the

Aerial view of the College in 1964 with the new machinery block shown top right

Boutflour Hall. Work commenced in the summer vacation of 1961 and the new building was opened rather later than was planned in the spring of 1964. Messrs R.A. Lister Ltd and Aubrey Rees & Son Ltd loaned equipment for practical demonstrations. On 8 May 1964 the Rt. Hon. Christopher Soames, CBE, MP, the Minister of Agriculture opened it at an official luncheon.

The future of the Steadings Farm was reviewed. It was decided that: no attempt should be made to demonstrate the Steadings as a smallholding; the Friesian herd should be treated as part of the whole farming enterprise; and later, at a suitable time, a plan should be prepared for establishing the Friesian herd in another part of the Farm in addition to the Fosse Hill herd, or as a separate unit. It was very necessary that the new machinery block be completed by then for there had been a fire in the old lecture facilities at the Steadings which had resulted in them being completely gutted. This brought up the need to make a decision on the future of these buildings, which, being on the other side of the Tetbury road from the College land, were isolated. At that time Cirencester Rural District Council were showing an interest in taking them over.

★

There were several prize funds by now at the College but Garner discovered that at least three had lain dormant for some years. A draft scheme for amalgamation of all the funds was prepared and eventually it was approved by the Official Trustee of charitable funds. It became known as the 'Royal Agricultural College Prize Fund'. As for external prizes the College students won many. From the Chartered Land Agents' Society they won the Talbot Ponsonby Prize for Agriculture and the Pendlebury Prize for Forestry. From the Royal Institution of Chartered Surveyors they won the Beadle Prize for Agriculture and the Mellersh Prize for Forestry. This maintained the long tradition of the College for scooping most of the prizes of the professional bodies of the land.

★

In 1963 the College was visited by Her Majesty the Queen, continuing the tradition of frequent royal visits. It took place on 29 April 1963. For a change the weather was fine with the daffodils in the main avenue in full bloom under the lime trees which were just starting to green over. Her Majesty the Queen and His Royal Highness the Duke of Edinburgh arrived to be greeted by His Grace the Duke of Beaufort who presented the Chairman and Vice-Chairman, the Principal and the Bursar. By now the Chairman of the Governors was Major P.D. Birchall,

The royal visit
1963. HM Qu
Elizabeth and
Duke of Edinl
arrive; introdu
by Major Pete
Birchall, Chair
of the Governe

242

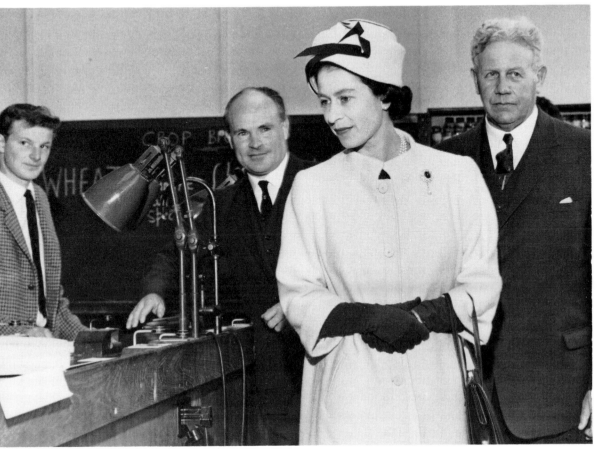

The royal visit in 1963. Frank Garner (*right*) and Dai Barling guide the Queen through the laboratories

elected following the death of Col. Chester Master and the Vice-Chairman was Mr Ivor R. Morris. A tour of the College was carried out before luncheon in the Boutflour Hall.

The tour was very thorough: in the morning the royal party visited the library, the tithe barn (where the Principal presented the College staff and their ladies), the Estate Management hall, the drawing office and the chapel. In the afternoon visits were paid to the botany and chemistry laboratories, the demonstration plots and a machinery exhibit. Finally the party went to Coates Manor Farm to see something of College farming and at Bledisloe Lodge they inspected the Beagles. Very little was missed by the Queen and the Duke and it certainly displayed the active interest of the Patron of the College.

Opportunity was taken during the visit to recognize the sterling and long-service work of members of the College. Silver cigarette boxes were presented to

Mrs Mary Boutflour, A. Noble, P. Haynes, H. St G. Rawlins, A.J. Ritchings and Dr J.H. Grove White, all of whom had served, or been connected with the College for long periods. Her Majesty and His Royal Highness were presented with bound copies of the brochure of the visit together with two silver paper weights suitably inscribed, as mementoes of the occasion.

★

The period from 1964 through to 1968 saw significant changes in the teaching standards, initiated by Garner. This started with a meeting that the Principal attended of the Principals of agricultural colleges with the Royal Agricultural Society of England to discuss the National Diploma of Agriculture examinations and the Farm Management course. The Society was not prepared to organize post-diploma examinations and was to raise the standard of the NDA by abolishing third class. In the past, students who obtained 50 per cent in the College examinations went on to take the NDA but with the new standard the Principal was of the opinion that only students obtaining the College Diploma Second Class (55 per cent or above), or 55 per cent in each of the NDA subjects, should go forward to the NDA. Garner was seeking to establish post-diploma courses in order to extend the range of College teaching. He put this to the Governors and they accepted that there should be a post-diploma course in Farm Management and a course in Estate Management for post-NDA students.

What he wanted in post-diploma courses was:
1. *Farm Management* – Lectures on Crop Husbandry, Farm Mechanization, Estate Management, Animal Husbandry, Farm Management and Work Study on the farm and estate. The rest of the course was to consist of case studies on farms and farming matters. This course would be called the Advanced Diploma Course in Farm Management. The entry requirements were to be an agricultural degree, a Second Class NDA, or the professional qualifications of the Chartered Land Agents' Society or the Royal Institution of Chartered Surveyors.
2. *Land Economy or Owner Occupation of Land* – This course was designed specifically for owner occupiers of agricultural land and would consist of lectures on Farm Buildings, Agricultural Law, Taxation, Scale of Enterprise, Forestry, Farm Management, Land Economy and Sporting Rights. The course was to be called the Advanced Diploma in Owner Occupation of Land and the entry requirements were to be NDA, an approved College Diploma in Agriculture or an agricultural degree from a recognized university.

His intention was to start these courses in the Autumn Term of 1964. Garner was in tune with the times. For the past few years the advisory services, notably the National Agricultural Advisory Service, had been concentrating on the economic side of farming and had been advising technical improvements in the light of the farm as a business. It was the time when one of the old students of the College, Derek Barber (later to be recognized for his contribution to agriculture and conservation of the environment by being knighted, and a recipient of the Bledisloe Medal), was writing with his co-author Keith Dexter and publishing their book *Farming for Profit*, an immediate best seller in the agricultural world. There was a demand for students from the College trained in the latest techniques in the management of farms and estates. The Advanced Farm Management course turned out to be one of the most succcessful of the courses initiated by Garner and continues to be so to the present day.

The Principal recognized that the standards required for the professional bodies were being raised and he foresaw that the time would come when these would recruit mainly degree holders. His solution was to suggest two courses, one a degree course for those who had the academic standards required by the profession, and a diploma course for those wishing to return home to manage their own farm or estate. Bearing in mind the previous close association that the College had had during the time when Boutflour was Principal, the university to approach might well be Bristol.

The Chairman and the Principal arranged a discussion with the Vice-Chancellor with a view to suggesting affiliation once again with that university. This came to nought for it was very evident from the outset that the terms would be dictated by the university and that it was more than likely that a degree course in Estate Management would not be acceptable to the professional bodies, in the same way that the degree course in Estate Management at Cambridge was not acceptable to them. The matter got no further.

The alternative was to make application to the Council for National Academic Awards (CNAA) for permission for the College to run its own degree course. The syllabus suggested to the Council set out the subjects to be taken over each of the three years as follows:

First Year – Principles of Economics and Accounting
Principles of English Law
Principles of Building Design and Construction
Principles of Land Surveying
Principles of Agriculture
Principles of Forestry

Second Year – Estate Accounting
Law Relating to Estate Management
Applied Building Design and Construction
Applied Land Surveying
The Practice of Forestry

Third Year – Estate Economy and Land Use
Law Relating to Control of Land Use
Valuations
Economic and Management Principles
Agricultural Economics
Forestry Economics.

After receiving and considering the proposed syllabus the Council suggested a number of major changes relating to teaching, personnel and facilities. The Governors felt that these changes would be very difficult to achieve without prejudicing the independence of the College. As in many cases before in the history of the College, when the Governors and Principal had attempted to obtain the help and cooperation of official bodies relating to agricultural education, the offers made were conditional on unacceptable changes in the structure of the College's teaching methods and facilities. The sticking point was nearly always the teaching ratio: to obtain the ratio demanded usually meant that the College would have to go into deficit financing and that they were not willing to do. It would make the College dependent on the provider who made up the deficit and thus restrict the independence that the College had, particularly in the choice of market that they wished to operate in. With the inauguration of the Diploma in Estate Management by Boutflour the College had always been able to look to a wider market than just agriculture and had encompassed the greater rural sphere. So the application was not proceeded with.

★

Garner did not let rest the matter of raising standards. On two fronts he sought to improve the College syllabuses. These were the two main streams of teaching – Estate Management and Agriculture.

For some time he had sought to lift up the Diploma course in Estate Mangement to a level where it would be acceptable by the three professional bodies, the Chartered Land Agents' Society, the Chartered Auctioneers' and Estate Agents' Institute and the Royal Institution of Chartered Surveyors, as granting exemption from their final written examinations – just as some university degrees were acceptable. The College academic staff prepared a syllabus for an Advanced Diploma course in Estate Management. The course, of three years, covered a wide range of subjects: Agriculture, Forestry, Building Construction, Accounting, Law, Economics, Valuations of Property and Estate Economy.

Full and detailed discussions with the three professional bodies took place and agreement was quickly reached on the establishment of such a course in Rural Estate Management. It has remained the same in its essential requirements up to the present day. Entry requirements would be passes in four GCE subjects (three at Advanced Level) including English Language, or Literature and either a mathematical or science subject, *or* passes in four GCE subjects (two at Advanced Level) including English Language, or Literature and Mathematics.

The terms of the agreement were:
1. The course was to be called the Diploma Course in Rural Estate Management.
2. It would be of nine terms' duration.
3. All students who passed the final examinations of the three-year course would

be given full exemption from all written examinations of the three professional bodies.

4. College students would be allowed to take the final (practical) examinations twenty-one months after leaving College.

5. From time to time the three professional bodies would arrange for a party of eight to visit the College and make a report to both the professional bodies and the College.

6. The College would furnish the three professional bodies with the names of assessors, one from the teaching profession and one engaged in practice, for approval. The final appointment of the assessors would be made by the professional bodies and would be for a period of three to five years, though it was felt undesirable for both assessors to terminate their appointments at the same time.

7. The assessors would agree all final examinations papers with the College staff. Each assessor would moderate in one or two subjects and read and check the marking of papers in order to estabish a standard, and, if they so wished, attend the examiners' meeting to agree class lists.

This new course started in October 1968.

This achievement by Garner marked a new and welcome stage in the lifting of the teaching standards to a higher level. In fact, it placed the College in the position of being the major full-time teaching establishment for the profession of the land so far as rural practice was concerned. It was a culminaton of the process started by Boutflour which had as its objective the combination of education in agriculture and in land economy and land management. At the time the College was unique in providing such a broad spectrum of advanced education in rural management. There remained only one further objective: to secure a degree course.

★

The other aim of Garner's, to uplift the agriculture courses, was, to some extent, foreseen by an Advisory Committee on Agricultural Education set up by the Ministry of Education in September 1963 which reported to the National Advisory Council on Education for Industry and Commerce in 1966. This was chaired by Sir Harry Pilkington, the Chairman of the National Council. The very wide range of representatives of agricultural organizations included Major P.D. Birchall, DL, MA, the Chairman of the Board of Governors of the College.

The report recommended four levels of courses:

1. Ordinary National Diploma type courses suitable for students with four passes at 'O' Level GCE or an equivalent.

2. Higher National Diploma type courses suitable for students with one pass at 'A' Level GCE or with the Ordinary National Certificate or Ordinary National Diploma.

3. Degree courses suitable for students with two passes at 'A' Level GCE or with equivalent attainments in an Ordinary National Certificate or an Ordinary National Diploma.

4. Post-diploma courses which were eminently suitable for dealing with specialist aspects of production which involve new and advanced techniques, and with farm organization and management.

It recommended the introduction of a new examination structure, the opportunity for institutions to secure the external assessment of internal examinations, and the creation of a central body for agricultural examination and of new award-giving boards, to be called the Council for Agricultural Education, members of which were to be appointed by the Secretary of State for Education.

During 1967/8 the agriculture courses were revised to correspond to the new concepts of the Pilkington Committee. Market research among potential employers revealed that while most were looking to recruit those with an HND, a considerable number wished to see students with special post-diploma training in Farm Management, Animal Husbandry, Dairy Husbandry, Crop Husbandry, Pigs and Farm Machinery. The College had the benefit of the advice of a Joint Committee set up by the Ministry of Education in deciding whether to prepare students for the OND or the HND. It was decided to concentrate on the HND and the Joint Committee opted for sandwich courses to include one year of practical training during the course.

The sandwich course was supported by the National Farmers' Union when discussions were held with them, but they appreciated the difficulties of such a course in agriculture due to the lack of experience of those who would manage it. However the Ministry of Education insisted on it. A scheme and syllabus was prepared by the academic staff: students would attend College for one term, then undertake their sandwich year of practical training to be followed by five terms in College. This structure of five terms allowed students full participation in College life which would not have been possible with a year-in-year-out scheme. Garner at first opposed any idea of a sandwich course and had told the Government Inspector so. He was stubborn but eventually agreed with the compromise.

The main subjects were: Animal Production, Crop Production, Farm Management, Farm Mechanization, Veterinary Science, Animal Nutrition, Soil Science, Agricultural Botany and Agricultural Zoology. The subsidiary subjects were Accounting, Taxation, Farm Buildings and General Studies. The entry requirements were: four GCE 'O' Level passes at grades A, B or C to include a subject showing command of English and two distinct mathematical or science subjects, plus one 'A' Level pass at grade A,B,C,D or E in a science subject, together with another subject studied to 'A' Level but not necessarily passed. All entrants also had to have had a year's practical work prior to commencing the course. The course eventually started in October 1969 and the NDA finally ended in 1973.

By that time (1968/9) all the courses at the College had been reviewed. There were four basic courses: the three-year Diploma course in Rural Estate Management, the Higher National Diploma course in Agriculture, the Advanced Farm Management course and the one-year farming course. It was thought that, as a contingency, if the numbers on the one-year farming course were to diminish, then an Ordinary National Diploma course could be established. The planning of any other advanced courses was left in abeyance.

★

It was in the next year that a further attempt was made by Garner to gain a degree course for the College. This time he approached Reading University. This was a reasonably obvious choice: Reading was by now a major contributor to agricultural education in England and a degree course in Estate Management taught at the College would complement their agricultural teaching. But the approach was unsuccessful. A further review of the courses on offer at the College resulted in a new Diploma course being suggested to run after the NDA examinations were discontinued, a Crop Protection course being set up and the syllabus of the one-year farming course being modified.

In Garner's time the standards of teaching had been significantly improved: the Rural Estate Management course had been extended to give successful students the right of exemption from all the final written examinations of the professional bodies; the College had carried out the change from the National Diploma in Agriculture to the Higher National Diploma, on the recommendations of the Pilkington Committee; the Advanced Farm Management course had proved to be highly successful, meeting the modern needs of employers and the one-year course had continued to thrive in spite of opposition from those who wanted to make its closure or radical alteration a condition of financial support to the College.

★

Over the period of these changes, with improvements in the educational standards and the increase in teaching staff, there was a corresponding increase in the numbers of students being accepted at College. In the session 1959/60, 462 students had been admitted. The progress in the ten years up to 1969/70 is shown below:

Students admitted 1960–70

1960/1	468
1961/2	482
1962/3	476
1963/4	479
1964/5	546

1965/6	565
1966/7	564
1967/8	595
1968/9	604
1969/70	639

If increase in numbers is any criterion of success then an increase of 36.5 per cent over the decade was a marked achievement for an independent college. The large expansion really took place over the last six years of Garner's time as Principal – a notable result of his resolution to raise the educational standard of the College.

★

To accommodate this increase in student numbers and to expand the teaching facilities Garner planned as early as 1962 for a new lecture block. He wanted additional office accomodation for staff and new lecture rooms. He envisaged a block with a large lecture room for two hundred students with two smaller lecture rooms and additional staff rooms. The space required would be about 5,000 to 6,000 square ft and the cost was estimated at £25,000 to £30,000. The new block would release the lecture room next to the tithe barn for student recreational purposes.

By 1964, with the machinery block completed, the matter was getting more urgent and the space needs had grown even more. The plans hardened into a lecture block to be sited between the Boutflour Hall and the new machinery block. It would include a drawing office for 50 to 60 students, one lecture room to hold 170 students, one for 120, one for 96, two for 60 and another for 40. Adding on eight tutorial rooms and offices made a requirement for 10,000 to 11,000 square ft. The aim now was to have it completed in time for the Autumn Term of 1967. Application for grant aid was made to the Department of Education and Science, and the cost was now estimated at £50,000.

The discussions with the Department proved fruitless because the answer given was that no grant could be forthcoming before October 1967. As the big jump in student numbers had already taken place and as the new courses were under way it was plain that this could not meet the College's requirements. Once again a government department simply could not keep up with the pace of the College's expansion. Garner had the same problem as Boutflour. This time the difference was that the Governors were able to authorize the go ahead utilizing the College's own resources. By now a substantial investment fund had been built up, mainly due to the prudent management of the capital funds by the Bursar, Jacobs. The project was built in two stages and the final cost was £48,669. It was opened on 13 October 1967, on time, by the President of the Chartered Land Agents' Society, Mr Martin Argles.

The new lecture halls
are opened in 1967
by Martin Argles,
watched by Major
Peter Birchall (*centre*)
and the Principal,
Frank Garner

The building developments under Garner had not finished: a new cricket pavilion was erected and the Governors contributed to the cost of a permanent pavilion at the Royal Show Ground at Stoneleigh which the Old Students' Association were funding.

★

In 1964 another attempt was made to purchase from Lord Bathurst the freehold of the land on which the College stood. It will be remembered that ever since the foundation of the College in 1845 the land and original property had been leased to the College and remained so through the generosity of the Bathurst family. The Chairman of the Governors had a meeting with Lord Bathurst and it was agreed that the matter should proceed, though the Governors felt that they could not give up any part of Field Barn Farm as in fact they would wish to increase the farmed acreage.

The College was held on a ninety-nine year lease from 1908 (the time of the reconstitution of the College's corporate structure and its adoption as a limited company) and the area comprised just over fifty-two acres. Until March 1944 the rent had been £225 per annum and this was increased subsequently to £400 per annum. The buildings on the land would become the property of the landlord on the expiry of the lease. These included the main building, Bathurst Wing, dining hall, kitchens, library, offices, common rooms, lecture rooms, changing rooms, toilets and bedrooms; the King George V Wing, tithe barn, drawing office, building materials room, chapel, car park, botany and chemistry laboratories, garages, squash courts, Cedar Hostel, domestic staff hostel, Bursar's house and two lodges. It was agreed that the Boutflour Hall and the new machinery wing would not be taken into consideration in assessing the terms of a new lease or the sale to the College. The Steadings, to which improvements had been made following the fire there, had been handed back to the landlord. The Bursar negotiated for the purchase with Mr John Lloyd, the agent for the Bathurst estate. The satisfactory result was that the College purchased the freehold of the whole property for £15,150.

★

To complete the expansion of this period College farming was greatly extended by the renting of Eysey Manor Farm. It was in 1969 that the Farms Director, Hughes, had been approached by one of the local agents to find out if the College would be interested in taking the tenancy of this farm of some 645 acres, nearly all arable, including sixty acres of grass. It was situated about ten miles from the College on the road to Cricklade. The farm was visited by the Chairman of the Farm Committee, the Principal, the Farms Director and the Head of the Agriculture Department. They reckoned that a satisfactory standard of production could be reached after three to five years of good management, though the soil types could lead to problems of cultivation and drainage. It would give an opportunity to develop a beef enterprise where several different systems might be demonstrated, and an extension of the existing dairy, pigs and sheep enterprises. They recommended the Board to accept the tenancy. This was done and four of the members, Messrs Morris, Coad, Owens and Trumper were authorized to negotiate with the agents for the owner and to plan a farm policy which would integrate the new farm with the existing College farms. So Eysey Manor Farm, Cricklade, was taken on a twenty-one year lease from Michaelmas 1970 at a basic rent of £7 per acre. The lease included seven cottages, the shooting rights and some fishing. The rent was to be subject to review at three-yearly intervals after the first five years.

The aim was that the farm should be of educational value to staff and students and that profitable enterprises should be chosen. This continued the general policies that the College had adopted over many years with little alteration. The enterprises chosen were based on a beef, cereals and potato system with a single suckling beef unit, semi-intensive beef production and an intensive barley/beef system, though the Farms' Director was given a certain amount of flexibility. K.L. Cameron was appointed Farm Manager and would lecture on beef production as well as conducting farm classes at the farm. He immediately organized a large scheme of drainage, hedge removal and realignment.

★

There was, while Garner was Principal, a relatively low turnover of staff. Most were able to give long service to the College and this must be illustrative of the regard in which Garner was held and of his style of management. While the numbers employed remained much the same, and the numbers of students had increased, the teaching ratio grew wider, but the effects of this were obviated by the more extensive use of tutorials.

Among those who left after long service was Arthur Noble, who had been Head of the Estate Management Department since his appointment by Boutflour in 1934. Save for a break during the war, when he practised land agency, he had been with the College for twenty-six years. Writing in the *College Journal* (Vol. LIV – 1965/6) P.A. Tucker, who succeeded him as head of that department said:

I suppose his most outstanding quality is his total involvement in the College and its activities. His prime concern has of course always been the Estate Management Department and the interest of the students studying within it. . . . But few can have known how much of his time and thought has been devoted to looking after the interests of students . . . in the relations with the professional bodies and helping them to obtain appointments on leaving. . . . He has maintained a comprehensive record of their progress in their professional careers. . . .

Goodness ! what a question

I must think this one out

It's enough to make a fellow weep

Just a moment

Comments
by Mr. V. R. Noble

Photographs
by H. M. C. Cooke

I'm getting there

That's it ! It's like this, you see

That being successfully disposed of—

Let's get on with the next point

A keen and considerable performer in his time he has always been closely associated with the Rugger and Cricket Clubs. His interest in the Chapel and all it stands for, his help and advice to the Estate Management Club are only a few instances of the very full part he has played in the corporate life of the College.

Noble was known to generations of students as 'Uncle Arthur' and this accurately describes the avuncular relationship that he had with students. He gained the appellation in the post-war years, lecturing to the influx of ex-service students, older than the eighteen or nineteen year old ex-schoolboys he had dealt with in the pre-war era. It is to his credit that he quickly adjusted to this more mature student who was set on working very hard and testing the lecturers with his insatiable desire for knowledge. Arthur Noble had an uncomfortable time to start with but very soon mastered his problems.

He had come to the College after eleven years lecturing in agriculture at Seale Hayne Agricultural College in Devon, with a National Diploma in Agriculture obtained in 1922. Just before leaving Seale Hayne, in 1933, he had taken his degree in Estate Management at London University, being awarded the gold medal for first place.

A serious man, taking most things at face value, he was devoted to teaching as a profession; for him it was a full-time career and once ensconced in the academic life of the College he was happy to practise his profession as a teacher. As he said, 'A man, by becoming a teacher of professional subjects, does not thereby become a professional educationalist. He merely lays himself open to the jibe (Bernard Shaw's, I believe), "Those who can, do: those who can't, teach," and, being a professional man, he does not like it. He hates to be considered unpractical. I prefer to phrase it another way, "If you can't do, you can't teach." ' Noble will stand comparison with some of the other great teachers of the College such as Wrightson, Fream, Kinch and Blundell. He served the College well. He has also left tokens of his affection for the College in his poems revealing his Christian attitude and his love of the Cotswolds.

★

In 1968 another link with the past was severed. K.N. Russell, who had been the energetic Vice-Principal and Farms Director at the College with Boutflour, died. He had left the College to become the Principal of Askham Bryan and then Shuttleworth Agricultural Colleges. The RAC Association, supported by the Governors, decided on a memorial in the form of the modernization of the library, and conversion to a conference room. These were completed in 1970 and the Kenneth Russell Memorial Room was opened by Mrs Russell during the old students' weekend in October.

★

Towards the end of 1970 Frank Garner announced his intention to retire at the end of the Summer Term 1971. He had been in post since 1958 and on reaching retirement age he would have been Principal for thirteen years. He had worked extemely hard, putting in long hours of earnest endeavour. Writing in the *College Journal*, J.A.R. Lockhart, a senior member of Garner's staff, said of him, 'He gained a reputation – mainly outside the College – of being a tough disciplinarian and that was considered desirable; he had no use for students with long hair; he could always be relied on to keep appointments and promises. . . . he and Mrs Garner worked tirelessly for the benefit of the College and all its personnel; they organised staff parties at the start of each term, children's parties, and wine and cheese parties which students were expected to attend.' The only time when his relaxation of discipline for the benefit of the students failed him was at the opening in 1959 of the Boutflour Hall. Obviously taken up with the idea of the celebration of this signal event in the history of the College he allowed sherry for the students before the luncheon and unlimited beer afterwards, with disastrous results!

His had been thirteen years of great development for the College: the student numbers had increased from about 450 in 1958 to nearly 650 by the time he left. The history of the College shows that during the first hundred years less than 5,000 had attended the courses; in the twenty-five years since the end of the Second World War over 6,500 had passed through, and of these over 4,000 had attended in the time of Garner.

For Garner, the prospect of following Boutflour, who had galvanized the College, must have been daunting, but he was a man who set objectives and then spared no effort by himself or those supporting him in seeking to attain them. He had transformed the facilities by providing a new Principal's house, building a large machinery block, and by extending two or threefold the teaching accommodation by an extensive block of lecture halls and rooms, later named in his honour 'The Frank Garner Lecture Theatres'. He had built extensions to the science laboratories, provided housing for the Assistant Farm Manager and had conducted numerous other smaller additions or improvements. He had seen the extension of the College farms with the acquisition of Eysey Manor Farm, thus giving the College the flexibility of three different soil types on which to carry out many varying farming systems both of crops and livestock.

But the two features that should be the enduring mark of his Principalship are the raising of the educational standards and the enhanced reputation that he gained for the College in the agricultural industry. Under him it became a truly national College of stability and high standards which could provide recruits to the many employers who looked for men of practical application with a professional, technical and scientific background. The College now offered courses which matched those at any other agricultural teaching institution and which were recognized by the professions as at a level equivalent to their own examinations and of a parity with degree courses. He had tried hard for an actual degree course to be taught at the College; he failed because he was ahead of his time – the universities were not ready to recognize the teaching as being at a standard they could accept. But he was not far off.

In a tribute to Frank Garner, Sir Emrys Jones, after he himself had been Principal of the College, said:

> . . . he will be remembered by most as a distinguished member of the agricultural 'establishment' and a very influential figure in the field of agricultural education.
>
> Frank Garner believed strongly that the Principal of a national college should get away from the campus and mix with as wide a cross section of the agricultural industry as possible. He was a member of the Farmers' Club for many years and as Chairman in 1966, he was very active and particularly keen to encourage the growth of the youth section. . . .
>
> He was a Liveryman of the Worshipful Company of Farmers and became Master in 1971/72. . . . Frank was a man of great integrity, but he was blunt, plain-spoken and adopted a 'no-nonsense' approach to life. He pursued his objects with a rock-like determination, with the result that his achievements often confounded those around him.
>
> Strangers, meeting him for the first time, were often taken aback by his brusque manner, but they were soon put at ease for there was always a twinkle in his eye and the faint quiver of a smile on his lips which endeared him to all who knew him.

Not a bad epitaph for the Principal who had, by exceedingly hard work, determination and single-mindedness, enhanced the College both physically, educationally and in its reputation.

Chapter Eleven

A SHORT TENURE THEN EXPANSION, 1971–8

The real challenge lies in finding the money to finance these very necessary and desirable developments.

Sir Emrys Jones, 1973

By mid-summer 1970 the Governors had appointed a new Principal to follow Garner. He was Dr Gordon R. Dickson, B.Sc. (Hons.), Ph.D.(Dunhelm) and the choice was of a person who satisfied the two essential criteria for the post, namely high academic qualifications with agricultural experience. He came at a time when the exciting prospect of the entry of the United Kingdom into the European Economic Community was commanding the attention of the agricultural world. In fact one of his early manifestations was a leading article in the *College Journal* for 1971/2 on 'The effects of EEC Entry on Farming'. He foresaw the considerable changes that were to take place in British farming, saying '. . . E.E.C. membership does offer a potential which is attainable through effort and initiative. . . . we must accept the need to be competitive in all aspects of marketing, and then seek greater levels of efficiency in production. . . . the immediate apparent benefits . . . will be considerably eroded by cost increases and inflation proceeding at far greater rates than price increments.' He was to be proved right in the coming years.

It followed that he was aware of the fact that, as well as the different regime to be faced by the UK farmers, the demand for education would change rapidly. He realized that greater emphasis would have to be given to developing the student's capacity for original thought and sound decision making, so that change could be accommodated and exploited, and that changes would be necessary in College. He envisaged the expansion of the HND course and the rapid development of the College Diploma course in Agriculture.

Dickson had been away from college life for fifteen years: he had come to take up his post from being manager of the farms of the Duke of Norfolk's estate at Arundel in Sussex. He was to start as from 1 September 1971, and prior to that he attended Governors' meetings by invitation. So he had a long lead-in to the job.

Gordon Dickson (*right*), Principal 1971–2, with Frank Garner

One of his early comments was that he was disappointed at the diminishing collegiate life which then appeared common to all centres of education. Although, as he said, this appeared to be an inevitable product of the times, he determined to encourage greater student participation in College activities. This was characteristic of the man for he was, by nature, an approachable extrovert, who found it easy to communicate with the agricultural student of the day. One of his earliest actions was to cooperate with the Royal Agricultural College Association (the Old Students' Association) because he saw scope for the greater involvement of that Association and for closer liaison between the Association and the College and in the support to be given to students in furthering their careers. He was glad to accept, on behalf of the College, a cheque given by the Association for the Frank Garner Travel Bursary Fund to be established. The amount of this award was later increased by the Governors; it was to be awarded annually to a student undertaking a study tour of agriculture in an overseas country during the College vacation who was required to submit a one thousand word account of his travels and impressions for publication in the *College Journal*.

Over the post-war years the Royal Agricultural College Association had grown in strength: it now had a representative in all the counties of the UK and in the Republic of Ireland; it also ran a regular reunion which was becoming an important item in the agricultural calendar with national figures being invited to address distinguished audiences. The reunion weekend included the Bledisloe Memorial Lecture, a highlight in which the speakers chosen were not only eminent in the field of agriculture but also of political significance. By 1972 the Association had grown to a membership of over 3,600.

At the start of Dickson's tenure the extension of the College farms by the acquisition of the tenancy of Eysey Manor near Cricklade was begining to show results. Reporting in 1971, H.V. Hughes, the Farms Director, was able to show that the farm had been reorganized from seventeen fields into four enclosures with two hundred acres drained, tree planting carried out to enhance the amenities, a suckler herd of eighty Hereford-cross Friesians and an 'eighteen month beef' unit of forty to fifty animals established with bunker silos constructed to hold one thousand tons of silage. On the other farms, the pig unit had been extended, enjoying, as the Director said, 'one of its efficient phases'! Loose housing for the dairy unit was replaced by cubicles to make it into a one-man operation. The College was now in a position to offer the students an even broader spectrum of farming to study than before. On all farms there were reasonably flexible systems that were prepared for modification to meet future circumstances.

In 1970, prior to Dickson taking over, the courses offered were reviewed and it was decided: to continue and expand the HND course; to re-establish the Diploma course in Agriculture following the discontinuance of the NDA examinations; to set up a Crop Protection course; to continue with the Advanced Farm Management course; and to modify the syllabus of the one-year farming course. The Crop Protection course was not pursued as it was offered elsewhere.

In the 1970/1 session there were some changes in the Governing Body in that the Royal Institution of Chartered Surveyors, now augmented by the amalgamation of the three professional bodies of land management, thus including the Chartered Land Agents' Society and the Chartered Auctioneers' and Estate Agents' Institute, would have three representatives. This reflected the importance that the teaching of Land and Estate Management had in the overall syllabus of the College.

Dickson took up the reins at the start of the 1971/2 session with 635 students in College. In the first term the College was visited by the Minister of Agriculture, Fisheries and Food, Mr James Prior, and by the President of the National Farmers' Union, Mr (later Sir) Henry Plumb, both of whom addressed the students. During the year Saturday morning lectures were discontinued for a trial period, later confirmed with an extension made to the weekday afternoon sessions.

Once in post the new Principal unveiled his plans for the future development of the College with suggestions for upgrading the courses. He proposed the construction of a separate Union Club building in line with modern university practice, to comprise a general purpose hall, bar and lounge; the modernization of all residential rooms to provide, where possible, single study bedrooms in groups of twelve to fifteen, each group to have kitchenette/launderette facilities; the construction of a new kitchen and dining block; an additional lecture room; the transfer of the administration and accounts departments to the existing kitchens and dining hall and the transfer of the library to the tithe barn. All this would need grant aid from the Department of Education and Science in order not to exhaust the entire capital reserve of the College as well as any appeal for funds.

This was a bold and imaginative plan designed to carry the College forward well into the 1980s and 1990s. It was intended to bring the College up to the standard of facilities being provided at the newer universities and to remove the remnants of the Victorian era still pervading the internal environment, yet keeping the external appearances of the more than century-old institution. Unfortunately the plan was never put into operation for the attempt to obtain a grant from the Department failed. Following a meeting with Mr Lloyd Jones, an Under-Secretary for Further Education, the application met with a refusal in 1973 and attempts to arrange a meeting with the then Secretary of Education, Margaret Thatcher, failed to find a suitable date and time. Perhaps the spirit of Boutflour was needed and a fortuitous train meeting planned!

★

At the next session there were some staff changes and the year began with slightly less students – 604. With the commencement of the new Diploma course in Agriculture, Arthur Williams was appointed as Lecturer in Agricultural Management and Head of the new Management Studies Department. He was sponsored by the Agricultural Mortgage Corporation. John Josephi (Forestry) took over from Cyril Hart and Major H. Jarvis (Economics) joined, whilst P.D. Carter took over the Estate Economy section of the third-year Rural Estate Management course.

There was, however, a much more significant staff change. Dr Dickson tendered his resignation as Principal on being offered the Chair of Agriculture at Newcastle University as from 1 October 1972. With such a promising beginning this came as a shock to the Governors and the staff, not forgetting the students, with whom he had developed a strong rapport and from whom he had earned respect. It put the Governors in the unhappy position of having to find another Principal within the short space of two years, having geared themselves to exploiting the new and exciting developments that Dickson had put forward and who was destined to see them through. It would be a difficult task to find someone of his calibre prepared to implement the plans with the energy he had generated and with the enthusiasm he had stirred in the staff and students.

The effect on the student body, which possibly reflected the reaction of the staff, was given in the views of the then Chairman of the Union Club, Simon Pott, reported in the *Journal* issue of 1972/3:

. . . [Dickson] came bursting with ideas for the College, a fresh wind that would blow through the lofty corridors of the College, bringing a new and more positive approach to agricultural education and bring the R.A.C. into the 20th Century. Within weeks the idea that the College independence and survival was at risk without the aid of external funds had been shattered with sound and logical debate. How much had these self imposed restrictions held the College back over the years? How much would the character of the College change following a substantial infusion of Government money, and was that a bad thing?

. . . Dr Dickson involved himself immediately with the potential as well as the problems of the College. . . . His involvement with the Union Club, and the help and advice which he gave in his capacity as President of that club were very greatly valued by those of us who had the opportunity to serve with him on the College Management Committee in the past two years. His sense of fun and good sportsmanship in the support he gave to the sporting teams and his splendid participation in Rag have left a lasting impression on many students.

. . . During the following year the atmosphere in the College improved perceptively. The student body as a whole applied themselves with increased vigour to whatever interests they pursued. . . .

. . . The news [of his departure] met with a stunned response from students, and it was only as the full reasons behind this move emerged that it was understood why he had accepted this post.

The full reasons were that he had been approached more than once by the University of Newcastle and had in the first instance refused. But for him and his wife the home ties with the north-east were too strong to resist for a second time. Dickson was a Durham man and the Chair was, to him, the ultimate achievement in the academic world. He perhaps regarded it as a higher peak than the Principalship of the first and original agricultural College of the United Kingdom.

It was a difficult decision for him, and no doubt his loyalties were torn, but it did leave the College having to find a successor in a short space of time and, bearing in mind the critical situation with plans awaiting to be executed which he himself had devised and which had been supported by the Governors, it became inevitable that a residual antipathy would arise. To this day, those with longer memories are inclined to see it as a discarding of the loyalty that the College has demanded of its servants. That such loyalty is expected may be misunderstood in this more commercial age of value for money and payment by results, does not remove the fact that it had been the cement that has enabled the College to prosper in good times and to weather the bad ones.

★

Finding a new Principal was difficult. The Governors decided not to advertise in the first instance but to conduct some independent enquiries in the search for a replacement. In the interregnum the post of Vice-Principal was resurrected and the Bursar, Jacobs, appointed to it and thus to act as Principal for the time being. Three possible candidates were considered in February 1973 but none was found suitable. The search was continued by the special committee set up for the purpose and the post was ultimately offered to and accepted by Sir Emrys Jones, then the Director-General of the Agricultural Development and Advisory Service of the Ministry of Agriculture, Fisheries and Food. With one exception this was a departure from previous policies that were applied to the appointment of Principals, in that the choice now fell on a person already eminent in the agricultural field and with great experience in agricultural extension and advisory work rather than someone yet to make his name in the field. The one exception was, of course, Boutflour.

Sir Emrys Jones, B.Sc., LLD had pursued a career in agricultural advisory work since his early days. A farmer's son, born in Carmarthenshire in 1915, he graduated from the University College of Wales at Aberystwyth with a First Class Degree in Agriculture with Economics and Political Science. He joined the National Agricultural Advisory Service at its commencement in 1946, having

Sir Emrys Jones,
Principal 1972–8

been Chief Cultivations and Technical Officer in Gloucestershire. Before this he had worked as a postgraduate scholar at the Hertfordshire Institute of Agriculture and also in Scotland. His career in the NAAS saw him rise very quickly to senior posts and by 1954 he was Deputy Director for the Service in North Wales and Director for Wales in 1957. In 1961 he was appointed Director of the NAAS and this was followed in 1967 by his becoming Chief Agricultural Adviser to the Minister of Agriculture, Fisheries and Food. In 1971 he became the first Director-General of the newly created Agricultural Development and Advisory Service. For his services to agriculture he was knighted in the Birthday Honours of 1971.

Sir Emrys was a member of many influential bodies, notably the Agricultural Research Council, and President of the Agricultural Education Association and of the Farm Management Association. He was a Fellow of the Royal Agricultural Societies and of the Royal Society of Arts. Academically, he became Honorary Professorial Fellow of the Department of Agriculture, University of North Wales, Bangor, and Honorary Professorial Fellow of the University College of Wales, Aberystwyth; the degree of Doctor of Law (*honoris causa*) was conferred on him by the University of Wales just after his appointment to Principal.

On 1 October 1973 Sir Emrys started with the College on a five-year contract. He inherited the need for the College to expand, on at least some of the Dickson proposals, but what was more important was for external funds to be obtained if any of these radical suggestions were to reach fruition. He asked heads of department to consider and put forward proposals for this future development. The outcome was that priority was to be given to increasing the intake on the agricultural courses to seventy to seventy-five, and to the improvement of student rooms, but the major need was to devote resources to the provision of a new building to house an enlarged library with lecture and workrooms. By now the application to the Ministry of Education and Science had been rejected and it was necessary to seek other sources of funds. It was here that the experience and contacts of the new Principal were to prove of immediate value to the College. Jones had entrée to many commercial firms and to trust funds; in particular he had satisfactory discusssions with the Parkinson Trust and the Hosier Trust, who were able to agree to support financially the proposed new library and lecture theatre. Dr P.N. Wilson, a Trustee of the Parkinson Trust, and Mrs D.E. King of the Hosier Trust visited the College and were prepared to recommend that their respective trusts put up the sums of £50,000 and £30,000.

The Principal also made contact with several commercial undertakings regarding sponsored lectureships. As a result of pursuing these, the Bath and Portland Stone Company, who owned subsidiary companies dealing with animal feeds, agreed to sponsor a lecturer in veterinary science and to covenant a sum worth £5,250 for seven years. Barclays Bank agreed to second a member of their own staff to the College on two-year attachments to lecture on finance, taxation, banking and accounting. The Agricultural Mortgage Corporation would finance the Chair of Advanced Farm Management at the College for an initial period of five years with the sum of £5,500 per year. In return the College were to allow the sponsored lecturer, or any other member of the staff, to advise them on loan situations and to visit farms. These arrangements for sponsored lectureships, Sir Emrys's innovation, were to prove extremely beneficial to both parties and the principle has been continued to the present day.

Emrys Jones was able to start his occupation of the post of Principal with the College in fairly good heart, though still upset at the peremptory departure of Dickson. He wrote:

> My predecessor, Dr Dickson . . ., wrote these words in 1972:
> 'On my arrival at Cirencester I was immediately aware of the enormous challenge of this post.'
> So am I! Not because the Royal is struggling for survival; quite the reverse. There are far more prospective students seeking places at the College than we can hope to accommodate and waiting lists are building up for two and three years ahead, especially on the Rural Estate Management Course. Moreover, the entry qualifications of the current intake of students on this course are well above the minimum requirements of the Royal Institution of Chartered Surveyors and are, in fact, equivalent to University entry requirements. There is indeed now a strong case for the expansion of the College itself, but there are those who believe that there is an even more urgent need to provide improved facilities for both learning and leisure within the campus. The real challenge lies in finding the money to finance these very necessary and desirable developments, particularly as there is no prospect of Government aid in the foreseeable future. . . .
> I have always believed that the Royal Agricultural College had a rather special role to play in the development of British Agriculture as a whole. . . . Its combination of courses and wide curriculum covers the whole spectrum of land management and land use planning and farm business management, in addition to agricultural science and technology. . . . One of the great advantages . . . is that most, if not all, of these disciplines are taught in one and the same educational establishment. This enables a dialogue between future landowners and farmers, future chartered surveyors and farm managers to commence at an age when the beginnings of permanent and fruitful relationships can be established.

Proof of the demand for places at the College was given by the increase in numbers accepted, from 616 at the start of the 1973/4 session to 671 in 1974/5. The College was certainly at the maximum capacity which it could comfortably accommodate. By now the fees had increased to £369 per year for tuition and £315 for residence. Some structural changes in the government of the College had been brought in, with a new Finance Committee and three separate Farm,

College and Students' Boards instituted. The College Board was charged with the task of, 'The formation and modification of College policies for approval by the Governing Body', while the Students' Board was to have terms of reference as wide as possible, to include lecturing and educational policy, social and sporting activities and living conditions in College. At a later date the responsibility for lecturing and educational policy was delegated to an Academic Board.

In 1974 there were changes on the Board of Governors: His Grace the Duke of Beaufort resigned and Major P.C.G. Shuter, representing Wiltshire County Council, and W.J. Clarke, representing the Old Students' Association joined. The academic staff were augmented by the appointment of A.J. Landers (Agricultural Engineering) and M.F. Ponting (Veterinary Science). The secondment from Barclays Bank, the first of the sponsored lectureships, was of A. Bishop, and the bank also loaned M. Hatton to lecture on taxation.

★

The advent of Emrys Jones saw the next large expansion of the College since the construction of the Frank Garner lecture block, both at the College itself as well as on the College farms. Jones and Hughes, the Farms Director, envisaged a new dairy unit at Coates Manor Farm. In early 1974 some preliminary discussions took place with two firms manufacturing and supplying dairy equipment: Messrs Hosier and Alfa-Laval. By April Hughes had produced plans for a two-man/one-hundred-and-eighty-cow unit and the two firms were asked to submit schemes to implement these.

Both firms had had earlier connections with the College going back to the Boutflour days and the scheme by Alfa-Laval was chosen because the firm were anxious to find a centre to cooperate with them in studying the problems of effluent disposal. They proposed that, in cooperation with the College, they would replace any slurry disposal system to be used in the new dairy unit with, possibly, their own Licon system and would bear the cost of any experimental or research work on the effluent disposal systems.

Before accepting this scheme Jones had been on an international tour in France, Holland, Denmark and Sweden. He had been a member of a party consisting of Sir Archibald Ross, who was UK Ambassador to Sweden and who became Chairman of Alfa-Laval, Sweden; Sir Henry (now Lord) Plumb, then President of the National Farmers' Union; and Sir Richard Trehane, Chairman of the Milk Marketing Board. This team, known as the 'Knights' Tour', was highly publicised, each member making a speech on facets of the dairy industry at each stop in Paris, The Hague, Copenhagen and Stockholm. At the last stop they met Hans Stalle, Chairman and Managing Director of Alfa-Laval; he was convinced by Jones's eloquent speech extolling the virtues of establishing the system at the College and agreed to supply the unit and to help to finance it.

The total cost of the new unit would be about £79,000: there would be a grant from the Ministry of Agriculture, Fisheries and Food of £11,000 under their Farm Development Scheme; Alfa-Laval were prepared to enter into a seven-year covenant with the College for £17,500; this would leave the College to find about £50,000. This attractive scheme was approved by the Governors and the Farms Director was authorized to proceed. It was another illustration of the policy adopted by the new Principal of liaising with commercial enterprises to provide facilities for the College, without having to appeal for external funds for development, which were to be of mutual benefit to both the sponsors and the College. It was very much a continuation of policies first initiated by Boutflour of keeping the College in the forefront of agricultural developments by involving the agricultural support industry and contributing to agricultural education in a practical manner. It had started with the fertilizer and feeding-stuffs firms in the 1930s and now many of the major agriculture suppliers as well as the banks were to be cooperators in the expansion of the College.

Not only was the College indebted to such supporters but also the contributions by certain private trusts were to prove invaluable. The plans for the new library and lecture-room complex had been approved by the Hosier and Parkinson Trusts, and the Ernest Bailey Charitable Trust, which had met the cost of 'Bailey Lodge', had shown interest also in being associated with the future development of the College. This Trust had £11,000 available and the Principal suggested that as accommodation was urgently required for the Advanced Farm Management course this could be met by incorporation within the proposed new complex. This the Trust was able to agree and so the new complex would consist of a well-equipped library to replace the old library, now woefully inadequate, a lecture theatre with modern facilities able to seat 168 and a tutorial unit for the Advanced Farm Management course.

The dairy unit was completed and in operation by 1 January 1976. The existing dairy herd at Fosse Hill was moved and expanded into the new unit. This new venture was viewed not without some warnings by the Farms Director, Hughes. Reporting prior to the start of operations, he said of this up-to-date unit:

> The new unit . . . includes a 12/12 herringbone parlour with automatic teat cup removal, cows housed in kennels and fed in winter via a forage box. The slurry will be contained in an above ground slurry store and used to best advantage with a view to reducing fertiliser expenditure. Like most capital expenditure it is very difficult to justify in the short term; it will materially add to our overhead costs via interest and repayment charges. Without tax relief these increased charges will amount to about £13,500, and with other increased costs will put great stress on the economic efficiency of the new unit, and will need high yields per cow associated with maximum utilisation of grass in the summer and winter. . . .

The Principal also warned against over-optimism: 'The arguments for and against [the new unit] attracted widespread interest and publicity and it certainly was difficult to justify such a costly investment, but we decided to go ahead with it. I still believe we were right to do so!'

These statements were, of course, made against a background of a year of depression throughout the agricultural scene. Costs were rising rapidly with inflation and some market returns were falling badly. Jones foresaw improvements to come in the economic situation on the expectation of recovery and based on the booming conditions on the world's stock exchanges. The outcome of the referendum on Britain's entry into the EEC was impending and if favourable it was anticipated that the agricultural industry would immediately benefit if the terms of entry were to be as anticipated.

It was not to be until 1977 that Hughes was able to report that the dairy unit was proving to be satisfactory in its performance and that the investment three years before was proving to have been sound. He reported that yields per cow and the margin over purchased food were being steadily improved.

The new library/lecture-theatre complex was completed ready for occupation in October 1976. Miss Hosier, Arthur Hosier's daughter, was invited to open and name the library 'The Hosier Library', and Mrs Fordham, of the Ernest Bailey Trust, opened that part of the complex to be the Advanced Farm Management Department. These openings took place on 26 October 1976, and on 16 December the lecture theatre was officially opened by an inaugural lecture entitled, 'Dairy Farming in the USA and the UK – A Controversial Comparison', delivered by Professor Peter Wilson, one of the Trustees of the Frank Parkinson Agricultural Trust. It was named 'The Frank Parkinson Lecture Theatre'.

★

During this year changes took place in the constitution of the Board of Governors. Mainly because there were material changes to the courses in the College, the reorganisation centred around the make-up of the Boards and the representation of outside interests on the main board. The changes were recommended to shareholders and accepted by a Special Resolution passed at a meeting held on 30 May 1975. The consequence was that after the retirement of several members, Earl St Aldwyn, Lord Banbury of Southam and Professor T.K. Ewer were invited to become Ordinary Governors.

The Governors had previously decided to create the posts of President and Vice-President. In view of his long association with the College, His Grace the Duke of Beaufort was invited to be the first President, and he accepted. The appointment of a Vice-President was left in abeyance for the time being.

The Governing Body now, therefore, comprised: as President His Grace the Duke of Beaufort, as Hereditary Governor Earl Bathurst, as Ordinary Governors Major P.D. Birchall (Chairman), Lord Banbury of Southam, Major A.

Biddulph, Mr C.H. Coad, Professor T.K. Ewer, Mr J.N. McClean, Sir William Mount, Bt., Earl St Aldwyn, Mr J.M. Stratton and Mr R.W. Trumper. The Representative Governors were: from the National Farmers' Union, Hon. R.C. Butler; from the Ministry of Agriculture, Fisheries and Food, Mr E.S. Carter; from Gloucestershire County Council, Mr J.R. Clapham; from the Old Students' Association, Mr W.J. Clarke; from the Royal Agricultural Society of England, Mr J.D.F. Green and Mr J.D.M. Hearth; from the Country Landowners' Association, Major G.B. Heywood; from the Royal Institution of Chartered Surveyors, Mr G.J. Holborow, Mr H.L. Knight, Mr E.W.T. Malcolm, Mr R.B. Sayce, and Mr E.R. Wheatley-Hubbard; from the Department of Education and Science, Mr E.M. Owens; and from Reading University, Professor E.H. Roberts.

There were four working committees: Finance and General Purposes Committee, and the Farms', College and Students' Boards.

Changes in the academic staff reflected the greater complexity of the courses now running at the College and Directors of Studies were appointed from the current staff. Hughes, the Farms Director, became overall Director of Studies and J.A.R. Lockhart and P.A. Tucker were Directors for Agriculture and Estate Management respectively.

Discussions were held with the Royal Institution of Chartered Surveyors to review the syllabus of the Rural Estate Management course resulting in an increase in the practical content, more emphasis on Capital Taxation, and a reduction in the number of lectures in Law and Forestry. The Institution also accepted the Advanced Farm Management course as part of the year to be spent in practical work prior to their final practical examination, a recognition of the worth of this recently established course.

The newly constituted Board of Governors met for the first time at the commencement of the 1975/6 session when there were 702 students in the College. This year saw some major changes at the senior level of management: Jacobs, Bursar and Registrar, was due to retire and Jones had indicated his desire to retire at the end of the five-year period for which he had been appointed, at the end of the Summer Term 1978. Tucker, Head of the Estate Management Department, was also soon due to retire. The Governors felt from their past experience that it was desirable for a period of at least a year to elapse between each retirement.

Jacobs, who had previously agreed to remain in a part-time capacity responsible for the College investments and student registration, was willing to stay on full-time until 1979, and Tucker also agreed to remain until the end of the Summer Term 1977 in order to organize the changes in the Rural Estate Management course. The Governors then promoted Hughes to be Vice-Principal, with the Directors of Studies for Agriculture and Estate Management reporting to him as from October 1976. Later on Lockhart was appointed to be overall Director of Studies.

A significant appointment at the start of that session and a harbinger of future developments was that of Miss A.M. Johns to teach animal husbandry. She was a graduate of Reading University and had been Demonstrator and Lecturer in Animal Production at the University College of Wales, Aberystwyth. This was to break the mould of the all-male staff that had existed since the role of Miss Ormerod as a visiting lecturer back in the early days of the last century.

★

With the increase in the numbers of students since the post-war period (from some 150 to over 700), the Union Club, which had developed from the Sports Club founded in the nineteenth century, had grown in the comprehensive nature of its activities, both sporting and social. A regular Rag Week was now being held each year, causing some confusion and astonishment to the citizens of Cirencester but raising appreciable funds for charity. Perhaps the oldest functions, the Beagles Hunt and the Rugby and Cricket Clubs, were operating at full strength. There were, in the 1975/6 year, thirty-three separate societies, covering a very wide spectrum of students' interests. It was unlikely that any new student could not find an interest to his taste, from the standard sports activities of athletics, both codes of football, hockey, cricket and tennis to more esoteric societies such as naturalists and field game. This demand for extra-curricular exercise had left the facilities somewhat behind and the Club pressed the College authorities for better facilities and improved living conditions for students.

★

The commercial connections continued to be built up: a consortium of companies engaged in the manufacture and distribution of agro-chemicals supported an annual in-service crop-protection course, 'Landmark'. Under the joint sponsorship of the Royal Agricultural Society of England, Barclays Bank and Imperial Chemical Industries, working in association with the Agricultural Development and Advisory Service, three Cereals Demonstration and Information Units were set up, one of which, the Cotswold Regional Group, (later to be called the Cotswold Cereal Centre, was sited at the College with Hughes, the Vice-Principal, as Chairman. These developments took the College further into extension work.

In March 1977 the Finance and General Purposes Committee met to consider who should replace Sir Emrys Jones on his retirement in 1978. The post was advertised with the objective of making the appointment by March 1977. The Governors agreed a shortlist and interviews held on 21 October 1978. Once again they were faced with the same set of criteria that had exercised the minds of all their predecessors during the history of the College, plus some others that had not applied in the early days. The ideal candidate would be one combining acadamic qualifications of note with agricultural experience. There was an additional factor: following Jones, who came to the College towards the end of a distinguished career in agricultural advisory work, with a national reputation already established, with the skills of public speaking and with influence that had been of benefit to the College, should they look for a character of similar standing and distinction?

Or should they seek a younger man (or woman, though at this time the male predominance was still much too strong to contemplate a female Principal!) who had his name to make and would seek achievement with the College as a base? Should it be an established academic with the knowledge and skills to run an agricultural college with over seven hundred students, a multiplicity of courses and a large farming enterprise? Discussions within the Board of Governors revealed two viewpoints, following the recommendation of the Finance and General Purposes Committee that the new Principal should be Hughes, the Vice-Principal. Here was a man on their very doorstep who had many, if not all, of the qualities that were needed save maybe one. He was not the already established national figure of eminence either in the academic or agricultural advisory and management field, so would not follow the pattern set by the retiring Principal. But he had the supreme advantage of knowing the College inside out, and he already had some recognition in the agricultural world, especially from his management of the College farms.

There was strong support within the Board for his appointment; that was one of the views. The other was the attraction of a candidate with high academic qualifications and an established reputation; he also had some of the characteristics of the outgoing Principal. The recommendation of Hughes prevailed and his appointment was approved, to take effect from the 1 October 1978. The College would suffer no traumatic effect from the change; Hughes could take over with little disturbance to the running of the institution. There were, however, some consequential changes, with several posts now to be filled: the Bursar and the Head of Estate Management were to retire and a new Farms Director was needed.

The post of Farms Director had to be re-created as Hughes had been Director of Studies before he was appointed Vice-Principal and that post was vacant. The new Farms Director would need to be a skilled and experienced person to follow in Hughes's footsteps, for in his eighteen years in charge of the farms he had produced for the College a total profit of over £453,000. It was decided to link the post of Vice-Principal with that of Head of the Estate Management Department, the largest on the campus, and the post of Bursar could be filled later when Jacobs retired.

The outcome of the search for these replacements, by the usual methods of public advertisement, shortlisting and interviewing, was that J.D. Young, B.Sc., FRICS became Vice-Principal and Head of the Estate Management Department, and J.A. Wilkinson, B.Sc. became Farms Director. Young was at the time head of the ADAS Unit at the National Agricultural Centre at Stoneleigh in Warwickshire and Wilkinson was Senior Lecturer in Farm Management at Writtle Agricultural College. Lloyds Bank agreed to sponsor Young's post and covenanted £7,500 for a first period of seven years.

Another change that was made at that time was the appointment of joint Vice-Chairmen of the Board of Governors in order to assist the Chairman, now carrying greater responsibility since the expansion of the College. Mr C.H. Coad and Major G.B. Heywood were appointed.

★

While all these arrangements for the future were being carried out the Principal continued to promote the College externally. He received an invitation to represent the College at the centennial celebrations of Lincoln College (now Lincoln University), Canterbury, New Zealand, and to give the inaugural speech. It will be remembered that the first Principal of this college, William E. Ivey, was an old student of the Royal Agricultural College and had thus forged a continuing connection between the two. By now Lincoln was the third largest college in the British Commonwealth and for some of its time had been run on similar lines as the College, thanks to the start by Ivey.

Sir Emrys was privileged to give the centennial oration, bringing greetings from the Governors, staff and students of the Royal Agricultural College to a highly distinguished assembly including the Governor-General of New Zealand, His Excellency Sir Keith Holyoake, GCMG, CH, Hon. LLD (Well.), Hon. LLD (Agric.) (Seoul Nat.) and the Prime Minister, the Right Honourable R.D. Muldoon, CH, Hon. Ph.D.(Seoul Nat.). The speakers were all highly distinguished scientists and academics eminent in the field of agriculture and food production.

Sir Emrys told of the history of the College and of the second college to be established in the Commonwealth, Ontario Agricultural College at Guelph in Canada, linking its origins with the Royal Agricultural College. Like the College it had got off to a stuttering start, its first Principal, Henry McCandless being dismissed for incompetence and as the result of a students' revolt! The second Principal was Charles Gay Roberts, a gold medallist of the Royal Agricultural College in 1864. He, however, did not last very long for he had a nervous breakdown and in temporary insanity jumped into the River Speed breaking his leg on a boulder. Sir Emrys then referred to the similarity with the RAC for the next Principal to be appointed, William Johnston (1874–9), was a man of vision and determination who laid the foundations of a highly successful college at Guelph. This paralleled the beginnings at the College with John Wilson following as second Principal after Hodgkinson.

So Sir Emrys revealed the close early connections of the three colleges and showed that one of the lectures that Ivey had attended at the College, given by the then Principal, John Constable, had influenced him when it came to setting up the syllabus of work for Lincoln College.

This culmination of Sir Emrys's tenure of the Principalship brought honour to the College and in reporting back he said, 'I was rather taken aback and, I confess, rather flattered with the respect and esteem in which the Royal Agricultural College at Cirencester is held by the rest of the world. It is, after all, the first agricultural college to have been established in the Commonwealth and has been copied many times since.'

★

Although he was only at the College five years Emrys Jones had undoubtedly enhanced its reputation and standing by his ability to project it to the wider public and by his successful adoption of commercial sponsorship for teaching and of financial support from trusts for the development projects to improve the academic facilities. He himself was honoured by the award of the Bledisloe Medal for his outstanding services to the College at a presentation luncheon to mark his retirement. The variation of the original Declaration of Trust for the award of the Medal (it was originally for outstanding services to agriculture by a former student) had the full support of the then Viscount Bledisloe. In addition he was granted the status of Principal Emeritus.

In October 1978 a new regime started under the Principalship of Hughes; the change was imperceptible for he had been working closely with Jones and the progression was a natural one following his long service to the College since his first days as a lecturer. The period now ending had got off to an unfortunate start with the precipitate resignation of Dickson but had finished on a note of continuing success and of stability. Hughes inherited a progressive and flourishing institution with the potential for further expansion.

Chapter Twelve

DEGREE TEACHING ACHIEVED WITH HUGHES, 1979–86

Management is not about today but about the future . . . we need to increase our facilities for more intensive teaching methods.

H.V. Hughes, 1979

In October 1978 when the new Principal took over there was another change in the senior management of the College. Jacobs had agreed to stay on until Hughes was in post and now he wished to retire. After advertisement, the post of Bursar was filled by Christopher H. Bailey, MA (Cantab.), an independent management consultant.

Neil Jacobs retired in April 1979, after a long and distinguished career with the College. He left a College extremely grateful for his work, not just in the posts he had at different times occupied of Lecturer, Bursar, Warden and Vice-Principal, but in the latter days of his incumbency as Financial Adviser to the Governors. He had run the College finances, particularly its investments, so effectively that there was, on his leaving, a capital fund of over £1,175,000, notwithstanding that while he was Bursar there had been capital development expenditure of over £257,000. It was by prudent management of the College's investment portfolio that he had accomplished this remarkable feat of helping to secure greater reserves than the College had ever had in its history.

His day-to-day management of the income and expenditure accounts was equally prudent; not a man to waste money, he was scrupulous in obtaining value for money especially in his dealings with architects and builders in the many development contracts carried out during his time. His desire for value for money may have led some to think that it was influenced by a certain degree of parsimony especially where the accommodation facilities were concerned. This somewhat spartan attitude towards the internal arrangements in the College must be tempered by the fact that, as he said, 'The question of accommodation in College for residents has caused me some concern but it is extremely difficult to effect any very great improvement due to the design of the building and to the fact that it was built as long ago as 1845. . . . I feel that it is generally adequate and that the students obtain pretty good value.'

Neil Jacobs,
Lecturer, Warden,
Bursar and Vice-
Principal 1934–8 and
1951–79

The tasks he undertook in his various guises became more extensive as the College grew from some 450 students in 1951 to over 750 in 1978. He had been at the College as a lecturer from 1934 to 1938 and then had returned in 1951 as Bursar following the untimely death of Harry Bailey. But he had already forged a close connection when in 1939 he had married Josephine, the daughter of Bobby Boutflour. For twenty-eight years he had been at the heart of the management of the College under four successive Principals, Boutflour, Garner, Dickson and Jones. Each in their way had contributed to the development and extension of the College and its large increase in the numbers of students, and Jacobs could be fairly said to have been responsible for the execution and financial control of the extensions as well as for the welfare of the students, sorting out their problems (as well as their transgressions!). A patient man, not given to any hasty decisions, and very rarely, if ever, appearing ruffled, for his services Jacobs was appointed MBE. The Governors asked him to continue to manage the College investment portfolio for a period of three years after his retirement; this he did so successfully that by the end of 1981 the investment portfolio had a market value of just over £2,353,000.

This was the end of the period that Jacobs had agreed to continue the management of the fund. The Governors felt that it would be too much to expect him to continue to carry this responsibility and so in addition to asking him to stay on as the investment manager for another year a committee to assist him was formed of the Chairman, Deputy Chairman, Principal, Bursar and two Governors, J.D.M. Hearth and P.W. Trumper. It found little need to make any suggestions or criticisms. Eventually, in 1984, Jacobs relinquished the post of investment manager when the market value of the portfolio was £3,328,210, a quite remarkable performance and one which crowned the efforts of one of the most effective of the Secretaries and Bursars of the College since its foundation. A professional adviser, Dr A.C. Copisarow, was appointed as investment manager.

★

The incoming Bursar, Christopher Bailey, arrived with experience in management consultancy. He had had a varied career before that: educated at Radley and having read Biology at Queen's College, Cambridge, he had worked as a farm manager in Kenya and on his return to Britain had been in industry. Before setting up on his own as a management consultant, he had been the administrative director of a group of companies involved in transport and distribution, timber manufacturing and engineering. He took over at a time when it was once again becoming imperative for the College to make provision for the increased student numbers and when one of the aims of the new Principal would have to be the raising of the academic standards in order to match the demands being made by an agricultural industry fast improving its technological performance.

★

Hughes, the new Principal (though hardly 'new' so far as his service to the College was concerned), would have to deal with two major steps forward that the College had to take if it was to hold a leading position in the world of agricultural education. Firstly, there was a need to increase and improve the facilities, not only the physical requirements, but also the academic resources, particularly to improve the staff/student ratio. The provision of the Hosier Library, the Ernest Bailey Seminar Room and the Frank Parkinson Lecture Theatre were a good beginning but student residential accommodation was becoming more and more insufficient as was the availability of social and recreational space. The students' bar was, in 1979, moved to the games room, once the only lecture room in Victorian days, and, with the tithe barn, once the chemical laboratory, it became the social centre for the College. The cost of these changes was borne equally by the brewers, the College and the Students' Union. A burning need was to upgrade the original students' rooms in the main building, most of which had hardly changed since the last century.

Hughes's early words on taking over reflected the situation in the industry: 'Management is not about today but about the future. If we dissipate our energies worrying about today, we're too late! Agricultural education is as dynamic an activity as the industry it serves. In College we need to increase our facilities for more intensive teaching methods. There must be greater emphasis on small group contact – a member of staff with three or four chaps. We can't not afford to do it. For this we need rooms.'

The second move forward so necessary was the establishment of the award of a degree taught at the College. The logical target to aim at would be a degree in Estate Management, for not only was the teaching of the Diploma in Estate Management up to the standard required by the professional body, the Royal Institution of Chartered Surveyors, it was not far short in professional terms of degree status. It would, of course, require a greater academic slant and a lower staff/student ratio and this would necessitate different teaching methods with more emphasis on tutorials and individual research and less on mainly taught subjects. The possibility of a degree course in Agriculture was to be considered later.

To pursue the possibilities the Governors decided that approaches should be made to appropriate universities. Professor Ewer, an Ordinary Governor, had already made contact with the Universities of Bath, Bristol and Oxford, of which the latter two, Bristol and Oxford, had had connections with the College in the past, Bristol being the last when granting degrees to students taught at Cirencester in the pre-war years under Hanley and Boutflour.

These contacts were not successful; there was no interest on the part of the universities concerned. The conclusion was reached that this would be long-term in achievement and that it would take at least two years. Two further approaches would be made: one to Professor Miles, Dean of the Faculty of Urban and Regional Studies at Reading University and the other to the Council for National Academic Awards. The former might prove to be fruitful since the Faculty already offered a degree in Estate Management, directly and to students at the College of Estate Management. It was realized that if a degree course was to be established it would need the appointment of at least three extra members of staff in the subjects of Accounting and Taxation, Law and Valuations and Land Economy. To enhance facilities the library would have to be extended and further tutorial rooms provided. The Principal was authorized to go ahead with recruiting the extra staff. The fulfilment of the College's ambition to achieve degree teaching was to take much longer than anticipated with protracted negotiations, producing agreement with the University only by 1982 so that the new degree course did not start until 1984.

★

There was one highly significant step taken by the Governors in 1979. This was to admit female students. The Governors of this all-male establishment, which had since its foundation not even contemplated the possibility of becoming coeducational, were not unaware of the change in the social milieu to equal opportunity for all, and of the growing entry into agriculture and land management of females. There was no legal requirement for a private institution to admit women students, but there had been representations from a local member of Parliament, from the Association of Assistant Mistresses, and a visit by members of the Equal Opportunities Commission. In addition, the Bursar had reported a growing number of enquiries from girls' schools about careers in agriculture and estate management and entry to the College. The Governors could hardly be expected to ignore the importance of equality of opportunity, nor, as a private, commercially run body, of the market as yet untapped for potential students. It may well have been this latter thought that tilted the balance in favour of the decision to admit women students on the Diploma course in Rural Estate Management in the year commencing October 1979. Eventually they were admitted to all courses. A pertinent comment on this episode is that the first two female students to complete the course appeared within the first five places in the final year lists: they were Susan Williamson (gold medallist) and Charlotte Cordy-Simpson.

★

In 1977, a cereal study group was started at the College, linked to the Royal Agricultural Society of England and based on the enthusiasm of local farmers for the expanding crop of winter barley; it was coordinated by John Wibberley of the Agriculture Department. Great interest was generated by the 'Barley '70' demonstration staged jointly by the College and the RASE at Fosse Hill Farm. Following this in autumn 1979, a highly successful venture in extension work was started which was to boost the reputation of the College, at first locally, and later on, nationally.

This was the setting up of the Cotswold Cereal Centre, later to become one of a national network of centres under the Arable Research Centre (Agricultural Research Council) with headquarters at the College. It was an initiative of Hughes and prominent farmers who came to the conclusion that there was a need for such a centre to experiment, obtain and diffuse information to farmers in the area. It was supported strongly by Tom Juckes, a Governor of the College and Chairman of the Committee. Hughes reckoned that the College could be a focal point for this function and that cereal growing should be studied in depth, with some thirty acres of College farm land needed for the experimental work. The facilities of the College laboratories were made available and the Centre – which was farmer founded and supported by ancilliary industries – would employ a researcher. Lockhart, Director of Agricultural Studies, with others, assisted in the initial work of laying out, drilling and monitoring the experimental plots prior to the arrival of the Centre's first Director, Michael Gibson, in November 1979. After Gibson's untimely death in 1984, Dr Michael Carver took over and continued the development of other regional centres under the new banner, Arable Research Centres (ARC), Ltd. The development of Arable Research

Centres, serving the major cereal growing areas, was especially valuable in that it anticipated future government intentions on farmer funding of 'near farm' research.

★

At the beginning of the 1979/80 session there were changes in the Governing Body and in the academic staff. Richard Trumper, a long-standing Governor and an eminent land agent, resigned; J.F.H. Edwards replaced E.R. Wheatley-Hubbard as a representative of the Royal Institution of Chartered Surveyors and Professor C.R.W. Spedding took over from Professor E.H. Roberts, representing the University of Reading. The Department of Education and Science decided, on the retirement of E.M. Owens, not to to be represented on the Board. The representative of the National Farmers' Union was N.J. Fiske, replacing the Hon. R.C. Butler. New staff posts were filled by R. Couchman (Valuations) and J. Mulholland (Law and Projects Officer), and R. Cornwell arrived from Askam Bryan Agricultural College to lecture on Farm Buildings.

★

Early in 1980 plans were prepared on a five-year basis for the building extension necessary and the first priority was given to the upgrading of the students' accommodation. The need for an extension of the library and for tutorial rooms was subsumed within an overall plan for the whole College site, including Bledisloe and Trent Lodges.

The Principal's estimate of the space requirements depended very much on the number of students attending courses and on the type of courses offered. Indeed, the key seemed to be whether a degree course in Estate Management would be commenced since this determined the increase in staff necessary and the student areas required to satisfy the degree awarding authority. He anticipated an increase in short in-service courses such as Farm Business Management for bankers and farmers, short updating courses for estate owners and their employees, and technology-based courses similar to the Landmark and UKASTA (United Kingdom Agricultural Supplies and Trading Association) courses already in existence. There would then be a considerable increase in library use leading to a need for quiet study areas as well as group study areas. More staff space was essential if the sharing of offices was to be avoided. There would be a corresponding shortfall in accommodation for residential students.

The renovation of existing student accommodation was commenced immediately. Plans for the library extension were prepared and for the erection of up to two hundred new student rooms, based on a first phase of sixty. These were estimated to require an expenditure of about £2,000,000, a sum which would be difficult to raise. To start to meet the cost it was decided to sell Bledisloe Lodge, together with some four acres of land. This building was in a poor state of internal decoration, would need a considerable sum of money to bring it up to modern habitable standards and was, in any case, inconvenient for the students being sited a considerable distance from the main campus and unsuitable for conversion to the desirable single study bedrooms.

To raise the balance of the money the Governors decided to launch an appeal for funds. An Appeal Committee was formed of Major Heywood, Messrs Coad, Hearth and Sir Emrys Jones with the Principal and the Bursar. It was decided that the maximum realistic sum on which an appeal could be based was £1,500,000. By now the College reserves were such that the income from them was contributing to the costs of running the College and, with the income derived from farming profits, fees could to be kept to a level which allowed the College to compete against other institutions financed by the government.

This was an important factor to be recognized and the independence of the College was felt to be a strong reason why the Appeal would be likely to attract sums from sponsors and donors. It was also made clear that the College was, in any case, making a large sum of money available to fulfill a modernization programme. It was hoped that donors would consider sponsoring an individual building as had been the case when the previous development programme had been carried through by donations from trusts, i.e. the Frank Parkinson Lecture Theatre, the Hosier Library and the Ernest Bailey Seminar Room. Three main groups of possible donors were approached: charitable trusts, industrial firms and similar bodies, as well as old students through the Royal Agricultural College Association. The appeal was launched that autumn.

A press conference was held to publicize this launch at 'The Royal Agricultural Showtime' during the Royal Variety Show in London on 1 December 1980. Dinners were arranged in various parts of the country in order to contact old students and those overseas were also notified of the Appeal. The Principal was assiduous in attending most of these functions and was met with enthusiasm. His message was straightforward:

> Our College is the oldest, and the only one independent of government funds. We save the Exchequer more than £1 million a year and we run at half the cost of government subsidised colleges. How do we do it? The College farms are highly profitable, there is considerable sponsorship from the Agro Chemical Industry and banks, tight management, and a soundly run investment portfolio. You can't exist on goodwill. You are only as good as the students you turn out each year. We are aiming for the 21st Century. Our students must be as well equipped for the real world as it is possible to be.

However, the response from institutions, charitable trusts and livery companies was disappointing – by the end of the year only £155,000 had been raised. The sale of Bledisloe Lodge made £216,000, so the total raised fell far short of the target. It turned out not to be the most propitious time to raise such sums: the country had run into recession, costs were rising and income was static or falling. By 1982 the position had not changed and a further effort to obtain funds, especially from past students, was made. In March of that year the Appeal was closed when the net proceeds stood at £480,276.28. A further £1,043.43 was received after closure and this and other small amounts were placed in a development fund. Essentially, the Appeal was a relative failure, in spite of the hard work by all concerned. It showed how critical the timing of such a venture was and how sensitive it could be to the economic climate of the day.

The failure of the Appeal did not restrain the Governors in going ahead with the planned developments; indeed, they were in no position to stop them, unless at the cost of having to reduce the student intake and restrict the amount of teaching, for the College was not just at capacity but was overflowing. Architectural plans had already been prepared for a new tutorial block and an extension of the library.

★

The siting and design of the new students' accommodation demanded great care and skill because it would be the first construction since the Boutflour Hall and the King George V Wing that would need to be in architectural sympathy with the old Victorian Gothic design. The machinery block and the Frank Garner Lecture Theatre block were strictly functional buildings and being at the back of the main site they did not contrast unfavourably with the old style, hidden behind the Boutflour Hall. The site chosen was to the west side of the main edifice and adjacent to the King George V Wing. It is on the boundary of the land owned by the College, from which there is an uninterrupted view over Cotswold farmland. David Lea, the commissioned architect, drew up plans for a courtyard design of an open 'U' shape with the open side facing west over the countryside. Eschewing any possibility of simply copying the Gothic design (it would have been extravagantly expensive) modern materials were used for the walling and an external appearance in keeping with traditional Cotswold buildings was achieved by the application of lime-based roughcast finish, broken by stone mullioned windows. The steeply pitched roof was covered in Cotswold tiles quarried locally which matched those on the older buildings. The internal design of the students' rooms was based on the 'staircase' principle of the older university colleges.

This new building of sixty study bedrooms, built to modern environmental standards, was also intended for use in vacations by conference delegates and other visitors. It would indeed satisfy several needs. Although close to the existing buildings it would give the students occupying it some sense of detachment. It complemented the adjacent King George V Wing; each building is enhanced by the presence of the other. It is essentially a Cotswold building and is accepted as such, being an attractive construction in its own right; it has since received favourable and appreciative comment, not least by the Prince of Wales, the President of the College since 1982, in his television documentary on architecture. The simplicity of design with no 'effort' made to render its style noticeable would also enable the new building quite rapidly to become a natural part of the building complex.

The final cost was about £¼ million, met from College resources. The work started in March 1982 and was finished by June 1983. The College had thus, as the Bursar reported, '. . . replaced our worst accommodation by building our best. The new study bedrooms on the College Campus were built after it was decided to sell a magnificent Georgian mansion two miles from the College, which had housed 60 students in rooms containing one to five beds.' In fact, wear and tear over twenty years had resulted in making not only renovation but internal redesigning too extravagant.

He continued, 'We also wanted to increase the sense of community on the main campus and bring the students more close to the library, teaching, social and sports facilities. The new building would have to offer equal – but not the same – advantages to students as the freedom of rented cottages. Although the College is an independent institution, we chose to use the University Grants Committee's financial standards as our yardstick, and to aim for a return on our capital with the help of full-time occupancy lettings during the vacations at "upper market" rates.'

Not unnaturally, the Governors, having toyed with other possible names for the new structure, decided to perpetuate the memory of the College's most illustrious old student and name it Bledisloe Court. It was officially opened by Robin Leigh-Pemberton, the Governor of the Bank of England, at the Bledisloe Memorial Lecture given by him on 6 January 1983.

★

Before this major project was carried out, other works had been necessary to modernize the College. In 1981 the stonework of the main building had to be renovated at a cost of £148,000. Considering that the masonry was over one hundred years old the Victorian founders had built an edifice meant to last. The changing rooms on the ground floor were refurbished from their stark male simplicity to herald the arrival of female students and further students' bedrooms were created out of the domestic staff hostel no longer required for that use. The additional offices for the academic staff were obtained by conversion of the Cedar Hostel, renamed Cedar Lodge. Evidence of the mobility of students of the day was the extension of the car park to take an additional 110 cars as well as the creation of a new park in the woodland near the aptly named Kill Devil Hill entrance for sixty more. It was given the important sounding title 'Westwood Car Park'.

College roofs.
Bledisloe Court
overlooks the
Cotswold landscape

In 1983 the kitchens were updated and changed to a cafeteria system at a cost of £506,000, the College drainage system was connected to the mains, and alterations to Trent Lodge improved the standards beyond recognition.

★

In 1980 Major Peter D. Birchall, Chairman of the Governors, retired at the summer meeting of Governors. He had been a Governor for thirty-three years (including seventeen as Chairman) devoting time to the affairs of the College. During his chairmanship major development programmes had been carried out – entirely new teaching facilities, including lecture rooms, tutorial offices, and the machinery wing. He had seen the College increase from some 250 students to over 700, and the College farms expanded from 620 to 1,300 acres. The freehold had been purchased and several severe financial crises overcome. He handed over the chairmanship to Major G.B. Heywood, the second old student of the College to hold the post since Lord Bledisloe.

In that year the post of Farms Director was taken over by Mr T.M. Limb from Mr J.A. Wilkinson, who had to resign on grounds of ill health. Limb had been the Assistant Farms' Manager at Coates Manor Farm under the Farms Director Henry Fell in 1959. He was a graduate of Leeds and Reading Universities. He had spent six years on his family farm in Northamptonshire and had been with

Imperial Chemical Industries for ten years. Wilkinson also relinquished the post of Head of the Management Studies Department and Dr T.F. Robson was appointed in his place. One of the new appointments was that of Dr H. Martin (Agricultural Science); the post was sponsored by Elanco Products Ltd. This was one of several sponsored lectureships, a practice started by Emrys Jones and continued by Hughes. Dr Martin's work was to benefit the newly formed Cotswold Cereal Centre. The use of part-time lecturers was another method adopted of increasing and improving the lecturing capacity of the College. C. Hayhurst-France, a local practising surveyor (Applied Valuations), A.J. Davies, a former Head of the Agricultural Service of the Agricultural Development and Advisory Service (Agriculture), R.B. Sayce, a Governor and former Head of the Land Service of ADAS (Rural Land Use), and A.D. Bird (Marketing) all lectured on a part-time basis.

★

Throughout the 1980s the College management had one continuing aim: to teach to degree standard. The College, after its long history of producing diploma students who were recognized as fully qualified to hold their own with any of the products of an agricultural education system that had flourished since its start in the nineteenth century, now found that universities, polytechnics and colleges, as well as some of the agricultural colleges (formerly the county institutes), were able to offer, or were moving to offer, courses leading to a degree. As far as the Diploma offered by the College in Rural Estate Management was concerned, this was, through the recognition accorded by the professional institutions, regarded as the equivalent of a university degree for all practical purposes, especially that of obtaining employment. This did not, of course, apply to the same extent to the Diploma in agriculture, nor, of course to the HND in agriculture. Yet, increasingly, it was the degree in agriculture or related subjects that employers were seeking; the Agricultural Development and Advisory Service was by now restricting itself to graduate entry and its example was being followed by the major firms in the agricultural industry recruiting from the colleges. If the College was unable to offer degree courses it would inevitably fall behind in the market place of education; as an institution independent of government assistance this clearly had to be avoided.

Some feelers had been put out with Bristol University but these had made no progress, though ironically it was Bristol which had courted the College at its inception in 1909. Bristol degrees had, pre-war, been awarded at the College but, as we have seen, the relationship had proved difficult, mainly because of a clash of personalities. Between 1980 and 1985 the agricultural component of a Bristol B.Ed. Honours degree had been taught at the College while St Paul's and St Mary's College at Cheltenham taught the educational components.

The Governors set up two working parties to pursue the objective of degrees in

Estate Management and in Agriculture. Of these it was always to be likely that the path towards a degree in Estate Management would be the easier, though the term is relative. In 1980 approaches were made to the Council for National Academic Awards. The response was not encouraging. For a start the Council wanted to see a staff/student ratio of 1:10 as well as improved library facilities over and above the proposed extension. It was apparent that the College could not attain these requirements without financial assistance and that the Council had applied the same criteria as they would to government financed colleges.

The College changed tactics and decided to continue with the Diploma course and to attempt to run a small degree course alongside it. This would mean the relatively modest change of adapting the Diploma syllabus, upgrading it and hoping that it would eventually be accepted as a degree course. On this basis John Young, the Vice-Principal, was instructed to approach the Estate Management departments of Oxford and Bristol Polytechnics, both CNAA (Council for National Academic Awards) awarding bodies, to see if they would cooperate with the College. Reading University was to be approached later when the new Dean of the Faculty of Urban and Regional Studies had been appointed.

These, and subsequently other approaches, leading to negotiations, were extremely protracted. Not unnaturally, the College had to make all the running and initiate talks. Those with the polytechnics ran into financial difficulties and validation hurdles proved difficult because the proposed liaison with them still involved the CNAA degree requirements and standards. However, by the middle of 1982, there was some hope of reaching agreement with Reading University. The College was made rather more welcome than elsewhere and progress was made on the basis that a degree course in Estate Management could be devised which would involve participation by selected students in the external degree at Reading. This was rather less than had been hoped for and would not do much more than put College students on the same footing as those who were registered by the University to take the external degree while working in professional offices. But it was a start and the first sign that the aim could be accomplished. More discussions were to be held in the autumn of that year.

The fresh discussions centred around a new degree to be offered internally rather than the external degree. Once the negotiations entered into a more detailed stage, there were two problems for the College. One was that the charitable status of the College might be lost depending on the legal framework entered into. The other was, inevitably, the financial arrangements, because association with the University was going to cost the College money. The College solicitor, Mr O.A. Logie, volunteered to resign so that specialist solicitors could be appointed. Mr R. Williamson, a Senior Partner in the firm of Morrel, Peel and Gamlen of Oxford, was appointed. They were solicitors to Oxford University and colleges. One other result of this appointment was to be that the corporate status of the College was amended and brought up to date.

By 1983 the negotiations with Reading University culminated in some firm proposals. A small number of students, not exceeding twenty annually in the initial stage, would be taught full-time at College for a B.Sc. Honours Degree in Rural Land Management. The University would ensure maintenance of academic standards by providing compulsory short residential courses at the University, and would be the examining body. On the College side, the library extension was to be completed and the necessary extra staff recruited to teach to degree standard and style. The course was to be under the direction of a Board of Studies consisting of nine members from the University and five from the College. The target date for the start of the course was October 1984.

The new course carried certain other implications. It would be running alongside the College Diploma in Rural Estate Management, which itself carried exemption from the final examinations of the Royal Institution of Chartered Surveyors (Land Agency and Agricultural Division) and of the Incorporated Society of Valuers and Auctioneers (Agricultural Practice Division). By agreement with these bodies the new course would, on successful completion, carry the same exemptions. Finally, the Governors decided that successful candidates would be granted Membership of the Royal Agricultural College (MRAC) in line with successful Diploma holders.

So far so good: the College had the prospect of being able to offer in its prospectus the B.Sc. (Hons.) Reading course to prospective students; the objective the Principal and Governors had set some four years previously. The final hurdle was the financial arrangements: these proved to be a sticking point. The annual cost was going to be £40,000 for improved teaching and £56,000 for the degree course as asked for by Reading. This was much more than anticipated; the College would be paying an excessive amount for the privilege of offering a degree course not of its own validation and under the control, ultimately, of another body. The Principal and the Bursar were instructed to renegotiate with the University. While they were doing so the basic syllabus was drawn up by the Board of Studies for eventual ratification by the Senate and Council at Reading.

Hughes and Bailey reached agreement over a reduction in costs. The College would pay Reading £37,053 in the first year, £30,150 in the second year and £36,730 in the third and subsequent years. In addition the College would pay Reading £500 for each student in excess of twenty in each year of the course. The Governors approved this and the first degree students arrived in October 1984. Although it had taken some four years to achieve and although the cost was higher than desirable (Reading had driven a hard bargain) this was not just a significant step in the history of the College, it was truly to be a milestone, for others were to follow in quick succession and degree courses would come to dominate the College prospectus. The credit for making this breakthrough must go to the staff, led by the Principal, with the Vice-Principal, John Young and the Bursar, Christopher Bailey, playing major roles. It was a nice touch that the start of the new course in 1984 coincided with the fiftieth anniversary of the Rural Estate Management course, started with such vision by Boutflour in 1934, and which had proved to be the salvation of the College in its dog days. A luncheon was held on 7 September 1984 in celebration.

★

The academic advancements and the development of further teaching facilities, the library extension and the building of the new residential accommodation were complemented by the modernization of the older parts of the building, notably the student rooms and domestic quarters. A result of this was that the Bursar could now offer vacation accommodation to hotel standard with modern conference facilities and thus earn valuable revenue for the College. There had always been some regular customers, notably the National Agricultural Advisory Service (later ADAS) and various firms in the agricultural industry. One constant visitor was the Transport and General Workers Union (TGWU) whose annual

TGWU summer school in the tithe barn

summer schools were to become a regular feature. But the catchment area was widening: it surprised some of the more staid members of the College to see advertisements such as that in the SAGA holiday brochure for the College as a centre for Cotswold tours. The summer vacation of 1981 was full throughout with two weeks of College-run conferences, five weeks of the TGWU, and seven weeks of holiday lettings. The target was, with the new accommodation, over £$\frac{1}{4}$ million a year gross as supplementary income. The College vacation courses were by then training bank managers to understand the needs of farmers, briefing chemical representatives to understand more about crop protection, teaching schoolchildren about careers in the countryside and bringing former students up to date with refresher courses.

★

The major step forward in education standards, made by the adoption of the Degree in Rural Land Management through Reading University which started in 1984, was made manifest by the fact that successful College degree students were to take part in the University Degree Awarding Ceremony at the end of the College year of 1986/7 and so the College Diploma Awarding Ceremony was resurrected and held in the Boutflour Hall on Saturday 19 July 1986. This lasted all day, in two sessions, and Lord Belstead, then Minister of State at the Ministry of Agriculture, Fisheries and Food, gave a short address at each session as guest of honour.

The advent of the degree course was, as far as Hughes was concerned, to be only the first advance in the provision of teaching to degree standard and he was assiduous in his pursuit of other liaisons or agreements with degree-awarding bodies in order to develop to the full the facilities now becoming available, both in educational material and accommodation and in staff resources. In 1985 there had been a number of meetings between Governors, academic staff and representatives of related industries to obtain some idea of the numbers and types of courses that should be provided to meet the future demand from those engaged in farming and allied industries. One outcome of these meetings was that there should be another degree course, possibly in agricultural business management, i.e. to use the jargon of the time, in Agri-Business. It was suggested that approaches be made to either a university or to the Council for National Academic Awards.

Following this up the Principal made contact with three Professors at Reading University, Giles, Miles and Speeding, to see if a syllabus could be drawn up for such a degree which would be acceptable to the University. He also had his eye on other universities such as Warwick and Bath and was casting widely by seeking publicity for College courses overseas through the British Council. This initiative by Hughes generated the need for a marketing strategy and a first move in this direction was to get the opinion of old students, who were, in any case,

The modern college in its Cotswold setting

one of the best sources of information operating as they did in the very field to be surveyed.

The result was a strong indication that the College should aim at Business Management and Marketing in Agriculture followed by some specialist subjects such as Crop Technology. The subjects proposed were, in order of priority, Business Management, Marketing, Agriculture, Specialist Technology, especially Crop Production and Agricultural Science. A wide range of subjects was suggested for short courses. Put to the Governors they took the line that bearing in mind that students' interest should come first the Principal should go ahead with seeking cooperation with other universities with a view to offering a degree in Business Management, as well as looking to start two or three in-service courses and reviewing the research and consultancy work of the College. They were also concerned that the College should be marketed nationally and internationally.

★

Armed with this guidance Hughes visited the University of Illinois with the objective of obtaining an international connection by developing courses in Agricultural Communications such as those being run at that University. He spent two and a half days there in discussions with the Dean of the College of

Communications, the Director and Assistant Head of the Office of Agricultural Communications and others. On his return he put forward plans for the College to:

1. Appoint a member of staff to develop the College marketing activities and to contribute to the development of a communication discipline in existing courses.

2. Undertake research to establish the career prospects for those with a sound agricultural training and education together with communications.

3. To seek to establish a cost-effective postgraduate qualification in Agricultural Communications and to develop appropriate relationships with educational bodies within and outside the United Kingdom.

These failed, however, to lead to a degree course in Agricultural Communications, but were a step in the direction of Business Management courses and a clear declaration that the College would be seeking to teach further degree courses in association with other degree-awarding institutions, with the possibility that in the future the College may become self-validating.

Chapter Thirteen

NEW STRUCTURES, 1987–90

Tempora mutantur, et nos mutamur in illis.

The academic advancement achieved by the establishment of the new degree course with Reading University, thus reinstating the degree teaching that had existed in the 1930s with the arrangement with Bristol University, warranted a review of the academic structure of the College. The result of the active and detailed discussions that took place by 1987 naturally extended to a close look at the very structure and organization of the academic side of the College, which with its two departments of Estate Management and Agriculture had remained virtually unchanged since their first establishment by Boutflour over fifty years before. The newcomers of Business Management and Marketing needed to be accommodated and it seemed right to set up another department. Furthermore, with one degree course already on stream and others projected, it seemed to the Principal and Governors that a structure more akin to that of a university was not only more appropriate but would be more effective in management.

As a result the academic departments of the College were renamed 'Schools' with the Heads of the Schools to be titled 'Deans'. Thus the divisions were: the School of Rural Economy and Land Management, the School of Agriculture and the School of Business Studies. With Young, the Vice-Principal and Head of the Estate Management Department, to become the Dean of the first School, the Principal took over, for the time being, as Dean of the School of Agriculture. A new Dean of Business Studies was to be recruited to take charge of that department. An allocation of the existing courses resulted in: the School of Rural Economy and Land Management offering the B.Sc. in Land Management and the Diploma in Rural Estate Management; the School of Agriculture offering the HND in Agriculture, the Diploma in Farm Management and the one-year farming course (the short course); and the School of Business Studies offering the Diploma in Advanced Farm Management. This did not mean leaving the Schools in isolated pockets; each was expected to contribute to the others in selected subjects.

It became immediately necessary to find a Dean for the School of Business Studies and then to discuss with him the direction in which the new School should aim. Before that the opinions of the academic staff were canvassed. They supported the concept and felt that from the strong base of the College in farm business management and rural affairs, advanced courses should be run in rural business as a wide-ranging topic and that the target should be validation for a degree by an appropriate university. A working party of the Governors had come to the same conclusion and the policy of seeking a degree course to add to that in Land Management was adopted.

Progress in appointing a Dean of Business was slow: it proved difficult to find a suitable candidate by 'head hunting', a technique of the day. So the Governors reverted to the more normal method of advertising nationally. This resulted in the appointment of Dr David J. Newton, though not until 1988; the School of Business was launched in the autumn of 1989 when the new Dean outlined its programme for the immediate future. It was to take over the responsibility for teaching in the Farm Management Department and control of the Advanced Agricultural Business Management course. Short courses would be run for the high street banks and the Agricultural Training Board and it would become involved in the courses preparing students for the final practical examination of the Royal Institution of Chartered Surveyors.

A series of meetings was held between the College staff and senior industrialists such as the Institute of Directors, the British Institute of Management, the National Association of Agricultural Contractors and UKASTA, with the objective of running short management courses for them. An innovation was to be the setting up of foreign language courses on a voluntary basis to support links with European countries, especially France and Holland, and an agreement of cooperation was entered into with the Institut Supérieur de Beauvais with whom links had been forged in 1985 by Young, the Vice-Principal. An important long-term initiative was to open discussions with Buckingham and Bath Universities for a B.Sc. Degree in International Agri-Business Management and for a European Master of Business Management course. A very useful beginning for the School was the agreement by the Agricultural Mortgage Corporation to sponsor a Chair in the School of Business as from September 1989 and the first occupant of this Chair would be Dr Newton. This new School, a significant departure for the College and one which was to enlarge its capabilities, got off to an excellent start. In 1990 the degree course in International Agri-Business was launched; it incorporates a sandwich period as well as compulsory tuition in foreign languages.

In 1987 when the academic structural changes took place there was success in establishing another degree course. Discussions were opened up with Reading and Bath Universities. Those with Reading about a degree course in agriculture were abortive. Agreement could be reached about the syllabus, the title of the course and the entry requirements but not about the financial arrangements. This was not surprising remembering that agreement over the Land Management Degree had proved difficult in this respect.

Much better progress was made with Bath University on establishing a course in Crop Technology and Resource Management, a subject in which there was evidence of a growing demand. The aim was to provide a practically oriented course of high technical standard which would integrate science, economic and management studies with agricultural and horticultural practice. For this purpose a sandwich course was necessary. What was agreed was a three-year full-time or four-year sandwich honours degree course taught jointly by the College and the University of Bath with a tropical study option. It was intended to appeal particularly to future managers of crop production enterprises in any part of the world, agricultural or horticultural. Most of the teaching was to be done at the College with some laboratory work at the University. This development was to enhance the syllabuses at the College by offering education on specialized subjects at a high level to meet the increasingly complex requirements for crop production management anywhere in the world.

★

The lifting of the academic standards at the College to university teaching levels, a long process in itself, demanded a greater engagement on research, particularly applied research, in addition to that of the Cotswold Cereal Centre, which was by now earning a national reputation. An evident field of work in which such research might prove fruitful and for which there was a growing need was that of the rural economy, to which greater attention was being paid because of the increasing demands being placed on rural resources by the expanding and diversifying urban population. For some time the Estate Management Department (by 1987 it had become the School of Land Economy and Land Management) had carried out minor consultancy work for, among others, the Countryside Commission. This experience encouraged the School to think that further research work could be obtained and carried out. It would be a source of income, it would enrich the teaching resources of the College and above all it would demonstrate to the public, to potential students and to the cooperating universities that such research would be a contributory factor in improving the educational standards. It would take the College back to the early days of pioneering research work on which it was founded.

The Centre for Rural Studies was started in 1987 just after the setting up of the new structure of 'Schools'. The initiative for the creation of such a centre originated with a Governor, R.B. Sayce, who, with the Dean of Land Economy and Land Mangement, had persuaded the Board of the necessity for the College to engage in rural research. There was little or no such coordinated research being carried on at the time and with a growing emphasis on the wider aspects of the countryside, especially in relation to agriculture and the farmer's role in the care and conservation of our rural heritage, it was appropriate that it should have focussed on the college. Dr D.M. Winter was appointed as Director, a man with known experience in his field of rural research. He had a degree in Rural Environment Studies from Wye College and ten years' experience in research at the Open University and the Universities of Bath and Exeter. He had done research into social and economic change in agriculture, agricultural policy and nature conservation policy. Dr Charles Watkins was appointed as the first Research Fellow. He had studied at London, Nottingham and Exeter Universities and had had experience with the Nature Conservancy Council. The funding of the Centre was based on the aim of being self supporting within three years. It helped that the two persons appointed were able to bring some research contracts with them. The official 'launch' of the Centre took place in September 1988; an address of welcome was given by Sir Derek Barber, Chairman of the Country-side Commission and an old student and holder of the College's Bledisloe Medal. With fresh contracts arriving, the Centre made a useful start; in the event it achieved its targets much earlier than the three years envisaged and became self-supporting.

★

The College corporate structure as a Limited Liability Company had been created in 1908 when the motive had been to obtain financial support from the government which was by then giving such support to the agricultural institutes in course of formation. This support had not been immediately forthcoming (the first annual financial contribution made by the government was not until 1922 and then only for five years) but the College had retained its structure as a private institution based on limited liability. In 1984 the Governors felt that change should be contemplated as there was an alternative form which might prove advantageous, that of a Trust. Put to the College solicitors their advice was that they could see no significant advantage in changing. However, the opportunity was taken to produce a new Memorandum and Articles of Association in order to control the purchase of shares and to re-define the structure of the Governing Body. The new Articles that were adopted allowed for the purchase of shares from disinterested shareholders; there would be no Hereditary Governor after Earl Bathurst, the current Hereditary Governor, had retired. This was to be, in line with other Ordinary Governors, at the age of seventy-two. It would mark the end, formally, of the long direct association of the College with the Bathurst family. Representative Governors were to be appointed for a period of three years and were not to be more than sixty-five years of age on appointment and would retire at the age of sixty-eight. The Chairman of the Governors would retire from the position at the age of seventy but could remain a Governor; the advisory offices of President, Vice-President and Principal Emeritus were included in the Articles and past Chairmen would be eligible for appointment as Vice-Presidents. These new Articles were adopted by the shareholders at an Extraordinary General Meeting on 14 December 1984. The changes brought the College more into line with current practice and were to ensure a greater turnover of Governors and thus bring fresh minds into the government of the College.

★

Although the College had, throughout its life, with minor exceptions, not received any government grants other than some assistance for capital works, it had been the practice for students to receive individual grants for their education. This started with the grants given to ex-servicemen who attended the College after the end of the Second World War. Thereafter students applied to their local authorities for annual grants for attendance at the College. This was not always necessarily straightforward. Such grants were discretionary and some local authorities were apt to refuse to award grants to otherwise eligible students on grounds which betrayed either ignorance of College teaching or, not to put too fine a point on it, political motivation. Examples were of those authorities who refused because they insisted that the student could go to the County Agricultural College or Farm Institute, overlooking the fact that such a student might be one accepted for the Rural Estate Management Diploma course, which subjects were not taught at the local institute. Some refusals could only be attributed to prejudice against a College reputed to be right wing in its outlook. The Principal and the Bursar were sometimes able to remedy such cases but not often. They took the matter up with the Department of Education and Science with little success since that Department was loath to intervene in what they regarded as local affairs, nor was it prepared to declare any of the courses as subject to mandatory grants.

When the new degree course in Rural Land Management was commenced the same difficulties were experienced. Reading University took the view that this was wrong and that the courses should attract a mandatory award because it was a university degree though the teaching was done at the College. There was a dilemma. If such mandatory awards were approved the maximum grant that the student could receive would be £530 (the rate in 1987), the parent would have to find the rest; discretionary grants awarded to students on other College courses could cover full tuition fees.

Following a visit by the local MP the Rt. Hon. Nicholas Ridley, a submission was made to the Secretary of State for Education and Science, but the response was not encouraging. It seemed that the Government would be introducing legislation to implement funding for universities, polytechnics and colleges but no thought had been given to the role of independent higher education. Here was another illustration, similar to many throughout the history of the College, of the difficulties faced by an independent college having to compete against government-sponsored institutions. Hughes and Bailey continued to press for support, seeking this from the Ministry of Agriculture and employing specialist advisers.

It was not until 1988 that any success in this matter was achieved. By then there had been a fresh submission on the advice of Mr Ridley and an informal visit by a Mr Peter Brown, one of HM Inspectors. The degree course in Rural Land Management was designated for receipt of mandatory awards; this had the effect of automatically allowing students to be eligible for consideration for maintenance

College life in 199

grants. Three more courses were later accepted: the degree courses in Crop Technology and Resource Management, in Agriculture and Land Management and in International Agri-Business.

But this created a discrepancy between the maximum mandatory award of £607 and the fees actually payable by the students, discretionary grants having been withdrawn from the newly mandated courses! It also had the effect that some counties took their marker from the mandatory maximum award level for students attending courses leading to the same professional qualifications. It seems that the Principal and Bursar had achieved one step forward and two backwards in spite of their long, drawn-out and time-consuming efforts.

This set-back caused the Bursar to examine the possibility of a loan scheme underwritten by the College; this would need a contingency reserve of £73,000. It would be a most unsatisfactory outcome to the efforts of the Principal and Bursar to overcome the illogicality of the grant system. Perhaps this had penetrated the inner recesses of the Department for it was subsequently announced that the grant for tuition fees would rise in 1990/1 from £607 to £1,600 and that in the later years this would go up to a maximum of £2,400 for engineering and science courses.

The College had obtained assurances that the new rates would apply; this was given in a letter from the Department of Education and Science. But the Department said that it was not being interpreted correctly. It was only after an interview that Hughes, Bailey, the Chairman and Vice-Chairman had had with the Rt. Hon. John MacGregor, the Secretary of State, that the interpretation by the College was acknowledged as correct! But this meant that, while the College would receive the higher rates for that year, thereafter the old rate of £607 would apply. This episode confirmed that students attending the College, an independent body, continued at a financial disadvantage to those at at institutions where the new higher rates were applied.

So the efforts were not rewarded, and it is illustrative again of the fact that, throughout the history of the College, its relationships with the government of the day were such that it had to fight its corner to receive any financial assistance at all let alone equality of treatment, since what was granted did not match the level given to others and was inconsistent between students – a penalty for resolute independence.

★

Hughes's management of the College farms was to continue the long-established principle that students benefitted most if they studied successful commercial farming. Therefore, while he was careful in spending money, he only conducted experiments and demonstrations where they did not intefere with farming profitably. When he became Vice-Principal John Wilkinson took over but he, unfortunately, had to give up for health reasons and tragically died shortly afterwards. He is to be remembered as a born communicator and a sensitive perfectionist.

Michael Limb was appointed Farms Director, a post he has occupied to the present day. Under his direction new buildings were erected at Eysey Manor Farm and a new sheep shed at Fosse Hill Farm. The College farms, like many other commercial farms, had successes and failures but always showed a profit to contribute to the income of the College. Limb took over following an excellent year under Wilkinson in 1978/9 when the profits very nearly reached six figures in total, or £200 a hectare. By 1980 he was reporting that the farms were commercially sound in spite of a current cost/price squeeze. The problem remained of the lack of flexibility in the choice of farming system especially on the heavier land at Eysey which precluded root crops and most vegetables as a practical proposition.

By April 1982 the farms had come through some difficult times, not only because of adverse weather conditions (mainly heavy rains in spring) but also against higher fixed costs, yet Limb was still able to report profitability at the same levels as in 1979/80. 'Our results this year typify the built-in economic balance of a mixed farming system but the inexorable rise in fixed costs is putting greater pressure on net farm income as product prices plateau and drop. Cash flow is reasonable because we are not big spenders but our role as a College Farm dictates a degree of diversity.' But by 1982/3 he had already increased profits by 30 per cent!

Even better results were to come: in 1984/5 the College farms' profitability increased slightly whilst the national results were down by 45 per cent. As the Principal said at the time, 'We always seem to buck the trend!'

In 1987 a unique opportunity was presented to the College to engage in 'organic' farming. This would not be to 'buck the trend' but possibly to go with it. Mr John Oldacre approached the College with an offer to share farm a holding which he had just purchased. The farm, Harnhill Manor Farm, was of 620 acres situated about three miles south-east of Cirencester, lying on the edge of the Cotswold limestone where it joined the alluvial soils of the Upper Thames Valley. Mr Oldacre had purchased the farm from Mr Robert Henly, who had for many years encouraged farm classes to study his methods of farming complementary with ecology and conservation. Agreement was quickly reached with Mr Oldacre on the basis that the owner would provide the land and the fixed equipment, including a grain drier and storage system and the College was to supply all machinery and labour costs. The variable costs of production were to be split between the parties on an agreed formula and the agreement offered opportunities for the terms to be renegotiated.

This excellent opportunity for the College to engage in a contemporary type of farming arrangement gave several advantages:
1. An increase in the size of the cereal enterprise based at Coates Manor, which could be managed with one set of farm equipment.
2. The ability to increase the size of the sheep flock without the need to increase winter accommodation.

3. An opportunity to engage in 'organic' farming by moving directly into such a system with 120 acres of land already available, having been converted to organic husbandry by Robert Henly's son-in-law, David Ursell, between 1984 and 1987.

4. Active involvement in share farming. Mr Oldacre joined the Farms Board of the College and, through the Oldacre Foundation, funded a three-year study on improving organic cereal husbandry on Harnhill Manor Farm.

5. The farm was one of a chain of 'Link' farms set up under the auspices of the Countryside Commission and the local Farming and Wildlife Group in Gloucestershire.

By 1988 Limb was reporting for the farming year 1987 a very satisfactory set of net farm income figures. The Cricklade and Coates farms contributed some £90,000 towards the income of the College. By 1989/90 the profit margins were lower but still a cause for satisfaction, for Harnhill Manor Farm had had to be incorporated on the new and different basis and experience gained in farming the 120 acres on the organic method. The total farmland of the College now stood at 1,800 acres, a far cry from the original forty acres to which it had been reduced in the previous century.

From the time when Boutflour took over and established the dairy herds at the Steadings and Fosse Hill under a regime of modern cow management, the College farms can show continuous success in producing a significant contribution to the general income of the College. In all the vicissitudes of financial crises that the College has undergone the one consistent factor has been the performance of the College farms. This must reflect great credit on the Farm Directors since Russell and has been a continuing demonstration to successions of students of how to engage in high-performance, high-income farming.

★

Towards the end of the period of Hughes's tenure as Principal there were two retirements of members of the senior academic staff who had devoted the greater part of their careers to serving the College. These were D.M. Barling and J.A.R. Lockhart, both teaching on the agricultural side. Dai Barling (for as such he was known to generations of students) had been Head of the Department of Agricultural Science since 1950. Jim Lockhart had been Director of Studies and Head of the Agricultural Department for most of his thirty-eight years at the College.

Lockhart had been recruited by Boutflour in June 1948 and had started as a lecturer in September of that year. His period at the College covered the changes in farming from the horse to the computer and he was, with A.J. Wiseman, a successful author of the standard textbook on crop husbandry which, in its various editions, served successive generations of students from 1966 onwards. Together with Frank Oldfield, he started the Cirencester Agricultural Discussion Society, an independent forum for thinking farmers which has continued at the

College since 1961. He was keenly interested in the Agricultural Education Association, being President in 1982/3. With Barling and Hughes, Lockhart was one of the remaining links with the Boutflour era. These two senior members of the academic staff may be ranked with the Kinches and Blundells of the former years, devoted to their work for the College and of inestimable value to the many students who passed through their hands.

Dai Barling had also been a Boutflour appointment in 1946. He was a lecturer in Agricultural Science for only a short time because when Dr George Redington, the then head of the Department, died suddenly, Boutflour promoted this young man in his place. It was an inspired move and Barling never looked back nor was he to be enticed away by the many opportunities that came his way. His reputation was founded on two solid bases: he was an articulate and enthusiastic lecturer and a recognized and leading researcher. His early work on grassland was surpassed by his field research into crop production. He had a facility to transfer science and research knowledge into a form appreciated and understood by the farmer. He was, with Lockhart, crucially responsible for the setting up and success of the Cotswold Cereal Centre. He walked with ease in the footsteps of the great College researchers of the past. He was succeeded as Head of the Agricultural Science Department by the College's able entomologist, W. Heath-erington, who, sadly, died in 1991 and who had been a most thorough overseer of the College library over the years on the academic staff.

Another loss to the College towards the end of the 1980s was caused by the death of Geoffrey Cragghill who had been a member of the Senior Common Room from 1956 to 1988. He lectured in animal production and his knowledge was based on sound practical experience. He had many other interests from which the College benefited. He did much to consolidate and improve the College Beagles and was Master of the Dummer Beagles for over a quarter of a century.

★

A significant retirement in 1989 was that of Frank Parker, the very conscientious Secretary to all Principals from Boutflour to Hughes. He was also Secretary to the Board of Governors. He was deservedly awarded an honorary MRAC, as was John Stevens, the long-serving and very able laboratory steward in the Agricultural Science Department. Frank Parker's association with the College was part of a longer link, for his father-in-law was Percy Haynes, the College caretaker from 1922, the one whom Boutflour had met when he returned to the College after the military had left it in 1945.

★

The College now possessed a flourishing Students' Union and an active Old Students' Association – the RAC Association. Students' facilities had been improved – the opening of a bar and games room in the old lecture theatre next to the tithe barn was an indicator of modern times and an acknowledgement of the maturity of those now attending the College. No longer did students have to rush down to town for a quick pint at lunchtime! Through the Students' Board suggestions were put forward for increased sports facilities, including further tennis courts, training facilities and an all-weather floodlit playing area. By 1987 the new pitch was completed at a cost of £16,000 on a site between the Tetbury road and the Rugby pitches, and opened by W.J. Clarke, the Chairman of the Students' Board.

In earlier days the Students' Union Club had been very much dominated by academic management; during the latter part of the previous century and up to 1932 the Chairman had always been a senior member of staff. Boutflour had changed this and given more autonomy to the students to manage their own social and sports affairs within the overall authority of the Principal. This had gradually increased over the years of Garner and successive Principals. In 1988 a further step forward was taken in response to a feeling by the Union that the status of their Management Committee should be upgraded and that their meetings should be held without senior members of staff being present. Up to that time some of the senior members had been active in supervising activities and in taking an active part in them. The support to the Beagles Hunt given by Geoffrey Cragghill was an example. The constitution and rules of the Union Club were amended to remove this attendance at the Club meetings; although the Principal would retain a veto on any matter and accounting would be undertaken by the College. This certainly gave the Union Club a greater freedom of action and enabled it to run a very diverse set of sporting and social activities among which two of the annual highlights are the May Ball and Rag Week.

The Rag Weeks, though maybe causing some trepidation among the citizens of Cirencester, usually proved their worth in benefiting charitable causes. In 1989 the Students' Union organized a very successful charity run from John O'Groats to Land's End (christened 'Le Jog'), in addition to the annual Rag Week. The total raised was £52,000: £14,000 from Rag Week and £38,000 from 'Le Jog'. This was distributed to the Cotswold Care Project (£15,000), the Meningitis Trust (£2,000), Riding for the Disabled (£2,000) and the Star Centre for the Disabled (£33,000). A room in the Cotswold Care Project, a hospice for the terminally ill, was dedicated 'The Geoffrey Cragghill Room donated by students of the Royal Agricultural College, 1989'. This reflected the respect in which he had been held. In Rag Week 1990 £17,000 was raised.

The success and popularity of these events are a manifestation of the exuberance and vitality of the typical agricultural student! As Jim Lockhart elaborated, 'Rag weeks and Club dinners have always been excuses for frivolity, e.g. a young Hereford bull in the Senior Common room; concrete block walls across corridors; monster footprints along streets and over houses in several local towns; tractors, cars and animals in unusual places. . . .' These high jinks also included a

Student activities in
1991

car, and, at another time, a cow, put on top of the tower, as well as the beating up of the College by student ex-service pilots in a Miles Magister in 1946!

The Royal Agricultural College Association, formed in 1946, but with antecedents going back to the Dinner Clubs of the nineteenth century, has maintained touch with former students of the College, encouraged by its first President, Lord Bledisloe. The reunion arranged every year in January has now become a major event in the agricultural calendar, with invitations to speak being accepted by leading agricultural and political figures. The highlight of these conferences has been the Bledisloe Memorial Lecture. Speakers since 1965 have been:

1965   C.A.C. de Boinville, Chairman of British Oil and Cake Mills
1969   D.G. Pearce, Chairman of the Farm Management Association
1970   Oscar Colburn, farmer and landowner
1971   A.T. Mitchell, Barclays Bank
1972   G.H.B. Cattell, Director-General of the National Farmers' Union
1975   Sir Nigel Strutt
1978   Dr Keith Dexter, Director-General of the Agricultural Development and Advisory Service
1979   Lord Winstanley, Chairman of the Countryside Commission
1980   The Rt. Hon. Peter Walker, Minister of Agriculture, Fisheries and Food
1981   Richard Butler, President of the National Farmers' Union
1982   Lord Middleton, President of the Country Landowners' Association
1983   His Grace the Duke of Westminster
1984   Robin Leigh-Pemberton, Governor of the Bank of England
1985   Sir Henry (later Lord) Plumb, Member of the European Parliament
1986   The Rt. Hon. Enoch Powell, MP
1987   The Rt. Hon. David Owen, MP
1988   Walter Goldsmith, Chairman of 'Food from Britain'
1989   The Rt. Hon. Nicholas Ridley, MP, Secretary of State for the Environment
1990   Sir Michael Franklin, Permanent Secretary, the Ministry of Agriculture, Fisheries and Food.

The Association provided a pavilion at the Royal Show, Stoneleigh, and in 1980 this was in need of renovation. The Governors agreed to share the cost of £4,000 with the Association. This was eventually taken over in 1987 and remains the responsibility of the College.

★

Even though, while Garner, Dickson and Jones were Principals, the lecture accommodation had been increased to accept the greater intake of students, by 1987 the space was limited and so an extension to the lecture block was carried out. By putting a pitched roof over the whole building two new lecture rooms each holding forty students, two demonstration rooms (Forestry and Building) and nine fresh offices were created on the first floor. On the second floor four new lecture rooms and two computer rooms were made available. The cost was £930,000 and the new areas were ready for occupation by October 1987. It was officially opened in 1988 by the Rt. Hon. John MacGregor, MP, Minister of Agriculture, Fisheries and Food who named it 'The Frank Garner Lecture Block'.

In this same year, 1987, the old library over the dining hall was renovated and converted into a conference room. It was named 'The Kenneth Russell Room' and opened in March 1987 by the widow of the late Vice-Principal and Farms Director.

★

In 1989, John Wibberley left his post as Head of the Agriculture Department to pursue overseas mission work and his own communications business, but he retained a visiting fellowship at the College. Dr John Alliston was appointed Dean of the School of Agriculture. He was previously Farms Director at the Animal and Grassland Research Institute, Hurley, Berkshire, but had before that been a lecturer at the College.

The years 1988 and 1989 saw another facet of the College's expansion and an acknowledgement of its international role. In the summer of 1988 the Director of Studies, Dr Paul Davies was able to accept an invitation to participate in an International Congress of Plant Pathology in Japan and to carry out an initial study of the Institutes of Agriculture in Malaysia. It was funded by the British Council, the Department of Agriculture in Malaysia, the Royal Society and the College.

The new contact with Malaysia was by good fortune. When an International Symposium, organized by the Royal Agricultural Society of England, was held at the College in 1987, Hughes asked a visitor strolling in the grounds if he needed any help. He turned out to be the Minister of Agriculture for Malaysia! This contact was assiduously followed by Davies.

During Davies's visit, arrangements were made with the University of Malaysia for some College students on the degree course in Crop Technology and Resource Management to gain experience and training in tropical agriculture at the University. He also visited China as part of that tour. The outcome was that in 1989 a follow-up visit completed the study and future cooperation with the College was agreed. The scheme drawn up between the British Council and the Government of Malaysia funded a scheme of cooperation for four years from January 1989. It mainly consisted of courses of study for Principals and staff of the Institutes of Agriculture in Malaysia with the objectives of managing their farms profitably, developing their curricula and achieving greater self-sufficiency. College staff were to visit Malaysia to give training in advisory work. This initiative resulted in a good working relationship with the British Council and an invitation to participate in a project in Turkey.

★

In the summer of 1989 the College was honoured by a visit from the President, His Royal Highness, the Prince of Wales. The Prince spoke to members of the domestic staff, visited students at work in the laboratories, drawing offices and lecture rooms, and attended a seminar at which the Vice-Principal, Young and the Farms Director, Limb, gave papers on Land Management Research and Organic Farming. This had followed a visit, by invitation, to Highgrove, the home of the Prince, by Hughes and Winter (Director of the Centre for Rural Studies).

Coincident with the launching of the School of Business, the Governors were studying a five-year development plan, necessitated by the seemingly never-ending

Prince Charles in one of the laboratories during his visit in 1989

demand for more residential accommodation for students. Rooms were needed for first-year students and for mature students. The 1988/9 session had started with 688 students and the prospect was that by the next session the number would be over 700. In fact there were 723 registered in the following year.

The long-term aim was for 140/150 extra rooms; the immediate objective being a design of forty-eight study bedrooms. In addition there would have to be a separate block of tutorial rooms for the School of Business. The site chosen for this new development was near to the Westwood Car Park, between it and Bledisloe Court. This involved the purchase of a parcel of land from the Bathurst estate. The whole project was estimated to cost between £10 – £12 million, of which £5 million would be spent on the School of Business.

This money had to be raised. The College, wisely in view of previous experiences, decided to engage professional advisers, fund-raising consultants Messrs Redmond Mullen. Their report made three basic recommendations:
1. To write a prospectus.
2. To establish a campaign office in the College, including the appointment of a Development Director, with a small supporting staff.
3. To appoint a fund-raising committee to give a lead; the committee to be limited to six people, each of whom would be a substantial donor in his own right either personally or through his company, and who would have a special interest in the idea of a new Business School at the College.

A development office was set up in the College, with a Development Director and assistant, their task being to raise the funds for the residential accommodation, £5–£7 million. In addition a Fund Raising Committee would be responsible for raising the £5 million required for the School of Business. At a luncheon on 21 November 1989 to launch the School of Business, to which some two hundred leading industrialists, academics and government officials were invited, the principal speaker was Sir Michael Caine, Chairman of Booker, PLC, supported by Mr Henry Lambert (Agricultural Mortgage Corporation), Mr Paul Ingram (Barclays Bank) and Mr George Gray (Rural Develpment Commission). With the publication of a prospectus for the School of Business the fund-raising campaign was started. Mr Tony Clegg, a strong supporter of the College and in sympathy with its aspirations, accepted the role of Chairman of that Committee. The membership was left to his discretion. Stuart H. Crocker was appointed Development Director, with an assistant and clerical support.

Work on the new residential block of forty-eight study bedrooms was not delayed and started in 1990 with a target date for completion of September 1991, five acres having been purchased from the Bathurst estate.

★

The developments during Hughes's period of office in acquiring degree courses, opened up the possibility of self-validation. This needed examination in the light of the College's constitution. In 1989, following the verbal assurance of the Clerk to the Privy Council that the College's Royal Charter still existed, he undertook to assist the College to operate within the framework of the original Chartered Body so that degree-awarding and validation status might be given under the new legislation. It was, however, pointed out that the provisions of the original Charter and its statutes would not be acceptable to the Privy Council for a body which was offering its own degree. This made it necessary to have a new document prepared for presentation to the Privy Council, together with a Supplemental Charter and modern statutes. The Bursar was authorized to engage a professional firm to proceed with the documentation after consultation with the College solicitors and the Department of Education and Science. The hope was that the draft to be prepared would take into account the usual university structures but would be streamlined to eliminate much of the administrative burden and delay that they introduced.

A draft Charter with statutes was prepared, approved by the Governors, and sent to the Department of Education and Science for their approval after full inspection of the College by HM Inspectors, and forwarding to the Privy Council. The Department, however, was carrying out a review of degree-awarding status of institutions with the Council for National Academic Awards, the result of which was not expected until 1991, and in consequence it was unwilling to consider the College on a 'one-off' basis. The College responded by pointing out that it should not be considered a part of the review with the Council for National Academic Awards. By 1991 the matter had still not been resolved and the College awaits its third Supplementary Charter.

★

By the spring of 1991 a successor to Hughes had to be found, for his retirement would fall due in the autumn of 1990. In July 1990 the post was advertised and on receipt of applications an Appointments Board was formed comprising C.H. Coad, Chairman of the Board of Governors, and members Barrett, Juckes, Law, Keene and Pearce. They short-listed fourteen from a field of fifty-five and invited six to visit them at the College.

The post was offered to and accepted by Professor Arthur S. Jones, B.Sc., (Dunhelm), Ph.D. (Aberdeen), C.Biol., F.I.Biol., FBIM, FRSA, who was at the time Professor of Agriculture at the University of Aberdeen and Principal of the North of Scotland Agricultural College.

★

Hughes had been at the College for thirty-four years, a very long period, not necessarily the longest of anyone who had served on the staff but certainly unique in the posts he had occupied. Arriving in 1950 as a new lecturer, after four years he was away for six years as Vice-Principal at Brooksby Hall, Leicestershire, then returned to be Farms Director for eighteen years (including two years at the end of this period as Vice-Principal). He was then Principal for twelve years. As has been mentioned, his promotion to Principal was by no means a cut and dried affair. The Governors, not unnaturally, had always hankered after another Boutflour whenever they had been faced with the problem of finding a Principal, remembering his scarcely believable success in uplifting the College to a pre-eminent place in agricultural education. There was no doubt that although Hughes was a known quality in his management of the College farms and his lecturing, he was in some need to prove himself as a Principal.

We can now look back on his performance, of which the peak must be the acquisition of three degree courses for the College. That and the reorganization of the academic structure with the introduction of the School of Business and the Centre for Rural Studies will endure as the benchmarks of his time at the College. These achievements may mask what he did as Farms Director: the improvement in the quality of the dairy herd; the success of fat lamb production when others were leaving the enterprise; moving the dairy to Coates Manor Farm; the first recorded three-ton-per-acre barley crop in the area; the acquisition of the tenancy of Eysey Manor Farm. The later oversight of the Harnhill farming agreement and the fostering of the Cotswold Cereal Centre are not to be forgotten. He established the Advanced Farm Management Diploma and started a separate Management Department which turned into the School of Business.

He had seen the admission of women students, provision of more residential accommodation and better lecturing and office facilities for the increased numbers in College, as well as a larger staff, both academic and administrative, to manage than any previous Principal. His relations with staff and students were based on approachability and availability – he had it in common with Boutflour that he was always 'Vic' to the students rather than 'The Principal' and that he saw that they could never be evaluated by their academic achievements alone. He must have learnt from Boutflour to assess the future potential of the whole person before him. His contributions to agricultural education were deservedly recognized by the award of CBE in the Queen's Birthday Honours in 1989.

It is possible that a more definite assessment of the period that Hughes was Principal and of the part he played will be made in later years and set in the context of the 150 years that the College will have been in existence by 1995; perhaps it is too close to events to make that assessment now. But the prima-facie evidence is of a period of quite substantial and critical progress sufficient to raise the academic standards to a level from which the College may aspire to being a degree-validating institution and thus directly comparable with the best in the land in agricultural education. Furthermore, this improvement, of itself, has a momentum which will remove from the College any vestiges of the reputation it did acquire from its early days for the teaching of select numbers not too serious about the need for hard work. Garner started to correct that; under Hughes the acceptance of sterner criteria and a wider context with the extension of teaching into the whole range of rural matters and the realization of the fundamental necessity for business training, will change the philosophy of the teaching at the Royal Agricultural College in the future.

Chapter Fourteen

ENVOI

Felix qui potuit cognoscere causas.

Virgil

History continues; the recording has to stop at a suitable point in time. The point chosen, with the appointment in 1990 of a new Principal, is a watershed in fortunes of the Royal Agricultural College. Over the past three decades the number of students has more than doubled, the facilities for lecturing, for accommodation, and for research and study have been improved and extended to meet the expansion.

The College's academic structure has been modernized with the three Schools of Agriculture, Business, and Rural Economy and Land Management. There should be no further need for any more changes: the structure should be able to provide the operational needs in whatever direction the education policy of the College may take within its aims and objectives. Such policies will be determined by external forces impinging on agricultural education, or, in a wider context, upon the whole of the rural resource.

The first of these is demographic trends. The Principal, Professor Arthur Jones, pointed this out in his first article in the *College Journal* (1989/90, Vol. LXXVIII):

The change in demographic trends is the most dramatic for many decades. By the mid 1990's the number of 18 year olds will have dropped by 30% compared with 1987. Most Universities and Polytechnics have been able to counter the fall in the number of students by concentrating on those subjects which have a high student demand, by allowing greater access to students with unconventional qualifications and by developing courses for mature students.

The Royal Agricultural College does not have the same ability to concentrate on areas of high demand. . . . There are special problems relating to agriculture and the number of agricultural students applying for further education has dropped by half over the last five years.

Thus any policy for the College is going to be dominated by these inexorable facts.

The other external factor of major consequence is the sea-change in the public perception of agriculture in a period, which has now lasted for a significant time, of over production of food – at least in the European Community, though not in the Third World. This changed perception takes note of the relationship between food and health (consumer habits are changing through concern over food quality and the incidence of heart disease, for example). The publicity of the problems associated with farm livestock processes such as salmonellosis, listeriosis and BSE (Bovine Spongiform Encephalopathy), together with the concern about the use of chemicals and artificial fertilizers and their effect on water supplies, have all led to greater public awareness and often to misconceptions. The more extensive knowledge that the community is gaining about the conservation of wildlife and the rural countryside has altered attitudes toward farmers, farming and food production. It is this that has caused legislation to be enacted which has restricted agriculture's freedom of action and has necessitated different management methods.

All these compound the difficulties that the agricultural industry is facing and will continue to face with the changes in the Common Agricultural Policy: the removal of land from food production with 'set-aside' schemes and encouragement for diversification of activities on the farm to non-agricultural enterprises as well as for conservation of precious nature sites and landscapes.

Jones continued, 'All these changes in how the public perceive agriculture actually create new demands and new opportunities for training and education in agriculture. More specialism will be required to meet the demands of high technology in the home-based industry. More training will be required as margins fall and farmers are required to become much more financial managers as managers of land.' This last point is of great importance. It means that those with responsibilities in rural areas, landowners, public and private, tenants and owner-occupiers, become, each in their own way, managers of the whole resource, and training in farming alone will not suffice. That is not all: there is an emphasis today, in all industries, on vocational education and training in specialisms, to the extent that it is encouraged by government who see Britain lagging behind by comparison with her competitors.

With this as background, the College management has set about defining the aims and objectives for the coming years. As would be expected the primary aim is to provide vocational education and training in land-based studies, and, reflecting on its history throughout the changing periods in which it has striven to provide an agricultural education, the College has hardly changed these objectives. Robert Jeffreys Brown had intended a College for vocational training in agriculture by the applicaton of scientific method. It was to be for the coming generation of farmers. The only change today from this original concept is the widening of its scope to include any who participate in the management of rural areas and of the food and agricultural industries, not just of farms.

Plans for the future envisage an increase in courses leading to a degree, with the retention of shorter courses of one or two years which will give access or act as a stepping stone to the higher courses. To be included are post-doctoral, master and postgraduate courses. Such a policy is intended to meet the new requirements for vocational education as well as those specialized demands for management of specific sectors of the food and agricultural industries.

In order to adjust to the demographic trend which will result in the reduction of the number of school leavers and potential students, the aim is to expand by attracting more students from lower-income families: it is felt that this would enhance the internal environment of the College and ensure that students are trained not only for the professions but also for management; that it would give additional scholarly talent and thus ensure the elevation of academic standards; and that it would enable the College to compete with other colleges engaged in recruiting from the same diminishing pool of potential students. While the first two reasons may be intellectually and philosophically sound the last is the more pragmatic. It is ironic that if this policy succeeds then the College will be making a return to the very first policy of the founders, in a way, for they sought to take the sons of tenant farmers, the lower-income groups in agriculture, and even some sons of farm workers.

★

The adoption of such policies by the College can only be contemplated if there is commensurate progress in: establishing degree courses of a specialist nature; widening the catchment area through international connections; improving and extending physical facilities and amenities; and in forging a closer relationship between the College and the industries it serves. As to the first of these desirable objectives, in addition to the existing degree courses, there is an intention to move into the following areas of study: Business Systems and Management Communications, Marketing, International Business Management, Rural Resource Management and international degrees in cooperation with centres of education in other countries.

The College has set up a development office; under its Director it is concentrating on certain of these aspects, namely: an extension of the School of Business; a computer laboratory; an extension of the library; and accommodation for more students to take the number from 800 to 1,000 by providing an additional 154 rooms. An international office has been formed to increase contacts.

To unlock these ambitious programmes of education there is one essential key: the self-validation of degrees. For this privilege the College will need another Supplementary Charter. It is very necessary that this be obtained in the near future. Then the College will not only have confirmed its ability to teach to the level of those degrees awarded by other cooperating establishments, but will have the authority to award its own. The College will then have arrrived at the same level as some of its sister institutions founded on the same principles as those of the first College in the English-speaking world and in some cases started by students or professors from the College. In effect the College would become the equivalent of a university college. Travelling down this road, with an emphasis on teaching vocational management skills for the whole of the rural resource and providing the food and agricultural industries with their highly trained and expert specialists, would lead to a College different in concept from the original foundation. Indeed, it may be that the concentration on business would, if successful, take the College to a point where the three present schools of Agriculture, Business, and Rural Economy and Land Management, would be of approximately equal size and influence. This would certainly create a College whose *raison d'être* is no longer the teaching of general agricultural subjects but one which teaches as well the subjects which increasingly influence farming towards the end of this century: environment, marketing, pollution and the wider European aspects. This might be a future which some supporters of the College would not view with equanimity but possibly with horror. The School of Agriculture may become very specialized in its curricula.

A College which has in its history faced up to crises of finance, of forced closures, of frequent changes in government policies on agricultural education, especially in the financial support to be given, and of some lack of impartiality from time to time in the attitude adopted by government, ought to be able to weather whatever variables may occur in the future, especially if it retains flexibility to change. This can only be done through resolute independence. It has done so before; it will do so again.

★

FLOREAT COLLEGIUM CORINIENSE

Hail, worthy College, hark to me!
Through livelong years may you be free
To shake off dull bureaucracy
And keep your own identity.
In British Isles and oversea,
O'er every clime, there may you be,
To keep alive with dignity
The spirit of the R.A.C.,
In hundreds (let them nameless be),
Uniting in one entity
In faithful pride and loyalty.
So, through the coming century
May you, most honoured R.A.C.
Add laurels to your history.

Arthur Noble

ROYAL AGRICULTURAL COLLEGE 1845 to 1990

PATRONS
HRH Prince Albert
HRH The Prince of Wales
HM Queen Victoria
HM Edward VII
HM King George V
HM King Edward VIII
HM King George VI
HM Queen Elizabeth II

PRESIDENTS
The Rt. Hon. Earl Bathurst
His Grace the Duke of Marlborough
His Grace the Duke of Richmond & Gordon
The Rt. Hon. Earl Spencer
His Grace the Duke of Beaufort
HRH The Prince of Wales

CHAIRMEN OF GOVERNORS
Sir Thomas Tancred
Edward Holland, Esq.
His Grace the Duke of Marlborough
The Rt. Hon. Earl of Ducie
The Rt. Hon. Lord Moreton
The Rt. Hon. Lord Bledisloe
The Rt. Hon. Earl Bathurst
Major Sir Frederick Cripps
The Rt. Hon. Earl St Aldwyn
Col. W.A. Chester Master
Major P.D. Birchall
Major G.B. Heywood
Charles Coad, Esq.

APPENDIX I

PRINCIPALS

Mr W.J. Scales
The Revd G.C. Hodgkinson
Professor J. Wilson
The Revd J.S. Haygarth
The Revd J. Constable
The Revd J.B. McClellan
Professor J.R. Ainsworth-Davis
Professor M.J.R. Dunstan
Dr J.A. Hanley
Professor R. Boutflour
Mr Frank H. Garner
Dr Gordon R. Dickson
Sir Emrys Jones
Mr H.V. Hughes
Professor Arthur S. Jones

Appendix II

THE FIRST STUDENTS

The names of the first twenty-five students enrolled in the College, when it opened in 1845, in the two houses in Thomas Street, Cirencester, under the tutelage of John Scales, with their geographical origins, were given in the minutes of the Council:

6 August 1845

1. John Coleman – Wandsworth
2. John George Stubbs – Cannock, nr. Stafford
3. Anthony Bliss Kittermaster – Meriden, War.
4. John George Rodney Ward – Over Stowy, Somerset
5. Henry Tanner – location not given
6. Edward Marston – Monk Hopton, Salop
7. Richard Carpenter – Wotton Underidge
8. Josiah Hanks – Harnhill
9. John Coling – Stratford-on-Avon
10. Henry Emmett – Egglescliffe Grange Farm, York
11. Richard Ridley Lander – Shifnal

20 August 1845

12. James Lowe – Wolverley, nr. Kidderminster
13. William Thomas Saunders – Wolverley
14. George Pudsey Aston – Wolverhampton
15. Alfred Morton – Stafford

3 September 1845

16. Edward Bell Hamilton – Leasowes in Bridgnorth
17. Martin Fitzwilliam Malden – Worcester
18. Samuel Bickerton – Sandford Hall, nr. Oswestry
19. Henry Woodcock Needham – Syston, nr. Leicester

1 October 1845

20. John Smith Meakins – location not given

5 November 1845

21. Henry Smith – Ironbridge
22. Robert Bartholomew Shaw – Stourton

19 November 1845

23. William Scott – Beverley
24. Septimus Brigham – Beverley

3 December 1845

25. John Henry Whitton – Banbury

The enrolments that followed widened the area from which students were drawn; the counties noted were Norfolk, Bedfordshire, Lincolnshire, Oxfordshire, Suffolk, Sussex, Cumberland, Wiltshire, Essex, Northumberland, Denbigh, Lancashire, Dorset and Devon.

THE COLLEGE PROSPECTUS, 1847

In 1847 an eight-page prospectus was issued, including the title page, but not including an additional seven pages comprising a list of shareholders. Some relevant extracts of interest appear below:

Patron
His Royal Highness Prince Albert

President
The Right Honourable Earl Bathurst

Vice-President
The Right Honourable Earl of Ducie

Seventy-five Governors were named and the Council had thirteen members. The staff named were:

Principal
Revd G.C. Hodgkinson, MA

Vice-Principal
Mr J. Wilson

Professors
Agriculture – Mr J. Wilson
Chemistry – Mr J.T. Way
Geology, Natural History and Botany – Mr S.P. Woodward
Mathematics and Natural Philosophy – Revd G.C. Hodgkinson, MA
Surveying and Practical Engineering – Mr Bravender
The Veterinary Art – Mr Robinson
Farm Superintendent – Mr Thomas Arkell

OBJECTS

'The object of this Institution is to provide such a course of instruction as will be most useful to the practical farmer. The benefits to be derived by the agriculturalist from a judicious application of scientific information are becoming daily more and more extensively acknowledged; while the means of obtaining that information, if indeed it can be obtained at all without for the time sacrificing a due attention to the practical operations of husbandry, are so scattered and costly as to be within the reach of very few.'

APPENDIX III

FARM

'The Farm is held on lease from Earl Bathurst, for a term of 47 years, determinable, *at the option of the Council*, at certain periods and imposing no restriction as to the mode of cultivation. It is situated a mile from Cirencester, and contains 450 acres (420 of which are Arable) of a varied character and soil. The best established system of tillage will be adopted; and the breeding and feeding of stock will be combined with a dairy. Every description of trial and experiment will be made, in such a manner, however, as not to risk general results, it being the determination of the Council that the system pursued on the Farm shall be the one most profitable, and such as the pupils may adopt with confidence in their future occupations: still a portion of land will be set apart for experiments.'

COLLEGE

'The College, which adjoins the park and woods of Earl Bathurst, is situated on the farm, about a mile and a half from the town; the principal front, 190 feet long, has a south aspect, and commands an extensive view over North Wiltshire. The ground slopes in every direction, and a more healthy or beautiful site could hardly be pointed out. The buildings include a large Dining Hall, Library, Museum, and Laboratory, besides the offices and ranges of sleeping apartments on two floors.'

MANAGEMENT

'The management of the College is committed to the Principal, who is responsible to the Council for the general well-being of every department. He has all matters of discipline under his immediate control, and vigilantly superintends the industry, progress, and moral habits of each student, reports of which will be sent, at least half-yearly, to the parents or guardians.'

COURSE OF INSTRUCTION

'The College course extends over two years, commencing from Midsummer, and this is the shortest time in which any student can proceed to the final examination.

  The *theoretical* department comprises

 1. Oral instruction in practical agriculture.
 2. Elementary Geometry applied to surveying, levelling, cubage of solids, &c.
 3. Mechanics applied to agricultural implements, to the erection of sheds, and the construction of roofs, &c.
 4. Hydraulics applied to draining and irrigating.
 5. Designing and drawing of plans for implements and buildings.
 6. Chemistry and General Physics   )in their various
 7. Geology and Mineralogy   )important relations
 8. Botany, Vegetable Physiology, and Natural History   )to agriculture.
 9. Principles of the Veterinary Art.
10. Methods of Farm Accounts.

  Practical Instruction – The students spend the half of each day on the Farm, and take part in all the manual operations of husbandry.'

ADMISSION OF STUDENTS

'Students are admissible only upon the nomination of a Proprietor, or Donor of £30: they are not allowed to enter the College under the age of fourteen years, and must, at the least, be thoroughly versed in the routine of a good English Education.'

CHARGES

'The charge for pupils at the College is £50 per annum, to be paid by half-yearly instalments in advance, together with such charges as the Council may fix for the maintenance of the Library, Museum, and Laboratory.'

OUT-STUDENTS

'Non-resident Students of any age will be allowed, upon the recommendation of a Proprietor, to attend the Lectures and avail themselves of the practical instruction of the institution. The annual charge is £30 to be paid in advance for the year.'

The prospectus invited the reader to become a Proprietor or Donor by purchasing a share or making a donation at a cost of £30; this then gave the right to nominate a student.

Appendix IV

'FARM AND COLLEGE'
BY
CHARLES DICKENS

Reprinted from All the Year Round, *No. 4949, 10 October 1868, pp. 414–21.*

That part of the holding of a farmer or landowner which pays best for cultivation is the small estate within the ring fence of his skull. Let him begin with the right tillage of his brains, and it shall be well with his grains, roots, herbage and forage, sheep and cattle; they shall thrive and he shall thrive. 'Practice with science' is now the adopted motto of the Royal Agricultural Society. Amateur farming by men whose real business lies in other trades, and who, without any true scientific training, play with a few of the results of science, cannot pay and never ought to pay. The farmer's occupation is the oldest, the most necessary, and, when rightly pursued, one of the worthiest a man can follow. Of late years it has risen to the dignity of a liberal profession, and the young Englishman may go through part of his special training for it in a well appointed college.

This is the Royal Agricultural College at Cirencester. After fighting an uphill fight for twenty years, it stands now upon higher ground than any other institution of its kind. There is, indeed, no other of its kind in England; but of institutions for the practical and scientific training of the farmer out of England; among the agricultural academies in France, Germany, and elsewhere; not one, we believe, is at the same time satisfactory and self supporting. The Imperial Model Farm and School of Agriculture at Grignon, founded in 1826, and the chief of several established by Louis Philippe, receives subvention from the State, and the pupils upon its one thousand two hundred acres are under highly qualified teachers paid by the French Government. The German academies and experimental stations are also endowed by their governments. In Ireland, again, our own Government has founded agricultural schools. An unendowed agricultural school, founded in 1821 at Bannow, Wexford, only lived seven years. But since that time the Commissioners of National Education have made agricultural training schools part of their system. The chief of these training schools is at Glasnevin, where there are also thirty acres of botanic garden; and a year ago the Museum of Irish Industry was reconstructed and opened on a seven years' probation as a Government school of science with a department of agriculture. Our English college, founded six and twenty years since, not by Government, but by working farmers, when a fashion had come up for recognising the new need of scientific training to their business, has not received one farthing of public money. It had to find its own way in the world, and paid so heavily for the experience by which it profits now, that there is a charge to be met of some twelve hundred a year, interest on debt incurred in its young days. For the last twenty years the college has paid this out of its earnings, while providing liberally from the same source for the minds and bodies of its students. Abandoning illusions and endeavours to achieve desirable impossibilities, it has attained a degree of efficiency which brings visitors from France, Spain, Germany, Sweden, and the United States to look into its system. It draws pupils also from distant parts of the old world and of the new. To this condition of a widely recognised efficiency the Farmers' College has attained, and it is working on towards yet higher attainable results. The number of students has, of late years, been steadily rising, and now mounts to seventy, which is within ten of the largest number that can be accommodated in the handsome gothic building set up by the sanguine founders of the institution. In a few years there will not be room for all applicants. A case in its natural history musuem shows how greatly the yield of wheat may be improved by the use of picked seed. When there can be a preliminary examination for the picking of the best prepared and aptest minds, and more or less exclusion of the weak and idle, the tillage of brains in the Cirencester College, already so successful, will show finer and more uniform results.

British farming always has been in the front rank of that form of industry. A Book of Husbandry, written more than three centuries ago by one of Henry the Eighth's judges of the Common Pleas, at a time when cultivated herbage and edible roots were unknown in England, is said to contain little that is not permanently true about the cultivation of corn, and clearly to point out errors of practice which have been transmitted from the untaught father to his untaught son, even to this day, in some English districts. Twenty-three years after the printing of that book of Fitzherbert's husbandry came to honour of verse in Thomas Tusser's Five Hundred Points of Husbandry, a book which indicates many a then recent increase to our agricultural wealth. Hops, introduced early in the century, had become a common crop; hemp and flax also were common crops; and carrots, cabbages, turnips, and rape, were grown for the kitchen. Clover, and probably also turnips, came to England in the reign of Charles the First, through Sir Richard Weston, who had been ambassador to the Elector Palatine and King of Bohemia, and who wrote a discourse on the husbandry of Brabant and Flanders. In sixteen 'eighty-four we have the first notice of turnips as a food for sheep; but even at the time when George the Third came to the throne, clover and turnips, essential as they are to the modern farming system, were scarcely cultivated by our common farmers in the north. It was at the end of the Stuart time, when we first begin to hear of the sheep eating turnips, that potatoes began to attract attention. Raleigh, who brought the plant from Virginia, had established it in Ireland, thence it had passed into Lancashire, where, at the end of the reign of Charles the Second, we learn 'they are very numerous, and now they begin to spread all the kingdom over. They are a pleasant food, boiled or roasted, and eaten with butter and sugar.'

Scientific farming may be said to have begun in the first year of the last century, when Mr. Jethro Tull, a Berkshire gentleman, reasoned to himself that plants feed on minute particles of earth taken up by their rootlets, and, therefore, began sowing his crops in rows or drills, so wide apart as to admit of tillage by plough and hoe in the intervals. His purpose was to break up the soil into what he called 'pasture' for the roots, and to eradicate the weeds which would steal part of 'this terrestrial matter.' He formed his land into broad ridges, with two or three rows of his crop upon each, then used horse-hoeing between the ridges and hand-hoeing between the rows. Jethro Tull was a generation ahead of his time, and his book upon Horse-hoeing Husbandry, produced vehement controversy. But in our own day his reputation has come up and ripened. His book appeared in seventeen 'thirty-one, eight years after the formation of our first Agricultural Society– 'the Society of Improvers on the Knowledge of Agriculture in Scotland.' The Earl of Stair, one of its most active members, is said to have been the first man who grew turnips in Scotland. He had a turnip head. But this society also was before its time, and lived only for twenty years. Mr. Maxwell, another of its active members, who gave lectures upon agriculture, published at its death a volume of its Select Transactions, and in that volume occurs the first mention of a threshing machine. It was patented, worked by water power, and recommended by the society as enabling one man to do the work of six.

The Royal Dublin Society, founded in 1737, had for one object the encouragement of agriculture. It still holds an annual cattle show, and has of late years established an Order of Associates in Agriculture. Holders of it are entitled to wear blue blossoms of speedwell in their button-holes.

Population increased, commerce and the arts added continually to the wealth and power of the nation, farms were enlarged, and so much new land was brought into use, that whereas before the reign of George the Third the whole number of enclosure bills that had been passed was only two hundred and forty-four, there were passed within that reign more than three thousand. In seventeen 'seventy-seven the Bath and West of England Society, for the encouragement of 'Agriculture, Arts, Manufacture, and Commerce,' came into existence, and began to hold its meetings. It met to exhibit breeding stock and implements, and offered premiums for reports on subjects affecting agriculture in the West of England. Six years later, that is to say, in seventeen 'eighty-three, the 'Highland and Agricultural Society of Scotland' was instituted, for the encouragement of Highland Agriculture, Fisheries, and Commerce. This was the year in which the country was relieved of the baneful pressure of the American War. It was the time, also, of Robert Bakewell's fame as an improver of the breeds of sheep and cattle. His improvement upon the long-horned cattle has been superseded by the application of his own principles to the short-horn or Durham breed; but the new race of sheep that he perfected, the Leicesters, still adds to the wealth of the county. The Bakewells of Cirencester go a step further, and are for the intellectual breeding of an improved race of farmers.

What is called alternate husbandry, alternation of green crops with grain crops, came also in those days into use. In seventeen 'eighty-eight the Swede turnip was accidentally discovered, and soon was in general cultivation. Swing ploughs and threshing machines were no longer rarities. Five years after the discovery of the Swede turnip a 'National Board of Agriculture' was established, and remained alive for twenty years, collecting statistical information and drawing up special surveys, documents which would have been more serviceable if they had been less extensive and less expensive. Agriculture next throve upon blood manure in the wars of the French Revolution.

Seventeen 'ninety-five brought us a deficient harvest, and Napoleon's cutting off of our supply of foreign grain. The price of wheat was nearly doubled. Upon this followed the Bank Restriction Act, suspending cash payments, and introducing unlimited speculation upon credit. The high price of wheat stimulated farmers to produce as much of it as possible, by improving arable land, reclaiming wastes, and ploughing up their pastures; the green crop of the new system of alternate husbandry more than compensating for the pasturages thus withdrawn. This lasted for twenty years. Wheat that in the preceding twenty years had sold for less than fifty shillings a quarter, rose till in eighteen hundred and twelve it came to one hundred and twenty-six shillings. The people suffered but the farmers throve, and agriculture made rapid advances. Within that period of twenty years the rental of land in Scotland advanced from two million to five million and a quarter.

Since that terrible war period there has been rapid and great increase of population asking to be fed, there has been great increase of wealth and great increase of knowledge. Law has struck off fetters with which it had crippled enterprise. The steam engine was first applied to a threshing machine in eighteen hundred and three; there were several machines so worked fifteen or eighteen years later. Steam on the farm, steam on the railway, making transit of stock easy, the marvellous development of mechanical inventions, and a still more marvellous development of the great science of organic chemistry, which has given a true basis to the practice of farming, have secured during the present century the progress of agriculture; although the majority of farmers, scattered over the land in much inevitable isolation from the great collective life of men, have kept pace slowly with the movements of their day.

Sir Humphrey Davy was the first chemist who took a real hold upon the agricultural mind, and this was when, in eighteen 'twelve, he lectured before the Board of Agriculture, and showed that agricultural chemistry had for its study all changes in the arrangements of matter connected with the growth and nourishment of plants; the comparative values of their produce as food; the constituents of soils; the manner in which lands are nourished by manure, or rendered fertile by the different processes of cultivation. But the great stir in this direction began with the publication, in eighteen 'forty, of Baron Liebig's work on Chemistry in its application to Agriculture and Physiology. Liebig's writings obtained a remarkably wide popularity. Everybody concerned in the management of farms was bitten by Liebig, and talked potash and nitrogenous manure. It was the fashion to believe that this great chemist had found the master key to agricultural success. There was a wholesome little mania for agricultural chemistry. The most wonderful immediate results of all kinds were expected from what Liebig called offering a small piece of the philosopher's stone as an oblation to the God of the Dunghill. But when these immediate results didn't follow, the more empty of those who had gone with the crowd turned back. Nevertheless an impulse had been given to true progress in the right direction. In eighteen 'forty-two a body of Mid Lothian tenant farmers started an 'Agricultural Chemistry Association,' and employed a chemist to conduct experiments for them. Their zeal died out in a few years, but the Highland Agricultural Society kept up the chemical researches. The Agricultural College at Cirencester originated in the same way in the same year 'forty-two. There was not only the Liebig mania in all its freshness and strength, but the tendency to work by association was then strengthening among the farmers as among other bodies of men. The Yorkshire Society had been formed in 'thirty-seven; the Royal Agricultural Society of England, which now has more than five thousand members, and is in close connexion with the Royal Veterinary College, in 'thirty-eight; the Royal Agricultural Improvement Society of Ireland in 'forty-one; the College at Cirencester, as before said, in 'forty-two; and in 'forty-three the chief of the Farmers' Clubs came into life, the Central Farmers' Club, with its headquarters at the York Hotel, Bridge-street, Blackfriars.

It was at a meeting of one of the many local Farmers' Clubs – that of Cirencester and Fairford held in November eighteen 'forty-two – that Mr. Robert Jeffries Brown delivered an address 'On the Advantages of a Specific Education for Agricultural Pursuits;' and this was the first move towards the founding of the Cirencester College. When the club met again, at the end of December, its members adopted formally a public address based upon Mr. Brown's views, saying that 'we cannot too highly estimate the importance of a specific education for those engaged in agricultural pursuits; and the great value to them of a knowledge of those sciences that are in constant operation in the cultivation of the soil, the growth of crops, and the rearing and feeding of domestic animals; and we think it most essential that the study of these sciences should be united with practical experience. The advantages of an institution of this kind to the landowner, as well as to the occupier, are too obvious to require comment; and we confidently rely on their cordial co-operation and support.'

They proceeded accordingly to wait upon landowners and occupiers; upon their own particular great man at Oakley Park, Earl Bathurst, and upon the other chief men of the district. They held meetings also at various market towns. Mr. Brown gave nearly the whole of the next year to the work he had begun. At a public meeting held in Cirencester in April, 'forty-four, it was moved by an earl – the late Earl Ducie – and seconded by a tenant farmer, that an institution ought to be provided in which 'The rising generation of farmers may receive instruction at a moderate expense in those sciences a knowledge of which is essential to successful cultivation, and that a farm form part of such institution.' Then Lord Bathurst offered a farm of more than four hundred acres for a long term of years, and an adjacent building site for ninety-nine years; a society was formed for the establishment and management of an agricultural college, the interest of noblemen and landowners in distant parts of the kingdom was raised to subscription point, and a proposed capital of twelve thousand pounds was thus obtained. In March, 'forty-five, a charter of incorporation was secured; but as it was now found that twelve thousand pounds would not do all that was expected to be done, it was provided by the deed of settlement that this capital should be doubled. Additional exertions did not quite succeed in doubling it, but they did bring it up a few hundreds over twenty thousand pounds. The managers, delivering themselves up to unrestrained enjoyment of a good dabble in – the mud-pie making of our maturer years – bricks and mortar, produced a handsome edifice, with a frontage of nearly two hundred feet, battlemented tower, gable roofs, and lofty gothic windows. Rooms made, of course, to the windows, instead of windows to the rooms, were often spacious only in height. Lofty they must be, because the ceiling is usually looked for somewhere above the top of the window; and the bottom of the window, itself lofty, would be so high above the floor that a student might have to stand on a chair to see the ground outside. There was a dining-hall so high that, without making it a bit too low, a very fine museum has been got by laying a floor midway across it. But on the whole, no doubt, a very durable and handsome college was erected, which by some trouble and thought has, in course of years, become as convenient and comfortable as if the architect himself had been vulgar enough to care for the convenience of its inmates. The architect – several of his craft have done the same within the present century – considerably exceeded his estimates. The managers of the new college were sanguine, and had all their experience to buy; there was no other agricultural college in the country by whose early mistakes they might profit; so they began, like heroes, with an offer of board, lodging, practical and scientific education, all for thirty pounds a year. What could be more desirable than that?

'How lovely the intrepid front of youth!' Experience the first showed that while each student paid thirty pounds a year for everything, he cost the college thirty-two for meat and drink alone. That being so, how was the debt on the buildings to be met? How were the teachers to be paid? Out of the profits of the farm? Aye, but that, too, was managed at a loss. There was a bright ideal notion that students should become practically acquainted with every detail of farm work – hoeing, digging, paring turnips, feeding sheep, and so forth; but that if they did field labour they gave service worth wages, and should be credited with wages of their work. Thus it was thought that their industry might pay some part of the cost of their maintenance. And, behold, there was a book kept in which every student was credited with the wages of such work as he did on the farm. Such work! Well. The same bright speculation is to be tried under different and far more hopeful conditions at the new Cornell University in New York.

The plan of the Cornell Institution, which has enrolled our countryman, Mr. Goldwin Smith, among its professors, is partly based upon the good later results obtained at Cirencester. About six year ago Mr. Ezra Cornell, of Ithaca, New York, who had made a large fortune by telegraphy, visited the college at Cirencester with Colonel Johnstone. He afterwards made his offer to the New York government of more than a hundred thousand pounds, in addition to the considerable grant of land from Congress to a state that would provide agricultural teaching, on condition that the whole should go to the founding of a single institution, not as a grant to be divided among several districts. The result is the Cornell University in the State of New York, one department of which is planned upon the model of Cirencester, and forms the only good agricultural college in the United States. There is a large agricultural school at Yale, but it is not very efficient. Mr. Cornell was told at Cirencester of the complete failure there of the system of paying students wages for field labour. Nevertheless he means to try it in America, but not in the same form. The large endowment makes the teaching practically gratuitous in his new university. The farmwork is not required of any as a necessary part of the routine, but it is open to all. Thus it is thought that the poorest father may send an industrious son to this new institution, with the assurance that while he receives intellectual training he may earn enough to pay his moderate expenses, finding also suitable work read to his hand, and a state of opinion among his fellows trained to recognise it as both useful and honourable. In fact, we are told by newspapers that in this first session of the Cornell University some youths enter three months before the classes opened for the sake of earning two dollars a day through haying and harvest towards their winter expenses. The Cirencester students did not work like men who labour for a living. When the poor students at a Scottish university, who supplies, doubtless, another of Mr. Cornell's models, is proud to earn by work of his hands in leisure time the money spent on cultivation of his intellect, he works nobly, indeed, but under the strong joint pressure of need and ambition. The common labourer works to feed himself and his wife and children; but the young student whose actual wants are paid for by his father's cheque, and who goes out with a troop of light-hearted young fellows in his own position to play at field labour in the name of education, and to have his earnings put down to his father's credit, is the most unprofitable of all known sorts of farm servant. He turns work into play, smokes under hedges, and even when he does get through a certain quantity of work, is not to be relied upon for doing it at the right time, or thoroughly. When the business of the college farm required that certain work should be completed in a certain field by a particular day, the chance would be that it was not done, or done badly, if it was entrusted to the students. To the students of that day: we speak of times completely gone, of difficulties conquered, partly by abandonment of efforts in a wrong direction; but the results of the first years of work in the Agricultural College at Cirencester were disappointing. In the year 'forty-eight the managers found that they had overdrawn their account at the bank to the extent of about ten thousand pounds. They were working college and farm at a loss, and had not much to say for the results produced. Even the art of managing the hearty, free-spirited farmers' sons, accustomed to much outdoor sport and little study, who then came to the college, had yet to be learnt. One day a rat was brought to the lecture room of an unpopular professor, let loose in lecture time with a sudden slamming of every desk, hunted, killed and thrown in the professor's face.

Then there was the very troublesome fact of the overdrawn ten thousand. The promoters met to consider whether the college was to be closed as a failure. The results of discussion was that the work of the place lay before it, not the less clear for its early errors and shortcomings. Earl Ducie, Earl Bathurst, Mr. Sotheron Estcourt, and Mr. Edward Holland, who had first offered himself to bear the whole responsibility, became, with Mr. Langston, answerable for all the college debts, and by right of this responsibility, they took upon themselves its management. Upon their personal security upwards of thirty thousand pounds were added to the original subscriptions and donations. These gentlemen now constitute the Council of the College, and under their supervision it has become what it now is, not yet the best conceivable thing of its kind, but the best and most successful agricultural college that has yet been founded anywhere.

It stands about a mile out of Cirencester, facing Oakley Park, whose beautiful woods were so familiar to Pope that in his later years he wrote thence to Martha Blount, 'You cannot think how melancholy this place makes me. Every part of this wood puts into my mind poor Mr. Gay, with whom I passed once a great deal of pleasant time in it, and another friend, who is near dead, and quite lost to us, Dr. Swift.' And he said that he felt in it 'the same sort of uneasiness as I find at Twickenham whenever I pass my mother's room.' Alas that Pope's melancholy should be perpetuated, for there is talk of placing a new cemetery midway between the town and the college, a cheerful addition to what now is an agreeable promenade. So planted, on high and healthy ground, six hundred feet above the sea level, and with no buildings but its own in sight, the college is as pleasant a place of residence as any one could wish who takes delight in English country air and scenery. The Farmers' College is as rural in all its surroundings as the farmer's occupation. Its massive and roomy farm buildings are a quarter of a miles distant from it. They include a fixed engine of ten-horse power, which works a threshing-mill, a pair of stones for bruising or grinding, the chaff and root cutters, and also the pumps. There are the feeding-boxes and cow-house, the chaff and root house, where all material is prepared for the stock, which is lodged close by in yards, and sheds, and styes. The cart-stable is so divided that each animal can move about at pleasure, and be fed at the head. An opposite line of buildings includes the slaughterhouse, tool and artificial manure house, office, and blacksmiths' and carpenters' shops, in which useful lessons may be taken by those students who are about to emigrate. Under the roofs of these buildings are shed-room, straw and hay lofts, and granary. Add to all these a roomy rickyard and the residences of the bailiff and tenant, an old student of the college, who took honours there in his time, is thoroughly interested in the college work, and goes through his business with all his methods of proceeding open to the daily observation of the students. This gentleman cultivates the five hundred acres on his own account. Farm management by the collective understanding of a body corporate could scarcely pay. By a turnpike road that intersects the farm is another of the outlying buildings, the Veterinary Hospital, under the management of the veterinary professor. The college is obliged usually to buy instructive cases of disease. Farmers are more ready to kill cattle when they begin to sicken than to incur doctor's bills of, say, a couple of pounds apiece on their account; and if they have a sick horse they don't take very well to the notion of its being argued over in clinical lectures before sixty or seventy students. They have a mistaken dread, too, of the humour for experiment in scientific men, and fear lest, when they send a horse to be cured,

> Dread feats shall follow, and disasters great,
> Pills charge on pills, and bolus bolus meet.

Still cases do come in the natural way for the safest and best treatment to be had in that part of the country, and the deficiency is made up by a discreet purchase of diseased beasts.

As to the farm, of its five hundred acres, forty acres are in pasture, the rest arable. The soil, which belongs to the Bath oolitic formation, is composed of clays, marls, limestones, and inferior brash, the last named and least valuable form of soil predominating. But the variations are so frequent that in a furrow of ten chains in length the plough will often pass through soil alternating from brash to rich loam, or it may be to a cold tenacious clay. There are twenty fields, varying in size from ten to fifty acres; two thirds of the land is handy to the farm buildings, the rest scattered, difficult of access, and with an irregular surface, costly therefore to cultivate. These differences of condition, which might

Appendix IV

vex a farmer who looked only to money profit from the land, are full of interest and informtion for the student who is well taught to observe.

The flock on the farm comprises two hundred and fifty breeding ewes, pure Cotswold; there are twelve milch cows, for the supply of college milk; nine carefully selected horses of the Clydesdale, Suffolk, and West Country breeds, and pigs, pure Berkshire. These are winning honours as prize takers. They have among them now, as far as prizes can bear witness to such a fact, the first pig of the nation. He was the second; but the first is killed and cured, so that he is now without known rival as the great Lord Bacon of the day.

We paid a visit to this college a few weeks after the opening of its present session, went through it, dined with the students, and took a lesson with them in the laboratory upon a subject not, we believe, generally popular with the townspeople of Cirencester, water. Our visit was paid on the monthly live-stock market day, perhaps the best of its kind, as to quantity and value of stock, in the West of England. There we found, on one of the hottest baking days of this memorable baking year, in a newly constructed market, some three thousand sheep and oxen unprovided with a drop of water. Provision for water supply not only had formed no part of the architect's arrangement of the market, but seemed to have been disdained as low art. Cirencester itself is content with water from the same bed into which its drainage flows, though an ample supply of good water from the fuller's earth below, is pumped close by, for a canal, and at the service of the town if it will have it. But it won't. When men themselves are content with a little bad water, no wonder that beasts are believed not to require any. While the unfortunate animals in the Cirencester live-stock market were panting in the sun, a stream of clear water, the overflow of a lake in the adjacent park, was running along a pipe but a few feet under the surface of the market ground. Somebody had suggested that it would cost little to tap that pipe and put a pump over it. A stone tank had actually been given to receive the water so obtained. But no pump has been placed over the waste water pipe, and we saw close to a flock of thirsty sheep the stone tank contemptuously turned bottom upwards, dry in the dust under a sultry sun. After their day of thirst in the live-stock market, there is no road out of Cirencester that would bring those parched animals to a drinking place within a distance of some miles. A benevolent quaker in the town, merciful to other men's beasts, has done what he could to mitigate this evil by setting up a tank at his own door.

But the Agricultural College has wells of its own, and we heard nothing about the town water from its chemical professor. Remote from great cities, the professors of this college must be resident within its walls, and the ample building accordingly supplies rooms to a professor of chemistry and to his assistant; to professors of agriculture, of natural history, and of anatomy, physiology and hygiene, as well as a teacher of drawing, who is a certificated master from South Kensington. The professorship of mathematics and surveying is held by the principal, whose house, once alone on the farm, with walls built as if to stand a cannonade, is the only old part of the building. We found the students very much at home during the quarter of an hour – which did not seem a bad one – before dinner. Each has his own cell, and was hived in it, or buzzing in upon a friend, or joining a small swarm in the library, a comfortable room freely supplied with books of reference and journals. The dinner in hall was plentiful and pleasant, as an English college dinner ought to be, and has a common English feature that will not be copied in the Cornell University, in its brew of college beer. In the United States beer is not given in any place of education, and it is said that no college authority would venture to introduce it. But might not the man be less ready to 'liquor up' if the boy had formed wholesome acquaintance with John Barleycorn?

After dinner there were the musuems to look at. Each professor lectures once a week in the museum itself on the specimens illustrating his subject. A museum, all alive and growing, is to be seen out of doors in the well-stocked botanical garden, with beds set apart for experimenting. The museums are remarkably well furnished with what is necessary for the illustration of the lectures. There is a herbarium containing three thousand specimens of British plants; there is a good series to illustrate geology and mineralogy, with many striking illustrations of the effect of soil or selection of seed upon produce. There is a fine set of wax models of every form of cultivated roots; there are samples of the seed of every plant used in English agriculture, and specimen plants of many varieties of important

327

cereals. The excellent chemical collection also tells its facts to the eye in a striking manner. Thus, one case contains a series of articles of food produced by the farmer, separated into their constituents. Side by side the student sees in substantial bulk the relative proportions of water and of flesh and fat or heat-producing elements, in wheat, barley, oats, peas, beans, and so forth. The percentage of water thus put for substantial comparison before the eye, looks very striking. A veteran, long past the pulpy time of youth, who gave up in his manhood wine for water, impressed by the fact here shown, has, in his age, left off drinking altogether, on the plea that his bread, meat, and vegetables contain quite as much water as he wants. Another fact that catches the eye immediately concerns another veteran, whom it will not be improper to name, Jack Sprat. Of this person it is said constantly that he could eat no fat. That is a popular delusion. For here is a mass showing how much fat there is in the lean of meat. Jack Sprat may have been himself under a delusion, but the truth is that neither he nor anybody else can eat the lean and not eat fat.

But, like the Cirencester market builders, we are forgetting the water. It so happened that on the day of our visit to the college the chemistry of water had been the subject of the chemistry professor's morning lecture, and the custom of the college is for the students to work out for themselves after dinner practically in the laboratory, what they had been taught theoretically in the lecture-room. This is the soundest way of teaching, but not always possible. At the Agricultural College, a spacious airy laboratory, for elementary study, with a laboratory for advanced analyses and a professor's room, have been constructed out of an old barn. It has been thoroughly fitted up, each student has plenty of room for his own operations, and probably there is no place of education in the kingdom with a laboratory more convenient for its pupils, or for the professional analyses made by its chiefs. The work of the day was the analysis of water for organic matter, lime, and so forth. The different ways of testing could be copied into note books from a writing on the wall; the meaning of them was briefly and clearly told by the professor, and all requisite practical directions were at the same time given. Then the students set to work for themselves with their evaporating pans, their retorts and reagents, taking counsel of their teacher wherever they met with any difficulty.

So, too, the professor of natural history works at fit time with his students in the open country, and there is, by-the-by, a curious want of uniformity in the surface formation of the country about Cirencester, which makes this region a very conveneint one for the out-door study of geology. The professor of agriculture takes his students about the farm. The veterinary professor has his hospital, and a capital series of casts showing the teeth of animals at different ages, preparations of diseased structure, and other delicacies. The principal, who is also professor of mathematics and surveying, goes abroad among his students with chain and theodolite. When a tree is felled in the park he teaches them to estimate the value of its timber. They apply under his direction mathematics to the measuring of haystacks, and at the annual valuation of the farm there is a prize for the valuation by a student which comes nearest to that made professionally.

Great attention is paid to the study of the true values of farm work and produce. At once, upon entering, each student begins farm book-keeping, and has punctually to post up the details of the college farm. In the second year this book-keeping takes a higher form, and becomes a scientific study. A book is given to the student showing among other things the size of every field, the successive crops it has grown, and a minute analysis of the soil. Blank leaves following the description of each field, are then to be filled up with a minute analysis of the form of work done on it, the number of hands, horses, time and money spent upon each detail of its cultivation, and a mathematical reference of each element in farm work to a fixed standard of value. There is so much to be learnt every day, and such strict testing of the amount learnt by weekly examinations – of which every student sees the result in a list of marks showing him how far he has failed or succeeded in his studies – that a short time at the Farm and College cannot be spent unprofitably by any one who thinks of coaxing bread and meat out of this mother earth.

Now here is the difficulty. Agriculture rightly studied has become one of the liberal professions. At a dinner of the Royal Agricultural Society at Chester, Mr. Gladstone hardly exaggerated its real dignity when he spoke of it as an art 'which of all others, perhaps, affords the most varied scope, and the largest sphere of development to the powers of the human mind.' But it is not yet so taken by many; perhaps not by many even among the students of Cirencester. It combines, like medicine, practice with science, and for its right pursuit requires a preparation not many degrees less thorough. A volume called Practice with Science contains some lectures which have been given at Cirencester college. One is by the principal, upon Agricultural Education; and in this he combats the notion of the Royal Agricultural Society, that a well-educated farmer means a man who has learned Latin and Greek, and the notion of a member of the Central Farmers' Club, who argued that the college had placed the standard of qualification for its diploma too high, and that a two years' course of study was too long. 'All that was necessary,' said this objector, 'was a sound knowledge of the principles of mathematics, chemistry, geology, botany, and veterinary surgery!' As if it did not cost a good part of a life to get a 'sound knowledge' of any one of those little amusements. Still the notion that one may gather the fruits of study without climbing the tree is very common; and although the number of the Cirencester students who go steadily through the prescribed course and fairly earn the college diploma is increasing, it bears no proportion to the numbers that have come and gone every year, and to the pains taken to secure system and thoroughness in the machinery of education. The cost of this eduction is not more than has been found requisite to meet its unavoidable expenses. A farm cannot safely be undertaken with less capital than about eight pounds an acre, and a well cultivated brain is, as we said at starting, the best part of a farmer's estate, besides being (in this country) all of it freehold; yet the cost of acquiring it bears only a small proportion to the other costs of a safe start in English farming life. The English farmer cannot rise to the full height of the position made for him by the growth of science, until he receives a sound school training, valid in every part, and follows it up with a thorough training for his business. He should read and speak, not Greek and Latin, but two living languages besides his own, that he may be able to converse freely with farmers from abroad, and profit by their treatises and journals. But of the time taken from Latin and Greek the greater part should be spent in a particular cultivation of arithmetic and mathematics, and of the first principles of natural science. Then let him, at the age of sixteen, pass from school to the farm, and for the next year see and share in the work done upon it. So prepared let him go to the Cirencester College and work firmly through the two years' course. If he spend his time well he will learn enough for his purpose, although even after he has taken his diploma he will feel that the two years' curriculum was all too short. His age now will be nineteen. Armed with exact scientific knowledge, which he has been taught how to apply to every detail of agriculture, let him proceed to work and watch for himself, during the next two years, on any large well managed farm, taking a salary, perhaps, for the assistance he can give. At the end of that term he has reached the age of one and twenty. It is his own fault then if he be not in his own profession, what his cousin who goes every October to his London hospital will hardly be till a couple of years later in life, a duly qualified practitioner. Their day may be long coming, but of some such sort must be the English farmers of a day to come.

TYPICAL EXAMINATION PAPERS,
DECEMBER 1878

AGRICULTURAL CHEMISTRY.

PROFESSOR CHURCH.

CLASS III.

1. What do you know about the relation of silica to the processes and products of vegetable growth?

2. Why do you determine K_2O, N, P_2O_5 and the Soluble Salts in soil-analysis?

3. How do you account for the deficiency of lime sometimes noticed in certain soils derived from calcareous rocks?

4. How is it that the occurrence of small quantities of apatite, of hornblende, or of zeolites, in certain rocks has an important influence upon the fertility of the soils produced by the decay of such rocks?

5. What are the chief defects of the precipitation processes for the treatment of sewage?

6. I have some superphosphate offered to me at 3s. per unit per ton for "bone phosphate made soluble," I find the manure contains 20 .per cent. of monocalcic phosphate. What is the price per ton?

7. Name the vegetable foods (*a, b, c*) the average composition of which these percentages represent:—

	a.	*b.*	*c.*
Water, . .	14	12	75
Albuminoids, . .	24	30	1
Carbohydrates, . .	52	28	21
Oil or fat, . . .	2	12	0
Fibre, . . .	5	12	2
Ash, . . .	3	6	1

8. What useful purposes in the animal economy may "indigestible" fibre fulfil?

9. Illustrate the various uses of the albuminoids as nutrients by a reference to sheep-feeding experiments.

10. Give the average composition of cows' milk, of whey, and of fresh butter.

11. What chemical changes occur during malting, and how are they brought about? Give analyses of brewers' grains and of malt coombs.

BOTANY.

PROFESSOR FREAM.

CLASS III.

1. What is meant by the Grand Period of Growth, and why is it necessary to distinguish such a period? How does the rate of growth vary during different parts of the same day?

2. Describe the life-history of the wheat-plant from the germination of the grain to the ripening of the fruit. Make special reference to the nature of the food required, the sources from which it is derived, and its final disposition within the plant.

3. Enumerate (a) the several means by which self-fertilisation is prevented, and (b) the various modes by which cross-fertilisation is effected, in hermaphrodite flowers. Give a few illustrative examples.

4. Is there any general connection between the annual area of leaf-surface and the appearance presented by a cross-section of the woody stems of Monocotyledons and Dicotyledons respectively? Discuss this question fully.

5. Distinguish between Gamogenesis and Agamogenesis, and describe the several kinds of the former process, with examples.

6. Describe the typical structure of the anther, pollen-grain, and anatropous ovule of Angiosperms. What are endosperm and perisperm, and how does an albuminous differ from an exalbuminous seed?

7. Explain the following formulæ, draw the corresponding floral diagrams, and name flowers illustrative of each:—

$$(a.)\ \text{Ca}_3, \qquad \text{Co}_3, \qquad \text{An}_{3+3}, \qquad \text{Gn}_{(3)}.$$
$$(b.)\ \text{Ca}_5, \qquad \text{Co}_5,\ |\ , \quad \text{An}_5, \qquad \text{Gn}_{(5)}.$$
$$(c.)\ \text{Ca}_{2+2}, \quad \text{Co}_{\times 4}, \quad \text{An}_{2\times 2}^2 \quad \text{Gn}_{(2)}.$$

8. Describe the structure and life-history of the potato-disease fungus, *Phytophthora infestans*. To what order and what class do you refer it, and why? What means would you take to exterminate it on a farm?

9. What do you understand by the term *carpospore?* Give the orders and families of the fungal *Carposporeæ*, and refer the chief fungi that are parasitic on cereal crops to their respective families.

10. Compare the process of fertilisation in a gymnospermous with that in an angiospermous ovule. Also, state what structures are respectively equivalent in Gymnosperms to the microspore, macrospore, prothallium, and archegonium of the higher Pteridophyta.

MECHANICS.
PROFESSOR TANNER.
CLASS III.

1. Define:—force, power, horse-power, mass, weight, momentum, moment of a force about a point.

2. How long will it take an engine working at the rate of 8 H.P. to raise 10,000 gallons of water from a depth of 165 feet?

3. An excavation is to be 300 feet long, 70 feet broad, and 30 feet deep. The earth has to be brought to the surface on ramps and then removed to a distance of 450 feet. The material requires 3 pickmen to 2 shovellers. How many labourers of each class are required to complete the work within 28 days?

4. Sketch a system of compensatory whipple-trees for three horses abreast, and explain the action.

5. Find the horse-power of an engine from the following data:—diameter of piston, 11″; length of stroke, 14″; number of strokes per minute, 143; pressure of steam, 70 lbs.; cut off at 3″; pressure in condenser 4 lbs.

6. What are the laws of motion?

7. Deduce the formulæ for falling bodies from the second law of motion.

8. A weight of 3 lbs. on a smooth level table is attached by a long string to a weight of 5 lbs. hanging over the side. The latter weight touches the ground half a second after the two are let go. How high is the table?

9. How is the value of g determined?

10. A ball is thrown with a velocity of 120 feet per second at an angle of 45° to the vertical. Find when and where it will meet the ground which is level.

COLLEGE REGULATIONS, MAY 1879

In the early days of the College the students were strictly regulated and lived and worked under a firm regime, especially during the time of Constable as Principal. These are the regulations as published in May 1879.

1. Students in College must attend Morning and Evening Prayers, and all Services in the Chapel.

2. Students must not be absent from Meals.

3. Students must attend all Lectures, Classes, and Examinations, from which they have not express leave to be absent.

4. Students must be in the College when the doors are locked in the evening.

5. Whenever a Professor is unable to deliver his Lecture or attend his Class, the Students are to devote the time thus left unoccupied to Practical Agriculture on the Farm, no official order to the contrary being issued.

6. Each Student must keep a Farm Journal, Cultivation Book, or such Farm Book as is assigned to his Class.

7. The boundaries within which Students are expected to confine themselves are those of the Farm. Students wishing to go beyond these boundaries at any time which is not occupied by the engagements mentioned in No. 1, are to write their names in the Porter's Book when they go out, with the hour of their departure, adding, when they return, the hour at which they come back.

8. Order and quiet must be observed at all times in the College.

9. All Students must be in their own rooms at eleven P.M. No lights are allowed after the gas is turned off.

10. The introduction into the College, or on the Farm, of Wine, Spirits, or Fermented Liquor, of Playing-cards, Fire-arms, Gunpowder, or explosive materials of any description, renders the offender liable to expulsion.

11. Students cannot be permitted to bring Dogs to the College or Farm.

12. The habit of Smoking is discouraged as much as possible. If practised in any public place, the Farm Buildings, or any thoroughfare, it will be dealt with as a transgression.

13. Students are forbidden to frequent any Inn, Public-house, or Billiard-Room.

14. A Student damaging any part of the College, the Windows, or Furniture, must report the same to the Porter, that the value of the repairs may be charged to his account.

15. No game of any sort is to be played during the hours allotted for Lectures or Classes.

16. Students excused from a portion of their duties on account of indisposition, must not go beyond the College ground (No. 13) without leave.

17. Certificates of attendance at Lectures will be given by the Professors to those Students only who have shown proficiency in their respective departments. This proficiency will be mentioned in the Certificate.

18. Out-Students having selected the subject or subjects in the College Course which they desire to study, are required to attend regularly the Lectures and Examinations connected therewith.

Notice will be given on the Notice-board in the Entrance Hall of the hours of Prayers, Lectures, Classes, Examinations, Meals, etc., and any changes will be notified in the same manner.

THE CONSTABLE–CHURCH LETTERS

Chapter 3 describes the affair of the dismissal of Professor A.H. Church by the Revd John Constable. Appended are the relevant letters exchanged between them which led up to the dismissal of Church.

'Southgate, N., 17th January 1879
Dear Sir, – You will doubtless be surprised to hear that within the last forty-eight hours I have proposed and been accepted! No immediate change in my relation to the College is necessary, and so we can talk over this aspect of the matter in due course.
Yours truly,

A.H. CHURCH

The Rev. John Constable'

★

'The Agricultural College, Cirencester, Jan. 19, 1879.
Dear Sir, – I am a little but not greatly surprised at the fact you kindly communicate, for it was only yesterday I destroyed a note which I had written asking you if the report that you were leaving the College was correct: having heard this from more than one quarter, I began to believe that there was *some* foundation for it. Most sincerely do we all wish you every happiness in your proposed alteration, and I must thank you for so speedily acquainting me with your resolution.
I am, dear Sir, yours truly,

JOHN CONSTABLE

Professor Church'

★

'The Agricultural College, February 4th, 1879
Dear Sir,- Conversations sometimes lead to complications, therefore I think it advisable to put on paper what the College interest seem to require in connection with the resignation of your Professorship. I do not feel able to accept your services as a Non-resident Professor unless you are kind eno' to give them as an occasional lecturer on Agricultural Chemistry, provided circumstances make me apply to you for them.

Believe me to be, yours truly,
JOHN CONSTABLE

Professor Church, The Agricultural College'

★

'The Agricultural College, Cirencester, February 8th, 1879.
My dear Sir, – In accordance with your request, I beg to repeat in writing the intimation which I gave you at the beginning of the present term of my intention to marry during the next College vacation, and of the consequent necessity for my no longer (after April 24th) living within the College walls. Further, I have to thank you of your ready acceptance, previously accorded orally, of the notice of my intention – a notice which lacked some days to make it one of a whole term. You speak in your note to me of the 4th inst., of the resignation of my professorship here. I must remind you that I have not resigned, nor have I any intention of doing so.

Very faithfully yours,
A.H.CHURCH

To the Reverend the Principal, Agricultural College, Cirencester.'

★

'The Agricultural College, Cirencester, February 14th, 1879.
Dear Sir, – I am at a loss to understand what you mean by my ready acceptance of the notice of your intention to marry. Officially I have nothing to do with such a matter if it does not interfere with the duties you are under contract to fulfil. But I do understand that you told me that it was your intention to give up residence in the College after the termination of the present term – which I interpreted and do still interpret to mean: that after that time you can no longer discharge the duties of Professor of Chemistry in this College – I certainly received that intimation as your practical resignation – call it what you like – and in that light I am still willing to accept it tho' it is given one month too late.

I am yours truly,
JOHN CONSTABLE

Professor Church, The Agricultural College.'

★

'The Agricultural College, Cirencester, 17th February 1879.
My dear Sir, – Thinking that you might reasonably expect an answer to your note of February 14th, let me say at once that if, as you decide, by non-residence within the College walls I vacate my professorship here, then it becomes vacant at the date previously named. Of course I assume that this decision of yours is that of the Governing Body of the College, – indeed you stated to me that this was so. I refer to this point since I was elected, in 1863, to my present post by the Council, and under the bye-law then in force, and not under the bye-law of 1870, which vested in the Principal all future appointments and dismissals of Professors. I believe most people do not attach the same meaning to the words 'resign' and 'vacate'. I, for one, do not wish it to be said that I *resigned* my post. Yet, however anxious I might be to continue to fulfil, though not resident in the College, all the duties of Professor of Chemistry here – duties so long fulfilled by Dr Voelcker – yet I could not wish to remain when you are eager for my departure. Thus I would not ask you to do more than recall to mind that you have several times said to me that marriage, and marriage alone, would entitle me to live out of College; while you once wrote to me to same effect when I was contemplating becoming a candidate for a post at Bristol. You object to my mentioning the reason why my residence within the College walls will cease with the present term. I cannot but think I should have laid myself open to the charge of rudeness had I announced this consequence without explaining its cause. I have endeavoured throughout our conversation and in my previous letter to maintain an uniformly courteous tone. And why should my pain on leaving the sphere of such long and happy labours be needlessly embittered?

Very faithfully yours,
A.H.CHURCH

P.S. – It has just struck me in closing this correspondence, that the four letters which constitute it will, if made public, correct any erroneous notions that may prevail as to the circumstances under which my connection with the College ceases.

A.H.C.

The Reverend the Principal, the Agricultural College, Cirencester.'

★

'The Agricultural College, Cirencester, January [*sic*] 18, 1879. Dear Sir, – In reply to your note just received I hasten to remove a misconception on your part, namely, that my decision as to the necessity of your residing in the College for the discharge of the duties of your office was the decision of the Committee of Management – I never meant to say anything of the kind, nor can I imagine what I could have said bearing on such an interpretation. Am I to understand that you desire the decision of the Committee of Management in this matter? I am not aware how any word, or letter, or deed of mine in this discussion has a tendency to embitter your separation from the College, I have had no such intention. I must recall to your consideration the remark you made in our second conversation, namely, that you were quite sensible that in the opinions which I expressed at our first conversation I was actuated by what I believed to be my duty to the College. A long experience has convinced me that the discipline of the College can be carried on successfully only by the residence within the College walls of the principal Professors. I shall feel obliged by an early answer to this note,

And am, yours truly,
JOHN CONSTABLE.

Professor Church.'

★

'The Agricultural College, Cirencester, 21st February 1879. My dear Sir, – I cannot but allow that the distressing ailment which has laid you up so often during the last year or two must have made you liable to forget some things you have said, and to say some things you would forget. I note, in passing, that your letter, handed to me on the 19th of the present month, bears the date of January 18th, 1879. In answer to that letter I have to state that I most certainly understood you to speak, and that repeatedly, of the final determination of the supreme authority of this College not to permit me to remain here as Professor of Chemistry, unless resident within the College walls. You cannot suppose that I should have accepted your decision had I not been assured that it had received the sanction necessary to give it validity. And in addition to your reiterated oral assertions as to your already having secured such sanction, your two first letters obviously implied your decision to be final, and therefore that of the ultimate Court of appeal. What other construction could be put on the terms of your letter of 4th February, when you wrote, "I do not feel able to accept your services as a non-resident professor?" And are not the following words in your letter of February 14th absolutely conclusive on this point? "You told me that it was your intention to give up residence in the College after the termination of the present Term – which I interpreted and do still interpret to mean: that after that time *you can no longer discharge the duties of Professor of Chemistry in this College* – I certainly received that intimation as your practical resignation – call it what you like". But if, as I gather from your third letter, you now think that your determination to dissolve altogether my connection with the College was *ultra vires* on your part, then I should certainly, as a matter of course, expect you to obtain, for your own satisfaction, the decision of the Committee of Management as to this matter. It would be satisfactory to me also, as my "contract" was with the Council.

I remain, dear Sir, faithfully yours,
A.H. CHURCH

To the Rev. The Principal.'

★

'The Agricultural College, Cirencester, February 22, 1879.

Dear Sir, – Had you stated at our first interview that which may be inferred from your note of February 17th, namely, that you disputed my power to deal with the question of your non-residence, and that it was only a formal resolution of the Committee of Management that you would regard as final in this matter, this ill-advised correspondence would have been avoided. Until receipt of that note, I spoke and wrote as I am entitled to do so under the Bye Laws of 1870. From your note of yesterday it is difficult to know what you want – I shall therefore act as if you had asked, in conformity with No. 54 old Bye Laws and No. 28 new ones, the permission of the committee of Management to live out of the College as Professor of Chemistry after the end of the present term, unless I hear from you to the contrary in the course of today.

I am yours truly,

JOHN CONSTABLE

Professor Church'

★

'The Agricultural College, Cirencester, 24th February, 1879.

Dear Sir, – Your note of Feb.22 gave me but twelve hours for my reply. As I wished to consult friends I not unreasonably deferred writing until today. For my part, I should have hesitated to stigmatised as ill-advised a correspondence begun by you on Feb.4, and forced on me. It is satisfactory to me to find that you now admit to having spoken and written as the final authority on this matter, and as not subject to revision. You say, "I wrote and spoke as I am entitled to do under the Bye Laws of 1870." But the 24th new Bye Law refers only to Professors appointed by the Principal; not having been so appointed I repudiated at the time (Dec., 1870) the application of that bye law to my case. Two of my then colleagues lodged the same protest with you. Doubtless you remember this. My letter of February 21 fully explained my views as to a decision of the Committee of Management being desirable – such decision being of course based, not on an *ex parte* statement, but on a full hearing of sides of the question.

I remain, dear Sir, yours faithfully,

A.H.CHURCH

The Rev. The Principal'

★

Following this correspondence the matter was referred to the Committee of Management and both sides were heard.

ADDRESS BY THE COLLEGE, 1893

𝕿𝖔 𝕾𝖎𝖗 𝕵𝖔𝖍𝖓 𝕭𝖊𝖓𝖓𝖊𝖙 𝕷𝖆𝖜𝖊𝖘, 𝕭𝖆𝖗𝖙., 𝕱.𝕽.𝕾., 𝕯.𝕮.𝕷., &c.,
AND
𝕵𝖔𝖘𝖊𝖕𝖍 𝕳𝖊𝖓𝖗𝖞 𝕲𝖎𝖑𝖇𝖊𝖗𝖙, 𝕰𝖘𝖖., 𝕸.𝕬., 𝕱.𝕽.𝕾., 𝕷𝕷.𝕯., &c.

From the Governors, Principal, Professors, and Members of the
Royal Agricultural College, Cirencester.

In joining in the congratulations which the Agriculturists and Members of the learned Societies of the kingdom, and indeed of the world, desire to accord to you on the occasion of the jubilee of the foundation of the systematic agricultural experiments at Rothamsted, established and carried on through your munificent liberality and unique abilities, we beg to express our highest appreciation of the character and results of those experiments, which are universally recognised as being without parallel at any other Station in the world, and of a value which cannot be over-estimated to the Agricultural communities of our own and other countries.

But while we join with all others in expressing our general admiration for your work, we recognise in an especial manner, and are glad to be able, as the oldest College in the kingdom for teaching the sciences applied to Agricultural practice, to testify to their immense educational value, which has imparted to the studies of ourselves and our Students an accuracy and an interest of the highest importance in this department, and laid all future Teachers and Students under the deepest obligations. Further, we take this opportunity of publicly tendering our grateful thanks for the great and unvarying kindness and courtesy shown to us on the occasions of our annual excursions to Rothamsted for the examination of the experiments in progress ; and also for the honour and benefit conferred upon us by Dr. Gilbert, as Honorary Professor of our College, in first communicating to us from time to time in our Lecture Theatre, and through us, in the pages of our *Agricultural Students' Gazette*, to the public generally, the results of much original work from the Rothamsted Laboratories and offices, notably on Barley, Root Crops, Potatoes, and the Fixation of Free Nitrogen by Plants.

As well, therefore, on these special, as on general grounds, we respectfully tender our heartiest congratulations and warmest gratitude, and express our earnest hope that He, "to Whom the earth and its fulness belongs," may yet long spare and prosper your labours and reward them, as you have wished them to be rewarded, in the improvement of that noble and fundamental industry to the interest of which you have now for half a century consecrated your wealth, your talents and your zeal.

Signed on behalf of the College,

JOHN B. McCLELLAN, M.A., Principal.

EDWARD KINCH, Professor of Chemistry.

RUSSELL SWANWICK, M.R.A.C., R. A. Coll. Farm.

July 29th, 1893.

Appendix IX

OCCUPANTS OF CHAIRS AT THE COLLEGE, 1845–1915

The original Charter and Deed of Settlement made reference to professors, though no specific number was stated. There were mentioned the Professors of Farming, Chemistry and Natural History and Geology; their particular responsiblities were defined relating to the management of the farms, the laboratory and the botanical gardens. Mention was made of '. . . *other Professors . . .*', but none was specified. The number of Chairs entitling the appellation 'Professor' increased as the number of subjects in the College syllabus increased.

This practice of having Chairs ceased in 1915, a few years after the major reorganization of the College's corporate structure, when the College closed. After that time the only person entitled to and using the title of Professor was Boutflour, when he held a Chair at Bristol University. This, too, ceased when the connection with that University was severed just before the Second World War.

In 1910 a list of occupants of Chairs up to that date was published in the *Annual Scientific Bulletin of the Royal Agricultural College*, (No. 1 for 1909), as well as a list of the staff in post at that time.

The Staff in 1910

Principal
Prof. J.R. Ainsworth-Davis, MA, (Trinity Coll. Camb.), FCP

Agriculture, Dairy Farming and Poultry Farming
Prof. Drysdale Turner, SEAC (Dip.), PASI
Chas D. Stewart

Estate Management and Forestry
Prof. H.A. Pritchard, FSI

Chemistry
Prof. E. Kinch, FIC, FCS
M. Kershaw, BA, Agric.Dip. (Camb.)
W. James

Physics and Applied Mechanics
M. Kershaw, BA, Agric.Dip (Camb.)

Land Surveying, Estate Engineering, Bookkeeping and Drawing
Prof. W. Thain, AMICE

Natural History
The Principal
R.G. Stapledon, MA, Agric.Dip. (Camb.)

Veterinary Science and Bacteriology
Prof. A.C. Duncan, MRCVS

Former Occupants of Chairs (as published in 1910)

Agriculture:
1845–6, W.T. Scales; 1846–51, John Wilson, LLD, FRSE (Prof. of Agriculture at Edinburgh, 1854–85); 1851–3, Robert Vallentine; 1856–62, John Coleman, MRAC; 1863–4, J. Lynch Fletcher; 1865–77, J. Wrightson, MRAC (afterwards President of Downton College); 1877–8, J.P. Sheldon; 1878–80, P.H. Cathcart, MRAC; 1880–2, John Scott; 1882–9, H.J. Little; 1882–5, Robert Wallace, FHAS (now Prof. of Agriculture at Edinburgh); 1885–9, W. McCracken, FSI, FHAS (now Agent to Lord Crewe); 1890–1, James Muir, MRAC, MRASE, FHAS (afterwards Prof. of Agriculture at Leeds); 1891–1908, Edward Blundell.

Estate Management and Forestry:
1903–7, Frank C. McClellan, MRAC; 1907, P.T. Maw, PASI.

Chemistry:
1845–7, J.T. Way, FCS; 1847–9, John Blyth, MD (Edin.), FCS (afterwards Prof. of Chemistry at Cork); 1849–63, J.C.A. Voelcker, Ph.D., FRS, FIC; 1863–79, A.H. Church, MA, D.Sc. (Oxon.), FRS, FIC (now Sir A.H. Church, KCVO); 1879–81, E.W. Prevost, Ph.D., FIC.

Physics:
1850, L.C. Edwards, MA; 1863–5, W.M. Lane, MA (Camb.); 1870–2, H.M. Andrew, MA (Camb.) (afterwards Prof. of Nat. Philosophy at Melbourne); 1873–4, W.A. Wall, BA (Camb.); 1874–5, Bion Reynolds, MA (Camb. and Lond.); 1875–9, H.W. Lloyd Tanner, MA (Oxon.), FRS (afterwards Prof. of Mathematics at Cardiff); 1879, F.B. de Malbisse Gibbons, MA (Camb.) (now Prof. of Mathematics at Dunedin); 1879–98, Hugo Ohm, MA (Camb.); 1898–9, J.A.H. Johnstone, MA (Edin.), BA (Camb.); 1899–1905, G.F. Locke; 1906–9, P.G. Gundry, B.Sc. (Lond.), Ph.D. (now Prof. of Physics in the Transvaal University).

Engineering and Land Surveying:
1846–8, J. Bravender, FGS; 1850, J.D. Pemberton, CE; 1851, J.G.B. Marshall, BA, CE; 1851–3, W. Sowerby, CE; 1858, J.A. Jarman, CE; 1860–1, A. de Morgan Hensley, MA (Camb.); 1880–2, A.R. Carrington; 1882–7, A.W. Thomson, D.Sc., CE (Glasgow) (afterwards Prof. of Engineering in Poona); 1887–1906, George Paton, CE, MIESS.

Natural History:
1845–7, S.P. Woodward, Ph.D., ALS (afterwards an assistant in the Brit. Mus., and author of many geological memoirs); 1847–63, James Buckman, FLS, FGS, FSA (author of many geological and biological memoirs); 1863–5, J. Bayldon, MRCP and MRCS (Edin.), B.Sc. and MB (Lond.); 1866, R.O. Cunningham, MD (Edin.), D.Sc. (Queen's Univ.) (afterwards Prof. of Nat. History at Belfast); 1866–7, R.H. Traquair, MD and LLD (Edin.), FRS (afterwards Keeper of Nat. Hist. Collections in the Royal Scottish Museum); 1868–70, W.T. Thiselton-Dyer, MA (Oxon.), B.Sc. (Lond.), Ph.D., FRS (now Sir W.T.T–D., KCMG, some time Director of Kew Gardens); 1870–1 (and part of 1874–6), W.R. McNab, MD (Edin.) (afterwards Prof. of Botany at the Royal College of Science, Dublin); 1873, R.J. Watson, MA (Camb.); 1875, J.F. Duthie, BA (Camb.) (afterwards Director of the Botanical Department, N. India); 1876, G.E.S. Boulger, FGS, FLS; 1876–9, W. Fream, B.Sc. (Lond.), LLD; 1879–81, Morton G. Stuart, MA (Camb.) (now 17th Earl of Moray); 1881–94, J.A. Harker, FLS; 1895–9, T.T. Groom, MA (Camb.), D.Sc. (Lond.); 1899–1906, G.S. West, MA, D.Sc. (now Prof. of Botany at the University of Birmingham); 1906–7, G.S. Gough, B.Sc., ARCS (now Inspector, Board of Agriculture); 1907–9, A. Rutherford, MA, B.Sc. (Edin.).

Veterinary Science:
1850–62, George T. Brown, FRCVS (afterwards Sir G.T.B., KCB, Vet. Adviser to Privy Council, President of the Royal Vet. College, London); 1863–5, A.J. Murray, MRCVS; 1866, W. Hunting,

FRCVS (afterwards Vet. Inspector to the LCC and President of RCVS); 1867–8, E. Nettleship, MRAC, FRCS, MRCVS (afterwards Ophth. Surgeon to St Thomas's Hospital, &c.); 1866–7, 1868–76 and 1880–2, J.A. McBride, Ph.D., MRCVS (afterwards Vet. Prof. in Tokio and Melbourne); 1876–80, T.W. Mayer, FRCVS; 1882–6, W.F. Garside, MRCVS; 1886–9, N. Almond, FRCVS; 1889–97, W.T. Wilson, FRCVS; 1898–9, J.W. Brittlebank, MRCVS; 1899–1900, H.A. Woodruff, MRCVS (now a Prof. in the Royal Vet. College, London); 1900–3, G.H. Wooldridge, FRCVS (now a Prof. in the Royal Vet. College, London); 1903–5, V. de V.H. Woodley, MRCVS.

THE GOVERNING BODY

The Governing Body of the College was, in the original Charter, the Council. Later on the direct responsibility for the management of the College was delegated to a Committee of Management, first created following the period when Edward Holland had sole charge from 1847 to 1849. This continued until the reorganization in 1908, when as a company under the Companies Acts the Governing Body become the Board of Governors. These authorities changed in composition from time to time. The membership, at selected points in the College history, is given.

★

College Council – 1845

The Earl Bathurst (President)	The Earl of Ducie (Vice-President)
Sir Michael Hicks Beach	T. Arkell
E. Bowly (Joint Treasurer)	D. Bowly
R.J. Brown (Secretary)	T.C. Brown
R. Cripps (Joint Treasurer)	C.G.B. Daubeny
G. Edmonds	J.H.H. Foley
N.H. Goddard	Edward Holland
H. Howell	T. Iles
J. Kearsey	C. Lawrence
P. Mathews	Revd T. Maurice
G.F. Newmarch	Revd J.M. Prower
E. Ruck	T.H.S. Sotheron-Escourt
T. Stone	D. Trinder

★

Committee of Management
under Supplemental Charter of 1870

Stipulated by the Charter

Edward Holland	T.H.S. Sotheron-Escourt

Elected by the Bondholders

Lt.-Col. R.N.F. Kingscote	The Earl of Ducie
Sir Michael Hicks Beach	A.L. Goddard

Elected by the Council

E. Bowly	A.A. Bathurst
W.J. Edmonds	Revd T. Maurice

★

Reorganization of 1908
Board of Governors

Hereditary Governor
The Earl Bathurst

Ordinary Governors

Lord Moreton (Chairman)
Sir John Dorrington
Col. J.F. Curtis Hayward
H.J. Bailey

Viscount Cobham
Col. T.W. Chester Master
Col. W.E. Carne Currie
A.F. Somerville

Representative Governors from:

Glos. CC (3)
Monmouth CC (1)
Wilts. CC (1)
Oxford University (1)
Bath & West Agric. Soc. (1)

Hereford CC (1)
Somerset CC (1)
Worcs. CC (1)
RASE (1)
Bristol University (1)

★

Board of Governors – 1922

Hereditary Governor
The Earl Bathurst

Ordinary Governors

Lord Bledisloe (Chairman)
The Marquis of Crewe
A.L. Goddard
W. Scotford Harmer
C. Turnor

Prof. E. Blundell
Maj. Sir F.W.B. Cripps
Sir J. Oakley
Hon. E. Strutt
Sir Archibald Weighall

Representative Governors from:

Ministry of Agriculture (1)
National Farmers' Union (1)
Bath & West Agric. Soc. (1)

Bristol University (1)
RASE (1)
Cirencester UDC (1)

★

Board of Governors – 1931

Hereditary Governor
The Earl Bathurst (Chairman)

Ordinary Governors

Viscount Bledisloe
The Marquis of Crewe
Sir Thos. Davies
W. Scotford Harmer
C. Turnor
Lord Clinton

C.P. Ackers
Maj. Sir F.W.B. Cripps
A.L. Goddard
J.H. Scrutton
Sir Archibald Weighall

Representative Governors

Hon. Claude Biddulph (RASE)
Maj. G.J. Buxton (Wilts. CC)
G.G. Harris (Glos. CC)
E.G.H. Massey (National Farmers' Union)
J.M. Scott (Glos. CC)

Prof. B.T.P. Barker (Bristol University)
Col. W.F. Fuller (Wilts. CC)
A.L. Hobhouse (Bath & West Agric. Soc.)
T. Loveday (Bristol University)

★

Board of Governors – 1945

Hereditary Governor
The Earl Bathurst

Ordinary Governors

Lady Apsley
Viscount Bledisloe
Prof. G.E. Blackman
Maj. Sir F.W.B. Cripps (Chairman)
A.L. Goddard
Sir William Marris
F. Peter
J.P. Terry
Sir Archibald Weighall

The Duke of Beaufort
C.P. Ackers
Lady Cripps
The Marquis of Crewe
Brig. E.B. Hankey
Lt.-Col. D. Macleay
S.J. Phillips
C.W. Whatley
Maj. G.J. Buxton

Representative Governors

Hon. Claude Biddulph (RASE)
Sir Arthur Hobhouse (Bath & West Agric. Soc.)
B. Swanwick (Glos. CC)
R.R. Ware (Ministry of Agriculture)

Col. W.F. Fuller (Wilts. CC)
Prof. M. Skene (Bristol University)
Prof. T. Wallace (Bristol University)

★

Board of Governors – 1952

Hereditary Governor
The Earl Bathurst

Ordinary Governors

Maj. Sir F.W.B. Cripps
The Earl St Aldwyn
J. Arnold-Foster
Viscount Bledisloe
T. Holland Martin
R.W. Trumper

Maj. C.P. Ackers
Lady Apsley
The Duke of Beaufort
Lt.-Col. W.A. Chester Master
J.M. Stratton

Representative Governors

Maj. P.D. Birchall (Glos. CC)
J.S. Hill (Ministry of Agriculture)
Hon. Holland-Hibbert (Land
    Agents' Society)
S.J. Phillips (Glos. CC)

Prof. G.E. Blackman (Ministry of Agri-
    culture)
G.A. Lister (RASE)
Prof. M. Skene (Bristol
    University)

APPENDIX X

J.P. Terry (Glos. CC)
Col. F. Trumper (Land Agents'
Society)
Prof. T. Wallace (Bristol
University)

The Earl Waldegrave (Bath &
West Agric. Soc.)
C.W. Whatley (Wilts. CC)
F. Peter (Royal Institution of Chartered Surveyors)

★

THE ROYAL AGRICULTURAL COLLEGE
1990

PATRON
HM The Queen

PRESIDENT
HRH The Prince of Wales

VICE-PRESIDENTS
The Rt. Hon. Earl St Aldwyn, PC, GBE
Maj. P.D. Birchall, CBE, MA
Maj. G.B. Heywood, MBE, FRICS

The Board of Governors – 1990

Chairman
C.H. Coad

Ordinary Governors

D.M. Backhouse
The Earl Bathurst
D.B.S. Fitch
A.C. Keene
D.G. Pearce

A.M. Barrett
C.H. Coad
T.S. Juckes
T.J. Lawson
P.W. Trumper

Representative Governors
C.J. French (National Farmers' Union)
R. Graham-Palmer (Country Landowners' Association)
J.D.M. Hearth (Royal Agricultural Society of England)
B.J.G. Hilton (Ministry of Agriculture, Fisheries and Food)
R.A. Law (Royal Institution of Chartered Surveyors)
Professor T.R. Morris (Reading University)
S.F. Pott (Royal Institution of Chartered Surveyors)
J.K. Royston (Royal Institution of Chartered Surveyors)
J.L. Tuckey (Royal Institution of Chartered Surveyors)
R.J. Wainwright (Royal Institution of Chartered Surveyors)

Appendix XI

COLLEGE STAFF AND COURSES IN 1990

DIRECTING ACADEMIC STAFF

Principal
Professor Arthur S. Jones,
B.Sc.(Dunhelm), Ph.D.(Aberdeen), C.Biol., F.I.Biol., FBIM, FRSA

Vice-Principal and Dean of the School of Rural Economy and Land Management
J.D. Young, B.Sc. (London), FRICS, FAAV

Dean of the School of Agriculture
J.C. Alliston, B.Sc., (Aberdeen), Ph.D. (Wales), C.Biol., MIBiol.

Dean of the School of Business and AMC Chair in Business Strategy
D.J. Newton, B.Sc., (London), M.Sc., Ph.D. (Bradford)

Director of the International Office and Director of Studies
W.P. Davies, B.Sc. (Wales), M.Sc. (Exeter), Ph.D. (East Anglia), C.Biol., F.I.Biol.

Farms Director
T.M. Limb, B.Sc. (Leeds), Dip. FM (Reading)

★

COURSES OFFERED

School of Agriculture
1. B.Sc. Crop Technology and Resource Management – a B.Sc. Honours Degree validated by the University of Bath and taught jointly by the College and the University.
2. B.Sc. Agriculture and Land Management – a B.Sc. Honours Degree validated by the University of Buckingham.
3. B.Sc. International Agricultural and Equine Business Management – a B.Sc. Honours Degree validated by the University of Buckingham.
4. College Diploma in Agriculture and Farm Management – a two-year course including Agricultural Science.
5. One-Year Farming course – a concentrated course which may lead to the College Diploma course.

School of Business
1. B.Sc. International Agri-business Management – a degree course validated by the University of Buckingham.
2. The School of Business also offers advanced managment courses, tailored to meet special requirements.

School of Rural Economy and Land Management

1. B.Sc. Rural Land Management – the course leads to the B.Sc. Honours Degree of Reading University which institution validates the teaching provided throughout the course by the College.

2. Diploma in Rural Estate Management – this is the only course available at diploma level giving exemption by the Royal Institution of Chartered Surveyors from their written examinations for rural surveyors.

★

COLLEGE FARMS

The College farms some 770 hectares comprising Coates Manor Farm, Fosse Hill Farm and Eysey Manor Farm. In addition the College recently started share farming a holding at Harnhill of 250 hectares including 50 hectares of organic cropping. The Cotswold Cereal Centre which started in 1978, and is funded and controlled by Cotswold farmers is mostly sited on the College farms. The Arable Research Centres Company is based at the College.

Appendix XII

THE ORIGINAL SHAREHOLDERS

His Royal Highness Prince Albert
Sir Thomas Dyke Acland
Edward Alton, Esq.
Daniel Arkell, Esq.
William Arkell, Esq.
Southgate Austin, Esq.

The Hon. Viscount Alford
David Archer, Esq.
Thomas Arkell, Esq.
W. Atkinson, Esq.

Edwin Bailey
Thomas Bailey, Esq.
Sir Edward Baker, Bt.
T.B.L. Baker, Esq.
W.H. Barrett, Esq.
Thomas Bascombe, Esq.
The Hon. W. Bathurst
Sir Michael Hicks Beach, Bt.
Col. Beauchamp
His Grace the Duke of Bedford
George Bengough, Esq.
J.B. Bevington, Esq.
E. Bloxsome, jun., Esq.
David Bowly, Esq.
Edward Bowly, Esq.
Richard Bowly, Esq.
C.H. Bracebridge, Esq.
John Bravender, Esq.
Thomas Broadbent, Esq.
Robert J. Brown, Esq.
John Browne, Esq. (Chisledon)
His Grace the Duke of Buccleuch
E.B. Bunny, Esq.

Joseph Bailey, Esq.
W.H. Baillie, Esq.
Samuel Baker, Esq.
David Barclay, Esq.
The Hon. Viscount Barrington
The Rt. Hon. Earl Bathurst
Joseph Baxendale, Esq.
Robert Beaman, Esq.
John Beddoe, Esq.
John Bell, Esq.
Henry Bethell, Esq.
Sir Francis Blake, Bt.
Sir J.P. Boileau, Bt.
Devereux Bowly
J.H. Bowly, Esq.
William Bowly, Esq.
T.W. Bramston, Esq., MP
Septimus Brigham, Esq.
Samuel Brooks, Esq.
Thomas C. Brown, Esq.
John Browne, Esq. (Upham)
Dr Buckland
The Rt. Hon. the Earl of Burlington

His Royal Highness the Duke of Cambridge
The Hon. Viscount Camden
Richard Carpenter, Esq.
James Chapman, Esq.
John Benjamin Churchill, Esq.
His Grace the Duke of Cleveland
R. Coleman, Esq.
Joseph Compton, Esq.
William Cosens, Esq.

William Capel, Esq.
Josiah Castree, Esq.
John Church, Esq.
The Rt. Hon. the Earl of Clarendon
The Hon. H.H. Clive, MP
R. Coling, Esq.
William Cooke, Esq.
W. Cotton, Esq.

The Rt. Hon. Earl of Craven
Raymond Cripps, Esq.
W. Crosskill, Esq.
Alfred Crowdy, Esq.
James Crowdy, Esq.

Frederick Cripps, Esq.
William Cripps, Esq.
Christopher Crouch, Esq.
H.C. Crowdy, Esq.

John Dallewy, Esq.
Dr Daubeny
The Rt. Hon. Lord de Mauley
Revd Luke Dennis
The Most Hon. the Marquis of Downshire
Samuel Druce, Esq.
P. Duncan, Esq.

The Rt. Hon. Earl of Dartmouth
The Revd E. Daubeny
The Rt. Hon. Earl of Denbigh
John Dent, Esq.
Joseph and S. Druce
The Rt. Hon. the Earl of Ducie

Sir John Easthope, Bt.
Charles Edmonds, Esq.
Matthew Edmonds, Esq.
The Rt. Hon. Earl of Effingham
Robert Emmett, Esq.
O.L. Evans, Esq.

Albert Edmonds, Esq.
Giles Edmonds, Esq.
John Edwards, Esq.
The Revd Dr Ellerton
T.G.B. Estcourt, Esq., MP
The Most Noble the Marquis of Exeter

John Ferrabee, Esq.
The Rt. Hon. Earl Fitzhardinge
James Foster, Esq.

Anthony R. Fewster, Esq.
J.H.H. Foley, Esq.

Henry Gale, Esq.
Robert Gill, Esq.
Ambrose Goddard, Esq.
Sir J.L. Baron Goldsmid & de Palmeira
The Revd S. Gompertz
Abel Lewis Gower, Esq.
The Rt. Hon. Earl Granville
C. Pascoe Grenfell, Esq.
Sir John Guest, Bt.

George Gibbs, Esq.
J. Gillett, Esq.
Horatio Nelson Goddard, Esq.
F.H. Goldsmid, Esq.
Robert Gordon, Esq.
His Grace the Duke of Grafton
G.W. Gratwick, Esq.
The Rt. Hon. Earl Grey
Sir John Guise, Bt.

Robert Kimber Habgood, Esq.
Daniel Hanbury, Esq.
E.W. Harding, Esq.
James Hatton, Esq.
Hedges & Keymer
Frederick Herbert, Esq.
William Hervey, Esq.
Robert Heynes, Esq.
William Fisher Hobbs, Esq.
Edward Holland, Esq.
Richard Hornsby, Esq.
Henry Howard, Esq.
Henry Howell, Esq.
William Hughes, Esq.

Richard Hall, Esq.
G.G. Harcourt, Esq.
Benjamin Harrison, Esq.
W.G. Hayter, Esq.
Joseph Hegan, Esq.
The Hon. Sidney Herbert
John Hewetson, Esq.
Henry Hoare, Esq.
Robert Stayner Holford, Esq.
F. Holland, Esq.
Henry Houldsworth, Esq.
The Rt. Hon. Earl Howe
John Hudson, Esq.
William Henry Hyett, Esq.

Richard Iles, Esq.
The Rt. Hon. Viscount Ingestre

Thomas Iles, Esq.

J.H. Whitmore Jones, Esq.

James Kearsey, Esq.
Dr Kinneir

The Rt. Hon. H. Labouchere, MP
William Jenner Lane, Esq.
The Most Noble the Marquis of Lansdowne
Chalres Lawrence, Esq.
The Rt. Hon. C. Shaw Lefevre
The Rt. Hon. Lord Leigh
The Rt. Hon. Earl of Liverpool
Sir John Lubbock
The Rt. Hon. Lord Lyttleton

The Rt. Hon. Earl of Macclesfield
S.S. Marling, Esq.
W. Marshall, Esq.
Peter Matthews, Esq.
J.J. Mechi, Esq.
The Rt. Hon. Viscount Milton
C.A. Moncke, Esq.
William Morse, Esq.
Richard Mullings, Esq.

John Nash, Esq.
George Newmarsh, Esq.
I.L. Nicholas, Esq.
James Norton, Esq.

Robert Palmer, Esq., MP
Sir Hyde Parker, Bt.
Thomas Parkin, Esq.
G. Parsons, Esq.
The Hon. G.D. Pennant, MP
A. Phillips, Esq.
D. Powell, Esq.
W.P. Price, Esq.
The Revd J.M. Prower

The Rt. Hon. Earl of Radnor
T. Ready, Esq.
The Rt. Hon. Lord Redesdale
E.W. Rich, Esq.
C.L. Ringrose, Esq.
George Robinson, Esq.
Joseph Ruck, Esq.
The Rt. Hon. Lord John Russell

The Rt. Hon. Earl of St Germans
Leo Schuster, Esq.
William Henry Sealy, Esq.

Thomas Kingscote, Esq.
Dr Kittermaster

John Lane, Esq.
J.H. Langston, Esq.
Sir Francis Lawley
Capt. Laws
The Rt. Hon. the Earl of Leicester
Sir Charles Lemon, Bt., MP
Samuel Janes Loyd, Esq.
J.W. Lyon, Esq.

Dr Malden
J. Marshall, Esq.
John Martin, Esq.
The Revd Thomas Maurice
Arthur Mills, Esq.
George Milward, Esq.
Alfred Morgan, Esq.
Joseph Randolph Mullings, Esq.
S. Mundy, Esq.

Jonah Newman, Esq.
John Newton, Esq.
The Most Noble the Marquis of
   Northampton

James Parham, Esq.
The Revd William Parker
John Parry, Esq.
E.W.W. Pendarves, Esq.
Dr Pennell
The Rt. Hon. Lord Portman
J.D. Powles, Esq.
William Price, Esq.
Philip Pusey, Esq., MP

M.W. Rand, Esq.
John Rebbeck, Esq.
David Ricardo, Esq.
His Grace the Duke of Richmond
The Rt. Hon. Earl of Ripon
Edmund Ruck, Esq.
Charles Russell, Esq.

The Hon. Viscount Sandon
George Poulett Scrope, Esq.
The Rt. Hon. Earl of Sefton

P. Selby, Esq.

Miss S.M. Shepley

E.J. Shirley, Esq., MP

G.R. Smith, Esq.

Henry Smith, Esq.

R.H. Smith, Esq.

The Rt. Hon. Lord Southampton

Richard Spooner, Esq.

Thomas Stone, Esq.

Jacon Sturge, Esq.

The Rt. Hon. Earl of Talbot

H.W. Tancred, Esq., MP

G. Thomas, Esq.

Sir Robert Throckmorton, Bt.

Mrs George Townsend

The Revd Richard Townsend

Representatives of Daniel Trinder, Esq.

Charles Turk, Esq.

F. Villebois, Esq.

Henry Vizard, Esq.

Charles Bruce Warner, Esq.

T.J. Wasey, Esq.

The Rt. Hon. Earl of Wemyss & March

Elizabeth Whitton

O.H. Williams, Esq.

W.B. Wingate, Esq.

William Woodward, Esq.

Col. Wyndham

Joseph Sewell, Esq.

The Rt. Hon. Lord Sherborne

C.R. Smith, Esq.

H. Smith, Esq.

Richard Smith, Esq.

T.H.S. Sotheron-Escourt, Esq., MP

The Rt. Hon. Earl Spencer

John Stanton, Esq.

Thomas Stronge, Esq.

The Rt. Hon. Lord Sudeley

Sir Thomas Tancred, Bt.

The Dowager Lady Tancred

The Revd Vaughan Thomas

George Tomline, Esq.

R.L. Townsend, Esq.

Nathaniel Tregelles, Esq.

Richard Tull, Esq.

The Hon. Viscount Villiers

W. Vizard, Esq.

Thomas Warner, Esq.

Thomas Wells, Esq.

William White, Esq.

J. Williams, Esq.

John Wilson, Esq.

F. Woodward, Esq.

The Rt. Hon. Lord Worsley

Appendix XIII

SHAREHOLDERS IN 1990

The Rt. Hon. Earl St Aldwyn

The Rt. Hon. Lord Banbury of Southam
The Rt. Hon. Earl Bathurst
S. Biddulph, Esq.
H.L.H. Birley, Esq.
P.D.C. Brown, Esq.

R.W.T. Chester-Master, Esq.
C.H. Coad, Esq.
J.P. Cripps, Esq.

H.W.G. Elwes, Esq.

N.J. Fiske, Esq.

Reps. of R.H. Garner, dec'd

Major G.B. Heywood
Official Custodian for Charities (*re* Holland Memorial)

H.N. Jacobs, Esq.
Sir Emrys Jones
Col. G.R. Judd

A.C. Keene, Esq.
Reps. of H.L. Knight, dec'd

T.J. Lawson, Esq.

A.W. Morris, Esq.
T.R. Morris, Esq.

W.J. Oldacre, Esq.

D.G. Pearce, Esq.

Reps. of H. St G. Rawlins, dec'd

Lady Abel Smith
J.M. Stratton, Esq.

P.W. Trumper, Esq.

N.M. Arnold-Forster, Esq.

Dr A.M. Barrett
Sir Thomas Bazley
Major P.D. Birchall
The Rt. Hon. Viscount Bledisloe
G.R. Burman, Esq.

Reps. of W.J. Clark, dec'd
The Rt. Hon. Vicount Cobham

D.B.S. Fitch, Esq.

R.H.W. Graham-Palmer, Esq.

Reps. of Mrs E.E. Jacques, dec'd
T. Juckes, Esq.

M.A. Kerr, Esq.
R.E.B. Knight, Esq

O.A. Logie, Esq.

N.R. Morris, Esq.

E.M. Owens, Esq.

Exors. of S.J. Phillips, dec'd

C.G. Stainforth, Esq.

C. Warde-Aldam, Esq.

THE COLLEGE CHAPEL

The College chapel, dedicated to St George the Martyr, was financed by private subscriptions of the Proprietors and Friends of the College. It was built and completed in 1847, two years after the main building of the College was completed. There was a separate appeal for funds.

It was built by Bridges and designed by Daukes and Hamilton, the same team that built the College. It is an excellent example of Victorian decorated gothic, measuring internally 73ft by 24ft. It is neatly pewed laterally and was originally decorated with fresco wall paintings, including on the north and south sides figures of certain of the prophets and apostles, and scripture texts on either side of the east window. These have since been covered over during internal renovation and decoration. The upper tracery of the east window is filled with stained glass, the gift of Sir Arthur Church, a former Professor of Chemistry at the College. The lower lights were filled in October 1963 by a beautiful stained-glass window depicting the Benedictine. This is a memorial to Robert Boutflour, the outstanding Principal from 1931 to 1958. His ashes, with those of his wife, Mary, rest within the chapel walls. This window was given by members of the Royal Agricultural College, Mrs Boutflour, family and friends, and was designed and made by Paul Quail.

Beneath the window, extending the whole width of the east wall, and along the north and south walls within the altar area, is a reredos comprising a series of arched panel recesses, erected in April 1860 by the staff and students in memory of the Revd J.S. Haygarth, the fourth Principal, who died in 1859. Four of the spaces are occupied by the Apostles' Creed, Commandments and the Lord's Prayer.

There are, on this reredos, memorial brasses with inscriptions to the 4th, 5th and 6th Earls Bathurst, the 2nd Earl of Ducie, Edward Bowly, Robert J. Brown, Raymond Cripps, T.H.S. Sotheron-Escourt, Edward Holland and J.H. Langston. These were the core of the original founders. There are also brasses in memory of the Revd J.S. Haygarth and the Revd John Constable. Frank Garner, Principal from 1959 to 1971, and D. Christopherson, a founder member and first secretary of the RAC Association are also commemorated.

The inscriptions on the brasses on the reredos are:

In memory of HENRY GEORGE FRANCIS, 2nd EARL of DUCIE
one of the founders of the Agricultural College
born 8th May 1802, died 2nd June 1858

ROBERT JEFFREYS BROWN
to whose zeal and industry the foundation of this College is mainly due
Died March 3rd 1859 Aged 63

The Revd JOHN SAYER HAYGARTH, M.A.
Principal for more than Eight Years of this College
Died April 7th, 1859 Aged 47

In Grateful Memory of their late Principal, the Revd JOHN SAYER HAYGARTH, M.A.
this Reredos was erected by the Professors and Students, April 1860

In Memory of JAMES HAUGHTON LANGSTON Esqre., of Sarsden, Oxon
many years MP for the City of Oxford
one of the founders of the Agricultural College
born 25th May 1796, died 19th Octr 1863

To one whose memory should ever be honored within the walls of the College which he assisted to establish, his long connection with it being marked by liberality and benevolence to all
HENRY GEORGE, 4th EARL BATHURST
born 24th Feby 1790, died 25th May 1866

In memory of Edward Holland, of Dumbleton, Worcestershire, for many years MP for Evesham, and President of the Royal Agricultural Society in 1873. He was Chairman of the College Council for a quarter of a century and it was chiefly by his steady support, untiring zeal and discretion that the difficulties of its early days were surmounted and its success ensured
Born Jany 11 1806. Died Jany 4 1876

In memory of the Right Hon THOMAS HENRY SOUTHERON ESCOURT of Estcourt
Gloucestershire
MP for Marlborough from 1829 to 1832
MP for Devizes from 1832 to 1844
MP for North Wilts from 1844 to 1865
Secretary of State for the Home Department 1859 and one of Her Majesty's Privy Council
Born April 4 1801. Died Jany 6 1876
His connection with the College is commemorated in the decoration of this Chapel

In memory of WILLIAM LENNOX, 5th EARL BATHURST
born 14 February 1791, died 24 February 1878
Fellow of All Souls College, Oxford, and for many years Clerk of the Privy Council, whose genial sympathy and liberal aid were always given to advance the interest of the Agricultural College.

In memory of ALLEN ALEXANDER, 6th EARL BATHURST
MP for Cirencester from 1857 to 1878 who assisted in upholding the interests of this College by his generous aid and support
Born Oct 10th 1832. Died August 2nd 1892

In memory of RAYMOND CRIPPS of Cirencester
one of the founders of the Royal Agricultural College
Born 1810. Died Feb 6 1852
Erected 1914

In loving memory of JOHN CONSTABLE, MA
from 1859 to 1879, Principal of this College
'Requiescat in Pace'

In affectionate Memory of EDWARD BOWLY of Siddington House, Cirencester
one of the founders of the Royal Agricultural College
Born July 29th 1808. Died 19th March 1882
Erected by his widow, March 1883

A stone screen separates the entrance vestibule from the chapel and supports the organ gallery. The chapel is now a local ecumenical project and is used for Anglican, Roman Catholic and Free Church services.

BIBLIOGRAPHY

The College has few archives of substance. In recent years the Librarian of the College has started a small collection of archival material and there is some of relevance in the historical section of the College library. To compile this history reliance has been placed on two primary sources: the minutes of the transactions of the Governing Body in the successive forms of the Council, the Committee of Management and the Board of Governors, and the Royal Agricultural College *Agricultural Students' Gazette*, later appearing as the *Journal* of the College. In the case of the minutes the record is missing from 1849 to 1864, covering the Haygarth years and part of the Constable period, and the *Gazette* commenced in 1875. There a few private papers and extracts from the press of the day available but little else. The reasons for this dearth of historical material are that (with some exceptions) throughout the life of the College there has been little conscious effort to preserve reports of events for historical purposes; the College has also twice had to be abandoned because of wartime circumstances and finally it is suspected that if any archives existed they may have been in the College tower which was gutted by fire in 1923. Researchers who have looked into the history of the College in pursuit of theses or dissertations for higher degrees will have had the same difficulties, but thanks are due to them for the availability of their works as source references; these writers are Tattersfield, Watkins and Wibberley. In the later chapters, within living memory, some of the material is anecdotal, and with the two primary sources mentioned above this has provided most of the information. A more detailed account, based entirely on the minutes of the Governing Bodies, has been prepared by Frank Parker, formerly Secretary to the Principal and the Board of Governors. It is available in the College library.

★

The place of publication is London unless otherwise stated.

General

The *Agricultural Students' Gazette* and *R.A.C.Journal*, Vols. I–LXXVIII (1875–1990).

Beecham, K.J., *History of Cirencester*, George H. Harman, 1886.

Journal of the Royal Agricultural Society of England, 2nd series, Vol. XXI, 1885.

List, E.J., *History of the R.A.C., Cirencester and its Developing Views of Agricultural Education* (unpub. article).

Minutes of the Transactions and Proceedings of the Council, Committee of Management, and the Board of Governors of The Royal Agricultural College, 1845–8, 1865–1990.

Tattersfield, B.K., 'An Agricultural College on the Cotswold Hills and the Origins of Rural Agricultural Education in England' (unpub. thesis, Reading University, 1985).

Watkins, G.N.J., 'The Royal Agricultural College, Cirencester, Its Origins and Development as a Specialist Institute of Scientific Learning, 1844–1915' (unpub. dissertation, Bristol University, 1979).

Wibberley, E. John, 'Sociological, Strategic and Comparative International Aspects of Agricultural Education' (unpub. dissertation, Reading University, 1985).

Chapter 1

Chambers, J.D., & Mingay, G.E., *The Agricultural Revolution 1750–1880*, Batsford, 1968.

Dictionary of National Biography, 'Daubeny, Charles Giles Bridle (1795–1867)', Smith, Elder & Co., 1888.

Journal of the Royal Agricultural Society of England, 1st series, Vol. III (1842); 2nd series, Vol. I (1865); 2nd series, Vol. XVIII (1882).

Morgan, Kenneth O., *History of Britain 1789–1983*, Sphere, 1985.

Wiltshire and Gloucestershire Standard, 1842–6.

Wood, A., *Nineteenth Century Britain 1815–1914*, Longman, 1982.

Young, G.M., *Portrait of an Age: Victorian England*, Oxford University Press, 1979.

Chapter 2

Anon, *A History of the Royal Agricultural College*, Cirencester, Charles H. Savory, *c.* 1859.

Blyth, J., private letters and MSS, 1852.

Dictionary of National Biography, Vol. XXVII, G.C. Hodgkinson (1891); Vol.XXXII, C. Lawrence (1892); Vol. LXII, J. Wilson (1900); Smith, Elder & Co.

Fleming, Ian. J., & Robertson, Noel, F., 'Britain's First Chair of Agriculture at the University of Edinburgh 1790–1990', East of Scotland College of Agriculture, 1990.

Journal of the Royal Agricultural Society of England, 2nd series, Vol. I (1865); 2nd series, Vol. II (1875); 2nd series, Vol. XXIV (1888).

Newton, A., Memoire of the late John Scales original MS *c.* 1884.

Report of Committee of Inquiry regarding the Rev. C.M. Cust, 1849.

Royal Agricultural College Prospectus, January 1847; June 1848; Brochure, Jubilee Celebrations 1895.

Scales, J., MS speech; letter to shareholders, 1847.

Scott Watson, J., *A History of the Royal Agricultural Society of England 1839–1939*, RASE, 1939.

Chapter 3

Arthur Herbert Church, extracts, private printing by Lady Church.

Blair, I.D., *The Seed They Sowed*, Lincoln College, University College of Agriculture, New Zealand, 1978.

Buckman, James, 'An Address to the Chairman of the Council of the Agricultural College, Cirencester', Cirencester, G.H. Harman, 1862.

Dictionary of National Biography, Vol. LVIII, Voelcker, John Christopher Augustus (1899); Supplement, Vol. III, Lawes, Sir John Bluett (1901); 2nd Supplement, Vol. I, Browne, Sir George Thomas (1912); 2nd Supplement, Vol. II, Fream, William and Gilbert, Sir Joseph Henry (1912); Smith, Elder & Co.

Dictionary of National Biography, 1922–30, Thistleton-Dyer, Sir William Turner; Oxford University Press.

Hudson, Kenneth, 'The Four Great Men of the Bath and West', Augustus Voelcker; Bath and West and Southern Counties Society; lecture at Abbey Church, Bath, 17 October 1973..

Jones, G.E., & Tattersfield, B.K., 'John Wrightson and the Downton College of Agriculture', *Agricultural Progress*, Vol. 55 (1980), pp. 69–77.

Journal of the Bath and West Agricultural Society, 3rd series, Vol. XIV, pp. 175–8: Notice of the late Dr Voelcker by Sir D. Acland, Bt., MP.

Journal of the Royal Agricultural Society of England, 2nd series, Vol. XXI (1885), p. 309: obit. Voelcker J.C.A.

Lincoln College Centenary Celebrations, 5–7 May 1978, notice of speeches.

Professor Church and the Agricultural College, Cirencester, a reprint of all correspondence, documents and opinions of the Press, Cirencester, G.H. Harman, 1879.

Smith, R.N., 'Dr J.A. McBride, M.R.C.V.S., Itinerant Professor Extraordinary', *Veterinary History Society*, 1980.

Voelcker, Dr Augustus, and Sons Ltd, private papers.

Who was Who, Vol. I, 1897–1915, 2nd edn.: Church, Sir Arthur, Adam & Charles Black, 1962.

Wiltshire and Gloucestershire Standard, 3 April 1987, 'The Buckman Family of Cirencester'.

BIBLIOGRAPHY

Chapter 4

Dickens, Charles, *All the Year Round*, No. 4949, 10 October 1868.

Dictionary of National Biography, 2nd Supplement, Vol. III, Miss Eleanor A. Ormerod (1912).

Ibid, Chapter 2. para. 12.

Journal of the Royal Agricultural Society of England, 2nd series, Vol. XVIII, p. 353.

Library of the Royal Agricultural College, documents and letters in the historical section.

The Report of the Departmental Commission on Agricultural and Dairy Schools, Cmd 5313, Chairman: Sir R.H. Paget, HMSO, 1887.

Chapter 5

Blundell, Edward, 'The Story of my Life', private papers.

Country Life, Vol. XCIX, No. 2574, 17 May 1946.

The 3rd Earl of Ducie, private diaries.

James, N.D.G., *An Experiment in Forestry*, Oxford, Basil Blackwell, 1951.

Medd, J.C., private papers.

The Report of the Departmental Committee on Agricultural Education, Cmd 4207, Chairman: Lord Reay, HMSO, 1908.

Report by J.B. McClellan on 'Re-Organisation' to members of the Governing Body, 12 November 1907.

Chapter 6

Agricultural Students' Gazette, July 1915, 'Roll of Honour; Royal Agricultural College and the War'.

Biographical Memoirs of Fellows of the Royal Society, Vol. 7, November 1961, pp. 249–70.

Board of Agriculture and Fisheries, 'Report of an Inspection of the Royal Agricultural College', February 1913.

Journal of the Royal Agricultural Society of England, Vol. 95 (1934), p. 115.

Ibid, Vol. 134 (1973), pp. 67–8.

Waller, Robert, *Prophet of a New Age, The Life and Thought of Sir George Stapleton, F.R.S.*, Faber and Faber, 1962.

Who was Who, Vol. III, 1929–1940, 2nd edn.: Ainsworth-Davis, James R., Adam & Charles Black, 1967.

Chapter 7

Departmental Committee of the Ministry of Agriculture and Fisheries Report on *The Re-Assessment of Annual Grants to Institutes Providing Higher Agricultural (Including Veterinary) Education in England and Wales*, pp. 24–106, Chairman: Lord Bledisloe, HMSO, 1927.

Dictionary of National Biography, 1951–60, Bathurst, Charles, First Viscount Bledisloe, Oxford University Press, 1971.

Ibid, Wood, Sir (Howard) Kingsley, (1881–1943).

Journal of the Bath and West Agricultural Society, 6th series, Vol. IV, (1929/30).

Journal of the Wye College Club, Agricola, Vol. IX: 48, (1938).

Principal's Quarterly Reports: 6 November 1922; 12 March 1922.

Principal's Terminal Reports: 20 June 1924; 11 March 1924; 26 June 1924; 5 November 1924; 25 June 1925; 29 October 1925; 3 March 1926; 24 June 1926; 13 December 1926; 28 February 1927.

Sandwith, G., private papers, letter 19 November 1985.

Sykes, J.D., private correspondence, Wye College, 23 July 1990.

The Times, 13 April 1923, 'The King and Queen at Cirencester'.

Who was Who, Vol. III, 1929–1940: Dunstan, Malcolm James Rowley, Adam & Charles Black, 1967.

Chapter 8

Boutflour, Mary, *Bobby Boutflour*, Crosby Lockwood, 1965.

Boutflour, Mary, *Combined Activity in Farming Progress*, private publication, 1968.

HISTORY OF THE ROYAL AGRICULTURAL COLLEGE

Boutflour, R., *Management of Dairy Cows*, NFU Kent County Branch, March 1946.
Ministry of Agriculture and Fisheries: MAF 33/342 TPB 444; 33/343 TPB 402; 33/43 TE 16970, Public Record Office, Kew.
Who was Who, Vol. VI, 1961–1970: R. Boutflour, Adam & Charles Black, 1972.
Wiltshire and Gloucestershire Standard, Saturday 30 March 1935.

Chapter 9
Boutflour, Mary, *Combined Activity in Farming Progress* private publication, 1968.
Boutflour, R., *Towards a 2,000 Gallon Average*, private publication, 1953.
Correspondence with Office of Works *re* College requisitioning, 1938–9.
Ministry of Agriculture and Fisheries: MAF 115/60 AE 1750; 115/15 AE 1020; 115/65 AE 2623. MAF (Ed) File ED 174/191 7413/8390/6, Public Record Office, Kew.
Moore, Ian, 'Agricultural Education – A Personal View', *Journal of the Royal Agricultural Society of England*, Vol. 132 (1971), pp. 18–25.
Report of the Loveday Committee, *Committee on Higher Agricultural Education*, Cmnd 6728, HMSO, 1946.
Trow-Smith, R., *Farmer and Stockbreeder*, 18–19 October 1955.
Who was Who, Vol. V, 1951–1960: Weighall, Lt.-Col., Sir (William Ernest George) Archibald, Adam & Charles Black, 1967.
Ibid, 1961–1970: Boutflour, Robert.
Wiltshire and Gloucestershire Standard, 25 May 1946.

Chapter 10
The Farmers' Club Journal, No. 105, July 1990, pp. 30–1.

Chapter 11
Blair, I.D., 'The Seed They Sowed', Lincoln College, University College of Agriculture, New Zealand, 1978.
Centennial Academic Congress, papers and speeches, Lincoln Agricultural College, Canterbury, New Zealand.
Jones, Sir Emrys, 'My Seventy Years in Agriculture', *Countryside 10*, 1985.
Ministry of Agriculture, Fisheries and Food, Press Notice, 14 March 1973: 'Sir Emrys Jones Appointed Principal of the Royal Agricultural College, Cirencester'.

Chapter 12
Architects' Journal, Vol. 181, No. 3, 16 January 1985, p. 35.

INDEX

All headings, other than names of persons and other institutions, refer to the Royal Agricultural College. Sub-headings are arranged as far as possible in chronological or logical order. References to illustrations are in *italics* with colour plate numbers in **bold**.
RAC = Royal Agricultural College